D1600489

AN INTRODUCTORY COMMENTARY
ON THE CONSTITUTIONS

The Constitutions of the Society of Jesus

AN INTRODUCTORY COMMENTARY

ON THE CONSTITUTIONS

by

Antonio M. de Aldama, S.J.

Translated by
Aloysius J. Owen, S.J.

ROME
Centrum Ignatianum Spiritualitatis

ST. LOUIS
The Institute of Jesuit Sources

This book is an authorized translation of *Iniciación al Estudio de las Constituciones* by Antonio M. de Aldama, S.J., 1979, published by Centrum Ignatianum Spiritualitis, Borgo S. Spirito 5, 00195 Rome, Italy.

First Edition
distributed in the Americas, Australia, and New Zealand
by the Institute of Jesuit Sources,
and in Europe
by Centrum Ignatianum Spiritualitatis.

Note: There is another edition, authorized for
sale only in Asia and Africa, which can be
ordered from Gujarat Sahitya Prakash,
Anand 388 001, India.

© 1989 The Institute of Jesuit Sources
St. Louis University
3700 West Pine Blvd.
St. Louis, Missouri 63108

Library of Congress Catalog Card Number: 89-80527
ISBN 0-912422-92-0 Hardcover
ISBN 0-912422-93-9 Paperback

CONTENTS

FOREWORD

The present book is one of a series of six published in Spanish by Father Antonio M. de Aldama of the Jesuit Historical Institute, Rome, about St. Ignatius' *Constitutions of the Society of Jesus*. In it the author aims to help Jesuits and other interested persons to return to the source, the wellspring of the founder's thought where the water flows fresh and pure. He views these *Constitutions* both as a legislative code and a source of spiritual inspiration. They unify the members of the Society and present the pattern for its apostolic work. A specialist thoroughly acquainted with the archival materials pertaining to the Society's foundation, Father Aldama often bases his interpretation of a passage on the history of the thought contained in it as ascertainable from the successive drafts from which it emerged.

This book, therefore, is a scholarly commentary, convenient to use because it treats all the *Constitutions* in one handy volume. The English version of this book is aptly called *An Introductory Commentary*. In the title the word "Constitutions" means the collected statutes contained in four treatises which St. Ignatius left in manuscript at his death in 1556, each with its own title: (1) the General Examen, an eight-chapter sketch of the Society's Institute intended for candidates; (2) the Declarations on the Examen; (3) the Constitutions of the Society of Jesus, with ten "Parts" which trace the admission, training, and later life of the members of the Society; and (4), the Declarations on the Constitutions.

These four treatises were grouped in the above order in the manuscript known as text B, the Autograph. They received their legislative force from their approval by the First General Congregation of the Society in 1558, and all their statutes have equal juridical value. They are St. Ignatius' detailed explanation of the Society's charism enshrined in the "Formula of the Institute" which became papal law in the bull of Pope Paul III, *Regimini militantis Ecclesiae*, dated September 27, 1540, and in the later bull containing slight revisions of Pope Julius III, *Exposcit debitum*, dated July 21, 1550. Both these bulls gave to Ignatius as superior general the "authority to establish constitutions leading to the achievement of the end proposed to us."[1] The word "Institute" means in this context "both our way of living and working, and the written documents in which this way is authentically and legitimately proposed."[2]

A brief sketch of a few highlights in Father Aldama's career will show how this and the other books in the series of commentaries came into being. He was born in Spain in 1908 and entered the Society of Jesus in 1924. He began his philosophical studies in Spain and, after the Jesuits were expelled from there shortly before the Spanish civil war, finished them in Marneffe, Belgium. He pursued his theological studies at Heythrop College, England. He became a military chaplain and then a professor of humanities to young Jesuits. From 1945 to 1950, during the generalate of Father John Baptist Janssens, he served in Rome as the Secretary of the Society of Jesus. Thereupon he was assigned to the Jesuit Historical Institute, Rome, to work and publish in the area of the Society's Institute. In this capacity he has published numerous articles and book reviews.

Father General Pedro Arrupe was deeply impressed by Father Aldama's extensive knowledge of his field and consulted him on numerous occasions when he desired expert opinion. Thinking that it would be a pity if Father Aldama's knowledge should be lost through advancing age or ill health, the general urged him to get his knowledge into print for the benefit of posterity. Father Aldama willingly complied and the Ignatian Center of Spirituality in Rome, "CIS," published his books in their original Spanish language. The order of their appearance was adjusted to circumstances of various needs and interests more than to steady progress through a preconceived plan. However, the completed set of six books falls into a very logical order, as follows:

> *Notas para un comentario a La Fórmula del Instituto de la Compañía de Jesús.* Rome: CIS, 1981. 126 pages.
> *Iniciación al estudio de las Constituciones.* Rome: CIS, 1979. 296 pages.
> *La vida religiosa de la Compañía de Jesús: Comentario a la VI Parte.* Rome: CIS, 1989.
> *Repartiéndose en la viña de Cristo: Comentario a la VII Parte.* Rome: CIS, 1973. 272 pages.
> *Unir a los repartidos: Comentario a la VIII Parte.* Rome: CIS, 1975. 289 pages.
> *El General de la Compañía de Jesús: su persona y su gobierno: Comentario a la IX Parte.* Rome: CIS, 1982. 179 pages.

In the later stages of this dedicated work Father Aldama was much hampered by increasing difficulties of vision and gradually became unable to read, though fortunately he retains his sight. He is presently engaged in

---

1   *Exposcit debitum,* [3]; in abbreviated editions, [1].
2   The 31st General Congregation, Decree 4, no. 2.

giving retreats and in spiritual counseling.

Father Arrupe also hoped that English translations of these books could be published. Some years ago the present writer, then Director of the Institute of Jesuit Sources, happened to be in Rome at the same time as Father Xavier Díaz del Río, Director in India of Gujarat Sahitya Prakash ("Gujarat Source of Light" in the Gujarati language), a division of Anand Press conducted by the Jesuits. We knew of Father Arrupe's desire and discussed the whole situation with Father Herbert Alphonso, Director of the Ignatian Center of Spirituality. All of us had overcrowded production schedules; but we resolved to do cooperatively everything we could to make these books available in English. The Commentary on Part VI is ready in Spanish but not yet published. Except for it, translations of all the works mentioned above are in our hands. The publishers involved plan to publish them as soon as their production schedules allow; but at present it is impossible to announce dates.

The English translation of this present volume by Father Aloysius J. Owen of St. Peter's College, Jersey City, New Jersey, was received with gratitude several years ago. But the press of other work made it impossible to do the time-consuming editing of this technical material. In time Jesuit confreres were found who successively did this work in the offices of the Institute of Jesuit Sources. Michael J. Woods and Eugene M. Turner each capably devoted much of a summer to it. After them John P. Leonard of Ireland became the chief editor and brought the typescript to readiness for publication, with help received along the way from John L. McCarthy, Philip C. Fischer, and the present writer. Martin E. Palmer prepared the page layouts and format. To all of these the Institute of Jesuit Sources expresses its gratitude. Father John W. Padberg, its present director, supervised all this work with patient understanding. Since I was Director of this Institute when the project of publishing this series of Father Aldama's books was planned and knew its earlier history, Father Padberg kindly invited me to write this Foreword. I comply with pleasure, and hope that my effort will be an expression of the gratitude I owe to Father Aldama, not only for this series of books but also for the invaluable help he gave me two decades ago when I was working on the English translation of St. Ignatius' *Constitutions of the Society of Jesus.*

George E. Ganss, S.J.
Director Emeritus
The Institute of Jesuit Sources
February 2, 1989

AUTHOR'S PREFACE

One of the most positive features of our age is surely the effort to return to the sources, to the origins, to the wellspring where the water flows fresh and pure, still uncontaminated and unsullied by its course through history.

In the Society of Jesus, a manifestation of this tendency has been the appearance of books and articles on St. Ignatius' *Constitutions of the Society of Jesus* and other writings. Such studies (apart from those on the *Spiritual Exercises*) have been more numerous in the past ten years than in former times, when authors were more inclined to focus their attention on the life and person of the saint himself.

This interest in studying the Constitutions is not without good reason. According to the letter prefaced to the first Latin edition of them, we are led to study the Constitutions by the grace of our vocation (or, as we might say today, by our "charism"). This grace or charism is set forth in the Formula of the Institute, but only in broad lines. It is in the Constitutions, the letter goes on to say, that we find "our Society's vital force, our order's solid foundation, the ties which must hold the whole body closely together so that the heavenly Spirit and the grace of God—the true life of a religious order—may dwell always therein. In them we shall find the pattern we should imitate, the path we should pursue, the light we should follow, the perfection we should aspire to, the mirror in which to examine our way of proceeding."

This book is intended as a modest contribution to the attempt at better understanding the grace of our vocation as presented in the Constitutions. We have entitled it *An Introductory Commentary* because our aim has not been to write a full-fledged commentary. Our intention was only to offer some clarifications, historical data, and perspectives which would be of help in reading this Ignatian work. We have aimed for the greatest possible objectivity, trying to insure that our interpretations were inspired by the text of the Constitutions themselves, by the way in which they took shape, by their written sources, by their historical context, and by similar means of determining the true mind of the author. We do not imagine that we have uniformly succeeded in this. Still, if our exposition stimulates others to bring fresh light, with different and even opposing points of view, we will be satisfied. Our wish is that Ignatius' thought become daily better known and more profoundly understood and thus be able to guide us more securely along the path of divine service we have undertaken.

It should be pointed out that our aim is at furnishing an introduction to the study of the Constitutions only, not of the Society's entire Institute. In other words, we limit ourselves to the law of the Constitutions and do not enter into the development this law has undergone with the changing times. Of course, this development presents many highly interesting aspects and deserves a study of its own. However, this would require too much space here and would distract us from our primary objective. Furthermore, in some cases we could not avoid controverting other opinions and other writers in the Society, and such controversies are always painful.

Every introduction is an invitation. Ours is an invitation to read the Constitutions themselves—to read them assiduously, so that one becomes familiar with the Ignatian text and and allows its expressions to sink into one's memory; to read them thoughtfully, so that (according to the reader's possibilities) one engages in a genuine study of them; and to read them meditatively, so that reading turns into prayer.

For this purpose the norm given by Jerónimo Nadal will be of help: one should read the Constitutions *spiritu, corde, practicê*:

Spiritu, "with the spirit"—rising from the letter to the spirit which animated Ignatius as he wrote. This is not to bypass the legal norms but to see them as informed and animated by the spirit which gives them their true meaning.

Corde, "with the heart"—opening the heart to the teachings of the man whom God has given us as a guide on this "road to Him." This should be with a sensitivity rendering us able to receive the imprint of his spirit; and with spiritual devotion, enabling us to "experience interiorly" the invitations that the grace of our vocation makes to us through the Constitutions.

Practicê, "with a view towards practice"—directing our reading towards practice, towards *living* the Constitutions and being transformed into the Gospel image of Jesus Christ which Ignatius contemplates in the Spiritual Exercises as the ideal of his life, which he was able to communicate through the Exercises to his companions—and which he left to us in the form of the Constitutions that it might also be the supreme ideal of our consecrated life.

Antonio M. de Aldama, S.J.
Rome, April 22, 1979

ABBREVIATIONS

AAS	*Acta Apostolicae Sedis*
ActRom	*Acta Romana Societatis Iesu*
ArchHistSI	*Archivum Historicum Societatis Iesu*
ARSI	Archivum Romanum Societatis Iesu
Autobiog	The *Autobiography* of St. Ignatius
C.G.	Congregatio Generalis
CIC	*Codex Iuris Canonici* (1917)
CIS	Centrum Ignatianum Spiritualitatis
CollDecr	*Collectio Decretorum Congregationum Generalium S.I.*
DicSpir	*Dictionnaire de spiritualité: ascétique et mystique*
Epit. Inst. S.I.	*Epitome Instituti Societatis Iesu*
Evang. Nunt.	*Evangelii Nuntiandi.* Apostolic Exhortation of Paul VI
Form. Inst.	The Formula of the Institute
GS	*Gaudium et Spes.* Vatican II, Pastoral Constitution on the Church in the Modern world
LG	*Lumen Gentium.* Vatican II, Dogmatic Constitution on the Church
MHSI	Monumenta Historica Societatis Iesus. The historical records of sources of the Society of Jesus in critically edited texts
Bobadilla	*Bobadillae Monumenta*
Direct	*Directoria Exercitiorum Spiritualium*
DocInd	*Documenta Indica*
EppMixt	*Epistolae Mixtae ex variis Europae locis, 1537-1556.* 5 vols.
EppXav	*Epistolae S. Francisci Xaverii.* 2 vols.
Laínez	*Lainii Monumenta.* 8 vols.
MonPaed	*Monumenta Paedagogica.* 1 vol. (The revision has 4 vols.)
Nadal	*Epistolae P. Hieronymi Nadal.* 6 vols.
PolChron	*Chronicon Societatis Iesu, auctore Polanco.* 6 vols.
PolCompl	*Polanci Complementa.* 2 vols.

MI	Monumenta Ignatiana. The writings of St. Ignatius of Loyola
Const	*Constitutiones et Regulae Societatis Iesu.* 4 vols.
Epp	*S. Ignatii Epistolae et Instructiones.* 12 vols.
Exer	*Exercitia Spiritualia S. Ignatii . . . et eorum Directoria*
FontDoc	*Fontes Documentales de S. Ignatio*
FontNarr	*Fontes Narrativi de S. Ignatio.* 2 vols.
Regulae	*Regulae Societatis Iesu*
Scripta	*Scripta de S. Ignatio.* 2 vols.
PC	*Perfectae Caritatis.* Vatican II, Decree on Renewal of Religious Life
PL	Patrologia Latina, ed. Migne
P.U.G.	Pontificia Università Gregoriana
Regula	Rule of St. Benedict
RevAscMyst	*Revue d'Ascétique et Mystique*
SC	*Sacrosanctum Concilium.* Vatican II, Constitution on the Sacred Liturgy
SpEx	*Exercitia Spiritualia.* The *Spiritual Exercises* of St. Ignatius
SpDiar	The *Spiritual Diary* of St. Ignatius
ZAM	*Zeitschrift für Aszese und Mystik*

Chapter I

THE IGNATIAN CONSTITUTIONS
(Genesis, Author, Character, Acceptance)

Upon first picking up the book of the *Constitutions of the Society of Jesus*, either in the original Spanish or in another language, a person may easily find two of its features rather confusing. In the first place, the work does not begin—as would seem logical—with Part I or with its Preamble. These are preceded by another document, the Examen, which, however, is not an introduction. In the second place, it is odd to find paragraphs in roman type interspersed with others in italics.

Actually, under the general title of *Constitutions of the Society of Jesus*, four books are included:

1. the Examen
2. the Declarations on the Examen
3. the Constitutions properly so called
4. the Declarations on the Constitutions.

In Ignatius' mind, these four books were distinct works. Soon, however, they began to be published as a single volume. The Declarations were printed in italics to distinguish them from the main text; they were set either in the margin or immediately after the corresponding paragraph in the main text.

As a result, the word "Constitutions" does not have a single meaning. In its narrowest sense it means only the third book in the above listing. In a wider sense it means that same book along with its Declarations. In a still wider sense it includes, as we said, all four books. In each case we shall have to determine by the context the sense in which the term is to be understood.

We think it advisable in this introductory chapter to describe the whole work in broad terms, discussing its origins and author, its particular nature or literary genre, and the kind of appreciation or acceptance the Constitutions have won.

I. GENESIS[1]

1. Preparation (1541-1549)

To study this topic with the fullness it deserves, we would have to begin by investigating Ignatius' spiritual development, his reading, his philosophical and theological formation, and his relations with members of other religious orders. For instance, we know that in the early days of his conversion Ignatius thought of entering the Carthusian monastery of Seville and sought information about the kind of life led by the Carthusians.[2] A letter written in 1536 to Gian Pietro Carafa shows that Ignatius regarded the two great founders of the mendicant orders, St. Francis and St. Dominic, as models,[3] though it is not clear that he had read their rules and constitutions[4] prior to the arrival of Polanco. Ignatius' contact with the patriarch of western monasticism, St. Benedict, merits special attention. The influence of the Rule of Monks (*Regula Monachorum*) can be observed in early Ignatian documents. An oral tradition of the monastery of Monte Cassino, unfortunately obscured by polemics, held that Ignatius read and studied this rule during the forty days he stayed there in the spring of 1538 while giving the Exercises to Doctor Ortiz.[5] However, the nature of the present work as a mere introduction to the study of the Constitutions does not permit us to investigate this aspect more deeply. We must content

---

1   We have developed this topic in the article entitled "La composición de las Constituciones de la Compañía de Jesús," published in *ArchHistSI*, 42 (1973), 211-245.

2   See *Autobiog*, no. 12

3   See MI Epp, I, 116; *ArchHistSI*, 44 (1975), 140-151. It is interesting to note that, judging by *Autobiog*, no. 7, it was the lives of these two saintly founders which made the greatest impression on him while he was reading the *Flos Sanctorum*.

4   The kind of poverty chosen for the Society in 1539 was certainly inspired by Franciscan poverty, but this poverty was defined in the decretals of the popes, which the first Jesuits knew well. Aloysius Hsü, S.J., in his doctoral thesis *Dominican Presence in the Constitutions of the Society of Jesus*, (ms., Rome: P.U.G., 1971), p. 23, interprets as references to the constitutions of other orders the signs in the form of a cross, which appear eight times in the *Determinationes Societatis* (MI Const., I, 10-14). But this interpretation lacks a solid foundation. The marginal crosses seem to indicate that the corresponding paragraph is a declaration or something that should go into the declarations.

5   The Benedictine authors who attest to this tradition were: A. Wion, *Lignum vitae et decus Ecclesiae* (1595); M. Scipione, *Elogia abbatum cassiniensium* (Naples 1630); C. Gaetani, *De Religiosa S. Ignatii sive Eneconis fundatoris Societatis per Patres Benedictinos institutione* (Venice 1641). Jean Rho, S.J., in his book *Achates* (Lyon 1644), answering the exaggerations of Dom Gaetani, admits that St. Ignatius read the Rule in Monte Cassino and even took notes from it.

ourselves with a summary of the stages through which the composition of the Constitutions passed.

Through an erroneous interpretation of the Preamble ([134]), some have thought that originally Ignatius did not intend to write constitutions, believing that the interior law of charity and love would suffice. In fact, from the very beginning he had determined to write constitutions. After the decision in mid-April of 1539 that the Society should become a religious order with its own superior, Ignatius and his companions remained together until June 24 in order to lay down the fundamental lines of the new institute—or, as Polanco states with precision: "to determine its form and its more substantial constitutions, desiring to imitate the apostolic model as best they could."[6] From these deliberations emerged the "Formula of the Institute," or fundamental Rule of the Society, in which it was foreseen that, in addition to it, there would be "constitutions"[7] in the Society.

The Formula authorized the superior general to draw up Constitutions, but in consultation with his brothers or companions. Consequently, when required to meet in 1541 to elect the first general, they took advantage of the occasion to settle some points of the Institute which had been left undecided or which experience had shown to require modification. The decisions then made were regarded as genuine "constitutions," though only provisional, and they are normally referred to as the "Constitutions of 1541."[8] They constitute an important source of the definitive Constitutions.

The fathers, however, quickly saw that the task of composing the Constitutions would be difficult if not impossible should they all need to be together to do it. Even on that occasion no more than six could be present and in fact the group never came together again. They then decided to leave the matter to the judgment of those who would remain in Italy. Eventually, since it was not easy to assemble even these, it was left to Ignatius alone.[9] Providence so disposed matters that the writer of the Constitutions should be Ignatius, to whom, according to the testimony of Francis Xavier, God had granted an interior perception of our way of life.[10]

Ignatius did not set out to compose all at once a complete and unified

6   MI FontNarr, II, 310.

7   Form. Inst., chap. I, no. 2.

8   Published in MI Const, I, 34-48. For instance, St. Ignatius alludes to them in the *Determinaciones antiguas*, nos. 1-5 (ibid., p. 211).

9   See MI Const, I, 23-24, 32-33, 69, 245.

10   MHSI EppXav, I, 176. The saint rejoices at the approbation of the Formula of the Institute, which he calls "our Rule and way of life," and thanks God for "having publicly manifested what secretly He gave His servant Ignatius, our Father, to feel."

text of the Constitutions, as is sometimes thought. His first step was to study particular points. He began with the question of poverty, which in the Constitutions of 1541 had become less severe than the original ideal. So, in the forty days of divine enlightenment described in his *Spiritual Diary*, he resolved to restore poverty to its original purity. Then he came to the subject, so central to the Society, of "missions." He wrote some pages on this under the title "Constitutions Regarding Missions," which were later to form the main nucleus of Part VII,[11] and some other pages on the ministry of teaching catechism to children,[12] and against ambition.[13] He also obtained from the pope the brief *Exponi nobis* in which the spiritual and temporal coadjutors were given their juridical position in the Institute and in which superiors subordinate to the general were introduced into the Society. He also composed the first text of the Examen; of this text only the declarations have been preserved.[14] Finally, he studied several other points of the Institute which were decided, it seems, only after the opinions of some competent fathers residing in Rome or passing through the city had been heard. These decisions he entitled "Early Determinations" (*Determinaciones antiguas*), "Determinations in the Lord" (*Determinaciones in Domino*), and "Notes for Determinations" (*Notas para determinar*).[15] They were later incorporated into the Constitutions, some of them almost verbatim.

As is clear, all this meant a great deal of work brought to completion by Ignatius himself, in spite of poor health and having to attend to the government of the Society at the same time. However, the preparation and editing of the Constitutions received its chief stimulus in 1547 when Ignatius named as his secretary the young Spaniard Juan Alonso de Polanco, a native of Burgos. Polanco was possessed of a mind that was clear, precise, and apt both for analysis and synthesis, quick to seize the implications of a situation or a doctrine, prodigiously methodical and good at organizing, not very original—though by this fact all the more capable of assimilating the ideas of others. He had received a solid philosophical and theological formation at the universities of Paris and Padua. He, then, was the ideal person to help Ignatius in his legislative labors.[16] In fact, his

---

11   MI Const, I, 159-164. In the first text of the Constitutions the folia containing these early norms were physically inserted.

12   According to the text of the document *Para fundar colegio* (ibid., pp. 49-65, col. 2).

13   MHSI MonPaed, 1st ed., 648-649, Index MI Const, I, 165-166.

14   MI Const, I, 248-256. The date which the editor tentatively assigns—1547-1549 —is unacceptable. It may be, at most, the beginning of 1547.

15   MI Const, I, 187-219.

16   For this characterization of Polanco, we have made use of the psychological profile by André Ravier in *Les Chroniques. Ignace de Loyola* (Nouvelle Librairie de France,

contribution was of such significance that it has given rise to the delicate and disquieting question of how much of the work is due to the founder and how much to the secretary.

First of all, Polanco sought to gain a deep knowledge of the Institute of the Society. He informed himself about its origins and studied the pontifical approbations and other documents prior to his time. In the second place, perhaps at Ignatius' behest or at least with his approval, he read and made extracts from the rules and constitutions of other religious orders.[17] The influence of these readings will be felt later on in the Constitutions of the Society, especially in Part III. However, as the evolution of the texts progressed, we shall see this influence become slighter and more remote. Nevertheless, the very fact of the influence is important since Ignatius has all too often been depicted as an absolute innovator who turned his back on the whole past of religious life in the Church. It is true that he ruled out monastic-style community and stability as incompatible with his ideal of the itinerant apostolic mission, yet he desired to place himself in the ancient tradition which distinguished the religious state in the Church. Also, to the extent that the charism proper to the Society allowed, he wanted to take advantage of the rich spiritual heritage found in the legislation of other religious orders.

Having informed himself about the Institute of the Society and the legislation on religious in the Church, Polanco did not proceed further without submitting to Ignatius the reflections and questions aroused in his mind about various aspects of the Institute.[18]

A final step was the composition of two preparatory treatises: "Measures Which the Society Should Use the Better to Attain its End" (*Industrias con que se ha de ayudar la Compañía para que mejor proceda para su fin*)[19] and "Constitutions of the Colleges" (*Constituciones de los colegios*).[20] The latter treatise was intended to help unify life in the schools which were being founded, though it was not sent out to the provinces—perhaps because at

---

1973), p. 325.

17 The codex containing these extracts, which for brevity we shall call *Collectanea Polanci*, is preserved in the archives of the Pontifical Gregorian University. Hsü made a careful transcript of it as an appendix to his doctoral thesis, which we cited in note 4.

18 See MI Const, I, 275-339. The documents which the editor calls series 5 and 6 are very diverse documents. They are questions proposed by St. Ignatius to some experts of the Roman Curia.

19 Published in MHSI PolCompl, 725-775. What the editor calls the 2nd series of *Industrias* (ibid., pp. 776-807) is only *Industria* 9, perhaps expanded.

20 Published in MI Regulae, 217-245.

that time the general Constitutions, which included references to schools, were already being composed. In the "Measures" (*Industrias*), it seems that Polanco, undoubtedly at Ignatius' direction, aimed not so much at organizing the legislative material he had gathered as at complementing it with some aspects of the life and activity of the Society which had not yet been properly considered. Both these drafts later became proximate sources of the Constitutions of the Society. The "Constitutions of the Colleges" influenced the composition of Parts III and IV. The influence of the "Measures" (*Industrias*) is to be found throughout the Constitutions, though to a lesser extent in Parts II, III, and IV.

2. Composition (1549-1556)

The composition of the Constitutions themselves took place in four stages:

(1) 1546-1547: the first extant text of the Examen, named by the editor "text alpha."
(2) 1549-1550: the primitive text of the Constitutions (called "text a") and the second text of the Examen (called "text A").
(3) 1550: text A of the Constitutions and text B of the Examen.
(4) 1551-1553: the definitive text of the Constitutions (called "text B").

The word "text" here refers not to the tenor of thought or content of the Constitutions, but merely to the manuscripts or copies made of them. As we shall see, these various manuscripts do not strictly speaking contain different editions (though we occasionally use this expression, for the sake of simplicity), but rather an evolutionary process in which a single edition is subject to corrections and successive changes. We shall speak of the textual evolution of the Examen in chapter 2 below.

The primitive text of the Constitutions has all the appearances of a first project or rough draft. In it the sources are copied literally, or almost literally, and at times even the folios containing them were incorporated into the text. There is no distinction between "constitutions" and "declarations," as had already been decided in 1541. Not infrequently quite tentative language is used: "It seems that there ought" (*parece que debría*).

This primitive text has often been given too much importance, as if it were the only accurate embodiment of Ignatius' thought. In fact, Ignatius' handwriting does not even appear in this text. Approximately three-quarters of the text (109 out of the 145 pages) are in Polanco's handwriting. The amount of corrected phrases and expressions, in proportion to the whole text, shows that he was neither copying a prior text, nor taking dictation, but actually composing the text himself.

The rudimentary and experimental character of this text is further demonstrated by the fact that, as soon as it was completed in the summer of 1550, another text, text A, began to be composed. This second text was more carefully constructed than the primitive text, although it occasionally lacks the freshness of the writings in the first attempt. In this text, the paragraphs taken directly from other sources are so worked over that their origins are not easily recognized; here the declarations appear distinct from the constitutions.

Text A was written by two copyists under Polanco's direction. He gave them appropriate directions on when to transcribe directly from the primitive text and when to insert different wordings which he had previously prepared. In general, the first four Parts underwent more changes than the last six, which follow more closely the wording of the primitive text.

We can find the handwriting of Ignatius at some 230 places in this text. At time, he corrects words or phrases, often showing a concern for even minor details of expression. At other times he adds, deletes, or substitutes entire paragraphs. Finally, he sometimes indicates the change to be made by means of a marginal note to Polanco.

Ignatius submitted text A of the Constitutions (along with text B of the Examen) to the judgment of the fathers who were able to meet in Rome in January 1551. Besides Ignatius himself, the only others of the first ten companions who could be present were Laínez and Salmerón.[21] Their observations,[22] along with a greater reflection on the whole matter in the light of experience, made necessary the composition of another text, the definitive text B.

The procedure followed in writing text B was the same as for the previous one. For the most part, text B was copied directly from text A, which had been corrected by Ignatius and Polanco for this purpose. However, there are some places in which substitutions are made for the wording of text A.

The more important of these changes are: the reduction of the number of chapters in some Parts, involving the combination of two, or even three, chapters into one; the transfer of some paragraphs from the Constitutions to the Declarations; the change in the order of the chapters in Part III and Part VI. Subsequently some important additions were made to the text, such as those in chapters 7 and 11-17 of Part IV.

---

21 Simão Rodrigues arrived somewhat later, and later still Bobadilla.

22 Some are preserved in writing and have been published in MI Const, I, 391-396. It is quite possible and very probable that others were communicated by word of mouth.

Again, Ignatius' handwriting appears many times, though less frequently than in text A. This is not at all surprising since not a few of the corrections in text A were made so that it might serve as an original from which the new text could be copied. Besides that, as the editing of a document nears the definitive stage, fewer corrections are necessary.

Text B was substantially completed in 1553, when a copy of it was entrusted to Nadal for him to use in the promulgation of the Constitutions in the provinces of Spain and Portugal. Ignatius, however, continued to make corrections in the text until his death in 1556. He did not want to give the text the final touches, believing this to be the duty of the general congregation. Doubtless, this was a sign of his fidelity to the Formula of the Institute, which gave the general the authority to draw up constitutions, but with the advice and deliberative vote of his companions.

The First General Congregation (1558) did as the founder wished and designated text B as *autographus Patris Ignatii*. This did not mean that the text was written entirely in his hand, nor was this a description in relation to earlier texts. It was meant simply in the sense of an original text used, corrected, and approved by Ignatius, of which all the later texts are mere copies. Among these are Nadal's copy (mentioned above), a copy (called text C) made after the death of Ignatius and approved by the same First General Congregation and a copy (text D) made in 1594 and declared official by the Fifth General Congregation.

II. AUTHOR

The question of authorship may hardly seem pertinent here. However, we think it needs to be discussed since it has more than once (and even recently) been an object of controversy.

There is a very old legend that the Declarations were actually added by Laínez, perhaps assisted by Salmerón.[23] Some have wanted to see in the book of the Constitutions a sort of mosaic in which the practiced eye could distinguish a small number of Ignatian fragments embedded in passages properly attributed to Nadal or Polanco.[24] In the proceedings of the French parliament against the Society in the eighteenth century, there was

---

23   As early as 1588 Aquaviva had to refute this view. See letter to the provincial of Andalusía, published in the photographic edition of the Constitutions (Rome 1908), p. 9. Among modern authors see H. Müller, *Les origines de la Compagnie de Jésus* (Paris 1890), pp. 228-229.

24   Quoted without name or any other reference by P. Dudon, S.J., *Saint Ignace de Loyola* (Paris 1932), p. 414.

someone who held that even if Ignatius had written a primitive text of the Constitutions it must have been considerably altered by his collaborators.[25] This opinion coincides with a recent one defended, in more scholarly fashion, by François Roustang.[26] None of these opinions can be supported in the light of the evidence in the manuscript texts.

A difficult and delicate question which deserves more attention is that of the collaboration between Ignatius and his secretary, Polanco. We shall begin by saying that the testimony of contemporaries speaks eloquently on this point: none of them hesitates to attribute to Ignatius the authorship of the Constitutions.[27] As an example we cite the introductory letter of the first Latin edition (1559), probably written by Laínez, then general, or at least under his direction and with his full approval. He said that the Society, dispersed in various parts of the world and engaged in the most serious occupations of faith and religion, had good reason to entrust the work of writing the Constitutions to our Father Ignatius, "its first author and founder." He added that Ignatius approached the task with such diligence and prudence, and so conscientiously, that for many years he gave himself chiefly to this work. During this time he begged the Lord with tears, constant supplications, and devout celebrations of Mass for the anointing of the Holy Spirit in order that under His inspiration and guidance he might accomplish through divine grace what he could not do through human wisdom. Laínez ends by saying that in this way Ignatius "with great effort composed all of the Constitutions and each one of its parts and carried the work to completion."[28]

Some comments of Bobadilla are also of interest for the light they throw on the question since these were written when, in a moment of temptation, he was trying to reduce the importance of the Constitutions by maintaining that the power of legislation belonged to the group of the first fathers. He wrote: "Despite this, Master Ignatius alone wrote them, since he was father and absolute master, and did what he wanted."[29]

25 See J. P. R. de Rippert de Montclar, *Compte rendu des Constitutions de la Compagnie de Jésus* (1762), p. 30.

26 *Constitutions de la Compagnie de Jésus*, II (Coll. Christus, no. 24), "Introduction à une lecture," pp. 11-138.

27 A. Codina has collected these testimonies in the prologomena to the critical edition of the Spanish texts. MI Const, II, pp. cxlvi-clv.

28 MI Const, III, p. cxlvi. "Constitutiones omnes et omnes earum partes summis laboribus confecit et suis numeris absolvit."

29 MHSI Nadal, IV, 733. Bobadilla forgot that St. Ignatius had submitted to his judgment the text of the Constitutions and that he had only made some observations of minor importance. See MI Const, I, 396.

When we approach the question of collaboration between Polanco and Ignatius, first of all we must set aside the Examen since, with the exception of some additions and later corrections, it was completed prior to the arrival of Polanco. As to the Constitutions proper and their Declarations, it has been wisely observed that "it is an impossible task to explain clearly the relationship between two people who complement each other so fully as to have almost become one person."[30] Supposing this to be the case, it would be wrong to present Ignatius—as has so often been done—as writing the Constitutions word for word in his own hand, or at least dictating every word and sentence, with Polanco being used merely as an amanuensis. It would be equally wrong to think that Polanco wrote the Constitutions on his own and that Ignatius later claimed them as his own work, as do some administrators with documents prepared by secretaries or experts.

The *material* author of the Constitutions is undoubtedly Polanco. In addition to the "Measures" and the "Constitutions for the Colleges," he wrote, in his own hand, nearly the entire primitive text of the Constitutions and in the writing of the other texts he was directing the copyists (assistants in the secretariat). At times he made editorial additions, which had to be inserted into the text as it was being copied. In this editorial work Polanco was neither following a prior Ignatian text nor was he taking dictation; he was composing. However, it cannot be said that he was composing entirely on his own. Before setting out on this work, he endeavored to know the mind of the founder, studying all the Ignatian documents pertinent to the Institute and submitting his own questions and ideas to Ignatius for clarification. We must remember too that Polanco was in constant contact with Ignatius, engaging in the ordinary affairs of governing the Society and observing how these were judged and resolved by the saint. Having known and assimilated the founder's ideas and "taken on his person" ([800]), Polanco endeavored to interpret them faithfully in the editing of the Constitutions. This task was easier and surer for Polanco than for others because he was gifted with a penetrating, though not original, intelligence.

The historical sources do not allow us with certainty to determine what part Ignatius personally played in the first phase of this task. It is very probable, at least, that during this stage the founder and his secretary discussed among themselves the plan of the work, the development of some of its parts, and other particular questions.[31] Already in the second stage,

---

30   The observation is by Angelo Martini, S.J., in *ArchHistSI*, 26 (1957), 102.

31   An indication, among others, may be the marginal note placed by Polanco in a rough draft of Part V, apropos of the vows of scholastics. See MI Const, II, p. 515, critical apparatus, 2nd col.

text A, we have seen Ignatius constantly intervening, removing and adding text, changing entire paragraphs, descending into details of style, and pointing out to Polanco various other alterations to be made. The same procedure can be seen in the editing of text B. Polanco's fidelity to Ignatian thinking is obvious from the care he took with these corrected paragraphs, preserving Ignatius' wording, even though he often had to change the syntax. This fidelity is further demonstrated by his willingness to submit each new change to Ignatius' judgment and approval. Only twice was he in doubt whether Ignatius had "reviewed" the correction (of a secondary matter). These exceptions serve only to confirm his general rule in other cases.

There is, then, no doubt that the Constitutions express the *thought* of Ignatius, though this does not mean that we can analyze each word and sentence as if they were all spoken or written by the saint himself. Only in those passages where the textual history indicates a direct intervention by Ignatius is such analysis justified. In general, the actual words and phrases are the means used by Polanco to express the mind of the founder. Doubtless some, or even many, of them came directly from Ignatius in conversation with his secretary, though we cannot be certain which ones these are.

III. CHARACTER

There have been many different attempts to find a key to the reading of the Constitutions.

Some, influenced by the current cultural atmosphere, have believed it to be found in the structure itself of the Parts and chapters; this is a dangerous path that easily leads to a priori and subjective judgments, a danger that has not always been avoided. The only recourse here is to adhere closely to the explicit indications of the author. In regard to the arrangement of the ten Parts of the Constitutions, Ignatius states explicitly that he is not following a systematic order, or order of intention, but rather the practical order of execution ([135-137]). A systematic order first presents the end and then the means to attain it, whereas the practical order of execution first presents the means and through them works up to the end to be achieved. In it the means are treated first and the achieved end last. In the order of intention the reverse is true. On another occasion, when enumerating the qualities proper to the general, he says that he is setting down the qualities in the order of importance ([724]), and we see that this order is: spirit, soul, body, and exterior gifts; and in the soul, the order of the faculties—memory, understanding, and will. We find the same order, at least partially, in the listing of the qualities proper to a candidate in Part I ([153-161]), in the arrangement of the chapters in Part III, and in the designation of the general's collaborators in Part IX ([698-807]). Also listed in order of importance are the reasons for dismissal in Part II ([209-217]), the means for the preservation of the Society in Part X, and probably the arrangement of the chapters of Part VI. At other times, we can see clearly that the author has in mind an outline of the various circumstances that could be involved in the topic being dealt with: who, whom (or what), how, and the like. Examples of this are to be found in the chapters of Parts I, II, and V, in the Declarations of the second chapter of Part VII, in chapters 2-7 of Part VIII and so forth. But apart from the danger of subjectivism already mentioned, this method of approaching the Constitutions runs other risks as well. It fails to give us the intimate feeling, the soul, that enlivens the whole work and thus it does not offer us a true key to reading it.

Another school holds that the Constitutions are the fruit of experience and should lead to experience. Since the experience that gave rise to the Constitutions was a "discerning" one, that is to say, one pondered with spiritual discretion, they ought not lead directly to activity, but rather to a spiritual discernment of what is to be done. More than a collection of norms, the Constitutions are an aid to discernment, offering us criteria for discernment. Some even say that the Constitutions are only a guide, a "vademecum" or manual pointing out not *what* we have to do but *the way* in which we ought to proceed.

All this could be a reaction against a certain rationalism or voluntarism which prevailed in the spirituality of the Society for a long time, itself a reaction in its day against quietism or the effect of an extreme fear of pseudomysticism. We ought to take care that—as frequently happens in human reactions—we do not fall into the opposite extreme. It is true that the Constitutions are the fruit of experience (what human law is not?), but not of experience alone. To experience must be added reflection on the demands of this vocation and on the specific end of the Society, and spiritual illumination. Read the *Spiritual Diary* of Ignatius. The Constitutions lead to experience. These laws are not philosophical propositions written for intellectual speculation; they are made for practice, to be observed. Likewise we grant that the observance of these laws (again as in the case of any other law) need not be literal, only conformed to the mind of the legislator. Equally, we grant that it is characteristic of the Ignatian Constitutions (as we shall discuss later) not to be merely procedural, but along with this to furnish a motive, and through it a spirit with which the procedures are to be observed. In all this, then, we are in agreement with the authors just mentioned. If, however, they mean to say that the Constitutions are not normative, that they do not contain laws, but are criteria of spiritual prudence; if they mean to reduce the Constitutions to something like an edifying book, such as the *Imitation of Christ*, then we cannot but disagree. Ignatius evidently wants the Constitutions to be observed "in full," though not under pain of sin ([602]), and he does not want us to lose the opportunity for perfection that could be obtained in their fulfillment ([547]). The general is to see that they are observed ([745, 790]) and although he may dispense from them, with consideration for their objectives ([746]), this very authority proves that they really are preceptive laws. He is not excused from applying a criterion of discernment.

How, then, are we to find the key we are seeking in order to read the text correctly?

All religious legislation aims at actualizing and preserving the original ideal through a juridical systematization. This juridical systematization is necessary in all societies and human communities "in order that the proper order necessary in every well-organized community may be preserved" (*ut congruus ordo servetur in omni bene instituta communitate necessarius*), as the Formula of the Institute states.[32] However, what illuminates, what animates and vivifies the law is the ideal that it aims to actualize and preserve. In other words, this ideal is the vocation proper to the Institute, "our profession," to use the Ignatian expression, or, as we are now accustomed to say (using a less exact term), our charism.

What is this original ideal of the Society? Ignatius spoke of it many times. As early as 1536, before the Society was established as a religious order, he disclosed to the archdeacon of Barcelona his intention to live "in a state of preaching in poverty."[33] Eight years later, in the "Deliberation on Poverty," he spoke more explicitly, alluding to the poverty that Jesus Christ taught his apostles as He sent them out to preach: "All ten [companions] choosing this [poverty] unanimously (*nemine discrepante*), we take as our head Jesus Christ Himself, our Creator and Lord, to go out under his banner preaching and converting, which is *our profession*."[34] Somewhat later, in the "Constitutions Regarding Missions," in a passage which passed almost

---

32   Form. Inst., chap. I, no. 2.

33   To Jaime Cazador, February 12, 1536 (MI Epp, I, 96). It is of interest to note that like expressions are found in the early writings of the Order of Preachers: "*In paupertate* evangelica, pedites, religiose proposuerunt incedere, et veritatis evangelicae verbum *praedicare*" (Document of 1215, published by M. H. Laurent, O.P., *Historia diplomatica S. Dominici*, [MonOFP Hist], XV, 66).

34   MI Const, I, 80, no. 13. See *SpDiar*, Feb. 11, 1544 (ibid., pp. 90-91).

literally into the definitive Constitutions, he declares that his promise or intention and that of his companions is "to wander through the world and, where they did not find the desired spiritual fruit in one part or another, to go on to another and another in succession, going through towns and other particular places, to the greater glory of God our Lord and for the greater spiritual benefit of souls."[35] Here, and in other passages which we can omit for the sake of brevity,[36] the "apostolic life" is described in the sense that this expression had taken on since the twelfth century and which St. Thomas, with his characteristic clarity and precision, defined, saying that the apostolic life consists in this, that the apostles, having left everything, went out through the world evangelizing and preaching, as is seen in Matthew 10.[37] In the Society this apostolic life came to full realization when Paul III reserved for himself the right of sending out those who were to practice it. Thus, it established itself as a "missionary" lifestyle, or a life on "mission," not because all members of the Society actually engage in a "mission," but because they "ought to be ready at any hour to go to some or other parts of the world where they may be sent by the sovereign pontiff or their own superiors" ([588]; see also [82, 308]). This apostolic life, or life on mission, determines and conditions the majority of the norms of the Constitutions, such as those which refer to selection, intellectual formation, the vows of obedience and poverty, central government, and so on.[38]

This life, however, is not to be lived individually or separately, nor joined with others merely by bonds of common aspiration; rather, it is to be lived by forming with others an organized body, a religious order in the Church. Such was the decision of the first fathers in the deliberation of 1539. The Constitutions, along with the ideal of the "mission," show us how the body, in which such a life is to be enfleshed, is organized; the manner of structuring the religious order in which it has to be realized. Ideal and realization, the spirit and body, "mission" and juridical organization (or, if we wish to use contemporary terms, charism and institution), are the two aspects or dimensions which together offer us the real key to reading the

---

35   MI Const, I, 160.

36   See, for instance, the letter to King Ferdinand of Austria, 1546 (MI Epp, I, 451).

37   St. Thomas, *Contra impugnantes cultum et religionem*, chap. 4. In the same sense an anonymous Dominican of the 13th century wrote: "Vita apostolica est omnia propter Christum relinquere, et paupertatem servando Ipsum praedicare" ("Tractatus de approbatione Ordinis Fratrum Praedicatorum," *ArchOFPraed*, VI [1936], 145, lines 21-22).

38   We have developed this theme in the article "La misión, centro focal de las Constituciones ignacianas," published in *Ejercicios-Constituciones. unión vital* (Bilbao 1974), pp. 262-286.

Constitutions. We will stress this point when speaking of the image of the body in the Preamble.

The Ignatian Constitutions are not, of course, perfect. They seem to be in need of a final revision to correct some defects in form. There are unnecessary repetitions, and some passages, due to the revision of the text or to mistakes by copyists, have remained obscure. Other additions do not seem to be in their proper places. Above all, the Constitutions have been criticized for descending too often into minor details, a trait especially distasteful to modern readers. However, note that very general laws are not very effective, and that the preoccupation with detail in the Constitutions is more than compensated for by their adaptability to circumstances, a feature we shall soon discuss.

Furthermore, these deficiencies in form do not obscure the great values contained in the Constitutions. We will be content to point out three here, which we judge to be the most characteristic.

The first is that, like the Rule of St. Benedict, but unlike the constitutions of the other older religious orders, the Ignatian Constitutions are not mere ordinances. The prescription of what is to be done is ordinarily supported and given life by a spiritual motive, or the "spirit" with which it is to be observed.

St. Gregory the Great said that the Rule of St. Benedict is notable for its discretion (*discretione praecipua*).[39] Without making an unwarranted comparison, something very similar could be said of the Ignatian Constitutions, designating this as one of their characteristic features. They observe, in effect, the "moderation" or the perfect mean which they recommend for all legislation in the Society, without leaning "toward an extreme of rigor or toward excessive laxity" ([822]). At various times the "iron discipline" of the Jesuits has been overemphasized. If it actually existed in any period, it was not in virtue of the founder's Constitutions. We need only point out that the Constitutions contain no penal code such as can be found in all or nearly all the ancient constitutions, even the Benedictine Rule.

The fruit of this discretion is a third characteristic, that is, flexibility or adaptability to various situations. The author always makes room for exceptions and accommodations to the general norm that these varied situations might require. Sometimes he mentions them concretely; at other times he gives general advice so that circumstances of times, places, and persons be given consideration. In more than twenty places in the text we encounter this advice. The purpose of the Declarations is to guide the

---

39 St. Gregory the Great, 2nd book of the *Dialogues*, chap. 36.

superior in the prudent application of the general norms.

These characteristics have insured that the Ignatian Constitutions have always retained their vitality and contemporary value. It is significant that in recent decades they have aroused even more interest and been studied with greater enthusiasm.[40]

IV. ACCEPTANCE

In the Society the Constitutions have always been accepted, and even venerated, as a priceless heritage of the saintly founder.[41] Laínez, for example, wrote that in them Ignatius had left "a great treasure, for they contain a very holy and prudent policy (or way of life) and will more than suffice for one who would want to be governed by them in order to become a great servant of God our Lord."[42] He added that the Ignatian Constitutions were enough even to govern and reform all the religious in the Church.[43] There was perhaps one exception [to this pattern of acceptance and reverence], that of Bobadilla under temptation, to which we alluded earlier.[44]

The Society especially manifested this esteem and reverence for the Constitutions when various attempts were made to change them. This occurred, for example, when under Paul IV an attempt was made to introduce a three-year term for the general, and when under St. Pius V the practice of choir and final profession prior to ordination were introduced.[45]

The same attitude was apparent at the general congregations. The First General Congregation, after approving and ratifying them, ordered that the Constitutions be observed "as they are in the original text of our Father Ignatius." It decreed that "the substantial constitutions of our institute" should not be subject to discussion and that the others should not be modified without previous trial or without a very clear reason.[46] These

---

40   See I. Iparraguirre, S.J., *Orientaciones bibliográficas sobre san Ignacio de Loyola* (Rome 1957), nos. 478-514; M. Ruiz Jurado, S.J., *Orientaciones*, II (Rome 1977), nos. 372-466.

41   See *CollDecr*, d. 2, §1.

42   Laínez to Juan de Vega, Dec. 30, 1556 (MHSI Laínez, I, 636).

43   Reference by Ribadeneira: MI Scripta, II, 160.

44   See MHSI Nadal, IV, 733 and 734.

45   See MHSI Laínez, VIII, 649 (Le Bas), 707 (Borgia), 725 (Goudanus), 741 (Pelletier); Nadal, IV, 166 ff.

46   C. G. I, dd. 15 and 16; see d. 49, and C. G. II, d. 6.

decrees have been confirmed in our own century by Congregation XXVII (1923) and Congregation XXXI (1965-66).[47]

Some have stressed the fact that Ignatius did not want to "close" the Constitutions, and have deduced from this that they should always remain open to whatever modifications the passage of time might indicate to be desirable. However, in Ignatian language, to "close" the Constitutions meant nothing more than putting the final touches on them and definitively approving them. Ignatius, out of humility and fidelity to the Formula of the Institute, did not want to do this; it was to be left up to the congregation of the whole Society. Once the First General Congregation had reviewed and approved them, they remained definitively "closed." In 1565, Polanco wrote: "it appears that nothing has to be changed in the Constitutions approved by our Father Ignatius and the [First] Congregation; for they have been established with much prayer and experience, *and the final touch has been given to them.*"[48]

The Ignatian text was even more firmly established by a decree of Congregation III (1573), confirmed by Congregation XXVII, which stated that, if a congregation wanted some prescription of the Constitutions to cease being observed, it must say this in a note without changing the original text, which must be passed on to our successors just as we received it from our Father Ignatius.[49]

These resolutions of the general congregations may be criticized (and already have been) as placing the Constitutions under a binding procedure that impedes their vital adaptation to changing times. The most compelling reason for this concern to preserve the Constitutions intact is (as has been said before) that the Ignatian code is not reducible to a set of regulatory norms. The regulations and prescriptions are supported and illuminated by their spiritual and theological motivation. The spiritual and the regulatory are so intimately linked in the Constitutions that—as someone said at Congregation XXXI—it is impossible to alter the latter without the former suffering harm or disappearing altogether. The Ignatian Constitutions are a monument to religious life which, like the Benedictine Rule, must be preserved and passed on intact to future generations.

---

47 C. G. XXVII *CollDecr*, d. 14; C. G. XXXI, d. 4, no. 3. [Editor's note: General Congregation XXXI did confirm the substantials of the Institute in its decree 4, no. 3; but it also made changes in decrees 12-16 found in the Collectio Decretorum, pp. 11-16. Among these changes was the abrogation of decree 13 on pp. 11-15, namely, the material which is in Epit. Inst. S. I. (1962), #22, pp. 320-323.]

48 ARSI, *Inst* 148, p. 151.

49 C. G. III, d. 23; C. G. XXVII, *CollDecr*, d. 14, §4.

Outside the Society these Constitutions have been little known until recent years. For this reason, the evaluations of the Society by various authors refer more to its activity and its organization in general than to the book of the Constitutions themselves.

The prosecutors of the French parliaments or courts of justice subjected the Institute of the Society to criminal prosecution in the eighteenth century and thus became acquainted with the Constitutions. However, their judgments are not worth citing, not because they are negative, but because the passionate bias that both animates them and robs them of all value is readily apparent.[50] Much the same might be said about the lectures on the Jesuits given a century later in Paris by Professors Michelet and Quinet.[51]

It will suffice to quote from an author who is better informed about the origins of the Society and, though a Protestant, more impartial: Heinrich Boehmer. In the first edition of his work *Die Jesuiten*, after analyzing the Ignatian Constitutions, he concludes by saying: "This organization is without doubt a masterpiece of its kind, and its author is one of the greatest organizational geniuses of all time." In the final edition he writes: "Considering the Constitutions of Ignatius of Loyola, one might dare to assert that, if a human association was ever perfectly organized, both internally and externally, for the mission it set out to accomplish, it is the Society of Jesus."[52]

All of this, however, pales before the judgment and approbation accorded by the Holy See. The Constitutions were approved by Paul III even before they were written. By renewing in 1544 the permission granted for their composition, he signaled, by this fact, that they were to be regarded as approved by apostolic authority.[53] Our fathers took as a real approbation the fact that, having had the Constitutions examined by two cardinals, Paul IV returned the document intact, even though it was thought that he would disapprove of them, especially after Bobadilla's intervention. Only later did Paul IV impose on the Society, by a verbal

---

50   A resumé of these judgments is in A. J. Brou, S.J., *Les jésuites et la légende* (Paris 1907), II, pp. 146-153.

51   Michelet et Quinet, *Les jésuites* (Paris 1844). An impartial judgment of this work by the Protestant Gabriel Monod may be found in the introduction to the French translation of H. Boehmer's book which we cite in the following note, *Les Jésuites* (Paris 1910), p. xii.

52   H. Boehmer, *Die Jesuiten. Eine historische Skizze*, 3rd ed. (Leipzig 1913), p. 42; in the last posthumous edition (Stuttgart 1957), p. 67. The first assertion has been commented on and developed by A. Favre-Dorsaz, *Calvin et Loyola* (Paris-Brussels 1951), pp. 306-307.

53   Paul III, *Iniunctum nobis*.

precept, choir and the three-year term for the general.[54]

Of special importance are the approbations of Gregory XIII, Gregory XIV, and Paul V. These three, in approving the Constitutions, used the solemn formula: "by our own desire, certain knowledge, and the plenitude of our apostolic authority, just as if the Constitutions were inserted verbatim in this present document" (*motu proprio, certa scientia, de apostolicae potestatis plenitudine, ac si [Constitutiones] ad verbum praesentibus litteris insererentur*). This formula, according to the canonists, denotes an approval "in specific form."[55] The force of this approval may be summed up in the following two points: (1) From a juridical viewpoint, documents thus approved are converted into papal and canonical documents. This, however, does not deprive the Society of the authority, given by the Holy See itself, to modify its own Constitutions; though clearly any modified passage would not enjoy this same papal approbation. (2) From a theological viewpoint, these approbations, without being dogmatic definitions, are expressions, in their own degree infallible,[56] of the Church's magisterium, which, at least on substantial points, excludes all doctrinal error. They give us, then, the guarantee that, in the observance of the Constitutions, we have a sure path to religious perfection and what is proper to our Institute.[57]

54 See Nadal, *Scholia* (ed. Ruiz Jurado 1976), pp. 307-308; O. Mannaerts, *Exhortationes super instituto et regulis* (Brussels-Roulers 1912), p. 81.

55 Gregory XIII, *Quanto fructuosius* and *Ascendente Domino*; Gregory XIV, *Ecclesiae catholicae*; Paul V, *Quantum religio*.

56 [Editor's note: The original Spanish uses the expression *en su grado infalíbles*. There are serious reasons for questioning such an extension of the word "infallible" in these circumstances.]

57 See Luis Mendizábal, S.J., "El hecho eclesiástico de la obediencia ignaciana," article in *Manresa*, 36 (1964), 410-414.

Chapter II

INSTRUCTION AND EXAMINATION
OF CANDIDATES

(Examen, chapters 1-3, 5-8)

I. PRELIMINARY REMARKS

1. Originality

The book of the Examen is of a unique character. We can find its origin and foundation in the Formula of the Institute, or fundamental Rule of the Society. On the one hand, the Formula exhorts those who wish to enter the Society to consider carefully before taking on this burden lest they deserve the rebuke mentioned in the Gospel: "This man began to build, but was not able to finish."[1] On the other hand, it cautions against the Society's admitting anyone whose life and doctrine have not been thoroughly examined (*explorata*).

The early monks, it is true, were very careful not to admit readily anyone who presented himself at the monastery. St. Pachomius made candidates wait at the monastery entrance for some days.[2] According to Cassian, a candidate was not accepted until he had spent ten days making the request, prostrated on the ground, in tears.[3] St. Benedict also counsels in his Rule that no one wishing to embrace the monastic life should be admitted until after four or five days, during which the candidate is to persevere in asking to enter and in enduring the delay and other difficulties.[4] The Constitutions of the Dominican Order prescribed that three competent friars be appointed in each convent to examine candidates and to report later to the prior and the chapter.[5]

Nevertheless, it is hard to find a book written for the purpose of being

---

1   Lk. 14:30.
2   *Regula Pachomii*, 49.
3   Cassianus, *Institutiones*, IV, 3; *Conlationes*, XXI, 1.
4   Regula, chap. 58.
5   *Constitutiones O.P.*, Dist. I, chap. 13. According to A. H. Thomas, O.P., *De oudste Constituties van de Dominicanen* (Leuven 1965), pp. 289-290, note 241, what is prescribed is of 1232-1235.

used in the examination of candidates. We know of one precedent, the "Function of the Examiner" included by Humbert of Romans in his book on the Instruction of Officials of the Order of Preachers (*De Instructione Officialium Ordinis Praedicatorum*). However, the differences between these two books are substantial. That of Humbert of Romans is only a guide for the examiners and only for the examination, while the Ignatian text is, as we shall explain shortly, for the purpose of informing the candidates. Besides this, when Ignatius wrote the Examen, he did not know of this Dominican legislator's book, so that we can affirm that his work was entirely original.

2. Structure

This Ignatian text is often cited, even in official documents of the Society, under the title of General Examen. But this is an incorrect title originating from an error made by the copyist of text D (the 1594 text). He omitted the title of the whole book, *Examen*,[6] which occupied its own page in the "autograph." The book consists of eight chapters, and the title, or more properly, subtitle *General Examen* covers no more than the first four. The last four contain the particular examens.

The character of the first part (or of the first four chapters) is well summarized in the first text: "What, before all else, ought to be proposed to the one to be instructed and examined on desiring to enter the Society of Jesus our Creator and Lord, is the following." "Instructed and examined": this indicates that it is not only a question of examining the candidate, but also of instructing him, of giving him an understanding of the kind of institute he wants to enter. This is done so that both sides, the candidate and the Society, may proceed with all possible clarity and without misunderstandings of any kind (see [18]).

The first part, or the General Examen, presents the candidate (in chapter 1) with the distinctive and particular features of the institute that he desires to enter.

There follows (in chapter 2) the enumeration of the various impediments and the reasons for their establishment. It would be useless for the candidate to continue if such an impediment existed. The Dominican constitutions also required the examiner to inquire discreetly of the

---

6   Text C says: *Examen en romance*. Roustang is in error when he writes that in text B the epithet "general" is placed after Examen, "comme s'il s'agissait du titre d'ensemble" ("Introduction à une lecture," in *Constitutions de la Compagnie de Jésus*, II [Coll. Christus, 24], 41). It is not so. Before this title, which is in folio 2, one finds in folio 1 the title of the whole book: *Examen*.

candidate whether he had any impediments.[7]

Once this difficulty has been overcome, the examiner proceeds (chapter 3) to gather more information about the candidate: his personal background, family, life, vocation, and so on.

Finally, in chapter 4 the requirements of the Institute are proposed to him so that he may understand them from the beginning and, if he is satisfied, accept them.

The first and fourth chapters are for the instruction of the candidate; the second and third pertain to his examination, in order that the Society may come to know him.

The second part contains four particular examens: one for priests and those destined for ordination, or scholastics (chapter 5); another for those admitted as temporal or spiritual coadjutors (chapter 6); a third for scholastics before and after their studies (chapter 7); and finally one for those admitted as indifferent, to enter the grade for which they will later prove most suited (chapter 8).

3. Development of the Text

Three successive texts, or editions, of the Examen have been preserved. The first cannot be dated from before 1547, since it is written in the hand of Fr. Miguel Botelho, who came to Rome in October of that year. It is probably nothing more than a clean copy of an older text, dating perhaps from 1546, which has since been lost. The second, composed to be added as chapter 5 to Part I of the Constitutions, dates (as does the primitive text of the Constitutions) from 1549-1550. The third and final text, presented at the meeting of the fathers in 1551, dates from the end of the previous year, though it was corrected during the following years up until the death of Ignatius.[8]

The most notable difference between the first text and the other two is perhaps that in the first text the particular examens contain everything necessary for examining candidates in each of the categories, with the repetitions which that entails; the other two texts avoid this repetition by distributing the matter in different places. They also omit a long final paragraph which discussed first probation and admission to second

---

7   *Constitutiones O.P.*, Dist. I, chap. 13, decl. b. The Rule of the Franciscan founder instructed ministers to examine those who asked to enter "de fide et ecclesiasticis sacramentis"; and the *Constituciones*, from those of Narbonne (Rubr. I, no. 6), added other questions.

8   See A. M. de Aldama, "La composición de las Constituciones de la Compañía de Jesús," *ArchHistSI*, 42 (1973), pp. 230-234.

probation, the learning and teaching of Christian doctrine, and the importance of natural gifts and qualities.[9] The matter of first probation is left to Part I of the Constitutions ([198-200]). Some texts on the learning and teaching of Christian doctrine were added to the fourth chapter ([80]). As for natural gifts, it was thought that the teaching in the first paragraphs of Part X ([813-814]) was sufficient. It is a pity, though, that this passage, so carefully considered and Ignatian in tone, was finally omitted.

Moreover, we can see more precise wording in the definitive text where it speaks of poverty ([4-5]), external features of common life ([8]), probation ([16]), the renunciation of temporal goods ([53, 55]), and the reduction of the number of impediments, as desired by Salmerón,[10] and the like.

Although three sets of Declarations survive, only the third merits consideration. The first set was written for a text that has since been lost and the second set properly corresponds to none of the known texts, though the editor of the Monumenta Historica has published it with the second text of the Examen. The third set belongs to the definitive text, which is the one that really carries declarations.

Being unable to go into great detail here, we will give only a brief explanation of the first three chapters of the General Examen and the four chapters of particular examens, indicating at the end some of the more important spiritual teachings contained in them. After that, we will examine chapter 4 in more detail since it is especially important.[11]

II. CHAPTERS 1-3 AND 5-8

1. Characteristics of the Institute ([1-21])

The title of the first chapter, "The Institute of the Society of Jesus and the Diversity of Its Members," added by Polanco in the definitive text, can lead to its being read from a mistaken point of view. Ignatius did not intend to give us either the essential outline of the Institute or its fundamental structure in this text. These substantial elements and their basic structure are, as Congregation XXXI declared, contained in the

9   See MI Const, II, pp. 122, 124-125.
10   See MI Const, I, 391.
11   The following commentaries of two contemporaries and disciples of St. Ignatius on the *Examen* are conserved: J. Nadal, *In Examen Annotationes* (incomplete) in MHSI Nadal, V, 134-205; D. Laínez, lectures given at the Roman College in 1559, published by C. de Dalmases, "Esortazioni del P. Laínez sull'Examen Constitutionum," in *ArchHistSI*, 35 (1966), 132-185. We shall henceforth cite this source as Laínez, lecture and marginal number (in *ArchHistSI*).

Formula of the Institute, which is the Society's "Rule."[12] Ignatius, in the Examen as well as in the Constitutions, always presupposes that this "Rule" has been read by the novice before entering and during the time of probation ([18]). The object of this chapter is to present to the candidate some characteristic features of the Society, especially those in which it differs from other religious orders. It is good that the candidate knows of them before entering, not only to avoid being surprised later, but also to examine his own vocation in conformity with them.

The unusual features of the Society discussed include the reason for its name ([1]), its apostolic character ([3]), the vow of poverty ([4-6]), the fourth vow of obedience to the pope ([7]), the externals of common life ([8-9]), the diversity of persons accepted ([10-15]), and the lengthy period of probation ([16-17]).

To begin with, there is the name, "Society of Jesus," which was, even then, unique and somewhat controversial. For that reason, great care was taken to declare that the name was given to the congregation by the Apostolic See when the Society was first instituted. However, it is made clear that this occurred when the Apostolic See approved, with its supreme authority, the Formula of the Institute, which included the name that the first fathers had chosen in Vicenza.[13] Ignatius received divine confirmation of that name in the celebrated vision at La Storta.[14] As Nadal rightly observes, it is necessary to go back even further and seek the origins of the name in the meditations on the Kingdom and the Two Standards.[15]

In [3] we should not look for a concrete definition of the end of the Society, as one might think. This concrete definition of the end of the Society is found in the first paragraph of the Formula of the Institute. What is intended here is a statement of the Society's apostolic character. The sentence is perhaps clearer in the first text: "This least congregation . . . has been erected and confirmed by His Holiness . . . , not only for the salvation and perfection of the souls of its members, but also to labor strenuously for the help and perfection of our neighbors."

The reason for the Society's existence, then, is not only that, as in the older orders, those who enter it may save and sanctify themselves, but that they may save and sanctify others. This is to be done "strenuously," not as a secondary goal but, as Suárez puts it, "with the full weight of the Institute"[16] or "putting into [this work] its whole life and efforts," as is

---

12 C. G. XXXI (1965-1966), d. 4, no. 3.
13 See MI FontNarr, I, 204.
14 See MHSI Nadal, V, p. 136, no. 1.
15 Ibid., no. 5.
16 F. Suárez, *De Religione Societatis Jesu*, no. 28.

stated in the so-called Letter on Perfection.[17]

Regarding what pertains to the three religious vows ([4-6]), Ignatius thinks that only the matter of poverty needs clarification. This is because, juridically, only poverty has any special features; these involve the double aspect of lack of fixed income and of stipends.

Neither individuals nor houses or churches of the professed Society may have a fixed income for their sustenance or any other purpose ([4]). The fact that individuals may have no stable income was, of course, common to all religious. That no fixed income could be held collectively by the professed houses of the Society was typical of the so-called "mendicant" style of poverty. However, there was a time in the Society when it was thought that a division could be made between two subjects of ownership: firstly, the house or church, which could have fixed income for some purposes (such as medicine, books, or travel expenses, but not for sustenance), and secondly, individual professed fathers, who could have no kind of fixed income. Excluding the case of houses and churches, the addition "for their sustenance or any other purpose" doubtless alludes to this distinction, which was considered and finally rejected by Ignatius during the forty days of divine communication described in the *Spiritual Diary*.

However, an exception is made for the scholastics: "Though the Society owns colleges . . . which have fixed revenues for the living expenses of the scholastics before they enter into the professed Society or its houses, . . . the revenues of this kind may not be used for any other purpose" ([5]).

Concerning that other characteristic aspect of our poverty, the same text says that we must refuse stipends "even though such acceptance would be permissible for others" ([4]). Nadal notes that there are other orders which have no fixed incomes (the mendicant orders), but that the refusal of stipends is peculiar to the Society.[18]

To the three religious vows, the Society adds a fourth vow of special obedience to the pope "in regard to missions" ([7]). This is so unique and proper to our institute that it encountered no small amount of difficulty when it was submitted for approbation.

Another characteristic of the Society is that "in regard to what is exterior, the manner of living is ordinary" ([8]). Differing from the practice of the older orders, the Society does not have any regular penances or austerities "which are to be practiced through obligation" ([8]). The manner of life is ordinary not in the sense that it is accommodated to the secular

---

17   MI Epp, I, 498 (also in William J. Young, trans., *Letters of St. Ignatius of Loyola* [Chicago 1959], p. 122).
18   MHSI Nadal, V, p. 148, no. 12.

lifestyle, as Nadal notes,[19] but because it is not monastic. Rather, it corresponds to the common and approved manner of life practiced by "upright" priests, that is to say, priests leading exemplary lives.

Another unusual feature of the Society is that not everyone who enters is received into the same grade. Some are admitted to make, after their probations, solemn profession of the four vows, others to take the vows of a spiritual or temporal coadjutor, others to be scholastics, and finally, others are admitted as indifferent, prepared to accept whatever grade may later be seen as suitable for them ([10-15]). In the older orders it is clear that everyone, priests, choir brothers, and laymen, make solemn profession after their novitiate.

Finally, the time of probation is longer in the Society than was generally the custom in the older orders ([16-17]). It consists of two years (of novitiate) and a year (tertianship) after the scholastics have finished studies. This was in place of the one-year novitiate commonly found in other religious orders such as the Benedictines, Dominicans, or Franciscans.

The chapter ends with a paragraph ([18]) perhaps inspired by chapter 58 of the Rule of St. Benedict.[20] Here the candidate is instructed to read the bulls of approval of the Institute as well as the Constitutions and rules, and to repeat this process of reading every six months until he takes vows ([18-21]). In these documents he will find a complete description of the Institute of the Society which he desires to embrace.

2. Impediments ([22-33])

After enumerating the various impediments ([22-29]) and explaining why they are imposed ([30]), the second chapter tells the examiner how to proceed when he discovers one of them in a candidate ([31-33]).

The impediments to admission were defined very early on in the history of the Society. Already at the 1541 meeting, before their final profession and the election of the first superior general, Ignatius and his companions saw that it was necessary to establish some impediments.[21] The fact that there were so many is deserving of attention. In the first text there were seven and three more were added in text A: two regarding common law (on marriage and slavery under the law) and one concerning mental infirmity. The number of impediments was reduced, at the suggestion of Salmerón, though this reduction was made not by dropping any of the impediments, but by reorganizing them into groups. Ignatius

---

19   Ibid., p. 156, no. 61.
20   Regula, chap. 58, 8-16.
21   See MI Const, I, p. 39, no. 18; see ibid., p. 180, doc. 25.

took care to provide a reason for each of them ([30]).

The motive is the same for the first two impediments (defects in faith or morals). The monastic orders accepted even robbers and assassins who had repented, because they came seeking conversion, penance, and the salvation of their own souls. In the Society, however, one enters to convert others, to work strenuously for the salvation and perfection of the souls of our neighbors ([3]). Those who enter will be more suited to this purpose in the measure in which they are less known to have been marked by the first and second impediment, that is, less open to censure in regard to faith or morals, because of "ordinary and common weakness" ([30]). What is the weakness alluded to? Does it mean the weakness of those who enter, who could fall again into their former faults? Or does it refer to the weakness of the neighbors they are trying to help, who will find it more difficult to accept the teaching of someone who is known to have lapsed in the faith or lost his good name? Without doubt it refers to the latter group. Ignatius explicitly says so in the declarations which were once attached to the text of the examen which has not survived: "The less a person is known to have been marked by either defect in the eyes of men, so much the more credit will he have with them and so much the more will he be able to help them make progress, . . . because of human weakness and negative dispositions in those who ought to receive the word of God."[22] That was the reason Ignatius, who had not wanted to defend himself during the persecutions at Alcalá and Salamanca, personally insisted, and very strongly, that a judicial sentence be given in answer to the accusation of heresy lodged against him and his companions upon their arrival in Rome in 1538. They had already formed a group and had begun to preach, and so, without the credibility from being cleared of these charges, their apostolic ministry would have suffered serious harm.[23]

The reason given for the third impediment (concerning previous entry into another religious order)—the first established in the Society[24]—was that a good Christian ought to persevere in his first vocation ([30]). But doubtless it is also mainly this third impediment which is in mind (though the motivation applies to all the others) too when the text continues: "in addition to the greater edification of our neighbors . . . the more they [the members of the Society] are all of one color or likeness, so much the more will they be able to preserve themselves in the Lord" ([30]).[25]

---

22   MI Const, I, 250-251, no. 4.
23   MI FontNarr, I, 10 and 268.
24   See MI Const, I, p. 36, no. 18.
25   See Ribadeneira, *Treatise on the Institute*, chap. VII, p. 60.

The motivation for the other two impediments is clear. In the case of the fourth, regarding the common law of marriage and legitimate servitude, justice intervenes, while in the fifth, regarding mental illness, the motive is charity toward the Society and the candidate himself.

Underlying all these impediments is always the "apostolic life" or "mission" proper to the Society, for which credibility is essential. The same reason is given in the Formula: "This Institute requires men who are thoroughly humble and prudent in Christ as well as conspicuous in the integrity of Christian life and learning" ([6]). In addition, since this apostolic life has to be lived in a religious order, there needs to be a certain homogeneity which will help to maintain unity among those dispersed in various places. This is also the reason for the impediment concerning mental illness: "It would be a notable detriment to the Society itself" ([30]).

There are two statements in this paragraph [30] which are worth a comment. The first refers to the vocation of the Society, defining it precisely as an "apostolic life"; the other defines the consecrated life in general. The latter is called "holy" because the one who enters it "has abandoned all the world and dedicated himself completely to the greater service and glory of his Creator and Lord." Such is the classical definition of religious life.[26] In contrast, it is specifically said of the Society that one enters "to be a good and faithful sower in the Lord's field and to preach his divine word"—or, as the primitive text puts it, perhaps more clearly, "to plant well and faithfully in the Lord's field, evangelizing and proclaiming his divine word."

3. Qualities Required ([34-52])

Once the problem of impediments has been settled, the Society will have to know more about the candidate before admitting him.

The plan or structure of this chapter is simple and logical. After the candidate has been questioned about personal details (name, age, place of birth [34]), further information is sought in three important areas.

First, about his family: their moral reputation, social condition, the possibility of their needing his assistance, the number of brothers and sisters ([36-39]). The question on whether or not his family were "new Christians" is intended not for the purpose of excluding them but merely to acquire more information about the environment in which the candidate has lived.

Second, more information is sought about the candidate himself and the circumstances of his life: possible difficulties arising from a promise to

---

26 Conc. Vat. II, *LG*, no. 44.

marry ([40-41]), his debts or other obligations ([42]), his education and abilities ([43]), his health ([44]), his prior reception of any ecclesiastical orders or profession of religious vows ([45]), his devotional life ([46]), and his willingness to accept direction regarding his opinions, scruples, or spiritual difficulties ([47-49]).

The third area concerns his vocation, his desire to leave the world, and his determination to enter the Society ([50-52]).

We will dwell on only three points.

The first concerns the explanation of an obscure passage, declaration C ([41]). In the earlier paragraph to which this declaration refers, the candidate is asked: "Has he at any time given a *palabra de matrimonio?*" ([40]). The declaration then explains: "If he gave it by present words, consummating the marriage, or by some equivalent way, he would be considered to have the fourth impediment, which prohibits acceptance into the Society" ([41]). The apparent meaning seems to be that the phrase "by some equivalent way" refers to the phrase that immediately precedes it: "consummating the marriage." However, this last phrase ("consummating the marriage") was added later, after the whole declaration had been written. We must therefore take it as parenthetical, and refer "by some equivalent way" to "by present words" (*por palabras de presente*). At that time, a distinction was made in marriages between *palabras de presente* and *palabras de futuro*. *Palabras de futuro* signified a promise to marry—in other words, a betrothal. *Palabras de presente* were a marriage properly so called. The idea is, then, that if it was not merely a betrothal but a true ratified marriage either by *palabras de presente* (the ordinary form of marriage) or by an equivalent procedure such as by signs or through a proxy, and the marriage was then consummated, the candidate would be considered to have the fourth impediment, which was mentioned in the previous chapter ([28]).

Another paragraph that merits attention is [48], concerning scruples and spiritual difficulties; it was added in the final text, as was [47].

The so-called "conscientious objection" or conflict between conscience and authority, seems a modern problem. Nevertheless, Ignatius foresaw it, and the way in which he resolves it can be seen in some observations on obedience that he dictated to Fr. Gianfilippo Vito: "When I think or judge that my superior has ordered me to do something contrary to my conscience or something sinful, and my superior thinks the contrary, then I ought to believe him, where there is no complete certainty. If I cannot achieve this myself, at least setting aside my own judgment and understanding, then I ought to submit the matter to the judgment and decision of one or two or three persons. If I cannot bring myself to do this, then I am very far from the perfection and qualities demanded of a true religious."[27]

Here the question extends to include "whatsoever scruples or spiritual difficulties" he who enters the Society "has or in time may have" ([48]). The declaration explains how "choice of these persons to whom the one in such difficulties should entrust himself" should be made. These persons can be chosen by the superior with the consent of the subject, or by the subject himself with the approval of the superior, and it is permissible for a person from outside the Society to be chosen ([49]).

Ignatius often used this method. One of his first companions, Bobadilla, had some difficulty or scruple about making his profession, perhaps because of the vow to teach Christian doctrine, the inclusion of which in the vow formula he had opposed. The people chosen in this case were the doctor Iñigo López, the doctor Miguel de Torres, and the master Cristóbal de Madrid. All of them were from outside the Society, though the latter two eventually joined it.[28]

We must admire here the Ignatian generosity of spirit, so contrary to the rigid militarism often used to characterize him. It is clear that this way of proceeding supposes a basic abnegation of one's own judgment. For this reason Ignatius places "notable obstinacy in one's personal opinions" among the secondary impediments to admission, adding that such obstinacy is "highly vexatious in all congregations" ([184]).

Finally, we would like to comment on the examination of vocation prescribed in paragraphs [50] through [52].

This proceeds in steps, from the more general to the more particular: from a vocation to the religious life to a vocation specifically in the Society.

In number [50] the candidate is asked about his determination to embrace the religious life in general, which is defined as "abandoning the world and following the counsels of Christ our Lord"; and about signs of such determination, constancy, and so forth.

In [51] the candidate is asked three questions about his specific vocation to the Society: (1) "Does he have a deliberate determination to live and die in the Lord with and in this Society of Jesus our Creator and Lord?" ([51]). We hear in these words an echo of similar ones in the *Exercises*: "It is my earnest desire, and my deliberate choice . . . to imitate you."[29] (2) For how long has he had such a determination? (3) Through whom was he first moved to make this choice?

If the candidate has been inspired to enter by a certain member of the

---

27   MI Epp, XII, p. 600; FontNarr, I, p. 595.
28   See MI FontNarr, II, p. 104. See also FontNarr, I, pp. 706-707.
29   *SpEx*, no. 98.

Society, Ignatius wisely orders that he be given more time to reflect before God about his vocation. Otherwise, in a time of temptation he might come to doubt its authenticity.

The final paragraph of the chapter is significant, for here Ignatius brings together the salvation of souls and the glory of God in a formula more complete than those used in other places. In the *Exercises* he usually speaks of the glory of God and the salvation of the soul of the individual exercitant. In the Constitutions he frequently speaks of the glory or service of God and of aid to or the good of souls, or of our neighbors. Here, he combines the two expressions. The candidate, after reflecting on his vocation, feels and judges to what degree it is expedient for him to enter the Society: "for the greater praise and glory of God our Lord and also that he may better save and perfect his own soul by helping other souls, his neighbors" ([52]). The greater glory of God is the end of every Christian, indeed, of every human being. The salvation and perfection of his own soul is the end of every religious, but the religious in the Society is to accomplish this by "helping the souls of his neighbors." As Ignatius once told Nadal: "The way to make spiritual progress is to attend to the salvation of one's neighbors."[30]

4. The Particularized Examens ([104-133])

The last four chapters consist of the *particularized examens*. In the final text each of them presents its own unique characteristics.

Chapter 5, intended for priests (those admitted to make solemn profession or to take the vows of a spiritual coadjutor) and for those destined to be ordained (the scholastics), consists of two parts, clearly indicated in the Spanish text, and even in the "autograph." In the first part ([104-110]) the examen deals in turn with the studies which the candidate has already completed, his aptitude for further study, and his pastoral experience. The theme of the second part ([111]), to which we shall return, is indifference of spirit.

Chapter 6, intended for both the spiritual and temporal coadjutors, is more informative. In it Ignatius gives some time to a description of this way of belonging to the Society, its spiritual value, and the nature of the coadjutor's vows. The only question posed to the candidate is whether he is disposed to accept his grade without hoping to pass on to another.

In the description of this grade of coadjutor, we should note that it is always spoken of as a particular vocation. In [116], we read that "If

---

30   MHSI Nadal, V, p. 143, no. 26. See MI FontNarr, III, p. 516, no. 22.

someone has been trained and examined to become a spiritual coadjutor, he ought to devote himself to the spiritual matters which are appropriate and suitable to his first vocation (*vocación*), and not to seek . . . to attempt some change from his call (*llamamiento*) to another, namely, from that of a spiritual coadjutor to that of a professed or scholastic or temporal coadjutor"; and further, that he ought to proceed to make his way along the path which he has been shown "by Him who knows no change and to whom no change is possible," that is, by God.

In the same way, the following paragraph speaks of the temporal coadjutor as giving himself "to the things which are appropriate and suitable to his first call (*llamamiento*)," and of persevering "in his first vocation (*vocación*)" ([117]).

When commenting on these passages, Laínez quotes the words of the first letter to the Corinthians: "Everyone should persevere in the state in which he was called."[31] This is no doubt an inappropriate quotation since the words had a very different meaning in their original context, but it does indicate that for Laínez this grade constituted a particular vocation. This is not to say a vocation distinct from that of the Jesuit vocation itself; rather, it means a particular vocation within the vocation common to all Jesuits. This presents no real difficulty since, just as there can be different charisms, so also there can be different vocations conforming to these charisms. This is suggested, in a certain manner, when the Formula of the Institute states that every [member of the Society] seeks to further the end of the Society defined therein, "each one, however, according to the grace which the Holy Spirit has given to him and according to the particular grade of his own vocation."[32]

In chapter 7, the examen for scholastics, what is notable is that the scholastics are considered less a part of the Society than was later the case. Thus, they are questioned about whether they would accept dismissal from the Society ([123]), allow themselves to be directed in their studies ([124]) and do so without seeking their own advantage ([125]); whether they are determined to enter the Society upon completion of their studies ([126]); and so on. Even stranger to modern readers is the presence of a new examen to be administered to scholastics who have completed their studies, but "before they enter the Society or any of its houses to be admitted into it for total obedience" ([128]). This is done in order that "the superiors may

---

31 1 Cor. 7:20.
32 See MHSI Nadal, V, 179-180; Form. Inst., no. 1; A. M. de Aldama, "De coadiutoribus Societatis Iesu in mente et praxi sancti Ignatii," *ArchHistSI*, 38 (1969), 392-393, 416-417.

refresh their memories and knowledge of the scholastics, and also better and more completely know their firmness and constancy, or any change if one occurred in the matters which were first asked and affirmed" ([129]).

There is no need at present to discuss chapter 8, concerning those admitted as indifferent.

III. SPIRITUAL TEACHINGS

Before discussing the fourth chapter, we may bring together some of the principal teachings which are to be found scattered throughout the other seven chapters.

The principal theme and the reason for the existence of the Examen is, of course, that of clarity, the absolute sincerity which Ignatius wants to dominate the proceedings. This means clarity both on the part of the Society regarding the candidate and on the part of the candidate regarding the Society. This is a sort of leitmotiv, repeated continually: "that both sides may proceed with greater clarity and knowledge in our Lord" ([18]); "that the candidates may become better known" ([34]); "to give better knowledge and understanding of candidates" ([104, 112]); "for a better understanding of the candidate who is to be examined" ([130]). For this purpose, opportunities for providing information about the Institute are increased (chapters 1 and 4, and the reading of bulls, constitutions, and rules every six months), and likewise the examens of the candidate (the general examen and the particular examen according to various categories). In addition to this, a serious obligation in conscience is placed on the candidate to tell the truth "in order to avoid the deception which could arise from the candidate's failure to open his mind sincerely to his superior" ([35]).

The spiritual disposition most required by Ignatius in those who enter is indifference. According to their gifts, charisms, and the "grade of the vocation" of each one, they can enter to be professed, temporal or spiritual coadjutors, scholastics, or as "indifferent" in regard to the grade for which the Society might eventually find them most suited. However, from the very beginning all are advised to have the attitude of those in the last category ([10]; see [15]). In fact, all the evidence leads us to believe that this was the case at the Roman house in the time of Ignatius. We do not hear of a distinction being made between scholastic novices and coadjutor novices. We find that the unordained were all simply called "brothers," or even "laymen." Ignatius sent on to studies those who had the necessary qualities, though he took into account their inclinations in the matter. For this reason he used to call Bartolomé Ferrão "the untemptable" (*el intentable*), since Ignatius, having tried many different means, "almost coercion," was unable to discover from him whether or not he had any inclination to study.[33]

On the contrary, Ignatius thought it better to refuse acceptance to, or to dismiss, one who had an inclination to study or to the priesthood but lacked the aptitude for it, since continuing on would disturb the man's whole life (see [150]).

Indifference is considered so important that everyone, even priests and "men of letters" (that is, those who enter having already studied at a university), are asked whether, if they have doubts regarding the grade to which they are most suited, they would be disposed to accept for their lifestyle the external circumstances of a temporal coadjutor for the benefit and aid of the Society ([111]). In the first texts it was laid down that this question be asked of them every six months.

Why is such stress placed on indifference? One reason relates this to the earlier theme of clarity or sincerity. Ignatius did not want the Society to commit itself to a decision about the admission of candidates to one of the various grades without first coming to know their natural gifts, their charisms or supernatural graces, "the grade of their vocation" (see [15, 111]). But another reason, perhaps more important, is "the greater humility and perfection" of the candidate ([111]). Basically, this is the same indifference as in the Exercises, where the exercitant disposes himself for a better knowledge of the will of God. It is the indifference in which Ignatius lived during the years before the founding of the Society, when, in the words of Nadal, "with a unique modesty of spirit, he was following the Spirit, not anticipating him," and "was being gently led to something which he did not yet know—being, so to speak, wisely imprudent."[34]

A third theme relevant to these chapters is stability in one's vocation. Ignatius wants the candidate, when he enters, to come with "a deliberate determination to live *and die* with and in this Society of Jesus our Creator and Lord" ([51]). We have already considered this particular manner of speaking. The novice is to read the bulls of approval of the Institute, and the Constitutions and rules every six months, because "the more the subjects' constancy has been tested, the more stable and firm they may be in the divine service and in their original vocation, for the glory and honor of His Divine Majesty" ([18]). The reason for not admitting religious from other orders is that "every good Christian ought to be stable in his first vocation" ([30]). The scholastics' vow to enter the Society (which was, for

33 See da Câmara, *Memorial*, MI FontNarr, I, pp. 597, 602-603.
34 MHSI Nadal, V, pp. 625-626.

some time, the only one prescribed[35]) was originally only a vow of stability in the vocation. The scholastics promised not to abandon their vocation and, when their studies were completed, to enter the Society as professed members if it would accept them. When the grade of coadjutor was introduced, this vow also took on the meaning of a vow of indifference to accept either of the definitive grades, professed or coadjutor. It did not, however, lose its character as a vow of stability in vocation. Therefore, the candidate was still asked: "Is he determined . . . to enter the Society in order to live and die in it for the greater glory of God?" ([126]). "To live and die": We are compelled to think that the young men who so easily abandon the religious life do not reflect on that very serious commitment to Jesus Christ, to whom (in the words of Ignatius) they have bound themselves (see [17]) and to whom they have promised to live and die in the Society.

The coadjutor too is told that he ought not to seek "directly or indirectly, through himself or someone else, to inaugurate or attempt some change from his vocation to another, namely, from that of a spiritual coadjutor to that of a professed or scholastic or temporal coadjutor. Instead, he should with all humility and obedience proceed to make his way along the same path which was shown to him by Him who knows no change and to whom no change is possible" ([116]). These last words allude to a favorite theme in Ignatian theology, the divine attribute of immutability. We read in the Deliberation on Poverty, among the reasons for not altering the primitive poverty of the society, that "It is characteristic of God our Lord to be immutable, and of the enemy to be mutable and variable."[36] In this case Ignatius assumes, as we have already said, that this immutable God is He who has "shown the path" in different ways and brought about a diversity of vocations to the Society, according to the diversity of grades ([116]).

The same desire for stability is reflected in the norm which, if applied today, is disconcerting because of the cultural evolution which has occurred. It seems to have been inspired by the rule of St. Francis.[37] The norm states that anyone entering as a temporal coadjutor ought not to seek more learning or culture than that which he had at the time of entry ([117]).[38]

---

35   See E. Olivares, *Los votos de los escolares de la Compañía de Jesús: Su evolución jurídica* (Roma 1961), pp. 9-10, 28-32.

36   MI Const, I, p. 81.

37   *Regula bullata*, chap. 10.

38   According to da Câmara, *Memorial*, no. 341 (MI FontNarr, I, 719), this norm was introduced through experience with the case of Juan de Alba, who was tempted by studies. He left September 23, 1555. See ibid., pp. 664, 715, 733, 734, 738.

Nevertheless, exceptions to this principle are still possible. For example, at the suggestion of Salmerón,[39] declaration A was added to the text of chapter 8: "However, when something occurs constantly to these candidates as being conducive to greater glory to God our Lord, they may, after prayer, propose the matter simply to the superior and leave it entirely to his judgment, without seeking anything more thereafter" ([131]). The Holy Spirit, who inspired these desires, is not to be ignored and He will supply for all the human methods and arrangements ([700]).

In conclusion, we will simply note some other teachings which are to be found in these Ignatian texts,

We ought not to accept stipends for our spiritual ministries from anyone other than God our Lord, and we ought to do everything "purely" for his service ([3]).

"In the eyes of our Creator and Lord, those gain greater merit who with greater charity give help and service to all persons through love of His Divine Majesty, whether they serve in matters of greater moment or in others more lowly and humble" ([13]).

Those who enter the Society less known or marked for defects in faith or morals will be the more suited to be good and faithful sowers in the Lord's field and to preach the divine word ([30]). This is because of the ordinary and common weakness of many persons.

In order to fulfill this office of sowing and ministering the divine word and of attending to the spiritual progress of our neighbors, it is expedient to possess a sufficient amount of sound learning ([109]).

The more the members of the Society are of one "color" or likeness, the more they will be able to preserve themselves in the Lord, through His grace ([30]).

To influence another to enter the Society can be licit and meritorious ([51]).[40]

The Lord has given care of his neighbor to everyone ([115]). This is implied in Scripture[41] and can be applied here to the desire to seek the salvation and spiritual perfection of the souls of our neighbors.

39   MI Const, I, p. 393, no. 17.
40   See *SpEx*, no. 15.
41   Eccli. 17:12.

Chapter III

REQUIREMENTS OF THE INSTITUTE

(Examen, Chapter 4 [53-103])

I. PRELIMINARY REMARKS

1. Meaning of Chapter 4 of the Examen

In his Rule, St. Benedict expressed the desire that anyone coming to enter the monastery "be informed about the difficulties and severities [*dura et aspera*] to be endured by one who is making his way to God."[1] Something similar is found in the legislation of other religious orders. The Customs (*Consuetudines*) of the Premonstratensians and, copying from them, the Constitutions of the Dominicans prescribed that, before granting the habit to a novice, the severity or austerity of the Order (*asperitatem aut austeritatem Ordinis*) should be explained to him.[2] St. Bonaventure uses the same expression in the Franciscan Constitutions: "The rules and austerities of the Order should be explained" (*Regula et asperitates Ordinis exponantur*).[3]

In our opinion, chapter 4 has no other meaning than this. There are differences, however, in that what is meant by the "severity" or "austerities" to be explained to the novices in these other orders are primarily fasts, abstinence, or bodily penances, while in the Society they consist above all in total renunciation and abnegation. Laínez summarizes the matter of this chapter in three points: renunciation of relatives, of temporal goods, and of self.[4]

---

1   Regula, chap. 58, 8.
2   "Asperitatem" is found in the Premonstratensian *Consuetudines* and the first Dominican Constitutions; "austeritatem" or "austeritates" in the text of Raymond of Peñafort and later texts. See A. H. Thomas, *De oudste Constituties van de Dominicanen* (Louvain 1965), pp. 142 and 324.
3   *Constitutiones Narbonenses*, Rubr. I, no. 6. See *ArchFrancHist*, 34 (1941), 39.
4   See C. de Dalmases, "Le esortazioni del P. Laínez sull'Examen Constitutionum," art. in *ArchHistSI*, 35 (1966), 33. Henceforth on we shall cite only the exhortation and in it the editor's marginal numbers. Very different is the presentation of chapter IV by Roustang: "d'abord de la pauvreté, ensuite des experiments, et enfin de la vie dans la maison sous l'obéissance de la Compagnie." (Not a word about renunciation or abnegation.) "Introduction à une lecture," in *Constitutions de la*

This is not to say that chapter 4 contains everything that pertains to the perfection of the Institute of the Society. "Difficult and severe" is not synonymous with "perfect." For example, there is no reference to that spiritual maturity (mentioned in Part VI) of the formed religious who, as "spiritual and sufficiently advanced," do not need external rules to govern their personal lives of prayer, mortification, and study ([582]). That is logical because this chapter 4 is dealing with the practices of the life of perfection which must be undertaken at the beginning by one who enters the Society and which prepare him for the life proper to our Institute. At times, however, as when it speaks of the love of the Cross, the text invites its reader to more lofty spiritual heights.

2. Structure

The chapter is divided into two parts or sections. The division occurs at [90], where the candidate is asked whether he wants to observe what has been said and explained up to that point. The impression is that the following paragraphs [91-103] were added later, as a sort of appendix.

The first section begins logically with the first step the novice must take, the great step of renunciation, the "the flight from the world" (*fuga mundi*): renunciation of temporal goods ([53-59]) and of his own family ([60-63]). The text about the manifestation and correction of faults ([63]) is added here, perhaps because of the abnegation of self-love that this entails.

The text continues with the six testing experiences of the Ignatian novitiate ([64-79]) which normally occupy the first semester of probation (see [71]), though they may be done later. They initiate the novices into the life of the Society.

Once these experiences have been completed, the novice should remain in the house of probation, occupying himself in devotional practices and in the observance of regular discipline ([80]). He ought also to learn the virtues more proper to the vocation of the Society: poverty ([81-82]), humility ([83]), and obedience ([84-89]).

Finally, the candidate is asked whether he will accept all of this (all these difficult and severe things) together with the penances that may be imposed on him for his faults ([90]).

In the first text, the second section covered only two topics: the account of conscience ([91-97]) and the love of the Cross ([101-103]). Between these, some paragraphs about immediate preparation for vows ([98-100]) were later inserted.

II. FIRST SECTION

1. *Renunciation of Temporal Goods ([53-59])*

The first step is, as we have said, the renunciation of the world, the *fuga mundi;* and, first of all, the renunciation of temporal goods.

Ignatius explains the motive behind this renunciation, as well as the time for and manner of accomplishing it.

a. Motive

The motive is explained by the fact that it was the intention of Ignatius and his companions to admit into the Society only "persons already detached from the world and determined to serve God totally, whether in one religious institute or another" ([53]).

Ignatius has been called a "worldly saint."[5] His spirituality has been labeled the "mysticism of the enjoyment of the world."[6] Some have used an even more debatable term, referring to his "conversion" to the world.[7]

There is no doubt that Ignatius was exquisitely well-mannered in his dealings with others. Nor can it be doubted that this "contemplative in action" found God in everything in the world. Certainly, after Manresa, he had an ardent desire (which he knew how to communicate to his companions) to "travel throughout the world" seeking "the greater glory of God our Lord and the greater aid of souls" ([605]). However, it is no less certain that his detachment from the world, which he achieved at the time of his conversion to God and which he wanted all who entered the Society to attain, was complete and definitive. There is no contradiction in this. For this "world" of which he is speaking is not that of the terrestrial realities, in which we should encounter God ([288]) and which we ought to value as instruments for divine service ([814]); neither is it the world of human beings, to whom—even to those who are the enemies of Christ—we are sent so that they may "gain their ultimate end from the hand of God our Creator and Lord" ([156]).

What is this "world" then? In the first place, it is secular life, in which people can, and do, enjoy their freedom, temporal goods, family life, and

---

5   See B. Schneider, "Der Weltliche Heilige Ignatius von Loyola und die Fürsten seiner Zeit," art. in *Geist und Leben* 27 (1954), 30-58.

6   See K. Rahner, "Die Ignatianische Mystik der Weltfreudigkeit," art. in *ZAM*, 12 (1937), 121-137.

7   See M. Madurga, *Conversión al mundo? Dimensiones teológicas de la vida y escritos de S. Ignacio de Loyola en el tema de la relación Naturaleza-Gracia* (Mexico 1972). See the review in *Manresa*, 45 (1974), 413-415.

other earthly realities and values. The religious life, in contrast, is one in which all these things are abandoned and which is consecrated exclusively to the divine service.[8] However, this concept of the world can take on a moral tone with a pejorative meaning. For secular people run a greater risk of overestimating or having an inordinate love for the worldly realities and values among which they live, even to the extent of forgetting eternal things and God Himself. Ignatius fixes his attention principally on the over-emphasis that the world tends to place on luxury, fame, acclaim, honors, and so forth (see [66, 101]).

This latter is the world from which those who enter the Society ought to be "detached," and "determined to serve God totally." Consecration to religious life, according to Jean Beyer, consists of two elements: separation from creatures—or, as is commonly said, leaving the profane sphere and entering the divine sphere.[9]

We must, however, note the forceful and radical meaning of the expressions used here: "*detached* from the world" and "determined to serve God *totally*, whether in one religious institute or another." The first expression means to disengage oneself from something, to let go of it, or to have nothing more to do with it. The second expression was added by Ignatius himself in his own hand, to indicate a break with the world so definitive that, if a candidate were refused entrance to the Society, he would seek out another religious institute, since in his soul a return to the world is something absolutely excluded forever.

b. Time

As to the time of this renunciation, Ignatius proposes both an ideal and an accommodation of this ideal to concrete circumstances.

The ideal, which corresponds to this spirit of a break with the world, is to renounce temporal goods from the very beginning, before entering, "before they begin to live under obedience in any house or college of the Society" ([53]). This is in imitation of what the Apostles did.[10] It is also what Ignatius and his companions did.[11] It means burning one's boats or, as Laínez said, it is like what the Lord did with the people of Israel by

---

8   In this sense the Constitutions usually prefer the word *século*. See nos. 14, 30, 50, 246, 734.

9   See J. Beyer, "De statu vitae professione consiliorum evangelicorum consecratae," art. in *Periodica*, 55 (1966), 39.

10 Lk. 5:11.

11 On St. Ignatius see *Autobiog*, no. 13. The companions deferred the renunciation until after studies were finished. See G. Switek, *Praedicare in paupertate* (CIS, Recherches, IX), pp. 82-88.

closing the Red Sea behind them and thus cutting off any return to Egypt.[12]

However, the abstract ideal is not always the most advisable in some circumstances. The candidate's vocation has not yet been proven and, in the event that he leaves the Society, it would be harsh to send him away deprived of any means of support. On the other hand, if he does stay, he will be able to make this renunciation with greater devotion than he could have done at his entry into religious life.[13] These and other reasons[14] counseled a postponement of the renunciation.

Ignatius knew how to harmonize the ideal with the reality of life. The candidate promises to give up promptly all his worldly goods one year after his entrance or whenever the superior orders him to do so ([54]). With this promise and attitude of readiness, the affective detachment in the ideal is attained. Leaving this matter to the judgment of the superior secures the advantage of a prudent delay where circumstances seem to demand one.[15]

c. Manner

The manner of this renunciation also reflects the total break with the world. The renunciation ought to be *universal*, that is to say, of all the worldly goods that one had or hoped to gain ([53, 59, 255]), *absolute*, *irrevocable*, casting away "all hope of being able to possess those goods at any time" ([53]),[16] and, above all, *spiritual* and *evangelical*. Ignatius emphasizes the third quality most of all. He notes, with St. Jerome, that, provided there are no debts or obligations to be considered, the Lord did not say in the Gospel "give to your relatives" but rather "give to the poor" ([54]).[17] Other spiritual advantages result from following this evangelical counsel: a greater example of detachment is given, the disadvantages of a disorderly distribution of goods are avoided, the door is closed to any further recourse to relatives and to useless recollection of them, thus confirming the renunciation, with greater security for one's vocation (see [54]). Nevertheless, Ignatius always kept the exceptions in mind. In the first place, among the possible obligations alluded to in the text were those

---

12 Laínez, Lect. 9a, no. 3.

13 See MI Const, I, 391-392, no. 6; II, 46, no. 5.

14 In the time of St. Ignatius some put off renunciation in order to be able to help with their patrimonial goods other poorer students. Thus Doménech in Paris, Canisius in Cologne, and Polanco in Padua.

15 For St. Ignatius' praxis see MI Epp, II, 102, 471; V, 343; VIII, 212, 343; IX, 446-447.

16 See MI Const, II, p. 46, no. 6.

17 See Jerome, *Epistolae*, Ad Hedybiam, no. 1; Ad Demetriadem. See MI Epp, I, p. 96.

that a son has to his parents or a father to his children.[18] It can happen that the obligation is not clear. Doubt can arise about "whether it would be more perfect to make the gift or renunciation of these goods in favor of relatives rather than others, because of their equal or greater necessity, and other just considerations" ([55]). This is one of the problems foreseen in chapter 3 ([48]) and the same solution is given here: "since there is danger that flesh and blood may draw the candidates to err in such a judgment, they must be content to leave this matter in the hands of one, two, or three persons of excellent life and learning" ([55]; see [256]).

If the renunciation is made in favor of the poor or, equivalently, "in favor of pious and holy causes" ([53]), Ignatius allows great freedom as to the choice of these poor or pious works. Each one will act "according to his own devotion" ([53]). Note, however, that devotion here is not synonymous with whim or human affection. This devotion is an interior movement of the Spirit which gives a sense of what is most conducive to the divine service with regard to the renunciation and distribution of these goods (see [254]).

2. Renunciation of Relatives ([60-62])

If the detachment from the world is to be total ([53]), it is not enough to renounce one's temporal goods. To this must be added renunciation of one's family. St. Mark notes that the sons of Zebedee also left their father in the boat in order to follow Jesus Christ.[19]

Ignatius spoke first of effective separation and later of affective detachment and the transformation of love for one's family.

In line with the whole tradition of asceticism, he explains that "especially in the beginning" it is necessary to break all contact—both by direct conversation and through correspondence—with one's relatives. Thus, during the time they spend in the house of probation, the novices should be willing to have their correspondence seen by someone whom the superior appoints ([60]).

The reason for this is that, while he is attending to his soul and seeking spiritual perfection, the novice will more likely be disturbed than helped by conversations with friends and relatives. These will usually disturb him by shifting his attention to the concerns of his relatives, reawakening in him feelings and affections for earthly things that he has renounced, and even, perhaps, by contaminating him with worldly ways of thinking.

Of course, Ignatius did not forget that this separation is important

18   An early declaration says this expressly. See MI Const, II, pp. 42-43, note 5.
19   Mk. 1:20.

chiefly "at the beginning." To his brother, who was surprised to receive a letter from him after so long a period of silence, he responded: "Do not be so surprised. In treating a serious wound, one ointment is applied first, then a different one, and finally another."[20]

The general norm that Laínez gave for conversation with family or other seculars was that we ought to be like a seal which leaves its imprint on them, not like wax which receives an imprint from them.[21]

But more important than physical separation is affective detachment, and this continues to be true even after the early stages of religious life. Ignatius said that everyone who enters the Society "should judge that he should leave his father, mother, brothers, sisters, and whatever he had in the world" ([61]). "Should judge": This implies that leaving them is something which is assumed, or taken for granted, a logical consequence of the complete break with the world. As in the case of the renunciation of temporal goods, this is based on passages in the Gospel. In Matthew, Jesus promises eternal life to those who for His sake leave behind father, mother, brothers.[22] In another place, in Luke, the Lord says that, if someone wants to be his disciple, he must "hate" his father, mother, brothers, sisters, and even his own life, his very self.[23]

We know that the Lord was not speaking here of real "hatred" in the sense that we normally give the word. Neither did Ignatius mean hatred, for he begins speaking of love in the next line. His thinking was not that love for one's parents ought to be extinguished, but rather that it ought to be purified and transformed, bringing about the death of carnal affection by converting it to spiritual affection ([61]).

Carnal affection or love springs from the "flesh" and obeys the instinctive tendencies of nature, the natural instincts of a human being. Spiritual affection or love is produced in the soul through grace, the breath of the Holy Spirit. Carnal love moves us to desire earthly goods for those we love: riches, human honors, temporal well-being. Spiritual love moves us to desire supernatural goods for them: divine graces, virtue, holiness, and eternal salvation.

In order that this detachment may be complete, Ignatius goes so far as to say that it is a "holy counsel" for those in danger of an inordinate affection for their family, as novices could well be, to say not that they have parents or brothers, but that they had them ([62]).[24]

---

20   MI Epp, I, 79.
21   Laínez, Lect. 9a, no. 8.
22   Mt. 19:29.
23   Lk. 14:26.
24   For the history of this declaration, see MI Const, I, 392; II, 50 (critical apparatus).

This is a hard and austere doctrine, but it comes from the Gospel. Contrary to his practice in other parts of the Constitutions, when speaking of renunciation Ignatius uses a number of quotations from the Gospel in support of his teaching. This doctrine, however, is not as negative as might appear at first sight. It is a renunciation, absolute, unconditional, and irrevocable, of the world, temporal goods, one's family, and even one's very self. But it is a renunciation that has a glorious compensation. In exchange for all that has been given up, the Jesuit receives Christ, for whom alone he lives, "having Him in place of parents, brothers, and all things" ([61]). This corresponds to the teaching of St. Benedict: "making oneself a stranger to the conduct of this world, preferring nothing to the love of Christ."[25]

3. Fraternal Correction ([63])

Perhaps no other passage in the Constitutions has, from the very beginning, met with such difficulty and opposition both inside and outside the Society as number [63] of the Examen, from which rules 9 and 10 of the old Summary of the Constitutions were taken. The principal objections are that it does not observe the order of fraternal correction given by the Lord in the Gospel of Mark (Mk. 18:15-17) and that it takes no account of the right to personal reputation.[26]

To answer these criticisms, General Congregation VI (1608) noted that since novices, both before they enter and many more times prior to taking vows, read the Examen and the rules and freely accept all contained in them (see [18, 90]), they renounce any right to a personal reputation that might otherwise impede the observation of these rules.[27] This is clear and removes any potential difficulty. We may, however, ask: Up to what point

---

St. Ignatius expressed what he thought about dealing with relatives in the letter he wrote his brother Martín in 1532. See MI Epp, I, pp. 77-83, esp. pp. 79-81.

25   Regula, chap. IV, 20-21.

26   See v.g. MHSI Nadal, II, 77-78, 176-177; ARSI *Congr 41*, ff. 108, 111, 137v, 158, 164v, 207 (replies of St. Francis Borgia to the provinces of Castile, Andalusia, and Toledo in 1568); P. Ribadeneira, *Tratado en el cual se da razón del instituto de la religión de la Compañía de Jesús* (Madrid 1605), chap. 34, pp. 278-302; G. González Dávila, *Pláticas sobre las reglas de la Compañía de Jesús* (Barcelona 1964), pp. 202-203; Sforza Pallavicini, *Vindicationes Societatis Jesu* (Rome 1649), pp. 260-280; Th. Raymond, *Opera*, XVIII (Lyons 1665), 161-162 (against C. Scotti); A. Astráin, *Historia*, III (Madrid 1925), 400-401; M. Mir, *Historia interna documentada de la Compañía de Jesús*, I (Madrid 1913), 349-362. In ARSI there are various explanations by G. Vázquez (*Inst 178*, ff. 364-382v), D. Ottolini (*Inst 25a*, ff. 396-398), G. Fuentes de Albornoz (*Hist Soc 180*).

27   C. G. VI, d. 32; *CollDecr*, d. 62.

is the right to a personal reputation, or the evangelical teaching on fraternal correction, in conflict with the observance of this rule?

In the Latin translation of the Examen, [63] is divided into two paragraphs. The first paragraph (rule 9 in the old Summary) speaks of the manifestation of the faults of others, and is directed not at those who perform this deed of charity but at those whose defects are manifested to the superior. These are asked "whether they will be willing [to be treated in this way] for greater progress in spiritual life and especially for greater lowliness and humility." Nothing is said regarding the method or order in which the manifestation is to be performed, as Ribadeneira notes.[28] This is logical since nothing is addressed here to those actually making the manifestation. This paragraph is so far from contradicting the evangelical teaching that Laínez links it precisely to the text of Matthew's Gospel: "This is based on the Gospel: 'If your brother sins against you, go . . . tell it to the church,' and so on."[29] He also cites examples from the rules of other religious orders, such as that of the Franciscans, which contain similar norms.[30]

In the second part of [63] (rule 10 of the Summary, following the Latin translation), the candidate is asked about his attitude towards three things: (1) receiving correction from others (*ab aliis corrigi*), (2) himself giving correction to others (*ad aliorum correctionem juvare*), and (3) manifesting the faults of others to the superior (*manifestare se invicem*) "with due love and charity." In the Latin text this threefold distinction is clear, and this is how the paragraph was understood by authors like Orlandini and Dirckinck, who used the Latin text only.[31]

It will be said that in the original Spanish text the first two actions ("aid in correcting and being corrected") were conditioned by the third ("manifesting one another"). In other words, the correction is not to be made directly, brother to brother, but through the superior, with each one manifesting the faults of the others to the superior so that he may correct them.[32] This reading is based on a false interpretation of the gerund "manifesting" (*descubriendo*) as if it were necessarily a modal gerund: "by manifesting." We know that in the language of Ignatius the gerund can

---

28 Op. cit. in note 26, p. 285.
29 Laínez, Lect. 10a, no. 1.
30 Ibid.
31 See N. Orlandini, *Tractatus seu Commentarii in Summarium Constitutionum et in regulas communes* (Roehampton 1876), p. 180; J. Dirckinck, *Exhortationes domesticae* (Bruges 1913), pp. 342-349.
32 This is how A. Coemans understood it. See *Commentarium in Regulas Societatis Jesu* (Rome 1938), p. 128, no. 233.

perform very different functions, including that of substituting for other verbal forms.[33] Here the gerund "descubriendo" is used as an infinitive. Its exact Latin translation is "ac manifestare."[34]

This interpretation of ours is not arbitrary, for, in the first text, Ignatius puts this verb into the infinitive form: "y para descubrir."[35] Afterwards, either because of his tendency to subordinate phrases instead of coordinating them or perhaps to give greater cohesion and harmony to the paragraph, he changed the infinitive to a gerund, which for him had the same grammatical value.

That explains why Laínez, who certainly knew both the Spanish text and the mind of the founder, saw in the phrase "to aid in correction" an application of the words of St. Matthew in the passage cited earlier. Laínez said: "Each one ought to be disposed to correct a companion, even though our fallen nature finds doing this unpleasant; and this is a Gospel precept: 'Tell him his fault, between you and him.'"[36]

In any case, it was certainly not the mind of Ignatius to exclude direct fraternal correction, brother to brother, from the Society. In addition to this paragraph, we find this teaching mentioned in other Ignatian documents, such as the "Constitutions of the Colleges"[37] and the replies to the scholastic Antonio Brandão.[38] Furthermore, the teaching is commonly defended by other Jesuit authors.[39]

The reader must pardon us for spending so much time on this question

---

33   See M. Rotsaert, *Description de l'emploie du verbe dans les* Ejercicios espirituales *de saint Ignace de Loyola* (ms., thesis defended at the University of Louvain, 1970), pp. 155-166.

34   A similar case in *SpEx*, no. 71: "I will consider how up to now He has always had so great pity and mercy on me. I will end with an Our Father." (Asimismo [traer a la memoria] cómo ha tenido de mí tanta piedad y misericordia, *acabando* con un Padre Nuestro.) J. Calveras interprets the gerund *acabando* by an infinitive, *y acabar* (J. Calveras, *Ejercicios espirituales: Directorios y Documentos* [Barcelona 1958], p. 64).

35   See MI Const, I, 256, critical apparatus, lines 14-15.

36   Laínez, Lect. 10, no. 3. In the same sense Mannaerts, *Exhortationes super instituto et regulis* (Brussels 1912), pp. 479-480. This explains the difficulties of this fraternal correction.

37   See MI Regulae, p. 226, no. 39.

38   See MI Epp, III, 512.

39   Besides the previous quotations (Laínez, Ribadeneira, Mannaerts, Orlandini), see I. Negrone, *Regulae communes Societatis Jesu commentariis asceticis illustratae* (Milan 1613), pp. 619-620; Suárez, *De Societate*, no. 977; N. Widmann, unpublished commentary on the Constitutions, in ARSI, *Inst 12*, pp. 175 and 841; J. M. Aicardo, *Comentario*, I, p. 277. Those authors, on treating of the old common rule 31, distinguish beween *reprehendere* and *corrigere* or *monere*. The same distinction is found in the rules of the Roman residence in the time of St Ignatius. See MI Regulae, p. 164, no. 32.

of interpretation. However, the controversy that surrounds this paragraph seemed to require it. Nevertheless we must not lose sight of the principal objective sought here by Ignatius, namely, the abnegation demanded by the full observance of this teaching: "to be willing," as he says twice in the text. To "be willing" or to accept with good grace having our faults manifested to the superior and corrected by him or another companion, requires humility and the abnegation of self-love. No less abnegation is required for us to correct others, since, as we heard Laínez say, our fallen human nature finds doing this unpleasant.

Laínez adds some very serious words, with which we will end the consideration of this matter: "Two sins are the cause of the loss of many: the sin of the flesh and negligence in fraternal correction; and the universal punishments sent by God are sent because of this negligence."[40]

4. The Six Principal Experiences ([64-79])

Having taken this first step in renunciation, the Jesuit novice must now face six principal "testing experiences" (*experiencias*) which were originally made prior to the single year of novitiate.

The text, after stating the obligation to make them ([64]), describes each of the experiences in particular ([65-70]), and specifies the period of time during which they must be made ([71]), the way those who make them should present themselves ([72]), and the testimonials they ought to obtain as to how they made them ([73-79]).

These experiences are not, as has often been thought, a test of endurance to which the novice's vocation is submitted, and even less are they practical lessons in the difficulties with which the men of this world must contend. They have a double purpose: the first is *to test*, to explore, to examine whether or not the novice has the qualities required by the Institute of the Society; the second is *to train*, to direct, to initiate him into the life proper to this Institute. Nadal confirms this many times. For example, at Alcalá in 1561, he said: "Probation is meant to test whether or not one is good for our Institute, whether he can train himself in it or not. The Society has its prayer and treats of it; the novice is given the Exercises to see how he finds himself in this prayer and how well-suited he is to spiritual things. The Society occupies itself with works of charity, with the service of the poor, and with traveling from place to place in order to help our neighbor; one who desires to enter the Society must test himself by serving in hospitals, by making a pilgrimage, and so with other matters. In

40 Laínez, Lect. 10, no. 3.

this way he proves his capability in coping with the conditions in which he will spend the rest of his life."[41]

Hence this choice of experiences is not an indifferent or arbitrary one.

Ignatius chose those things which he and his companions had done, since they had lived the Society's way of life, the apostolic life, before converting it into a religious order.

All of them, following Ignatius, began this life with the Spiritual Exercises. Ignatius was a great pilgrim throughout his life; his companions came as pilgrims, on foot, from Paris to Venice and later to Rome. In Venice they devoted themselves to the service of the sick in hospitals. So it is not strange that in the spring of 1539, when they drew the main lines of the new Institute, they decided that all who would seek to enter it should also undergo these three experiences.[42]

In Venice and Rome they engaged in domestic tasks and also gave themselves to the apostolic ministries of teaching Christian doctrine, hearing confessions, and preaching. At first they did this "more for mortification than for any other reason," according to Laínez.[43] As a result, all these experiences were later added by Ignatius as experiences or tests for those wanting to follow his way of life.[44]

In his lectures on the Constitutions, Laínez emphasized the example that our Lord and his apostles gave us for each of the six "experiences" or "practices."[45] This only confirms what we said earlier, since we already know that Ignatius and his companions wanted to imitate the *apostolic life* in the Institute of the Society.

However, to this element, or objective, in the testing and training of a novice for a future life in the Society another is added, namely, the renunciation and abnegation of one's his own self, one's self-love. This element or objective is not completely distinct from the previous one, since

---

41   MHSI Nadal, V, p. 380; see pp. 73-75; IV, p. 175. [Editor's note. In the context of *Cons* [12, 64-79], Ignatius' Spanish word *experiencias* means experiences which bring knowledge to the candidate and are also tests of his suitability for life in the Society. In the Latin translation of the Constitutions of 1558, *experiencias* was translated by *experimenta*, which also means "experiences." But this Latin word in turn led, in many English-speaking regions, to Ignatius' testing experiences being called "experiments"—a rather inadequate translation because so many take the word to mean something like tentative procedures. See *ConsSJComm*, fn. 23 on p. 82 and fn. 7 on p. 96.]

42   MI Const, I, 12. See p. 40.

43   MI FontNarr, I, 118, 120; see II, 84, where Nadal relates that the first word St. Ignatius used in a sermon was "hojourdi," thinking he was speaking Italian.

44   They already appear in the first text of the *Examen*.

45   See Laínez, Lect. 10, nos. 4-6.

the apostolic life demands a man "dead to the world and to self-love, and who lives only for Christ our Lord" ([61]). There is no doubt that the first fathers had this also as their objective in all their pilgrimages, service in hospitals, and other practices of mortification.

Some experiences reflect one of these elements more than another. The teaching of Christian doctrine ([69]), preaching, and hearing confessions ([70]) clearly have the character of tests or training for the future apostolic life of the Jesuit.[46] In the domestic tasks, called the "humble" experiences ([68]), it is principally the virtues of humility and obedience that are exercised, virtues fundamental to the Jesuit vocation.

The two experiences of the hospital ([66]) and the pilgrimage ([67]) are very closely linked, to such an extent that from the beginning they were considered to be interchangeable ([67]).[47]

To be on pilgrimage, to go from one part of the world to another at the command of the vicar of Christ or, in his place, of the superior general of the Society, is the Jesuit vocation (see [82, 304, 308, 605]). Our fathers went on foot, they lodged with the poor in hospitals, and they offered spiritual and corporal service to both the sick and the well.[48] Serving the sick in hospitals is also one of the works which the Society can exercise ([605]).

Much more important than the material circumstances of traveling on foot without money, circumstances which change with the passing of time, is the interior disposition, the spirt of the "pilgrim." St. Ignatius always felt himself to be a pilgrim and in his autobiography he calls himself "the pilgrim." Peter Canisius likewise urges each of us "to regard himself as a pilgrim" (*existimare se esse peregrinum*).[49] The pilgrim has no permanent home. As Ignatius wrote: "his foot is ever raised,"[50] "ever shod and ready to go and spread the gospel of peace."[51] "Accustomed to bad food and

---

46   Nadal in the exhortations at Alcalá stresses the note of testing. MHSI Nadal, V, pp. 379-380.

47   See MI Const, I, p. 12.

48   F. Widmanstadt relates the impression which Salmerón, Nadal, and Canisius made on him in 1552, when sent from Rome to Bohemia, Austria, and Poland. Since they traveled on foot, their bodies were worn out by fatigue and bad weather, and yet they gave signs of great erudition and freedom of spirit: "tota corporis constitutio patiens laboris et molestiarum apparebat; tanta simul eruditio, tanta libertas, tantus animi candor et pietas in illis elucebat, ut totam Vienam in admirationem raperent, et ego mihi non vulgares homines, sed Apostolos Dei intueri viderer" (J. Warszawski, *Vocationum liber autobiographicus* [Rome 1960], p. 308).

49   *Exhortationes domesticae* (Roermond 1876), p. 448.

50   MI Epp, II, 346.

51   MI Const, I, 183.

lodging" ([67]), he has the apostolic "independence" (*autarchia*) of St. Paul, knowing how to walk in the midst of abundance as well as poverty.[52] The pilgrim can rely on nothing transitory; he must "with genuine faith and intense love place his reliance entirely in his Creator and Lord" ([67]).

This requires, of course, a great renunciation and abnegation of one's self, yet no less a victory over self is required for work in the hospitals, and the text emphasizes this: "in order to lower and humble themselves more, thus giving clear proof of themselves to the effect that they are completely giving up the world with its pomps and vanities, that in everything they may serve their Creator and Lord, crucified for them" ([66]).

The Jesuit ought to be a man of prayer and a man of God. The Exercises are a school of prayer. So much so that, as Nadal wrote in 1554, the Constitutions have little to say about prayer because they assume that one has already made the Exercises.[53] In the light of this, we recall that passage in the primitive text of the Constitutions according to which the month of the Exercises helps the novices to know Jesus Christ better, inflames them with his love, and consequently makes them more fervent in the practical affairs of their lives.[54] Nevertheless, to the novice the Exercises are not just a school of prayer; they are a test as well. Nadal said: "The Exercises are given not only to instruct [the novice] in prayer and to give him a method to follow in spiritual matters, but also to test his capability in spiritual matters. . . . He might have so little ability in dealing with the interior life that he would not be fit for the Society."[55]

5. In the House of Probation ([80-90])

The six experiences constitute the principal, though not the only, initiation of the novice into the life of the Society. In the next section ([80-89]), the candidate is introduced to some of the virtues fundamental to the Jesuit vocation, virtues which he ought now to begin acquiring.

After an introductory paragraph on the life of cloister, piety, and the regular observances of the novitiate ([80]),[56] the candidate is made aware of the necessity of three great virtues: poverty ([81-82]), humility and self-denial ([83]), and obedience ([84-89]).

We cannot spend much time on these topics, and will only indicate

52   See Phil. 4:11-12.
53   MHSI Nadal, V, 95.
54   MI Const, II, 166, no. 6
55   MHSI Nadal, V, 380.
56   The texts A and B added in this number the reference to learning Christian doctrine and the practice of preaching. The original text put it at the end of the book.

here some ideas which deserve more attention.

a. The Life of the Poor

In the first chapter, the candidate was told about some of the characteristics of the vow of poverty in the Society, namely, the lack of fixed or stable revenue and the gratuity of ministries. But even without fixed incomes, and living entirely on alms, one might still have a comfortable life, like that of the rich. What is described here is, in practice, more difficult: the manner and measure to be observed in the use of things needed and appropriate for living, such as provision for sustenance, clothing, furnishings, and the like.

We are now coming to a problem similar to what the Franciscans experienced in their practice of poverty; it was called the *usus pauper*, "use characteristic of the poor," and was at the heart of the medieval controversy between the "spiritual" and Conventual Franciscans. At that time it was said that simply denying ownership of the temporal goods held for the community's use was not enough: their use too must be regulated to be like that of the poor, moderate and restricted to the necessary.[57]

Ignatius' norm is that the things to be used for sustenance, clothing, or residence should be like those of the poor. Some have believed that this was intended not in the social but in the religious sense, that is, to live like those who have professed poverty. However, the norm indicated below by Ignatius, "to reach the same point" as the earlier fathers, excludes this interpretation.

Socially the term "poor" covers a wide variety of meanings, though within certain limits. A beggar is poor, as is a common laborer and even a low-salaried employee. However, an industrialist, a merchant, a lawyer, a doctor, or an engineer cannot be called poor, even though they must work for their living. There will always, of course, be intermediate and undefined areas between these extremes. In order to know better how Ignatius wanted this norm to be understood, it is necessary to know how he applied it in practice.

It is not possible to go into adequate detail here. We cite only one example. When dealing with scholastics, who he thought could lead a life more free of care because of their studies and the fixed incomes of the colleges in which they lived (see [297]), Ignatius regarded a college as securely established if its fixed income yielded four escudos per month per person. At that time, four escudos was equivalent to the monthly salary of

---

57 See Gratien de Paris, *Historia de la fundación y evolución de la Orden de Frailes Menores en el siglo XIII* (Buenos Aires 1947), pp. 277-280 and 358-365.

a laborer.

In the rules for rectors, Laínez wrote: "The rector should take care that poverty is observed in his college in such a manner that not only does no one own anything, but also the usage of poverty is observed and loved, in regard to food, clothing, and furnishings. Thus, they are to wear cheap (although functional and durable) clothing. The alms to be accepted are to be either the food that the common people (*plebs*) are accustomed to eat or the money to buy it. Delicacies or expensive things are to be refused unless there are some sick in the house for whom they would be helpful."[58]

As for the novices, they are to be given "what is worst in the house" ([81]), the clothing most worn out and patched. This is done that they may learn by experience "the impact of poverty, that they may find it later within their own souls," as Ignatius said in the first Declarations on the Examen.[59]

Leading the life proper to the poor implies, at times, begging for alms.[60] Ignatius was not content with the candidate's merely knowing this; he thought the candidate should have some experience of it, at least before he commits himself through final vows. During the lifetime of Ignatius, for some time those assigned to beg alms in Rome went along the streets with knapsacks, calling at the doors of houses, shouting, "Give me alms, out of the love of God, for the Society of Jesus." This spectacular method of begging did not at all please the founder.[61] The method more proper to the Society is simply to explain the nature of the need in the presence of one who might offer some relief.

If we now investigate the reasoning behind these practices, we will find the same motives as we did in the six experiences. In the first place, the novices are made to do this "for their greater abnegation and spiritual progress" ([81]) and in order that "contrary to common human opinion, they may be able in God's service and praise to humiliate themselves more" ([82]).

At the same time, thought is given to the future, to the apostolic life, for which the novice ought to be trained: "Another purpose is to enable them to find themselves more disposed to do the same begging when they are so commanded, or when it is expedient or necessary for them as they travel through various regions of the world,[62] according to what the

58 ARSI *Inst 220*, f. 117.
59 MI Const, I, 253-254; 257-258.
60 "It is our profession to live on alms," in a letter to Simão Rodrigues, May 2, 1556 (MI Epp, XI, 320).
61 See MI Const, I, 675-676.
62 In the Spanish text the gerund *discurriendo* is a circumstantial gerund: as they

supreme vicar of Christ our Lord may order or assign to them, or, in his place, the superior of the Society. For our profession requires that we be prepared and very much ready for whatever is enjoined upon us in our Lord and at whatsoever time, without asking for or expecting any reward in this present and transitory life, but hoping always for that life which in its entirety is eternal, through God's supreme mercy" ([82]).

Ignatius also looks to the past. He twice refers to the "first members of the Society" and exhorts us to imitate them ([81, 82]). This is not a question of nostalgia or conservatism. The deeper reason is that the vocation (or charism) of the Society was lived out before its elements were set down in writing. One of the ways of coming to know this charism is to know more about the early Society and the life of Ignatius its founder. Nadal was quite convinced of this.[63]

b. The Life of Humility

The literal meaning of number [83] is somewhat difficult to grasp.

In the first place, what is meant by the absolute gerund *particularizando?* Some translators have taken it to mean "descending to details," but this is not what actually happens in the paragraph; it continues in the same vein as the previous paragraphs. We think that Ignatius is here using another accepted meaning of that verb, namely, to favor or prefer; hence, to show greater preference.

Another difficulty arises from the inclusion in text A of the verb *tomar,* to take, which is not found in the primitive text. Text B resolved this difficulty, but only by adding a twist or different meaning to the paragraph which reduced it to a simple ascetical norm: to take on more readily what is more repugnant to human nature.

In our opinion, the mind of Ignatius is most clearly expressed in the first text: "Con esto"—despite this, despite all the experiences mentioned previously—attention is to be given in particular (in a particular or preferential manner) to some other tests of humility which should be very readily carried out, for the purpose of self-abnegation. These consist in being engaged in lowly and humble tasks such as working in the kitchen or cleaning the house, and in performing all the other jobs, experiences, or services in which one finds greater repugnance, when one has been commanded to do them.[64]

---

travel.
63   See MHSI Nadal, V, 262-267, 661.
64   See MI Const, II, 68. If it were not presumption, we would be tempted to doubt whether the one who introduced in text A the verb *tomar* (Polanco?) correctly

The object is always to show the candidate what is hard and severe (*dura et aspera*).[65] It is required, then, that the novices be given some exercises in humility and self-abnegation, which are repugnant to their nature, and that they do these promptly when they are so ordered. Even more, these exercises ought to be the object of special, preferential attention: "particularizando."

c. The Life of Obedience

That obedience is one of the fundamental virtues of the Jesuit is well known and hardly merits repeating here.

In the Constitutions, obedience is discussed many times, under various headings (see [284-286, 424, 547, 550, 659-660]). Here it is presented to the candidate in a setting that makes it look more difficult, namely, the lack of certain human qualities in the one who commands. Thus, the first case proposed is that of obedience to the cook ([84]), though this is later extended and applied to all others with official authority ([87-88]) and to the doctor or infirmarian in times of illness ([89]).

Returning to the initial limit case of obedience to the cook, we already see here the basic doctrine of Ignatian obedience. True obedience looks not at who it is that gives the orders, whether he is the superior or the cook, whether he has certain qualities or not. It looks to God alone, "considering the matter with sound understanding" (that is, understanding it accurately and without error) and believing that in the cook or the superior one obeys God alone ([84]). The inference is not very clear at first sight, so an explanation is given in the next paragraph ([85]), where we read that the cook as well as the superior gives orders in the place of Christ.

This idea that the superior "takes the place of Christ" or (as the Letter on Obedience explains) "takes his place and authority"[66] forms the nucleus of Ignatian obedience. It is not surprising, then, that the founder often repeats this phrase in the Constitutions (see [284, 342, 424, 432, 527, 661, 761]) and had already introduced it in documents prior to them.[67] The expression used in the Formula of the Institute is even stronger: in the superior, the subject ought to recognize Christ as present, and offer him the proper reverence.[68]

---

understood the wording of the first text.

65   Form. Inst., no. 9.
66   MI Epp, IV, 671-672.
67   See MI Const, I, 217.
68   On this argument see L. Medizábal, "Naturaleza del orden de subordinación primariamente pretendida por San Ignacio," art. in *Manresa*, 37 (1965), 134-138.

Consequently, the one who obeys "ought to consider and weigh the order which comes from the cook, or from another who is his superior, as if it were coming from Christ our Lord" ([85]).[69]

Could it be that this Ignatian idea shows the influence of the Rule of St. Benedict? In that document too we hear that the abbot "takes the place of Christ," that "the obedience paid to superiors is paid to God himself," and that one ought to comply with what the superior orders "as if it was ordered by God."[70]

On the other hand, the instruction that the cook should not request but command, in order to show that he speaks in the place of Christ ([85]), is original. It was so original, in fact, that Salmerón questioned it on the grounds that Sacred Scripture also shows God as requesting and that more love is shown in asking than in ordering.[71] Ignatius' reply, addressed to Polanco, was: "Both are good, asking and commanding. Nevertheless, in the beginning, it helps one more to be commanded than to be asked. But, despite this, if you think something should be changed, change it."[72] Polanco wrote declaration D ([86]), making use of Ignatius' words and softening some of the expressions in number [85].

The section ends with an investigation of the candidate's willingness to be obedient in everything described and ordered up to that point and to endure any penances that may be imposed on him. All this is done "for the surer achievement of everything hitherto stated and for the candidate's own spiritual progress" ([90]).

III. Second Section

As already mentioned, this second section originally contained only two topics: the account of conscience ([91-97]) and the love of the Cross ([101-103]). Later, in text A, three paragraphs about immediate preparation for vows ([98-100]) were inserted between these two. It might have been better to add these paragraphs, of a rather juridical tone, at the end of the chapter so as not to disturb the spiritual and thoughtful tone with which these two subjects were being discussed. On the other hand, perhaps the actual arrangement was chosen so that the chapter would close, as with a golden clasp, with the love of the Cross.

69   See MI Const, I, 217.
70   Regula, chaps. 2, 2; 63, 13; 5, 15ª, 5, 4. The word *maiores* for "superiors" is also used by St. Ignatius.
71   MI Const, I, 392.
72   MI Const, II, p. 71 (critical apparatus).

We do not think it necessary to treat more than the two main topics here.

1. Account of Conscience ([91-97])

The obligation to give a manifestation of one's conscience to the superior is one of the points (very few in our view) in which Ignatius can be called an innovator in the religious life. Of course, it is possible to cite precedents from early ascetical writers like Basil, John Climacus and, above all, Cassian.[73] However, these authors speak of the manifestation of one's soul to a director or spiritual father so that these may offer their help in overcoming difficulties in the interior life. This is also to be found in the *Exercises*, [326], and in Part III of the Constitutions, [263]. In sharp contrast, the account of conscience that Ignatius is discussing here is made to the superior and with the purpose of being governed by him in his capacity as superior. For that reason it is given at fixed intervals, not when the person has some difficulty.

Ignatius, aware perhaps that he was treading on new ground, did not take this step without consulting a great Dominican theologian, Egidio Foscarari, Master of the Sacred Palace and later Bishop of Modena. Foscarari told him that the whole concept seemed to be based on revered sources and Gospel teaching and, as such, was worthy of being observed.[74]

The passage, after considering the convenience and necessity of superiors' having a full knowledge of their subjects and giving the reasons for this ([91-92]), lays down the obligation of giving an account of conscience, the time and the manner of doing so ([93]), and how often the practice is to be repeated later ([94-97]).

One is struck by the carefully considered words used here by Ignatius, who is normally very reserved in his language.[75] This may be one of those matters which, as Polanco said, "he received in a more than human fashion."[76] Indeed, Ignatius introduces the topic by saying: "through reflection in our Lord, what follows has seemed good to us in His Divine Majesty" ([91]). From his *Spiritual Diary* we know what "reflection in our Lord" and things seeming good to him "in the Divine Majesty" meant for Ignatius.

When treating of the reasons, he puts them in a hierarchical order. It

---

73   See F. N. Korth, *The Evolution of Manifestation of Conscience in Religious Rules* (Rome 1949).
74   MI Const, I, 342-346.
75   See MI FontNarr, I, 659; IV, 805.
76   Ibid., I, 204.

is always "a matter of great and even extraordinary importance" that superiors have a complete knowledge of their subjects. This is true for two reasons: first, that the superior may better direct, govern, and guide them in the way of the Lord ([91]); second, so that "with greater love, diligence, and care" the superiors can "help the subjects and guard their souls from various inconveniences and dangers" ([92]). We might say that these principles are confirmed by the experience of all religious (and even secular) governments: the more the superior knows of his subjects, the more he will be able to govern them and deliver them from greater dangers.

But there is a particular reason for manifestation in the Society: It is required by our vocation to the "apostolic life." Ignatius continues, saying "Later on," that is, in times to come, whoever enters the Society ought, "in conformity with our profession and manner of proceeding," to be ready to "travel about in various regions of the world, on all occasions when the supreme pontiff or our immediate superior orders him." In such circumstances, which constitute the proper life of the Jesuit, "it is not only highly [as in the previous case] but even supremely important" that the superior have complete knowledge of those under his care: their natural "inclinations," spiritual "motions,"[77] and the sins to which they have been or are moved and inclined. This too is for two reasons: first, in order to insure that, for such missions, the right man is sent to the right place and for the right task, even in missions from the pope (since it pertains to the general to keep the pope properly informed) ([607]); second, in order that no persons are placed "beyond the measure of their capacity in dangers or labors greater than they could in our Lord endure with a spirit of love" ([92]). We should not overlook this last phrase. Although the subject ought to be disposed to work and suffer for Christ (as we shall see shortly), the superior not only must not expose him to dangers and labors beyond his strength, but should even shield him from those which he cannot support "in a spirit of love."

Having said this in passing, we must stress that Ignatius saw the manifestation of conscience as intimately linked to the vocation of the Society. This explains his deep reflections on the theme. For this reason, General Congregation V (1594) declared manifestation to be one of the substantial points of the Institute.[78] At the time of the promulgation of the Code of Canon Law, Father General Ledóchowski sought special papal approbation for the practice. Pius XI granted this, after having had the

---

77 See *SpEx*, no. 313.
78 C. G. V, d. 58.

appropriate paragraphs of the Examen read to him and having asked for time to reflect, make consultations, and pray.[79]

In the last text, another reason was introduced, in Polanco's hand: "that the superior, while keeping to himself what he learns in secret, may be better able to organize and arrange what is expedient for the whole body of the Society" ([92]). However, this deals with an end or reason not so different from the previous ones. Oswald calls this a subsequent end (*finis consequens*) and Coemans a mediated end (*finis mediatus*).[80] That is to say, from the proper governing of each of its members follow the proper order and welfare of the whole body.

Ignatius goes on to speak of the external manner and the internal spirit with which the account of conscience is to be given.

As to the external manner, he leaves the individual free to give his account "in confession or in secret or in another manner which may be more pleasing or spiritually consoling" ([93]).

The adverbial form used here, *en secreto*, is ordinarily understood as *bajo secreto*, "under secrecy." However, there is some difficulty in understanding the term this way. Naturally, the subject cannot insist that the superior not make use of what he hears in the account of conscience, for this would frustrate its purpose. As to not revealing what is said, this can be taken for granted since it was spoken as an entrusted secret (*in secreto commisso*). *En secreto* has another accepted meaning in Spanish, which is perhaps more common: "in private," that is, in personal conversation with the superior, not in public. That seems to have been the way that Laínez understood it.[81] If it is to be understood thus, the "another manner which may be more pleasing or spiritually consoling to him" might be, for example, the interior consolation of the Spirit moving one to confess one's defects in public.

It might be objected that the purpose of the account of conscience is also frustrated when it is made "in confession." However, it is well known that, in the time of Ignatius, the seal of confession was not understood as strictly as it is now. It always excluded the revelation of anything heard in

---

79   The account of the two audiences granted by Pius XI to Father Ledóchowski is in ARSI, new Society, *S. Sedes*, 4-9. The pontifical approbation was published in *Statuta C. G. XXVII*, p. 261.

80   A. Oswald, *Commentarius in decem partes Constitutionum* (Roermond 1902), no. 562; A. Coemans, *Commentarium in regulas Societatis Iesu* (Rome 1938), no. 500.

81   Laínez, Lect. 13ᵃ, no. 4. He sets "*in secreto*" in contrast with "*in publico ad ognuno*" and adds: "*benché a dirlo palesemente l'uomo guadagna maggiore vittoria.*" Thus also S. de Goiri understands it (*La apertura de conciencia en la espiritualidad de san Ignacio de Loyola* [Bilbao 1960], p. 288).

confession, but not the possibility of using the information. This too was the teaching of Sts. Thomas and Bonaventure.[82]

The manner or interior spirit with which the account of conscience is to be made is "with great humility, integrity, and charity" ([93]). Without humility, one can hardly open one's conscience to the superior. St. Benedict names the opening of one's heart to the abbot as the fifth step of humility.[83] "Integrity," sincerity, and truth are also needed ([263, 518]). Above all, great charity is needed—which in the thought of Ignatius translates as great zeal for the glory of God and the spiritual good of souls. Toward this end a great help will be found in being well governed and directed in the ways of the Lord by one's superior.

2. Love of the Cross ([101-103])

These last three paragraphs are the most inspiring part of the chapter, of the book of the Examen, and indeed of the entire Constitutions.

In an early index of the first text we find a summary of this section's contents which will serve as a good introduction to it: "Of the love of things in accordance with the cross of Christ and the abhorrence of those which the world loves."[84] The subject here, therefore, is love in conformity with the cross of Christ, or love following the teachings of the cross, or simply the love of the cross.

First of all, Ignatius presents the ideal, which is the love of the cross ([101]). Yet, conscious that the ideal is too lofty to be demanded of one who has just entered the Society, he proposes it as something to be desired, yet as something to which the candidate ought to aspire ([102]) and towards which he ought to begin to move ([102-103]).

a. The Ideal ([101])

This paragraph begins with the word "likewise," which connects it directly with the reflections on the account of conscience ([91-97]), since the intervening numbers [98-100] were, as mentioned earlier, added at a later date.

The emphases are, however, even more important: "It is likewise highly important to bring this to the mind of those who are being examined (through their esteeming it highly and pondering it in the sight of our Creator and Lord), to how great a degree it helps and profits one in the spiritual life . . ." ([101]). Later this interior attitude is described as "a state

---

82   See Alphonsus de Liguori, *Theologia Moralis*, III, 677-678.
83   Regula, chap. 7, 44.
84   MI Const, II, 729.

of desires like these which are so salutary and fruitful for the perfection of his soul" ([101]), "holy desires" ([102]), and "this grade of perfection so precious in the spiritual life" ([103]). We know through Nadal that this doctrine was very close to the heart of Ignatius.[85]

What does this doctine mean? Fundamentally it consists in love of the cross for the sake of Christ. But Ignatius proposes the doctrine through a strong "black and white" contrast between the world and Christ, between the minions of the world and the followers of Christ.

The "men of this world who follow the ways of the world" are those who, as we said at the beginning, overestimate earthly values and love them inordinately, while forgetting eternal values and, perhaps, even God himself. These persons can easily become "enemies of the cross of Christ,"[86] and they "love and seek with great diligence honors, fame, and esteem for a great name on earth" ([101]).

In contrast are those who "truly" follow Christ our Lord: "where [here 'where' means 'if'] there would be no offense to His Divine Majesty, and no imputation of sin to the neighbor, they would wish to suffer injuries, false accusations, and affronts, and to be held and esteemed as fools (but without their giving any occasion for this)" ([101]).

Ignatius notes the importance of a decisively negative attitude toward the first tendency: "to abhor [or withdraw from[87]], wholly and not partially, all that the world loves and embraces." The break with the world is something already decided on right from the beginning of this chapter.

In contrast, the insults, affronts, false accusations, and the like constitute the "livery" of Christ. "Livery" was the set of identifying garments worn to distinguish the servants of one lord or prince from those of another. It was also the uniform worn at tournaments to distinguish one team of knights from another. (It was not a military term.) This explains why those who follow Christ "truly" will "love and desire intensely" to put on this livery. The reason for this is that Christ "for our spiritual profit . . . clothed Himself as he did. For he gave us an example that in all things possible to us we might seek, through the aid of His grace, to imitate and follow Him, since He is the way which leads men to life" ([101]).

The connection between this doctrine and the Third Degree of Humility in the *Exercises* is clear. Dr. Ortiz, commenting on this Third

---

85 See M. Nicolau, *Pláticas espirituales del P. Jerónimo Nadal en Coimbra* (Granada 1945), pp. 108-109; MHSI Nadal, V, 390-391.

86 Phil. 3:18.

87 Like *contemptus mundi*, abhor (in Spanish *aborrecer*) does not seem to include any judgment of value; it simply designates a practical attitude of not taking into consideration.

Degree of Humility even before the Examen was written, said: "In the most abject state . . . one imitates more fully our Lord Jesus Christ . . . who walked the world in the livery of this state and who gave it to his beloved apostles and the desire for it to all the martyrs."[88]

There is, however, a notable difference between the two passages. In the *Exercises* the phrase "ignominy with Christ filled with insults" is joined to the phrase "poverty with Christ poor." Here in the *Examen* there is no mention of poverty. Fr. Gil González Dávila says that Ignatius is here speaking of "people so freed from the flesh and detached from everything that all that remains is for them to wage war on this enemy, honor and self-esteem."[89] Certainly the renunciation of temporal goods is presupposed here. In fact, this has already been discussed at the beginning of the chapter, in very radical terms. For this reason we think that, although only the desire to suffer injuries is mentioned here, it is in substance the doctrine of the love of the cross.

This doctrine enjoys little popularity today, as if it were opposed to the dignity of the human person. This is not the place to enter into controversies. It is enough to answer with the words of Ignatius: Jesus Christ put on this livery and He is "the way which leads men to life" ([101]). Even more vigorous is the expression used by the Second Vatican Council in the constitution *Gaudium et Spes*, the document which has most insisted on the dignity of the human person: "Whoever follows Christ, the perfect human being, becomes himself more a human being."[90]

b. The Way

As we said, Ignatius is conscious that this love of the cross, these desires to suffer injuries and affronts, presuppose great perfection and cannot be required from all at their entry. Therefore, the one thing demanded of them is that they have "desires to experience them" ([102]), that they have desires to arouse in themselves this love of the cross, these "ardent desires" to suffer injuries and affronts for Christ.

But if these desires to have a love of the cross are authentic, then they will not remain mere desires; they will move one to take steps to "better reach them in fact" ([102]).

Ignatius proposes two kinds of steps, with a gradation from the lesser to the greater, the easier to the more difficult.

The first is to undergo suffering with patience. Since the one who

---

88   MI Exer, p. 636; see MI Const, I, p. 80.
89   G. González Dávila, *Pláticas sobre las reglas* (Barcelona 1964), pp. 232-233.
90   *GS*, no. 41.

enters does not have the strength to love the cross or to desire it, at least he can accept it when it comes and be ready "to accept and suffer with patience, through the help of God's grace, any such injuries, mockeries, and affronts entailed by the wearing of this uniform of Christ our Lord, and any other affronts offered him . . . returning them not evil for evil, but good for evil" ([102]).

The second means, "the better to arrive at this degree of perfection which is so precious in the spiritual life" of the love of the cross, is increasing self-abnegation and constant mortification of inordinate affections. Ignatius says that one who enters the Society ought to consider this abnegation and mortification as his endeavor, even "his chief and most earnest endeavor" ([103]), the work which ought to absorb all his attention and strength. This effort to make progress in mortification and abnegation is complemented by the superior, in his duty to help the subject in it "to the extent that our Lord gives us His grace, for His greater praise and glory" ([103]).

We would like to conclude this discussion with the words of Nadal, or rather, the words of Ignatius as recorded by Nadal. Nadal wrote: "I remember walking onetime with our Father in a corridor, and I asked him to tell me something by which I could profit. He told me that what I knew was sufficient and that I ought to put it into practice. When I persisted in asking that for the love of our Lord he should tell me something that would be of use to me, he answered with very grave and solemn words: 'Master Nadal, desire to suffer injuries, hardships, offenses, accusations, to be considered a fool, to be despised by all, *to hold to the cross in everything* for the love of Christ our Lord, and to put on his livery; because in this is the way of perfection, and spiritual well-being, happiness, and consolation.' With these and similar words, he showed much devotion."[91]

91   See M. Nicolau, op. cit. in note 85, pp. 108-109.

Chapter IV

THE PREAMBLE TO THE CONSTITUTIONS
(Constitutions [134-137])

I. PRELIMINARY REMARKS

The Constitutions of the Society, in their final state, might be compared in form to a fourth-century Christian basilica. In these buildings there was usually an atrium that served as an entrance; it both symbolized and actually effected one's passage from the profane world into the sacred precincts. From this atrium a stairway led up to the porch, or narthex, whose doors opened onto the nave, or rather the three or five naves, of the basilica proper.

The book of the Examen is a like grand atrium of farewell to the world. However, before going on to the Constitutions, divided like ten naves into their ten Parts, we find ourselves in a double entrance porch: the two preambles, one to the Constitutions proper and one to their Declarations.

Historically, the preamble to the Declarations ([136]) is older than that to the Constitutions. It is found in all of the texts, though in the beginning it formed a part of the Constitutions proper. Only in the last text did it become attached, in a fairly modified form, to the Declarations.

In contrast, the preamble to the Constitutions ([134-135]) did not exist in the early texts. It appears for the first time, in Polanco's handwriting, in the rough draft of the definitive text (text B).[1]

Mario Scaduto suspects that the first of the two paragraphs in this preamble reflects Bobadilla's attitude. As superintendent of the college in Naples in 1552, Bobadilla was of the opinion that the rules of the Society were not necessary. He, as superior, ought to keep his subjects in a state which he called "Christian liberty," so long as they were not lacking in solid virtues. This procedure caused some very serious problems.[2] However, we think that this connection with Bobadilla is at least rather uncertain. By

---

1   ARSI *Inst* 7, f. 19
2   See Polanco, *Chron*, II, p. 522; M. Scaduto, *L'epoca de Giacomo Laínez*, I, p. 38.

that time the preamble already should have been composed. Besides, these two paragraphs cannot be separated, since in Polanco's rough copy they appear to have been written at the same time and the same thought runs through both of them.[3]

The two paragraphs respond to a double question which might readily occur to a reader of the Constitutions. First: Why were the Constitutions written? Are they really necessary? ([134]); and second: Why are they written in this particular order, which does not seem to be the most logical? ([135]).

The purpose of the second preamble ([136]) is to explain the reasons for the Declarations, which are a peculiar feature of this work.

We will begin with the preamble to the Constitutions, which should have preference in the logical order.

II. REASONS FOR HAVING CONSTITUTIONS

1. The Interior Law ([134]) and the Exterior Laws

The preamble sets up as a premise that "the Supreme Wisdom and Goodness of God our Creator and Lord" is that which "deigned to begin" this Society ([134]). There is a parallel to this in Part X, where we read that the Society "was not instituted by human means" ([812]). This is something that Ignatius and his companions never doubted.

Suárez asks how this is to be understood. His answer is that, inasmuch as the Divine Wisdom and Goodness illuminated Ignatius with a special inspiration, it aroused and moved him toward the realization of this great work of the Society.[4] He adds that this is what the popes thought as well. Paul III said that Ignatius and his companions had acted "under inspiration of the Holy Spirit, as is piously believed."[5] Ten years later, Julius III repeated the same affirmation, omitting the prejudicial "as is piously believed," meaning by this omission that experience and the fruits of the Society's work had removed all doubt.[6] Gregory XIII spoke in the same way: "The Holy Spirit stirred up Ignatius and his companions," and "Ignatius, through divine inspiration." More recently, Pius XI said that Ignatius, while writing the Constitutions, had acted in obedience to a divine

---

3   In any case, any "polemical intention" is to be excluded.
4   Suárez, *De Societate Iesu*, no. 45.
5   St. Ignatius himself, in a letter to King Ferdinand of Austria, told him of this pontifical affirmation (MI Epp, I, 431).
6   The same observation was made by Nadal in 1561. See *Pláticas de Coimbra*, p. 73.

inspiration (*divino afflatui parens*).[7] What is more, Nadal does not hesitate to assert that the Holy See approved the Society as inspired by God.[8]

Suárez goes on to say that to confine this inspiration to the ordinary assistance of divine grace would diminish it too much, for such inspiration is necessary for any good work. It must be admitted, at least, that in what refers to the substance of the Institute, namely, the determination of its end and its primary or principal means, the Holy Spirit not only prompted Ignatius but also guided him in a very special way so that he would not miss something which was beneficial to the Church; and the Holy Spirit also enabled him to imagine and then serve as the architect of this work of such prudence and grandeur. If there had been something more, if the saint had had some explicit revelation or extraordinary guidance from the Holy Spirit, Suárez does not exclude it, although, writing as a theologian and not as an historian, he does not feel the need to assert it.[9]

From this premise the preamble deduces that, since the "Supreme Wisdom and Goodness of our Creator and Lord" is that which deigned to begin the Society, it will also be that which "will preserve, direct, and even carry [the Society] forward in his divine service." He would not have begun it if he did not intend to preserve it and carry it forward. Now, if God has taken upon himself the direction and advancement of the Society, why is it necessary to have Constitutions?

Sometimes it is said that divine direction does not preclude the existence of human law. This direction of human acts by divine wisdom is the eternal law, which has God as its governor and supreme regulator and to which "on our own part," in what refers to us, our other laws must correspond. These laws guide us to the ends and acts which the eternal law requires.[10]

The preamble answers that "on our own part," for what refers to us, what helps most must be "more than any exterior constitution, the interior law of charity and love which the Holy Spirit writes and engraves upon hearts."

The author is inspired here by St. Thomas, who in his own time followed the teaching of St. Augustine in his treatise *De spiritu et littera*.[11]

This interior law is the new law, the gospel law, which, according to Thomas, consists principally in the grace of the Holy Spirit and, in the

---

7   Brief "Paterna Caritas," *ActRom*, VII (1933), 275.
8   MI FontNarr, II, 4.
9   Suárez, *De Societate Iesu*, no. 54.
10   St. Thomas, 1-2, q. 91, art. 2; q. 93, art. 1, 2.
11   St. Thomas, 1-2, qq. 106-107.

words of Augustine, is "the very presence of the Holy Spirit."[12] More explicitly, Thomas says in another place: It is "the Holy Spirit which, living in the soul, not only teaches the understanding what is most expedient, but also inclines the will to do it."[13]

This law is the "law of charity and love" because, unlike the old law, which secured observance by the threat of certain penalties and was thus called the "law of fear," this new law inclines one to virtuous acts out of love for virtue, not because of any punishment or reward.[14] This is called the interior law, *indita* or "infused," by St. Thomas, who cites words from the prophet Jeremiah which also apply to our text: "Behold, the days are coming, says the Lord, when I will make a new covenant with the house of Israel and the house of Judah." Declaring what this covenant will be, he adds: "But this is the covenant which I will make with the house of Israel after those days, says the Lord. I will put my law within them, and I will write it upon their hearts; and I will be their God, and they shall be my people."[15]

This interior law must help to preserve, govern, and carry forward in divine service the Society, "more than any exterior constitutions." Commenting on the opposition found in St. Paul between the letter and the spirit, Thomas has some profound reflections on the priority of the interior law over the exterior. The exterior law can do no more than give us knowledge of what sin is, without removing its cause, which is concupiscence. Therefore, this exterior law is not evil, but it is imperfect and, without the Spirit which imprints it on hearts, it is an occasion for sin and death. This is why the law of the Spirit was necessary, to bring forth charity in the heart, and to vivify it.[16] Quoting Augustine, Thomas notes that the "law that kills" is not only the Mosaic law, but any exterior law, even the moral precepts of the Gospels. Laws which would "kill" are those which lack the interior grace of faith.[17]

In commenting on the words of the Apostle "where the Spirit of the Lord is, there is freedom,"[18] St. Thomas says that a person is free when he is his own master, and enslaved when he belongs to another. Therefore, he who does good or avoids evil out of an interior impulse acts freely, while he who does the same things only because they are mandated or prohibited

12   St. Thomas, 1-2, q. 106, art. 1; St. Augustine, *De spiritu et littera*, chap. 21.
13   *In Rom.*, chap. 8, lect. 1.
14   St. Thomas, q. 107, art. 1, ad 2; see *In 2 Cor.*, chap. 3, lect. 3.
15   Jer. 31:31, 33; St. Thomas, 1-2, q. 106, art. 1, "Sed contra est."
16   *In 2 Cor.*, chap. 3, lect. 3, nos. 90-91.
17   St. Thomas, 1-2, q. 106, art. 2.
18   2 Cor. 3:17.

by the exterior law does not act freely. The interior law of charity, which is the Holy Spirit, infuses into a person an interior principle of action, moving him to do good and avoid evil out of love. A human being is free, then, because, though he submits to the exterior law, he holds to an interior principle of action that moves him to comply with the requirements of the exterior law.[19]

All of these considerations have been negative, tending against the necessity of writing the Constitutions. Now, as in the *Summa* of St. Thomas, we come to the *Sed contra est*, the reasons in favor of writing them. We can isolate four such reasons.

2. The Four Reasons

The first reason is that "the gentle arrangement of Divine Providence requires cooperation from His creatures."

In these words there is a clear allusion to the words of the book of Wisdom: "She orders all things well."[20]

However, we must ask in what manner the Constitutions cooperate with the Supreme Wisdom and Goodness of God in order to preserve, govern, and carry forward the Society.

We ought not to forget that, though we have been reborn in Christ, we have no more than the "first fruits" or "guarantee" of the Spirit.[21] Yielding to the passions, we can place ourselves in a state in which the interior law loses its efficacy. Then we are left with the exterior law to show us the dictates of God's will. This law will be for us as the Mosaic law was for the Jews, in the words of Stanislas Lyonnet, "a pedagogue for the journey to Christ."[22] Emile Mersch maintained that even without arriving at such a sad state, "man does not have a soul so silent and docile that it can always hear the gentle whisperings of divine invitation. His heart is too disturbed for him to discern in it every supernatural sign."[23] In such cases the exterior law is a clear norm, dispelling all vacillation. We stand in the order of things brought on by the Incarnation. God wants to save in conformity

---

19 *In 2 Cor.*, chap. 3, lect. 3, no. 112; see S. Lyonnet, *L'opposition paulinienne "la lettre et l'esprit" à la lumière de l'interpretation de Saint Thomas* (Communication to the International Congress commemorating the seventh centenary of the death of St. Thomas Aquinas [Rome/Naples 1974]; in the appendix there is a collection of the saint's principal texts).

20 Wis. 8:1.

21 See Rom. 8:23; 2 Cor. 1:22.

22 Gal. 3:24. See S. Lyonnet, "Liberté du Chrétien et loi de l'Esprit selon Saint Paul," art. in *Christus* 1/4 (1954), 22.

23 E. Mersch, *Morale et Corps Mystique* (Desclée de Brouwer 1955), p. 265.

with our human nature, which is both corporal and spiritual. Therefore, since we have said that the exterior law without the interior is slavery, the desire to do away with the exterior law on the pretext that only the interior law is important does not, given human nature, lead to the condition of "Christian liberty" described by Bobadilla, but rather to license and, eventually, to another slavery, the slavery to the passions, to propaganda, or to pressure groups, and the like.

The second reason is that "the vicar of Christ our Lord has ordered this."

Nadal said that "we deduce this from the documents which confirm our Institute."[24] In effect, the first Formula of the Institute, approved by Paul III in the bull *Regimini militantis Ecclesiae*, grants the superior general of the Society the power to compose, with the advice of his companions, "Constitutions which aid in the construction of this end that we have proposed" (*ad constructionem huius propositi nobis finis conducentes*). The Formula of the Institute can be conceived of as a plan in which the general lines of the edifice of the Society are laid out. Later on there was a need for Constitutions to fill out these general lines with more particular details and to realize the projected construction.[25]

Following this way of thinking, the second Formula of the Institute, approved by Julius III in 1550, refers several times to more explicit determinations of the Institute which will be written into Constitutions: "following the declaration of our Constitutions," "as will be explained in the Constitutions," and "as will be explained at greater length in the Constitutions."[26]

These references in the Formula to the Constitutions, as to a complementary document, are not made without good reason. They can be considered both as a pontifical mandate to write the Constitutions and as a reminder that the Constitutions are an authentic interpretation of the Formula.

The third reason is that "the examples of the saints . . . teach us so." This is clearly an allusion to other founders. As we noted when speaking of the origin of the Constitutions, Ignatius, despite his reputation as an "innovator," always had the example of other founders in mind. We can see this, for example, in his letter to Gian Pietro Carafa.[27]

The final reason is that "reason itself teaches us." This is not meant in

24   *Scholia*, no. 134.
25   Form. Inst., no. 2.
26   Form. Inst., nos. 2 and 9.
27   MI Epp, I, 116.

the sense that, besides the reasons listed here, there are others which have been left unmentioned. Ignatius wanted to say that right reason dictated what had been done: it was reasonable to have Constitutions. In fact, it is inconceivable that a social body should be without some legislation. Even the Church, with its divine origin, does not lack legislation.

Reason and the example given by the saints teach us "in our Lord." These words "in our Lord" or their equivalent are used some 120 times in the Constitutions.[28] They are often used with the verbs to teach, to judge, to appear, and the like, but also with those which refer to other human activities, such as suffering, rejoicing, attempting, and the like. This gives us a glimpse of the meaning of this expression, which is not easily defined. It describes the act of relying entirely on the Lord, trusting that he will illuminate our judgments and perceptions and sustain us in all our activities, rather than trusting in our own feeble powers and dim lights.

For these four reasons, the first paragraph concludes, "we think it necessary that constitutions should be written to aid us to proceed better, in conformity with our Institute, along the path of divine service on which we have entered."

The Constitutions were written only in order to *help*, yet even this aid is secondary. After all that has been said, it should not be necessary to emphasize this. He who is to preserve, govern, and carry forward the Society in his holy service is Christ our Lord; "on our own part" the principal aid comes from the interior law of charity and love.

However, the fact that the Constitutions occupy a position secondary to the interior law does not preclude their being necessary. The four reasons have proved this. They are necessary for us to proceed better, in conformity with our Institute, along the path of divine service, a process which God our Lord deigned to set in motion.

There is no need to argue over the adverb "better." To proceed in just any manner, the Constitutions would not need to have been written. They help us to proceed better, to advance, or to improve.

On the other hand, it is important to take note of the insertion "in conformity with our Institute." Each institute has its own way of proceeding, its own method of imitating Jesus Christ, its own special vocation, its "grace" (as Nadal called it), or its charism (as we say today).[29] In order to understand this and proceed in conformity with it, one must have recourse

28 98 times "in our Lord"; 14 times "in Domino"; 3 "in the Lord"; 2 "in the Lord of all"; 1 "in Him"; 1 "in His divine Majesty."
29 See Pius XI, Apostolic Letter "Unigenitus," *AAS* 16 (March 19, 1924), 133-134); Conc. Vat. II, *LG*, nos. 44-46.

to the Constitutions.[30]

III. ORDER OF THE CONSTITUTIONS ([135-137])

The second paragraph of the preamble ([135]) cannot be read without its declaration ([137]), which antedates it and for which it was written.

Two main ideas are developed: the number and content of the Parts into which the Constitutions are divided, and the order in which these Parts are arranged. The image of a body is used throughout.

There are ten Parts. Three of these treat the body of the Society in general ("the body of the Society taken as a whole" [135]): how to maintain its unity (Part VIII), how to govern it (Part IX), and how to preserve it (Part X). The other seven refer to its members: their admission (Part I), their dismissal (Part II), their spiritual advancement (Part III), their advancement in learning (Part IV), their incorporation or attachment to the body (Part V), and, after their incorporation, their life in the body, both personal (Part VI) and apostolic (Part VII).

If one were to write a speculative treatise on the religious state, the logical order would be to begin with the body in general (its unity, government, and preservation). The purpose of writing the Constitutions is that the body of the Society should be better governed and preserved. This is the first and most important purpose: "In the order of our intention, the consideration which comes first and has more weight" ([135]).

However, this is not what is being done here. Instead, following the metaphor used in the Formula of the Institute, Ignatius is treating of "constructing" the edifice of the Society. And in this order of practice, as the declaration states, "it is usually best . . . to proceed from the less perfect to the more perfect" ([137]), or in other words, from the incomplete to the complete, from the parts to the whole. In addition to this, a scholastic principle holds that "what is first in the order of execution is what was the last in the order of consideration."[31] In the consideration, the first thing is the end that is intended, the last are the means that aid in attaining that end. In execution, on the other hand, the first things are the means toward the intended end. In the Constitutions, therefore, it is useful to begin with the means, which are imperfect (the components which make up the Society as a whole): their admission, formation, incorporation, and behavior are the

---

30 See Pius XII, "Discourse at Second Congress on States of Perfection," *AAS* 56 (1958), 38.
31 See St. Thomas, *In IV Sent.*, disp. 49, q. 1, art. 1.

means to the end of uniting, governing, and preserving the body of the Society.

We have said that the whole Society is conceived of as a body. It is worthwhile to take time to reflect on this particular point.

The difference between the Society of Jesus as a way of life and as a religious order should be kept clearly in mind. Even chronologically they are distinct. Ignatius began to live this "way of proceeding" of the Society after Manresa. His companions took up this sort of life at least from the time that, upon completing their studies, they left Paris for Venice. In contrast, only in the spring of 1539 did they decide to institutionalize this way of life, converting themselves into a religious order so that they might better govern and preserve themselves in it. It is interesting to note the expression that they used then: "We must confirm and consolidate our union and congregation by forming ourselves into a single body" (*reducendo nos ad unum corpus*).[32]

As we begin to examine the juridical organization of the Society, intended equally for its better governance and preservation, we again find the image of a body, though a more developed one. It is a body composed of members, who must be "incorporated into it," a body with a head that governs it, and a body which must be preserved and advanced in its well-being.

This way of life, which it was so desirable to organize and make incarnate in this body, is summed up—as we have already said—in the life of apostolic mission. We can speak of two themes or elements, mission and body, as the warp and woof of the Constitutions, which form the fabric of the whole work. The "mission" element pertains to the charism, the spirit, the soul; the "body" element pertains to the institution and the juridical organization. Always in accord with the proper end, the "mission" element prevails in some Parts (such as Part VII), while the "body" element prevails in others (Part V).

Should we risk forming a more uncertain hypothesis and say that in the first case (concerning mission) we have a more direct intervention of the inspired thought of Ignatius, while in the second (concerning the body) the organizational talent of his secretary Polanco is more evident?

Actually, the application of the image of the body to the Society, despite all that has been written about it, does not appear to be Ignatian. We do not find it in any of the writings redacted by Ignatius himself, nor in any of the corrections in his handwriting. It is not present, for example, in the "Constitutions Regarding Missions," nor in the first text of the Examen.[31]

---

32 MI Const, I, p. 3, lines 60-82; see lines 49-50; and pp. 23-24, lines 6 and 14.

31 Moreover, neither in the *Diario espiritual* nor in the *Deliberación sobre la pobreza* nor

It does appear in two documents on the foundation of the Society, the "Deliberation of the First Fathers" and the "Determination of the Society." However, these documents were not composed by Ignatius but by one of his companions. Moreover, the expression appears there in less defined forms: "unite ourselves into a single body," "united in one body," and "those who are of our body." We do not encounter the expression again until the arrival of Polanco in 1547. He begins to use it in his *Dudas*, though in the same less defined manner,[32] and later, in the first text of the Constitutions, where the metaphor is fully developed.

Nevertheless, the image is one thing, the idea it is intended to represent is another. We are inclined to think, given all that we have said, that the image of the body as applied to the Society in the Constitutions, is Polanco's work. By this means, however, Polanco intended only to mold the idea of the institution or juridical organization into the form which, after 1539, Ignatius and his companions had decided to give the Society.

IV. The Declarations ([136])

We began this work by pointing out that four books are included under the general title Constitutions of the Society of Jesus: the Examen, the Declarations on the Examen, the Constitutions proper, and the Declarations on the Constitutions.

The author now explains the reason for the existence of these Declarations. He begins with the purpose of the Constitutions: the proximate end "to aid the body of the Society as a whole and also its individual members toward their preservation and development" ([136]); "to proceed better, in conformity with our Institute, along the path of divine service on which we have entered" ([134]); and the more remote end of "the divine glory and the good of the universal Church" ([136]).[33]

The formal qualities that the Constitutions ought to have are deduced from this end. These qualities are—apart from the obvious appropriateness and usefulness that ought to characterize each norm in its attainment of what it is intended to do—that the Constitutions should be complete (*cumplidas*), clear, and brief.[34]

---

in the previous documents entitled by the editor *Constituta et annotata* (MI Const, I, 187-219).

32 See MI Const, I, 296, 307, 328.

33 See the parallel place in Part IX, chap. 3, no. 8 [746]. There is no mention here of the Church; but the spiritual help of neighbors is included in the "divine service."

34 In 1547/1548 Polanco wanted similar qualities in the Formula of the Institute. See

It seems that it would be difficult, if not impossible, to be complete and at the same time brief, or to be both brief and clear. The Latin poet Horace said so long ago, "Striving for brevity, I fall into obscurity" (*Brevis esse laboro, obscurus fio*).[35] In order to resolve this difficulty, it was thought at one time that a series of constitutional documents of greater or lesser length ought to be written, with individual documents destined for superiors, subjects, and externs and with a directory about how they should be used.[36] However, this idea was eventually abandoned, and it was decided to go back to the first plan of two documents or codes (separate from the rules, which we will discuss next): the Constitutions proper and the Declarations.

In fact, from the time of the 1541 meeting, convened for the election of the first superior general and the making of final profession, Ignatius and his companions were convinced that there should be "declarations," or explanations, which should be in the hands of superiors.[37] Both the "Constitutions Regarding Missions" and the first text of the Examen had them.[38]

What is their objective? The preamble says that they will allow the Constitutions to be more universal and summary, more "manageable."

Every legislator finds himself in this dilemma: Should he confine himself to general norms (as, to be humble, charitable, of service) or should he descend into the details of everyday life? The former is more applicable to the diversity of circumstances, but less efficacious. The latter is more efficacious, but difficult to adapt to all times and places.

Ignatius' idea was to make Constitutions that are "universal" and "complete," or that deal with principles for action and, as far as possible, cover every situation. Despite this he wanted Constitutions which are "summary" or brief, such that subjects could easily remember, can be shown to externs, and are "easy to handle" or manageable. All of this would help toward better observance.

Such constitutions, with these sorts of qualities, often present difficulties when they have to be applied practically to a real life situation. Thus, the Declarations have the purpose of guiding the superior so that he will know how to apply the constitutional norm in various circumstances and how to

---

MI Const I, pp. 295-296.

35 Horace, *Ars poetica*, 25-26.

36 See MI Const, II, 136 (first text). It is preserved substantially in text A. See ibid., p. 262.

37 MI Const, I, 43.

38 See ibid., pp. 162-164 and 249-258. Indexes on pp. 230-231 and 237-239.

do this in conformity with the mind of the legislator.[39]

We can find no antecedent, in other religious legislation, for this particular solution, which seems so inspired, though it sometimes suffers from an imperfect realization in the book of the Constitutions. Some might point to the Dominican constitutions. It is true that they also have declarations, and in a typographical arrangement similar to that used in the Ignatian document. In the first place, however, the actual typographical arrangement used for our declarations does not reflect the thinking of Ignatius, who envisaged two distinct volumes: one containing the Constitutions and meant for everyone, and one containing the Declarations and given only to superiors. In the second place, the character of the declarations in the Dominican constitutions is very different. They are ordinances or interpretations from general chapters, which were not incorporated into the text at the time of its writing. They were inserted after each paragraph, with a reference letter, by the first editor of the text, Vicente Bandelli.

It is primarily the Declarations that give the Jesuit Constitutions their flexibility, their adaptability to diverse circumstances, their quality of being valid for all times, places, and persons and, consequently, their consistency and perennial vitality. In fact, Ignatius wanted the Constitutions to be "universal and unchangeable." Of course, he meant a relative immutability, since the Formula of the Institute gives the Society gathered in general congregation the power to change them.[40] The first text said *"more* universal and unchangeable." Nevertheless, it was clearly the mind of Ignatius that the Constitutions should have a certain stability and remain, at least fundamentally, unchanged. He wanted to obtain a papal document that would render some of the more substantial points unalterable.[41] In fact, the identity of the Society demands this.

V. THE RULES

In spite of all this, Ignatius was very sensitive to the diversity of circumstances. He was not content with the application of the Constitutions made by the superior with the guidance of the Declarations. He desired further that in every house or college there should also be "ordinances" or rules as well, even for each office. These rules could be accommodated to times, places, and persons and could undergo changes that these circum-

---

39 See MI Const, I, p. 249, lines 12-15.
40 Form. Inst., no. 2.
41 See MI Const, I, p. 231; see p. 312.

stances might demand. He himself composed not a few sets of these rules: for the novices (as early as 1546-1547),[42] for the house in Rome, for the various offices that were exercised in it (1549), to say nothing of the well-known "Rules of Modesty."[43]

His intentions are clear. First, he wants a set of rules for each place, rules common to everyone in that place, and he wants particular rules for each of the offices. Second, although a certain variety will be demanded in them by local circumstances, he wants all the rules used in the Society to have a "uniformity," "insofar as possible." When he sent Nadal to Spain and Portugal in 1553, Ignatius gave him the rules used in the Roman house, not so that he might impose them, but that they might serve as a norm.[44]

The Constitutions refer to the rules, or presume their existence, in seven places: in the Examen ([18]), and in Parts I, IV, VI, VII, and X ([198-199, 395-396, 428, 585, 654, 811]). Bobadilla, then, was wrong when he wanted to do away with the obligation of rules for all those who were not lacking in solid virtues. His thinking did not coincide with that of Ignatius on this point.

---

42   See MI Const, I, pp. 207-209.
43   See MI Regulae, pp. 157-208.
44   See MI Epp, V, 13; X, 17. In Part IV, chap. 7 [396], the rules of the Roman College are indicated as a norm for other colleges. See also the reply given to Mannaerts when he was rector at Loreto (MI FontNarr, III, 434, no. 24).

Chapter V

ADMISSION

(Constitutions, Part I)

I. PRELIMINARY REMARKS

1. Structure

Following the order of execution as indicated in the Preamble ([135]), the Constitutions begin with the admission to probation.

The structure of this Part is simple and logical. After establishing who has the authority to admit, the first chapter continues by charging these individuals to use this authority very selectively. This "proper" selection requires a dual understanding: an abstract understanding of the norms or criteria according to which the selection must be made and a concrete understanding of the subjects who, in conformity with these norms or criteria, are to be accepted into or excluded from the Society. The norms or criteria for the first understanding are given in the second and third chapters: from a positive viewpoint in chapter 2 (qualities) and from a negative viewpoint in chapter 3 (impediments or defects). The manner of coming to know the subjects and examining their vocation is set forth in chapter 4.[1]

2. Sources

The principal source is Polanco's second *Industria*, entitled "On the Selection of Persons." A large part of it was copied word for word into the primitive text of the Constitutions.[2] The manner of making the first probation ([197, 198, 200]) is based on some rules dealing with this subject which Ignatius had recently composed[3] and on the book of the Examen. We will speak of other particular influences at the appropriate points in the

---

1   In the first text this last point preceded the norms or criteria for selection, and the secondary impediments were treated together with the positive characteristics. The primary impediments were not mentioned, for it was intended to add the Examen at the end, as Chapter V.
2   See MHSI PolCompl, II, 729-734.
3   See MI Regulae, 197-198.

text.

Basically, the ideas developed in this Part can be reduced to two: who has the authority to admit and how he is to use this authority.

II. AUTHORITY TO ADMIT ([138-141])

St. Francis of Assisi granted the faculty of admitting into his order to the provincial ministers.[4] In the Dominican Order, the Constitutions give this faculty to the prior of each convent along with the conventual chapter.[5] It is clear from one of the decretals in the Corpus Iuris of Boniface VIII that monastic discipline with regard to this question was not uniform. In some monasteries the abbot alone had the authority to admit, in others it was the abbot together with the community.[6]

In the Society, from the very beginning, from the deliberations of 1539 on, Ignatius and his companions decided that it ought to be the *praepositus* (the "superior"; and at that time, there was only one superior, the general) who, after having been properly informed, alone (*ipse solus*) ought to decide freely about the admission of those who desire to enter.[7] As the practice in other religious orders, to which we have just referred, was known to the first fathers, this emphasis on "the superior alone" (*ipse solus*) is intended as a declaration that in the Society any deliberative vote of a council or chapter is excluded.

A few years later, in 1546, Ignatius obtained from the pope permission for the single superior of the original scheme to have vicars or lesser superiors to whom he might delegate the faculty of admission.[8]

So it is clear that "the authority to admit to probation will belong to those whom the superior general of the Society thinks fit" ([138]). From him, as from the head, all the authority of the members of the body of the Society has to derive (see [666]). He will also know how to communicate this authority, attending to "what is conducive to greater service to God our Lord" ([138]). However, Ignatius does not fail to give him in the declaration some norms to guide him as to how this delegating is to be done (see [141]).

Those without authority to admit ought to refer to those with this authority anyone having a possible vocation whom they might have

4   *Regula bullata*, chap. 2.
5   *Const. O.P.*, Dist. I, chap. 13.
6   6 *de regul.*, III, 14, in Sexto.
7   MI Const, I, 13-14; see p. 39.
8   See MI Const, I, 172-173.

encountered in their apostolic life ([139-140]). It was hardly necessary to say this, but perhaps it was due to the influence of the Rule of St. Francis, which contains the same advice.[9]

III. SELECTION ([142-146])

Having said all this about the authority to admit, let us move on to the second point, the manner of exercising that authority.

The dominant thought of the rest of this Part is expressed in the first lines of [142]: It is very important for the divine service that there be a proper selection (*delecto*) of those who are to be admitted.

Selection is a relative term. It is not intended to mean receiving only a few of the applicants: "This does not exclude the number, even though it is very large, of persons who are suitable" ([658]). To make a selection means to accept no more than are "suitable for our Institute" ([819]).

To this end, probably inspired by the Dominican constitutions,[10] Ignatius allows to one with the authority of admitting the aid of an examiner who is discreet and has some skill in dealing with persons of various types and temperaments. This man will converse with those who want to enter, examine them, and judge the aptitude of each one ([142]).

There is a certain tension here between two legitimate desires: that of increasing the numbers of the Society and that of selecting those who are to be received in it; or, in the well-considered words of declaration C, between "endeavoring to secure in the Society an increase of workers for the holy vineyard of Christ our Lord" and admitting "only those who possess the qualifications required for this Institute and for the divine glory" ([144]).

In the evolution of the text, we note a shift in emphasis from one side of the tension to the other. In text A, Polanco had included a lengthy declaration, taken from his first *Industria*, in which there were no less than eighteen means "for getting people." Ignatius objected to this and wrote in the margin: "Take them all out, or, leaving a few, still make it very difficult." That is to say, suppress all eighteen of these means of fostering vocations, or reduce them to only a few while continuing to make it difficult to enter. Polanco omitted the whole declaration and, by altering the order of the components of Declaration C, he inverted the relative

---

9   *Regula bullata*, chap. 2.
10   The influence appears more clearly in the first text, where there is mention, not of an examiner, but of "some one or several persons."

importance of the two sides of this tension. Initially the declaration said: Although a selection is to be made of those who enter, an effort is to be made to secure an increase of workers in the vineyard of Christ. Now the declaration says: Although an effort is to be made to secure an increase of workers in the vineyard of Christ, much consideration ought to be given to the choice of those to be admitted.

Perhaps this change in the text reflects a change of attitude in the mind of Ignatius. Ribadeneira says of him that "although in the beginning he did not make it difficult to enter the Society, he later came to tighten his grip and to say that, if there was anything that would make him desire to live on (though he had decided nothing definite on this point), it was that he might be more stringent in admitting into the Society."[11]

Hence the instruction to the one who has the authority to admit and to the examiner who helps that they ought to be "very moderate in their desire to admit" ([143]). He wanted them to moderate that desire, even though legitimate, to increase the number of subjects in the Society and wanted them to "know the Society's concerns" (what the Institute demands) and "be zealous for its good progress" so that "no other consideration will be so strong as to deter [them] from what [they] judge in our Lord to be more suitable for His divine service in this Society" ([143]).

From the primitive text we know that the "considerations" spoken of by the legislator were the recommendations of important persons, benefactors, friends, or relatives. Therefore, in order to avoid any danger of passion, it is prescribed that the examiner ought not to perform his office in any circumstances where a disordinate affection could blind him, such as when the candidate is a relative or friend ([143]). This is a norm established by the first fathers in the deliberations of 1539.[12]

The examiner will have, in addition to the book of the Examen, the rules of his office, which guide him as to the manner of fulfilling it ([145-146]). However, Ignatius knew that all the written norms were insufficient without discretion and supernatural illumination. Therefore he adds that "the holy unction of the Divine Wisdom will teach the mean which should be retained in all this to those who have charge of that matter, which was undertaken for His greater service and praise" ([161]).

---

11   See MI FontNarr, III, 611; II, 475-476, no. 23. Polanco testifies to the same in his *Industrias*, MHSI PolCompl, II, 772.
12   MI Const, I, 13. There the examiner was not formally treated, for none was as yet appointed, only the *Praepositus*. But the principle was the same.

IV. Qualities Required ([147-189])

We have said that, above all, selection demands an abstract understanding of the norms or criteria according to which one should act. Although the definitive text of the Constitutions separates the positive qualities from the impediments or defects, we will speak of them both at the same time, since they tend to clarify each other.

1. General Norms

We can distinguish two classes of norms, general and particular. The following are the general norms.

Charity and zeal for souls, in which the Society exercises itself according to the purpose of its Institute, move the Society to open its arms to help "all sorts of people" attain eternal life. However, when there arises the question of not just helping them but of incorporating them into the Society, this same charity demands that it admit no more than those judged useful in the attainment of its end ([163]). It would be a mistake to argue that, although some might be useless to the Society in light of the purpose of its Institute, it would not be useless to them to be admitted ([152]). This is a mistake because the one admitting "should be vigilant that charity for an individual does not impair the charity for all, which should always be preferred as being more important for the glory and honor of Christ our Lord" ([189]). This principle of preferring the good of the Society to the good of any particular individual could lead to contradiction if not rightly understood. It does not mean the sacrifice of an individual for an institution; rather, it means preferring the good of the many to the good of the one when the two come into conflict. This understanding is an ancient principle, invoked in papal documents and the constitutions of other religious orders under the formula: "The utility of many is to be placed before the utility of one" (*Plurimorum utilitas utilitati unius praeponenda est*).[13]

Nevertheless, there can be a difference in the degree of suitability for the purpose of the Institute. "The greater the number of natural and infused gifts someone has from God our Lord which are useful for what the Society aims at in His divine service" the more suitable the candidate will be ([147]), and the more useful for the Society ([161]). It is true that there are some impediments "which bar admission absolutely" ([164]) or

---

13 See, for example, *Corpus Iuris Canonici*, c. 35, C. VII, q. 1 (Pelagius II); c. 18, X, *de regularibus*, III, 31 (Innocent III); *Constitutiones Ord. Praed.*, dist. I, chap. 19, decl. b.

"necessarily" ([146]), "for compelling reasons which move us in our Lord" ([164]), such that neither the general nor the whole Society can dispense from them ([176]). However, not all of the impediments have that absolute character. The others, the second group, only have the effect of making one who wants to enter the Society less suitable ([117]; see also [189]), a fact that can at times be compensated for by some "outstanding virtues and gifts of God" ([186]; see [178, 187]). Furthermore, even in the case of the first group of impediments which exclude absolutely, Ignatius did not want to close the door so completely that, if a candidate had extraordinary qualities and sought a dispensation from the Holy See, he still could not be admitted ([176]). Thus, he was disposed to accept St. John of Avila even though he had the third primary impediment, having been a friar.

Proceeding to the particular norms, the definitive text begins with those admitted as temporal coadjutors ([148-151]). At first sight this arrangement is surprising. The author is doubtless following the method that we have already observed, of going from the lesser to the greater, from the candidates of whom fewer qualities are demanded to those from whom more are required.

2. The Temporal Coadjutors

The qualities of those to be received as coadjutors in temporal affairs are determined by the end which motivates their admission, which is "the need to be aided which those have who are laboring in the Lord's vineyard or who are studying to labor in it later, that they may apply themselves to pursuits which bring greater service to God our Lord" ([149]). This relief or aid is symbolized by the "lot of Martha" mentioned in [148]. The lot of Martha is not the active life in contrast to the contemplative or apostolic life. The lot of Martha is that which Martha was exercising by serving the Lord and the apostles in her own house when they came together there to rest from the apostolic mission.[14]

In conformity with this aim, the temporal coadjutors ought not to be greater in number than "is necessary to aid the Society in occupations which the other members could not fulfill without detriment to the greater service of God" ([148]). Such occupations are, above all, the "more burdensome" offices (see [364]) which demand all of a man's time and activity. In declaration A, some of them are enumerated as examples, with

---

14 In the source (*Industria* 2ª) the title or marginal note on the content of the paragraph, written by Polanco, was "Satisfied with Martha's *office*." Similarly, Miró, writing in 1546 about Brother Jacobo Ponzone, said, "Omnino videtur natus ad *officium* Marthae" (MHSI EppMixt, I, 301).

the note that circumstances may be different and that the final decision is to be left to the superior's discretion ([149]).

Temporal coadjutors are not required to have intellectual gifts but are to be "edifying to those inside and outside the house" ([148]).

Their preaching is to be more by good example than by words, though the Examen exhorts them to improve their neighbors by means of spiritual conversations, since the Lord has given each one the care of his neighbor.[15]

The life of the temporal coadjutors is more domestic and community-oriented. For this reason, there is no special mention, as there is in the other grades (see [156]), of fortitude in enterprise; rather, mention is made of the social virtues, that they be "men of good conscience, peaceful, docile" ([148]). For the same reason, their life is more secluded and contemplative, and requires that they be not only "lovers of virtue and perfection" as all religious should be, but also "inclined to devotion" ([148]), that is, to the exercises of piety.

The temptation of those in this grade was, in Ignatius' time and ever since, to be discontent with the "lot of Martha"—with service in domestic offices to those who work in the vineyard of Christ or who study to work there later—and to aspire to the priesthood or to studies. For this reason, one of the qualities of these candidates ought to be contentment with their lot and office, as Martha was content to serve the Lord and his Apostles. They will have this quality if they love the Society and desire to help it for the glory of God our Lord ([148]).

However, Ignatius was a realist. In the declaration, he advises that one who had an inclination toward studies or the priesthood not be admitted as a temporal coadjutor. Such a candidate would lead a very disturbed life ([150]).

Regarding physical qualities, it is clear that the temporal coadjutor ought to have the health and strength demanded for domestic offices and an aptitude for them ([151]; see [305]). However, there is a great variety here, for the same strengths are not required for the office of cook as for that of secretary ([433]) or procurator ([591]).

3. Those Admitted for Spiritual Ministry

In the determination of the proper qualities for those admitted "to serve in spiritual matters" ([153]), that is, to help one's neighbors spiritually, the two coordinates we mentioned when commenting on the Preamble, "mission" and "body," come together, though in very diverse proportions.

---

15   The last words are a quotation from Eccli. 17:12.

The dominant presence is always the "mission," the apostolic end: "for the help of souls" ([153]).

(1) One who enters a religious institute ought to have the right intention, not one "mixed with human motives" ([180]), and be "desirous of all virtue and spiritual perfection" ([156]). For the candidate to the Society, this intention is expressed concretely by being "zealous for the salvation of souls. For that reason they should also have an affection toward our Institute, which is directly ordered to help and dispose souls to gain their ultimate end from the hand of God our Creator and Lord" ([156]).

(2) The "missionary" character of the Institute involves many serious difficulties. As early as 1539 the first fathers declared in the Formula that they knew this from experience.[16] Above all, fortitude and constancy are required to carry forward the enterprise of divine service against any difficulties ([156]), and such an enterprise is not for inconstant, weak, or cowardly souls ([181]). The inconstancy that could move one to abandon one religious order to enter another is one of the reasons that former religious cannot be admitted into the Society ([171-172]); for "every good Christian ought to be stable in his first vocation" ([30]).

(3) On the other hand, the relations that those in the Society have with their neighbors demands a "peaceful" soul ([156]), that is to say, one not disturbed by "passions which seem uncontrollable, or sinful habits of which there is no hope of much emendation" ([179]). In the "apostolic life" individuals who have such passions can cause great harm to souls, no matter how much goodwill they may have.

(4) The works of the itinerant apostolate also demand health and bodily strength ([159, 185]) as well as a suitable age, neither too young nor too advanced ([160, 185, 187]).

(5) "In order to be good and faithful sowers in the Lord's field and to preach His divine word" ([30]), those who enter the Society are required to have "a sufficiency of sound learning" ([109]). The candidate must, then, have "doctrine" (or theological knowledge) and doctrine which is "sound" or orthodox ([154]). "One suspected of some erroneous opinion in a matter concerning the Catholic faith should not be admitted while such a suspicion lasts" ([24]). If he has not already completed his studies, the candidate ought at least to have the intellectual gifts and aptitude necessary to acquire such doctrine or knowledge ([154, 155, 183]).

(6) In the apostolic life, however, it is not enough to have knowledge. There is the need to be able to present it to the people ([814]). One requirement is the ability to speak properly, with "neither embarrassment

16 See Form Inst., no. 2.

nor hesitation" (as it says in the primitive text); "In regard to the exterior, a pleasing manner of speech, so necessary for communication with one's fellowmen, is desirable" ([157]). This "pleasing manner of speech" was a skill for which Ignatius himself was well known.[17] In some old declarations for the Examen, Ignatius added in his own hand: "In a clear voice, or speaking clearly."[18]

(7) Another requirement for the apostolic life is prudence. The Formula of the Institute had already said that no one ought to make profession who was not "prudent in Christ" (*prudens in Christo*). To his speculative knowledge the candidate must add "discretion in respect to things to be done," in other words, discretion in practical affairs. In the case of inexperienced youths, they ought to at least show some "good judgment" (or natural wisdom) which will help them acquire this discretion ([154]). The harm that imprudent persons can do to souls is sometimes greater than that which can be done by those with uncontrolled passions or bad intentions.

(8) The office of preaching the divine word also requires credibility, because of the "ordinary and common weakness of many persons" ([30]). This need for credibility excludes, above all, those who have "separated [themselves] for a time from the bosom of the Holy Church" by denying the faith, by heresy or schism ([165-167]), and those who have committed murder or are infamous for having committed "enormous sins" ([168-170]).

(9) For this same reason of greater acceptance by those being evangelized, there is also the Ignatian requirement of a "good appearance" ([158]) or a decent exterior appearance. This seems strange or even scandalous to us, as if it were something worldly. On the other hand, it should not be exaggerated. In contrast with the defects which exclude, it simply means not admitting persons with "notable disfigurements or defects such as humpbacks and other deformities" because these are disadvantages in the priesthood and hindrances to the edification of others ([186]).

(10) This same purpose of edification, and that "vigilance [which] should be shown that no occasion of scandal or disturbance is taken," are what prevent the admission of those who have debts or other civil obligations ([185, 188]). In addition to the "restlessness" or disquietude "foreign to our profession" ([593]) which such candidates might experience, it could appear that they entered a religious institute to flee justice.

(11) Finally, the exterior gifts of nobility, riches, and the like have to be taken into consideration "to the extent that they aid towards edification"

---

17   See, for example, MI FontNarr, I, 659; MHSI Nadal, V, 833.
18   MI Const, I, 251.

of others. Though they are not necessary, they make one who has the other qualities even more suitable since, by leaving everything "for the gospel,"[19] he gives clear witness to the faith that he preaches.

Turning now to the second coordinate, that of the "body," the fact that the Society is organized into a body requires unity and thus a certain uniformity. This is another of the reasons given for not admitting religious from other orders ([171-172]; see also [30]). As Ribadeneira said: "He who had been a Hieronymite friar might judge that we should have choir and attend to the cycle of divine liturgy, a Carthusian that we ought to fast and withdraw from the world, a Carmelite that we should do more penance and study less."[20] It would then be difficult for the body of the Society to remain "of one color or likeness" ([30]).

Living the apostolic life in an organized congregation also requires that no one be accepted who suffers from mental illness ([175]), since this "would be a notable detriment to the Society" ([30]); similarly one who is notably obstinate in his opinions, since this is "highly vexatious in all congregations" ([184]).

V. KNOWLEDGE OF THE CANDIDATE ([190-203])

Inspired by the practices of the eastern monks as reported by Cassian,[21] St. Benedict prescribed in his Rule that admission should not be conceded easily to anyone who comes to embrace the monastic life. On the contrary, the advice of John should be observed: "Test the spirits to see whether they are of God."[22] If the candidate continues to request entrance and patiently endures the difficulties and objections made, he should be admitted, though not immediately to the monastery, but to the guesthouse, where he will stay for a few days before going to the novitiate.[23]

It is possible that this passage of the Benedictine Rule, if it is true that Ignatius actually read it, is responsible for giving him the idea of first probation. During the twelve to twenty days that first probation lasts, the candidate to the Society is also housed in a guesthouse (this is the meaning of the word *aposento*, "lodging," used in [190]), a house "separate and near our house" or, where this is not possible, at least in an "apartment" or

---

19   See Mk. 10:29.
20   Ribadeneira, *Tratado en el cual se da razón del instituto de la Compañía* (Madrid 1605), p. 60.
21   See I. Cassianus, *De Institutis coenobiorum*, Bk. IV, chap. 3.
22   1 Jn. 2:1.
23   Regula, chap. 58, 1-5.

habitation separated from the others ([191]).

The reason for this institution is that which we have pointed out before: As well as an abstract understanding of the norms or criteria according to which it is made, selection requires a concrete understanding of the individuals who are to be selected. It is necessary "to know their abilities and vocation well" ([142]). However, understanding the candidate's vocation involves the mutual exchange of information: the candidate is informed of the concerns of the Society and he sees whether or not they correspond to his own spiritual aspirations, and the Society comes to know him better in our Lord ([190]).[24]

Let us now accompany this candidate of the Society, following the course he must take to enter it.

1. Before Entering

The guest-like nature of the house of first probation might lead one to believe that anyone who comes with the desire to be a Jesuit is admitted. This is not the case. Those who "clearly appear to be fit to serve God our Lord in the Society" may be received ([192]). On the contrary, those who do not appear to be fit are to be sent away immediately, though they can be "helped by counsel and whatever means charity may dictate" ([192]).

There remain the borderline cases. These are not to be admitted immediately to the house of first probation. After seeing if such a one has any of the primary impediments (if they do, it would be useless to continue) and after presenting to him "the substance of our Institute as well as the experiences and difficulties" as described practically in the first and fourth chapters of the General Examen, the response to his request and the final decision on admission ought to be deferred for some time. This is to be done even though he exhibits a strong intention to enter the Society, "to live and die in it," without which—as emphasized in the Constitutions— no one should be admitted to first probation ([193]).

There is a double motive behind this delay in replying. The first is that the case can be considered and commended to God our Lord, and additional efforts made to know the vocation of the candidate better. The second is, as in the Rule of Benedict, to test the candidate's constancy

---

24 This no. 190 was missing in the first texts. It was added in the preparation of text B. Therefore Roustang has no reason for suggesting, when contrasting the first text to text B, that in the latter the candidate appears as one who must know the Society; on the contrary, in the first text the mutual knowledge was required. See "Introduction à une lecture," in *Constitutions de la Compagnie de Jésus*, II (Coll. Christus, no. 24), 50. We see that in the definitive wording the knowledge is reciprocal. See below, note 27.

([193]).

The measures that can be taken to better know the vocation of the candidate are various. (a) He is to be given a summary examen, on which see [146, 196]. Ignatius worked on a document which would serve as this examen, though he does not appear to have finished it.[25] (b) Apart from the examiner, other persons appointed by the superior might converse with the candidate. (c) Information might be gathered from externs who know the candidate. (d) He might make frequent confession in our Church. The confessor could either confirm him in his resolution or dissuade him if he is not suitable for the Society.[26] (e) If the doubt continues, "to have him make spiritual exercises will aid not a little toward gaining the clarity needed in his regard for the glory of God our Lord" ([196]).

2. First Probation

With these doubts favorably resolved, the candidate is received into the house of first probation, "dressed as he customarily was" or "in a manner in which he finds more devotion" ([197]). It might be, then, that if his manner of dress had been very luxurious he would experience greater devotion by dressing in poor clothes; or, if he had led a very worldly life, by dressing in more religious garb.

The first day he lives as a "guest" ([197]), that is, without any obligation.

On the second day, he is told "how he should conduct himself in that place" ([197]). The main thing is the withdrawal or isolation in which he should spend the days there, speaking to no one except those designated by the superior. This is intended that he may "with greater freedom deliberate with himself and with God our Lord about his vocation and intention to serve His Divine and Supreme Majesty in this Society" ([197]).[27] In fact, we have the teaching of the *Exercises* on this point: When one is alone, "not having his understanding divided among many things, but concentrating on one only, . . . he uses his natural powers with greater freedom, in order to seek with diligence that which he desires so much"; and "the more our soul finds itself alone and apart, the more apt it becomes to approach and reach its Creator and Lord, and the more it approaches Him, the more it is disposed to receive graces and gifts from

---

25   It is published in MI Const, II, 734-736. In 1565 Polanco wrote about this Examen: "non est confectum" (ARSI *Congr 20a*, p. 93).
26   So clearly in the first text: MI Const, II, 136.
27   These words also can only be found in text B.

His Divine and Sovereign Goodness."[28]

After this the candidate is left to himself for one or more free days, to commend himself to God and think about his situation.[29] The broadmindedness and consideration in this provision is notable.

"When two or three days have passed after he entered the probation" ([198]), the candidate uses up the remaining twelve to twenty days of probation with the following exercises: (1) He ought to be examined "more in detail" ([198]) according to the "complete" examen mentioned in the first chapter ([146]), that is, according to the whole book of the Examen, which should be lent to him so that he can read it more slowly.[30]

(2) He should consider the bulls, that is, the Formula of the Institute approved in the bulls of Paul III and Julius III.

Likewise, he should look at the Constitutions that he is to observe. The legislator proposed that a summary or extract be made for this purpose ([199], see also [20]). This was the origin of the so-called Summary of the Constitutions. It is not surprising that the first edition of this summary contained no more than some passages from the Examen and Part III, which were the constitutions that the novices had to observe (see [20]). Having been changed by Laínez to include the rules "which are to be observed by all,"[31] the summary was expanded in subsequent revisions and has recently been replaced by a "new Summary" in which the original value of the extracts from the Constitutions is preserved.[32]

In addition to the Constitutions and the summary of them, the candidate will also read "the rules which must be observed in the Society and the house he enters" ([198]).[33]

St. Benedict said: "This Rule ought to be read to him and he should be told: 'Here is the law under which you want to serve. If you can observe it, enter; if you cannot, feel free to leave.'"[34] We have already seen in the first chapter of the Examen that, perhaps inspired by this passage in the Benedictine Rule, or at least in the same spirit, Ignatius wanted the Formula of the Institute, the Constitutions (or their summary), and the

---

28 *SpEx*, no. 20.
29 So the first text: MI Const, II, 137.
30 About the office of examiner, which is mentioned in no. 198, see above, note 13.
31 See MI Regulae, 547.
32 We have developed this argument in the article "Origen, fin y naturaleza del Sumario de las Constituciones," published in *CIS*, IX (1978), 3, pp. 11-30.
33 We have changed the order of the sentence because we think that this is the meaning. The first text said "las reglas de casa." The first reading of B was "las reglas que deben observar en la Compañía." Afterwards Polanco added "y casa donde entran."
34 Regula, chap. 58.

rules read by those who are entering, not just once but every six months during the time of probation, up until the time of vows. He said: "This is done that both sides [the Society and the candidate himself] may proceed with greater clarity and knowledge in our Lord, and also that the more the subjects' constancy has been tested, the more stable and firm they may be in the divine service and in their original vocation, for the glory and honor of His Divine Majesty" ([18]).

(3) In the third place, the candidate should give some experimental proof of his aptitude for the apostolic ministry, especially in what pertains to doctrine and its presentation ([198]). For this purpose each of them will give a lecture on each of the faculties or branches of learning that they have studied (literature, philosophy, theology). This norm had already been established by Ignatius in the first text of the Examen. In the Examen he prescribes that the candidate give an exhortation or sermon; the reason for this is that his office of sowing and proclaiming the divine word and attending to the spiritual progress of others requires a "sufficiency of sound learning" ([109]).

(4) Finally, during the time of first probation the candidate will give an account of conscience to the superior, as described in the Examen ([93]), and by means of a general confession he will confirm his break with the world and his past life ([200]).

3. Entrance

When the first probation is completed to the satisfaction of both parties, the candidate enters "the house of common living and association where the second probation is made during a longer time" ([200]). Before doing this, however, he should write down and sign a statement that he is content to observe everything that has been proposed to him ([200]). This is a means of acknowledging his own responsibility.[35]

The entrance is properly completed with the Eucharist. The constitution says, "After being finally reconciled and receiving the most Holy Sacrament they will enter" ([200]). With a general confession and Communion, Ignatius began at Montserrat his new life as a knight of Christ,[36] and, as we will see in the description of the vows in Part V, he wanted all the most important events in his life, and in the life of the Jesuit, to be sealed and confirmed with this most holy sacrament of Christ's sacrifice.

---

35 He also notes the things he has brought, undoubtedly in order that they may be given back to him in case of dismissal.
36 See MHSI Nadal, V, 40.

4. *After Studies*

The last paragraph of the chapter, and of this Part ([202]), needs a little clarification since, given the actual development of the Society and its Institute, it now seems strange to us.

According to what it says, after their studies the scholastics are to go through a type of first probation again—one similar to that which they made at the time they first entered the Society. This was to be done for the same reasons too: that they might know their vocation better and the Society might know them better, "so that in proportion to the greater clarity in the procedure, each candidate may be just that much more stable in his vocation, and the Society may be better able to discern whether it is expedient for him to remain in it for the greater glory and praise of God our Lord" ([202]).

The problem is made greater by the knowledge that this paragraph did not exist in the first text. The norm was included in text A and expanded in the definitive text around the years 1550-1552, when the institution of the colleges was fully developed and the number of scholastics was increasing.

The solution will probably be found by connecting this paragraph to the second section of chapter 7 of the Examen. There it says that the scholastics who have completed their studies, before entering the houses of the Society and being admitted to the condition of total obedience, ought to be subjected to a two-part interrogation, which corresponds to the double purpose assigned to this probation. One part consists of questions about their vocation: "Whether they remain firm in their determination, vows, and promise which they made to God our Lord" ([128]). The other part covers their qualities, so that "the superiors may refresh their memory and knowledge of the scholastics, and also better and more completely know their firmness and constancy, or any change if one occurred in the matters which were first asked and affirmed" ([129]).

So it was that the scholastics, with each probation, became more bound to the Society, until they came to be parts or members of its body (see [511]), though Ignatius never considered them fully integrated into it. This, then, explains the additional probation and examen after studies, as well as the vow to "enter" the Society and the so-called third probation, which is actually another novitiate prior to definitive incorporation into the Society.

VI. FINAL OBSERVATION

A first reading of Part I can leave one with the impression that the juridical element dominates the spiritual. If, however, we apply our familiar double consideration of "mission" and "body" elements, we see that, in the determination of the qualities which candidates to the Society ought to have, the first element ("mission") largely prevails, though both are present. It is, above all, the aptitude for the apostolic life that is taken into account as an indication of the suitability of one who desires to belong to the Society.

The first paragraphs speak of authority and of those who hold authority, and this is fitting because the Society is organized as a juridical body. In the rest of the Part, however, it is the selection that dominates, as we have noted—a selection linked with the apostolic and missionary end of the Society, in other words, with its charism.

It is clear that in some details, such as the essential impediments and some circumstances surrounding the manner of making first probation, the legislator has had to descend to juridical norms, though always appealing to the discretion of the superior and, for the last word, to supernatural illumination. This is because "the holy unction of the Divine Wisdom will teach the mean which should be retained in all this" ([161]).

Chapter VI

DISMISSAL

(Constitutions, Part II)

I. Preliminary Remarks

1. Structure

It may be said of Part II that it is the negative of Part I. In both of them the dominant idea is that of selection. In Part I this idea appears under the positive aspect of admitting only those who are suited to the end of the Institute of the Society. In Part II it appears under the negative aspect of dismissing those found to be unsuitable for or harmful to the Institute.

Thus, the distribution of the material in both Parts is very similar. A comparison of the chapters of each Part will make this clear:

Part I	*Part II*
Who admits (chapter 1)	Who dismisses (chapter 1)
Who are to be admitted, their qualities and impediments (chapters 2-3)	Who are to be dismissed, reasons for dismissal (chapter 3)
How to admit (chapter 4)	How to dismiss (chapter 3)
	Those who have been dismissed (chapter 4)

2. Sources

Norms covering the authority to dismiss and the use of this authority existed in the Society from the time of the *Constituciones de 1541*.[1] It seems that, when the order and division of the definitive Constitutions was first being considered, it was not thought necessary to dedicate an entire Part to this question of dismissal. It was believed that it would suffice to insert

---

1   See MI Const, I, pp. 39-40, nos. 15, 16, 20, and 21; and with reference to the same Constitutions, pp. 204-205, no. 28; p. 211, no. 3; pp. 216-219, no. 23.

a few norms into the other Parts—Parts I and III, for example.[2]

This should not be surprising since no other religious legislators had dedicated a special section or chapter to dismissal. However, these older sets of legislation usually included a penal code in which dismissal was included as the maximum penalty. This is the case in the Rule of St. Benedict and in both the Dominican and Franciscan constitutions.[3] The Constitutions of the Society have no penal code; the correction of faults is left to the discretion of the superior ([269-270, 754]). We can see, then, why it was expedient to devote an entire Part to this matter of dismissal. This was a good idea since it freed the other Parts of the Constitutions from discussing this painful subject.[4] In addition to this, it provided the opportunity for developing the subject in all its aspects so that this "amputation" from the body of the Society might in practice always be accomplished with the proper consideration and charity.

II. DISMISSAL

1. *Relative Difficulty ([204-205])*

Among the many legends about the Society fabricated by its enemies is one saying that no one is secure in the Society: On the day he least expects it he will find himself cast out. Everything depends on the whim of the superiors and above all on the omnipotent general.[5] Even some Jesuits, perhaps impressed by certain passages in the *Memorial* of Gonçalves da Câmara, have thought that Ignatius was somewhat inclined to dismiss people. No matter how one chooses to interpret the cases related by da

---

2   It is the opinion of A. Codina in MI Const, II, p. clxxxvii. It is based on the following argument. In the indexes Polanco made of the documents prior to his time as secretary, he put in the margin a series of numbers indicating the Parts of the Constitutions to which each document belongs. So then, a first series of numbers (later erased) shows a division of the Constitutions into only nine Parts, among which there is none dealing with dismissal. For example, in the margin of the *determinación in Domino* which spoke of the dismissal of scholastics, Polanco first wrote no. 3, which he later corrected to read 2. In the margin of the *Regla de casa* (house rules) dealing with one who is determined to leave, he put no. 1 and afterwards erased it, writing 2 instead. Also in the *Industrias* dismissal is mentioned only in the 3rd, as a means of preserving those who were chosen (see MHSI PolCompl, II, p. 735, no. 7).

3   See St. Benedict, Regula, chap. 28, 6-8; *Const. O.P.*, dist. I, chap. 19; *Const. O.F.M. Narbonenses*, Rubr. VII, no. 14; Polanco, *Collectanea*, ff. 26v and 60v (in the transcription of A. Hsü, pp. 114, 231).

4   It remained, nonetheless, in Part VIII, no. 664.

5   See Aicardo, *Comentario*, V, 501-502.

Câmara,[6] this is the place where Ignatius explains his thought clearly and formally.

Dismissal is necessary at times: "Just as it is proper . . . to preserve and multiply the workers who are found fit and useful for carrying this work forward, so it is also expedient to dismiss those who are found unsuitable, who as time passes make it evident that this is not their vocation or that their remaining in the Society does not advance the common good" ([204]).

Nevertheless, even given this necessity, "just as excessive readiness should not be had in admitting candidates, so ought it to be used even less in dismissing them" ([204]). This "even less" is the thing that is surprising for many. It is not, however, inadvertent. The primitive text developed the idea by means of a comparison which could have been inspired by Benedict: "As in the case of bodily infirmities, where lancing and cauterizing are usually the last remedies tried, so it is here with dismissal, which is used only when other remedies are seen to be ineffective."[7] The definitive text also suggests that it be used only "if the remedies which charity requires before dismissal do not suffice" ([214]). That is a grave obligation for superiors. They cannot easily relieve their consciences of personal responsibility for their subject if they do not watch over him, advise at the right time, correct him, or keep him from danger and its occasion.[8]

2. Gradation of Dismissal

In reference to Part I, we said that, though everyone who enters the Society ought to be suited to the end of its Institute, there are differing grades of suitability. Something similar must now be said about the difficulty of dismissal. In all cases it is, to use the expression of Benedict, like amputating "with a sharp scalpel" (*ferro abscisionis*) someone who to one degree or another was integrated into the body of the Society. The more he was incorporated into it, the more painful and dangerous the amputation will be. However, no matter how much one is incorporated into the Society, he can always be separated from it ([204]).

The declaration ([205]) explains the whole gradation, from the case of those in first probation to that of the professed.

6   The instances treated in nos. 26-59 indicated by Ribadeneira, occurred over a period of some five to seven years. Besides, da Câmara confuses names. Contrast the passage with MI FontNarr, II, 387, no. 98.

7   St. Benedict: *Quod si nec isto modo sanatus fuerit, tunc iam utatur abbas ferro abscisionis* (Regula, chap. 28, 6). Cassian had previously used the same comparison in *De Institutione coenobiorum*, X, 7.

8   See what J. B. Janssens has to say in *ActRom*, XIV, 327.

Those in first probation can scarcely be said to have as yet entered the Society. Those in second probation can only be said to be testing their vocation through the experiences of the novitiate. It is clear that anyone in these two categories can be dismissed more easily.

Concerning those who have bound themselves to Christ in first vows (see [17]), the Society considers them more united with itself even though their vows were not accepted "into the hands" of anyone.

The approved scholastics already form part of the body of the Society (see [511]). In 1550 Polanco, ordered by Ignatius, wrote that scholastics should not be dismissed "without serious reason."[9] It is clear that this adjective "serious" is intended here in a relative and not juridical sense.

The formed coadjutors, both spiritual and temporal, along with the professed, "in a more precise" sense constitute the Society which the scholastics promise to enter (see [511]). They cannot, then, be dismissed without "highly sufficient reasons" ([120]).

That leaves only the professed, the Society "in the most precise sense" (see [511]). The declarations say that they can be dismissed "no matter what their rank and dignity in the Society," alluding here to the case of the general himself. The case implied here is one in which "it is judged that to retain them would be harmful to the Society and a disservice to God our Lord" ([205]). In other religious orders, the expulsion of a professed with solemn vows is only justified on the grounds of incorrigibility. Ignatius, too, took this extreme case into account (see [208]). He thought that there might be other reasons for dismissal, as we see both here and in Part IX (see [774]), though he still regarded the dismissal of a professed to be somewhat extraordinary.

To this principal norm, that of greater or lesser integration into the Society, Ignatius adds two secondary norms. One is the greater or lesser obligation which the Society has toward that particular person on account of the benefits received from him. Gratitude was one of the characteristic virtues of Ignatius. However secondary, this norm must be given its proper weight: More consideration ought to be given to one to whom much is owed. The other secondary norm involves the qualities with which the person was endowed for the purposes of the Society and the aid of souls. The divine service demands that more remedies be used before dismissing one more gifted for it, for such a man could still be a capable laborer in the vineyard of the Lord in the Society (see [205]).

9   MI Epp, II, 656.

III. AUTHORITY TO DISMISS ([206-208])

The principle of greater or lesser integration into the Society comes into play even in the discussion of the superiors who have or can have the authority to dismiss. However, it is combined here with another principle, that of subordination.

The principle of subordination is more explicit here than in any other place in the Constitutions, with the exception of Part VIII ([666]). The authority to dismiss belongs to the superior general. "The other members of the Society participate, each one, in this authority to the extent that it is communicated to them by the head. But it is wise that it be communicated amply to the provincial superiors, and in proper proportion to those local superiors or rectors to whom it seems good that it should be communicated, in order that the subordination arising from holy obedience be better preserved in the whole body of the Society, in proportion to the better understanding by the members that they depend on their immediate superiors, and that for them it is highly profitable and necessary to be subject to these superiors in all things for Christ our Lord." ([206]) This subordination, of which we shall speak at greater length in reference to Part VIII, is that which confers true organization on the body and, consequently, its very ability to function.

All of this is clear and logical because we omitted the first lines of [206], where it is said that "the authority to dismiss will be vested chiefly in the Society as a whole when it is assembled in a general congregation." The legislator had to add these lines to cover the particular case of the possible dismissal of a superior general, which could not be accomplished without the Society meeting in a general congregation. However, this involves an extraordinary and extreme set of circumstances. If the head is diseased, the Constitutions provide the Society with the means for preventing the infection of the whole body, even if this involves choosing a new head and removing the old one (see [774]).

Apart from this extreme case, it is the general who has the faculty of dismissing, as he has that of admitting (see [736]). Thus, the rest of the Society has the authority delegated to it by the head, not by the general congregation. The legislator did not forget to add that "the superior general will have the same authority in all other cases except one involving himself" ([206]).

We note, however, a certain vacillation in the earlier documents regarding the dismissal of professed. In 1541 Ignatius and his companions established that the dismissal of one still in probation would be under the general's jurisdiction but that dismissal of a professed needed a deliberative vote of the other professed.[10] A few years later, two of the "early determina-tions," obviously in reference to this norm, establish that dismissal be under the jurisdiction of the prelate or superior, both before and after profes-sion.[11] The primitive text of the Constitutions, though in a hesitant manner, returns to the norm of 1541: "It seems that the professed, as the principal members of the Society, ought not to be able to be dismissed by the general without a general congregation of the Society and without a majority of its votes in favor of dismissal." Was the writer of this paragraph aware of the two "early determinations" cited above?[12] In any case, the paragraph was removed and did not pass into the later texts.

The principle of greater or lesser integration into the Society enters into the matter of delegating the faculty of dismissal to subordinate superiors.

Four grades of integration can be distinguished here:

(1) Those in first or second probation can be dismissed by the same men who have the authority to admit them, unless special circumstances intervene.

(2) Those who have made first vows, and approved scholastics, can be dismissed by the provincial in accordance with the faculties delegated to him by the general.

(3) Formed coadjutors ought not to be dismissed without the consent of the general unless they are in some very remote region.

(4) It is understood that it should be very difficult to delegate the faculty of dismissing those with final profession. However, Ignatius does not deprive the general of the power to do this (see [736-738]).

IV. GROUNDS FOR DISMISSAL ([209-217])

As we have shown, dismissal is like a surgical operation, which demands great delicacy, conducted out of love and charity.

Contrary to what might be expected, the word "charity" appears proportionally more often in this Part than in any other. We find many occurrences of the word in Part III, but it is used even more frequently (more than a third more times; nearly double) here in Part II, much more

10   MI Const, I, 39.
11   MI Const, I, 214, no. 17; 217, no. 23.
12   A reason for doubting is that some of the observations written by Polanco in the margin of these *determinaciones* seem to indicate that he read them (perhaps more attentively on a second reading) when the Constitutions were already composed.

frequently than in the other Parts.[13] Here we find the text speaking of "discreet charity" ([212, 237]), "true charity" ([213]), "love and charity" ([225]), and the like. The virtue and affection of charity seems to infuse and animate this entire Part.

In order to guide the one who dismisses, the text gives a series of reasons organized into a scheme, which is not intended as a sort of penal code or catalogue of offenses which merit dismissal. To the contrary, some of the reasons listed are involuntary in nature.

Therefore, it is advised beforehand that the "discreet charity" of the superior consider whether or not there is sufficient cause for dismissal ([209]). Charity being the foundation and bond of all the virtues, as Ignatius wrote in 1546, we ought to have recourse to it and commend ourselves to it, desiring to be directed and led by it, for the greater divine glory.[14] This means charity toward God, toward the Society, toward the people that the Society helps spiritually, and toward the man whose dismissal is being considered. However, this must also be a "discreet charity," a charity bound with discretion so that it will be, in the first place, a "well-ordered charity" ([237]), which preserves the proper order among the various objectives involved, which takes account of concrete circumstances (see [211]), and which knows the most expedient means for accomplishing these things (see [219]). This discretion is not merely something natural or human; rather it is a "discretion of the Holy Spirit" ([219]) or, as Ignatius wrote here in his own hand, a discretion "had from the Holy Spirit" with which, in a climate of prayer, the superior is to ponder the whole matter "before God our Lord" ([209]; see also [211]).[15]

This treatment of charity is perhaps the inspiration for the scheme of the reasons for dismissal: charity toward God ([210-211]), toward the Society ([212-215]), toward the Society together with the one dismissed ([216]), and toward those outside the Society ([217]). This classification is not entirely adequate since, for example, the Society appears in it twice.[16] Therefore, prescinding from this, we do not think that it would be unfaithful to the mind of the author if we were to distinguish three sorts of reasons: lack of a vocation, scandal, and incorrigibility.

Being "incorrigible in some passions or vices which offend His Divine Majesty" ([210]), even if they are not scandalous, is a reason for dismissal

---

13 Here are the numbers: Examen, 5 times; Part I, 4 times; Part II, 9; Part III, 9; Part IV, 6; Part V, 0; Part VI, 6; Part VII, 3; Part VIII, 4; Part IX, 4; Part X, 3.
14 MHSI, MonPaed, 1ª edit., p. 648.
15 The expression "discreet charity" already appears in Polanco's *Industrias*. We will speak of it in Part VI while treating of the third chapter of that Part, no. 1 [582].
16 We suspect that this arrangement, the same in all the texts, is due to Polanco.

in all religious orders.

Scandal is here understood in the theological sense. It consists of giving others an occasion to sin, by one's example or "all the more so if by persuasive words he entices them to some evil, especially to instability in their vocation or to discord, or if he attempts something against the superiors or the common good of the Society" ([215], see also [664]). The Constitutions warn: "To tolerate this is not to be attributed to charity, but to its contrary on the part of the one who is obliged to preserve the peace and well-being of the Society of which he [the superior] has been given charge." A well-ordered charity demands that the good of the Society, which is universal, be preferred to the good of a particular individual.[17]

Scandal was what induced Leonard Kessel, the rector at Cologne, to dismiss from his college nine or ten scholastics who had been incited to rebel by a certain Dutchman named Gerard. Ignatius approved of Kessel's way of proceeding, but observed that if the remedies had been applied from the beginning it might have been enough to dismiss only one or two.[18]

The preference of the universal over the individual good does not prevent Ignatius from looking at times for ways to save the particular individual without dismissing him, even though there may have been a scandal. He did this when the fault involved was not so serious and the individual had, moreover, been a good subject. Declaration D leaves it to the discretion of the superior whether or not it might be expedient to send the individual to some distant place rather than dismissing him from the Society ([215], see [665]).

Finally, there is the lack of a vocation. All the other reasons are reduced to this one reason or group of reasons: that impediments are discovered which were not apparent when the individual entered ([212, 216, 217]); that the experience of the novitiate demonstrated that the individual would be unprofitable or very unsuited to the ministries or offices of the Society ([212]); that he has some sickness or lacks the physical strength to endure the labors of our Institute ([212-213, 216]); that he cannot or will not adapt himself to the Society's way of proceeding, either out of obstinacy or any other character defect, whether natural or acquired ([216]). It is clear that this last case applies primarily to those still in probation.

In the case of illnesses, a distinction is made between those contracted before entering and those contracted later. If one enters healthy and becomes ill "in the service of the Society," it "would be unjust" to dismiss

17   On this principle see what we said in Part I, text corresponding to note 13.
18   See MI Epp, IV, 361; Chron, II, 279-280.

him without his consent. The words in the text "would be unjust" are due to a correction in Ignatius' handwriting. Prior to this correction, the text read "there would be no reason." The general congregations have interpreted the phrase "ill in the service of the Society" to mean that the individual contracted his illness after first vows.[19]

V. MANNER OF DISMISSING ([218-230])

The third chapter is the most perfectly structured of the whole Constitutions. Only the first chapter of Part VIII could be compared with it. There are *three* points of view: that of the one who dismisses, of the man who is dismissed, and of the others inside and outside of the house. Under each of these points *three* measures to be taken are included. The whole process is to be characterized by the manner "which before God our Lord is likely to give greater satisfaction" ([218])—that is to say, greater peace of mind to everyone concerned. This peace, however, is "before God," of the spiritual, not human, order. One is reminded here of the "finding one's self in peace in God our Lord" in the Exercises and, even more, of the "the quieting and soothing [of the soul] in its Creator and Lord" involved in spiritual consolation.[20]

Throughout the chapter the treatment of the question is primarily concerned with those still in probation and, in the second place, with the formed scholastics. The dismissal of one of the professed is assumed to be an exceptional case. The primitive text says that it is likely, with divine assistance, that no professed would do anything for which he ought to be dismissed. If God would permit it to be necessary to dismiss a professed, "the charity and discretion of the Holy Spirit will indicate the manner which ought to be used" ([219]).

Turning back to the ordinary cases, let us examine the three points of view.

19 Humbert of Romans, O.P., *Liber de instructione officialium*, chap. V; "Numquam autem repellendus videtur novicius pro . . . defectibus qui ab initio noti fuerunt Fratribus, nec propter infirmitatem supervenientem, nisi a principio receptionis facta fuerit protestatio expressa quod pro huiusmodi casibus, vel pro sola voluntate, possint eum Fratres repellere, si vellent." See Polanco, *Collectanea*, f. 33v (in the transcription of A. Hsü, p. 143).
20 *SpEx*, nos. 150 and 316.

1. In Regard to the One Who Dismisses ([218-222])

In order that the one who dismisses might remain before God in "satisfaction" or with peace in his soul, the following three measures are to be taken:

First, he should pray and have prayers said in the house that the will of God may be clearly known (though he need not reveal the intention for which the house is praying) ([220]).

Second, he should consult one or more persons in the house who "seem more suitable" ([221]).

Third, "ridding himself of all affection," and keeping in mind the greater glory of God, the common good of the Society, and, as far as possible, the particular good of the subject in question, he ought to consider the reasons for and against and then determine whether to dismiss the man or not ([222]).

These three paragraphs are much more important than they may appear to be at first sight. This is because, through this example of dismissal, Ignatius is giving us the procedural norms which superiors ought to follow for all the difficult questions in government. This is the method Ignatius himself used and taught other superiors to use.[21] He described this method in one of his "early determinations" in his characteristic style with sentences and words laboriously chosen to convey the full meaning:

"The superior, according to his greater or lesser doubts about the matters over which he has charge, ought to have greater or lesser recourse to those who are his brothers or sons in the Lord—the more the difficulty that he experiences, the more he ought to confer and discuss such doubts with other persons or with all those who live together in that house, as the matter becomes more involved; prayers are to be said in the house and Masses are to be celebrated by all the priests, or by a suitable number of them, for a few days, more or less days as the doubt seems to increase or diminish (see [220]). And so, celebrating Mass and praying, each in the manner to which they have been called or ordained, with all simplicity, purity, and charity, bringing themselves to God our Lord, as much as the Holy Spirit gives them grace to do so, each one of them (looking only to the service, praise, and glory of the Divine Majesty) ought to write down what he thinks or feels in our Lord and, having either sealed or closed the letter without revealing its contents to any other person, give it to his superior or tell it to him by word of mouth, according to what was ordered in our Lord for the greater glory of His Divine Goodness (see [221]). Later,

---

21   See MI Epp, I, 621; IX, 226-227; FontNarr, I, 728, 732.

when the superior has read all of the written reports or considered what
has been told to him, having set aside all feelings that might move him to
any passion, he ought to have recourse to his Creator and Lord, presenting
all the opinions to him and setting aside his own (if he has one), seeking
nothing but His greater glory and praise in all things. Following this, he
ought, in conformity with his conscience, to make that decision which he
felt in our Lord or which seemed better to him, for the greater glory and
praise of His Divine Majesty (see [222])."[22]

2. In Regard to the One Dismissed ([223-226])

The three measures that are to be taken to insure that the dismissed
remains "satisfied" and in peace "before God" appear to have been inspired
by the *Officium Magistri Noviciorum* ("Office of the Master of Novices") of the
Dominican, Humbert of Romans.

In the first place, he should leave without shame or disgrace, as far as
this is possible, and should take with him everything that had been his
([223]). Second, he should preserve the love and charity that he had for the
community and leave it as consoled as possible in our Lord ([225]). Finally,
an effort should be made to find him another means of serving God,
whether in religious life or outside it. He should be helped by means of
prayer and advice and "whatever in charity may appear best" ([226]).[23]

This last phrase ("whatever in charity may appear best") was added in
Ignatius' own hand. Charity is what animates this entire passage. It is that
which dictates that the man leave without disgrace, that he leave consoled
and still loving in spite of the wounding inherent in dismissal. Charity is
what moves the superior to help him, even after he leaves, with his future
way of life, by means of prayers, advice, and any other means that charity
might inspire.

3. In Regard to Others ([227-230])

Charity also dominates the next passage, which deals with the
"satisfaction" or peace which ought to remain with everyone, both inside
and outside of the house.

---

22 MI Const, I, 218-219.
23 Compare this with the following passage of Humbert of Romans in loc. cit.:
    "Dandum est ei consilium et auxilium quod in aliqua religione sibi magis
    competenti ponatur. . . . Providendum est . . . quod tam urbane et occulte et cum
    omnibus suis quae portare voluerit recedat, quod aliis non sit scandalum nec ipse
    scandalizatus recedat, sed potius, quantum fieri poterit, aedificatus et cum amore
    Ordinis et Fratrum."

In the first place, charity will try to prevent confusion in the minds of others, but without harming the reputation of the one who has been dismissed. Thus, one who requires it should be given a satisfactory explanation of the dismissal, though one which touches as little as possible on those defects of the dismissed which may not have been widely known ([227]). When some scholastics were dismissed from the Roman College[24] in June 1555, Father Olave, charged to do so by Ignatius, spoke to the other scholastics of the college, explaining that the dismissal was necessary so that the little flock of Christ would suffer no harm or stain.[25] Perhaps this was inspired by these words in the Rule of St. Benedict: "that one sick sheep may not contaminate the whole flock."[26]

Secondly, charity toward the dismissed person calls for an effort to prevent others remaining "disaffected" or ill-disposed toward him, or, as far as possible, ensuring that they have no unpleasant thoughts about him. Rather, they should have compassion for him since he has lost the great treasure of life in the Society. Of this treasure Ignatius said in his Letter on Perfection to the Fathers and Scholastics at Coimbra that "not only among men but also among angels no more noble exercises can be found than those of glorifying their Creator and leading His creatures back to Him, inasmuch as they are capable."[27] However, Ignatius was not content with mere compassion. The constitution continues by saying that those who remain should love the dismissed and commend him to God in their prayers, "that God may deign to guide him and have mercy on him" ([229]).

How different is this Ignatius from the cold, calculating, implacable, and unfeeling administrator some authors have depicted![28]

Nevertheless, this love and spiritual aid for the dismissed does not mean that he should continue to be treated as if he were a member of the house.

Three of those scholastics dismissed from the Roman college were Sicilians. Ignatius wrote to the provincial of Sicily that they could be admitted to our colleges as students but they were not to have any conversations, brief or lengthy, with any member of the Society unless it was with one to whom the provincial had decided to give permission,

24   See MI FontNarr, I, 721-722.
25   See MHSI PolCompl, II, 581.
26   Regula, chap. 28, 8.
27   MI Epp, I, 498.
28   See E. Castelar, *La revolución religiosa* (Barcelona 1883), IV, 129; L. Marcuse, *Ignatius von Loyola, ein Soldat der Kirche* (Hamburg 1956), p. 177.

knowing him to be firm in his vocation and in the practice of virtues.[29] This was done so that the abandonment of a life consecrated to God and confirmed by the serious commitment of perpetual vows might not come to be equated with something as insignificant as withdrawing from a club.

The dismissed person is not the only object of charity here. Charity also includes anyone else involved, both inside and outside the Society. For some the departure, far from being a source of confusion and scandal, can be an occasion of spiritual growth and edification. So, in the third place we find some observations on the ways others can be affected, apart from the one dismissed.

Those inside the Society who are not acting in a manner as edifying as is proper should help themselves by means of this example or helpful warning and should come to fear what might happen to them if they are not willing to accept help or correction ([230]). Excessive tolerance or permissiveness gradually lowers the spiritual level of communities and religious institutes.

Those outside the Society should take some edification in knowing that in the Society nothing is tolerated which ought not to be tolerated for the greater glory of God. There is no doubt that externs are edified at seeing the zeal of the Society in protecting the flock of Christ from any contamination, just as they are scandalized by the contrary behavior and lose their confidence in the Society because of it.

VI. AFTER DEPARTURE ([231-242])

In the fourth chapter of this Part, there is an implied quotation from Paul which gives us, if not the key to the interpretation of the whole chapter, at least the environment created in it: "a spirit of gentleness" ([236]). When writing to the Corinthians, Paul said: "What do you wish? Shall I come to you with a rod, or with love in a spirit of gentleness?"[30]

There are three distinct topics treated in this chapter: the situation of the dismissed, bringing about the return of fugitives, and receiving those who return.[31]

---

29 MI Epp, IX, 240; see p. 339.
30 1 Cor. 4:21.
31 The arrangement would have been better had no. 231 been put immediately before or after no. 241.

1. Situation of Those Dismissed ([233-234])

It is clear that those who are dismissed no longer enjoy the privileges granted to the Society by the Holy See. These are understood to cease as soon one leaves the Society to which they were granted ([233], see [511]).

On the other hand, concerning the scholastics and formed coadjutors (the dismissal of a professed being an exceptional case, as already mentioned), all obligations also cease. Among these, the most serious are the obligations of the religious vows which, if made according to the formula used by the Society, do not require a dispensation for one to be freed from them ([234]).

In fact, these vows are simple and conditional. They are taken with the condition "if the Society desires to retain" those who take them ([536], see also [539]). At the moment of dismissal, in which the Society is declaring that it does not want to retain them, this condition is fulfilled and the vows cease. As Polanco explained to Salmerón, the Society has no faculty of absolving or dispensing from the vows other than this one.[32]

In this the Society exhibits the spirit of gentleness. In the older orders, which all have solemn profession immediately after novitiate, those who are dismissed remain bound by their vows (as do professed members of the Society who are expelled). Such people find life in the world very difficult since they lack the protection of their order while remaining bound by the vows.

2. Bringing Them to Return ([235-238])

For the same reason—namely that in the older religious orders not only the apostate and the fugitive but also the dismissed remain bound by their vows—a decretal of Gregory IX placed superiors under an obligation to seek out such people every year. If it is possible without detriment to discipline (*salva disciplina*), they should receive them into some monastery or convent; if not, a convenient location might be arranged for them to do penance.[33] The reason for this is, as the Dominican constitutions say, that the sick sheep, though separated from the flock, still belongs to the shepherd.[34]

In the Society, with members being religious with simple vows, this difficulty does not exist.[35] Ignatius saw everything from the point of view

---

32   See MHSI Salmerón, I, 319.
33   c. *Ne religiosi*, 24, *de Regularibus*, III, 31.
34   Dist. I, chap. 19, decl. b.
35   After Urban VIII had urged that Gregory IX's decretal be observed, the Sacred Congregation of the Council, on being asked whether the Society of Jesus was

of the divine service and, in conformity with it, of the place where each one is called to give greater glory to God.

One could bring up the case of one who leaves "without permission" and without being dismissed. He must have been a subject little suited for the Society, since we know that there are degrees of suitability. To this lesser aptitude there can now be added obvious inconstancy and instability in his vocation (see [181]). All of this indicates that he might be able to serve God better in an institute or way of life other than that of the Society. Rather than make many efforts to bring about his return, it is better to direct him to this other institute or way of life. However, since the superior has not intervened by stating his decision that "he does not want to retain him in the Society" his vows do not cease. In order that the man might "remain without scruple" and quiet his conscience, the superior ought to communicate this decision to him ([235]).

The contrary of this situation is also possible: the case of the fugitive from the Society who, given his aptitude and his vocation, which were examined upon his entrance, has nevertheless left on account of some strong temptation which has confused him or perhaps on account of others who have led him astray. Then the service of God demands not that he be left as a fugitive but that every effort be made to bring him back. These efforts involve persuasion above all. Paul III also granted the Society the right to impose canonical penalties for this purpose and even to use physical coercion. However, at least in the time of Ignatius, it does not appear that the Society made use of these privileges.[36]

There is one exception to this norm: the case of a fugitive who enters another religious order. If he takes the habit of that order he contracts the fifth primary impediment (see [171]). In addition to this, there would be another reason not to bring about his return, that is, peace and concord with the religious of that order. Although it may be judged that the subject is suited for the Society, as the Declaration says, "the Society ought not to litigate" ([237]). Here again, the "spirit of gentleness" (*spiritus mansuetudinis*) intervenes.

included, replied, "non comprehendi."

36 Nadal in his *Scholia*, no. 236, says that the Society had never imposed excommunication on apostates.

3. On Readmission ([239-242])

Those who regard Ignatius as rigid and militaristic cannot imagine him readmitting someone who had been dismissed from the Society. On the contrary, we know that he was always disposed to welcome back a prodigal son unless concerns for the greater divine service precluded doing so.[37]

The first norm in the Constitutions is that no one is to be received into the Society in one place who has been dismissed from or left it in another place without the superior of that place being informed or without the permission of the superior general ([231]).

This is an old norm of the Society,[38] a prudent one: "The purpose here is to prevent the lack of knowledge and information from being a cause of some error in disservice to God our Lord" ([231]).

In the case of the return of one who left the Society "without permission" (a fugitive), if it seems his place and vocation is to be in the Society, it ought to be first investigated "whether he brings a genuine intention to persevere," since by his flight he showed a lack of constancy. Consideration should also be given as to whether or not he wants to make some sort of reparation or probation. Otherwise, as the constitutions rightly observe, it would seem that he has not returned in genuine penitence and repentance and as such does not deserve to be accepted ([239]).

In case of doubt about this will to persevere, he could be made to go through some of the experiences of the novitiate again, such as serving in a hospital. This could also serve as a penance for his lack of constancy ([240]).

In the case of one who had been dismissed seeking readmission, the first matter of concern is whether or not the reasons for his dismissal still obtain. If they no longer do and if the dismissal was for a culpable cause and the dismissed is willing to offer some sign of reparation, the door of mercy ought not to be closed to him ([241]).

Without doubt, discretion demands that a new change from the worldly to the religious life not be made without some steps being taken to help carry out this transition. The first is an examen; evidently not the "complete examen" of the first probation (see [146, 198]), but rather one like that given to the scholastics upon completion of their studies, which has as its principal object knowledge of their will to persevere (see [128, 202]). The second step is a general confession, which will confirm the break with

---

37   See Aicardo, *Comentario*, V, 627-629.
38   See MI Const, I, 202, no. 17 (the whole paragraph in the hand of St. Ignatius). A similar norm is found in the Dominican Constitutions, Dist. I, chap. 20, no. 3.

that period spent in the world. The third step is an indefinite period of probation to be determined by the superior, for the edification of all and for the edification and spiritual growth of the one being readmitted, for the glory of God our Lord ([242]).[39]

Not only fugitives and the dismissed who spontaneously seek readmission, but also those who return as a result of the Society's efforts to bring them back, must repair the damage they may have done to others by their leaving. Ignatius leaves it to the discretion of the superior to judge whether they should offer some satisfaction or reparation for this damage and how much or whether it would be better to proceed in a full spirit of gentleness, for their good and the edification of the others ([236]).[40]

The discretion "had in the Holy Spirit" is that which knows how to combine the demands for edification of those who have suffered from the scandal with gentleness towards the one who caused it.

VII. FINAL OBSERVATION

In contrast to Part I, in this Part II consideration of the social "body" predominates over the consideration of "mission."

The motive of "mission," of the apostolic life, does enter into this Part where it is stated that a subject ought to be dismissed if he lacks a vocation or aptitude for the Society, and consequently that this ought to be taken into consideration if he seeks readmission.

In everything else, however, the social "body" is the primary object of consideration. The subjects of the Society can be dismissed from it with greater or lesser difficulty according to their degree of incorporation into its body. The authority to dismiss resides in the head and subordinately in the members to whom he delegates it. This principle of subordination, vigorously expounded here, has as its justification the organization of the Society into a body. Among the reasons for dismissal, a very important place is given to the "scandal" or harm done to others by example or word. The reason for this was explained by Ignatius when discussing one of these cases with Gonçalves da Câmara: "It has to be seen that the body is clean."[41] Even the manner of dismissal assumes that it is taking place in the atmosphere of an organized community. Furthermore, it is considered

---

39 Neither does the Church now require that the noviceship be repeated. See *Renovationis causam*, no. 38.

40 Although this is said of those who are brought back, declaration C [238] extends it to all those who return.

41 MI FontNarr, I, 722.

primarily in the case of the dismissal of those still in probation (see [219c]).

Despite all this, Ignatius knew how to infuse a breath of charity and a spirit of gentleness into these juridical norms, with the result that this Part, which from the nature of the subject ought to be the most negative and harsh, is actually the one that contains the most gentle accents.

Chapter VII

PROBATION OF NOVICES

(Constitutions, Part III)

I. PRELIMINARY REMARKS

1. Sources and Structure

More attention needs to be given to the structure of Part III than to the others, for two reasons: firstly, because there were notable changes in the arrangement of the material in the transition from the primitive text to the subsequent texts; secondly, because it is principally on Parts III and VI that the authors who believe they can find the key to the reading of the Constitutions in the order of the chapters base themselves.[1]

In the primitive text this Part consisted of three chapters: the first, "on the preservation of the body"; the second, "on the preservation of the soul," protecting it from what might harm it or hinder its greater progress in spirit"; the third, "on the means for disposing oneself more for the practice of virtues." In text A the second and third chapters are combined into just one, entitled: "on the preservation of what regards the soul and progress in virtues." In this same text A (not in text B, as noted previously a number of times), the single chapter on the soul and the virtues comes before the chapter on the body.[2]

Why were these changes made? In our humble opinion, if we want to make an objective examination of the author's thought we must look at the positive data he himself gives. One positive datum is the formation of the text; another is the author's explicit statement in some other part of the Constitutions where the same arrangement is found.

The source of the chapter on the body (the first in the primitive text,

---

1   See F. Roustang, "Introduction à une lecture," in *Constitutions de la Compagnie de Jésus*, II, (Coll. Christus, 24), pp. 58-66; id. "Sur le rôle de Polanco dans la rédaction des Constitutions S.J.," art. in *RevAscMyst*, 44 (1966), 194-197; D. Bertrand, S.J., *Un corps pour l'Esprit* (Coll. Christus, 38), pp. 100-106.

2   In text A. Although the chapter on the body was written before the chapter on the soul, afterwards in the titles of both the word "primero" was changed to "segundo," and the word "segundo" to "primero."

the second in those following) is the "Constitutions of the Colleges." Two
sections of this document, not just one, are found here, dealing respectively
with health and with the material goods of the colleges.³ We discover from
this that, despite the title, two themes are treated in this chapter: the
preservation of bodily health and strength ([292-304]) and the preservation
of "external things" or material goods ([305-306]).

The composition of the second chapter reveals characteristics that are
quite different from that of the third.

In composing the second chapter (corresponding to [204-275] of the
definitive text) the author again made use of the "Constitutions of the
Colleges" and also of other internal sources such as the *Determinaciones
antiguas* and Polanco's *Industrias*. But he had recourse as well to the rules,
constitutions, and other documents of other religious orders. In the chapter
we find excerpts, taken at times literally, from the rules of St. Augustine,
St. Benedict, and St. Francis, from the Franciscan and Dominican constitutions, from Humbert of Romans's work *De instructione officialium*, and from
the commentary of Cardinal Torquemada on the rule of St. Benedict. In
using these sources, he mixed and combined them in such a way that at
times a single paragraph derives from two or three distinct sources.

On the contrary, the third chapter (corresponding to [276-291] of the
definitive text) is an original composition. We could only distinguish two
or three references to antecedent documents of the Society.⁴ Perhaps the
chapter includes a description of Ignatius' own method in training novices,
unless it is the transcription of a previous document that has not been
preserved. The latter hypothesis would explain the repetition of topics
treated in the previous chapter, for instance, frequenting the sacraments.

Moving on to text A, we find that the fortunes of these two chapters
were also quite different. The second was completely reconstructed: some
paragraphs were suppressed; some recast completely, as we shall see later;
and all were reordered according to a different norm. The third chapter
also underwent some corrections, but only partially and in matters of minor
importance,⁵ the order of paragraphs remaining unchanged.⁶

3   MI Regulae, 233-238. Only a few original new numbers are added on the
     distribution of offices and the change of climate [302-304].
4   That the older members sometimes take on the office of those who serve [276]
     and that there are no studies in the houses [289] is found in the *Constituciones de
     1541*. Bringing to the attention of the superior the obligation to insist on
     observance [291] is found among the *Notas para determinar*. That is all.
5   There are corrections in nos. 276-282. Nos. 284-291 are copied directly from the
     first text.
6   There is an exception: the exercise of preaching was placed before the exercise
     of obedience and humility.

As was mentioned earlier, these two chapters of the first text (the second and the third) were reduced to one in text A. This is not unusual; the same procedure was followed elsewhere in the Constitutions, the first chapter of Part VIII, for example, being formed from three chapters of the first text. However, bringing the material under one title did not mean that the subjects were unified. The title itself of the new chapter reveals the twofold subject-matter developed in it: "preservation pertaining to the soul and to progress in virtues," and the first words of [276] indicate the start of a new topic: "toward progress in the virtues."[7]

We also mentioned that in text A this single chapter (consisting of the second and third of the first text) was placed before the chapter on the preservation of the body and on material things. Why was this done? Let us note the order brought about by these changes: (1) preservation pertaining to the soul, (2) progress in virtues, (3) preservation of the body, (4) preservation of material things; in short, soul—virtues—body—exterior things. In the development of the first theme (the soul) one may perhaps find the order of the powers of the soul: memory, intellect, and will. That, however, is rather obscure and problematical and we content ourselves with the suggestion.[8] At any rate, this is the order in which the qualities of the candidate are enumerated in Part I ([154-161]) and those of the general in Part IX ([723-733]). And in Part IX the author explicitly states that this is the order of importance ([724]).[9]

In saying all this, we have now indicated the sources of Part III. Nevertheless we need to delay a little longer on the subject. In view of the use that was made of the rules and constitutions of other religious orders, it has been asserted that this Part is the least Ignatian of all. The assertion is a serious one since Part III, along with Part VI, is the one that has the greatest amount of spiritual teaching. In the first place, the problem is not as serious as it seems: the influence of the legislative documents of other religious orders is limited to the second chapter of the primitive text, and not even to the whole chapter but to only twelve of the sixty-four numbers that make up this part in the definitive text. In the second place, the

---

7   These words, added in text A, take the place of the title which the third chapter had in the first text.

8   The order would be: (1) (memory) forgetting and keeping apart from the world [244-249]; (2) (intellect) instruction of novices [250-264]; the expressions are repeated: take into account, be instructed, instruct, teach . . . (3) (executive will) corrections and union of minds [265-275].

9   In the qualities of the general the virtues are placed first and afterwards the soul. But the reason is clear: there the qualities which the general should have when he is elected are dealt with; here, progress in virtues, which logically comes after the preservation of what regards the soul.

influences in question, while clear and noteworthy in these paragraphs of the primitive text, disappeared during the recasting they underwent on passing to text A—to such an extent that it is difficult at times to recognize their sources. While the subject matter of each of these paragraphs was preserved, concrete minor details by which the topic was developed were omitted. More important, new motivations were added. Now it is to these new motivations, stemming from Ignatius, that the spiritual value of this Part is mainly due.[10] We shall see later on an example of this recasting.

2. *Those Addressed*

To whom is Part III addressed? Directly to the novices, for the title says: "The preservation and progress of those who are in probation." However, many of the norms have a more extensive application.

In the first place, the second chapter is also directed to scholastics, as explicitly stated in Part IV ([339]). More than that, we think it is intended for all: it is the only section of the Constitutions that develops the subject of the care of health and bodily strength. There is, however, one exception, namely, that the professed and the formed coadjutors, in regard to work and penance, will have to understand this according to the rule of discreet charity (see [582]).

But there are also in the first chapter norms which by their very nature go beyond the time or the house of probation, either because they expressly refer to older members ([276]) or to preachers in our churches ([281]), or because they are intended not merely for the formation of the young but also for discipline in the houses and colleges ([266-271]), or also because they are ascetical norms of perennial value which, of course, the novices ought to learn during probation, but in order to observe them with ever-increasing perfection throughout their whole lives (see [272, 273, 288] and passim). We must not, then, exaggerate or make excessive distinctions which do not exist in the Constitutions. There is no doubt that, globally speaking, Part III is intended for novices and Part VI for formed religious. But is it "infantile" to live the life of prayer and union with God as taught in [288]?

---

10   This is also noted by A. Hsü in his doctoral thesis, *Dominican Presence in the Constitutions of the Society of Jesus* (ms., Rome: P.U.G. 1971), restricting himself to the Dominican sources.

II. PRESERVATION OF WHAT PERTAINS TO THE SOUL

1. *Seclusion ([244-249]))*

To enter the promised land one must pass through the desert. Besides, what we can call the novitiate in Ignatius' life, his period at Manresa, was a form of eremitical life, a desert experience.

Perhaps because of the two experiences characteristic of the Ignatian novitiate, the hospital and pilgrimage, it has sometimes been thought that Ignatius formed novices in contact with the world and wanted them so to be formed. The first numbers of this Part III prove the contrary.

The Constitutions establish a twofold principle. Those in probation should avoid "all communication," by conversation and letters, "with persons who may diminish their ardor for the goals they have set themselves." On the other hand, "while they advance along the path of the spirit," they should "deal only with persons and about matters which help them toward what they were seeking when they entered the Society for the service of God our Lord" ([244]).

Those who could weaken them in their resolutions are above all relatives and friends whose conversation, as Ignatius had already stated in the Examen, tends to "disturb rather than help those who attend to the spiritual life, especially in the beginning" ([60]). But others too, for example, religious of other orders, might bring about instability in a vocation which is not yet firm.

To avoid these and similar problems, if a novice at some time needs to speak with his relatives or friends, or leave the house, he is to have a companion ([246, 247]). If that is not enough to save his vocation and his peace of soul, then more radical measures are to be taken, namely, sending him to another place "where he can apply himself better in the divine service" ([245]). For the same purpose, written communication, correspondence, should be shown to someone appointed by the superior ([246]).

One must not think that these were disciplinary norms common to all religious orders at the time, norms which Ignatius had to follow despite their being counter to his mentality. On the contrary, the practice of Ignatius was even more severe. He did not permit a novice to go alone even to a church of the Society when there were outsiders in it.[11]

In the house the novices are to speak "only with persons and about matters which help them" ([244]). One method of forming novices, which later passed into canon law,[12] tended to segregate them from contact with

---

11 See MI Const, I, 207-208, no. 4; MI Regulae, 283 and 401.
12 See Clement VIII, *Cum regularem* (March 19, 1603); Cod.Iur.Can., can. 564.

older members. Ignatius, inspired perhaps by Benedict, follows a contrary system. Novices, still unformed, can give only a little help to one another. It is better that they "keep silence among themselves" and that they speak with "mature and discreet persons"; and these are not necessarily all those who are old, but those whom the superior will indicate. For the same reason the novices will never live by themselves but will have some older members living among them who will teach them by their example.[13]

There is no doubt, however, that in the thinking of Ignatius this greater seclusion was more applicable to the first months of the novitiate. As the novice matured he was granted more freedom, and in the second year he was readily sent to a college to pursue his studies.

2. Instruction

a. The Exterior Man ([250-253])

In this environment of seclusion the first thing to be formed in the novice is the exterior man, training him in the right use of the senses and members of his body.

This is one of the passages of the primitive text where the inspiration or derivation from other religious legislation is more obvious. Specifically, it is from the office of the master of novices by Humbert of Romans.[14] Many of the sentences are almost literal translations from the Latin of Humbert. At the same time, this passage is one of those which more clearly shows something that we mentioned before, namely, that on passing from the primitive text to text A, this influence or dependence on sources almost completely disappears. Text A, in fact, (and with it the definitive text) preserves only the subject matter: guarding of the senses from disorder; speaking discreetly; maintaining bodily deportment; being temperate in the refection of the body; saying grace at table; listening to reading during meals. All the details by which these themes were developed in the first text now disappear.[15] On the other hand, something much more important is

---

13   See St. Benedict, Regula, chap. 22, 7; MI Regulae, 402, no. 8.

14   On Humbert of Romans (or de Romanis), fifth Master General of the Order of Preachers, see M. H. Vicaire, O.P., in *DictSpir.*, VII, col. 1108-1116; R. P. Mortier, O.P., *Histoire des Maîtres de l'Ordre des Frères Prêcheurs*, I (Paris 1903), 415-604. The Office of Master of novices forms part of the *Liber de instructione officialium*, published with the *Constituciones O.P.* See Polanco, *Collectanea*, ff. 33v-37 (in the transcription of Hsü, pp. 142-152).

15   Hsü (op. cit. in note 10, pp. 133-134) shows how these details appear in the rules of the Master of novices (MI Regulae, p. 397, nos. 14 and 15). It is probable, though not completely certain, that this distribution of the matter between the

introduced: the motivation. The reason given for the careful guarding of the senses from all disorder, namely, that they are "gates" ([250]) through which the outer world enters man's interior, is new. Especially new is the idea that external modesty should shine forth from interior modesty; in such teaching one hears echoes of Benedict's "steps" (*gradus*) of humility[16] and, even more, images of the "poor of the Lord" and "the meek and humble of heart" are evoked.

Peace and true humility of soul tend to be manifested through silence and, if one must speak, in words that are well-considered and edifying, following the example of the "servant of Yahweh," who did not "cry, or lift up his voice, or make it heard in the street."[17] The silence Ignatius desired was precisely the kind that avoids disturbing the peace of the house and troubling those who want to pray or study.[18] Peace and true humility of soul are reflected in modesty of countenance, at once serene, amiable, moderately joyful. Peace and true humility of soul are manifested even in walking and other bodily movements. If peace reigns in the heart, there will be not levity or rashness but maturity; if there is true humility, the novices will not be moved to impulses of impatience or to pride.

But there is more: one who keeps himself in peace and true humility of soul, "gentle and humble of heart," puts himself in the last place, "in everything striving and desiring to give the advantage to the others." Even that is not enough: following the teaching of the Apostle: "Humbly regard others as more important than yourselves,"[19] such a one shows even outwardly, "in an unassuming and religious manner," the respect and reverence befitting each one's state ([250]). Even the superior ought in his heart to esteem subjects as if they were better than himself though outwardly his status and that of his subjects do not allow him to show them the same reverence that they should show him. As the rule of St. Augustine states, in the presence of the subjects he takes precedence, in the presence of God he should prostrate himself at the feet of everyone.[20] In this way, each one, observing the virtues and gifts of God with which others are adorned, will increase in devotion and will praise God our Lord, whose image will be recognized and revered in one's brothers ([250]).

Behind these norms lies a more transcendental principle. Much has been said recently about the witness that religious should give; to such an

Constitutions and the rules was made deliberately.
16 See Regula, chap. 7, the last four steps.
17 Isa. 42:2.
18 See MI Regulae, 18-22.
19 See Phil. 2:3.
20 *Regula ad servos Dei*, toward the end.

extent that some want to reduce all the value and purpose of religious life to this one point. But witness cannot be something merely external; that would be artificial and ineffectual. It must be the outward manifestation of genuine interior holiness. The words of Father John Baptist Janssens at the Second Vatican Council, words which 679 fathers of the Council made their own, are well known: "The religious state is not of value because it is a sign, rather it is a sign (or witness) because it has a sanctifying and redemptive value."

With regard to eating, all that remains from the primitive text, apart from grace at meals, refers to temperance and decorum in the very act of eating, and to reading at table. Here the terminology used to express these two actions, "refreshment of the body" and "of the soul," is of interest ([251]); it simply indicates the purpose of bodily nourishment, necessary recuperation of physical forces, and the purpose of the reading, which— as William of St. Thierry said—is to avoid immersing oneself in eating.[21]

Without delaying on the following number, which deals with avoiding idleness and helping those overburdened by work ([253]),[22] let us move on to the formation of the interior man.

b. The Interior Man ([254-265])

As we have just seen, Ignatius does not think that the formation of the exterior man should be done without inculcating interior virtues. However, from [254] on he deals more directly with the interior man: dispossession of property, spiritual combat, frequentation of the sacraments, and the need for spiritual direction.

Dispossession of Property ([254-259])

The first requirement, as in the Examen, is dispossession of property,[23] the denial of the instinct to own and control. The novices are not "poor"; they retain or may retain ownership of their patrimonial goods, in the Society even after the vows of scholastics, until they make the renunciation of their property ([53-54]). We also saw in the Examen that Ignatius knew how to combine wisely the ideal of a desire for dispossession from the

---

21   "Cum manduces, nequanquam totus manduces; sed corpore tuo suam refectionem procurante, mens suam non neglegat" (*Ad Fratres de Monte Dei*, PL 184, 330).

22   The first part seems to be inspired by the *Constitutiones generales antiquae* of the OFM, by way of the second series of the Polanco's *dudas*. See MI Const, I, p. 278, no. 28. The second part is derived from the Benedictine rule, chap. 33, 18.

23   We use this word in the etymological sense, not in the specific sense which it had later on in French spirituality of the seventeenth century.

moment of entrance, with actual circumstances that at times make it advisable to defer this renunciation ([53-54]). We will not delay on this; nor is there need to dwell on the instruction given in [258] about the special case of an inheritance renounced in favor of the Society. At the beginning Ignatius felt a certain aversion to accepting such renunciations. Later he thought it was for the greater glory of God to propose a norm which would combine a greater disinterestedness on the part of the one renouncing with a better application of the goods renounced, leaving this judgment to the one in charge of the whole Society.[24]

Yet, even though the novice is not "poor," even though he retains ownership of his goods, he must begin to "experience" the practice of the virtue of "holy poverty." He should be taught to be poor and so not have the use of anything of his own "as being his own" ([254]). We learn of the specific things to which there is reference here from the source, the "Constitutions of the Colleges," which lists money, books, or something similar.[25] What has to be learned is not having the use of anything as one's own, independently of the superior, used as by an owner who does what he wants with what he has.

If this is true for personal possessions, it has even stronger application for common property. The novices may not "lend, borrow, or dispose of anything in the house unless the superior knows it and consents" ([257]).[26] In Ignatius' time, to appropriate something belonging to the house as one's own was a case reserved to the superior.[27]

Spiritual Combat ([260])

Interiorly dispossessed of temporal goods, the novice ought to make efforts toward acquiring those which are eternal. He is to be taught the spiritual combat, a combat at once defensive and offensive.

He has to learn how to guard himself from a double assault, and first against the "illusions of the devil in his devotions" ([260]). This refers to the deceits of the bad angel who takes on the form of an angel of light in order to enter the devout soul and to bring it to his own purposes.[28] Ignatius wrote his rules for the discernment of spirits so that one could learn how to guard against such "illusions."

---

24 See MI Const, I, 247-248; Epp, II, 133-134.
25 See MI Regulae, 223, no. 21.
26 Here too the immediate source is the "Constitutions of the Colleges," ibid., no. 22.
27 See MI Reg., 205, no. 3; FontNarr, III, 652, no. 29.
28 *SpEx*, no. 332.

The other assault comes from temptations. The novice will have to know how to defend himself against them all and conquer them. Polanco, in the second appendix of his *Directorium ad confessarii et confitentis munus rite obeundum*, proposed specific remedies for each kind of sin or vice.

In the defense against the attacks of the enemy, one must add the positive action of the pursuit of "true and solid virtues, whether this be with many spiritual visitations or with fewer, by endeavoring always to go forward in the path of divine service" ([260]). Suárez says that "St. Ignatius calls true virtues those which are so not in external appearance or in the opinion of men but in the sight of God, and are practiced with the pure intention of the divine glory and out of affection for the very goodness of virtue. Virtues founded on true humility and contempt for temporal things are solid and based on the pure love of God."[29]

Reception of the Sacraments ([261-262])

Sacramental grace is necessary for this entire combat. The norm of weekly confession and communion is laid down ([261]); this was the practice of Ignatius himself from the time of his "primitive church" at Manresa, and also of his companions in Paris.[30] With regard to the frequency of Holy Communion, this norm seems inadequate to us today but in his day it was the most that was usually allowed. The definitive text added here the daily examination of conscience, which has a certain relationship to penance and the sacrament of reconciliation.

We are also surprised at the requirement that there should be only one confessor for everybody ([261]). As usual, this needs to be understood with a sense of history. In former Church discipline (which lasted until Clement VIII), just as the ordinary faithful were obliged to confess to the pastor of their own parish, so in the same way religious had to confess to their own superior or to a confessor appointed by him.[31] Characteristically, Ignatius shows himself more liberal in this matter for he permits more than one confessor, not only when one is not enough because of the number of penitents, but also when the penitents could be "aided more" by a different confessor than the ordinary one ([262]).

The essential point is that each one have his own "regular" or fixed confessor "to whom he should keep his conscience completely open" ([261]). Ignatius gives such importance to this total openness of conscience to one's own regular confessor that, if in special circumstances someone confesses to

---

29   F. Suárez, *De Societate*, no. 1014; see A. Coemans, *Commentarium in Regulas*, no. 349.
30   See *Autobiog*, nos. 21 and 59; MI FontNarr, III, 27 and 438.
31   See Wernz-Vidal, *De religiosis*, no. 167.

another, he wants him later on to open his whole conscience to his fixed confessor "so that he may better be able to help him, ignorant of nothing about his conscience" ([278]). This is an indication (and not the only one) that for Ignatius the confessor is what we understand to be a spiritual director. Hence the confessor is also the one who regulates corporal penances so as to avoid excess ([8, 300, 582]).

c. The Master of Novices ([263-264])

What has just been said, however, presents a problem. What is the purpose of the office described immediately afterwards in [263]? Above all, to whom does it refer? Some doubt arises because the first texts expressly mentioned the master of novices: "It will be helpful to have a master of novices." Later the title master of novices is omitted in the Constitutions ([263]); and instead declaration K ([264]) was added, which seems to say that the office described in [263] is different from that of the master of novices, for it can be exercised either by the master of novices or "by whoever the superior appoints as being more fit for this charge."

But this declaration has to be properly understood. There is question here, not of two distinct individuals (the master of novices and another who is more fit), but of two distinct names or titles. The intention is merely to avoid all formality. There can be a "master of novices" officially so appointed, but if it should not be thought necessary to have one, because of the fewness of the novices as well as for other reasons, the superior may put someone else in charge who would seem to be fit to hold the office even though he does not have the title or formality of master of novices. Apart from this, both source and context indicate that [263] is dealing with the master of novices. The first lines take their inspiration from the description of this office in the Dominican constitutions;[32] the remainder is in conformity with what is said about him in the contemporary rules for the master of novices.

The master of novices can be the confessor, as Father Wischaven[33] was in the time of Ignatius, and as continued to be the practice in the early Society. The rules to which we have just referred are composed precisely for a master of novices who is at the same time their confessor.[34] But the two offices are not identical. The office of master of novices has a threefold purpose: first, to instruct the novices about their conduct; second, to

---

32   See *Constitutiones O.P.*, Dist. I, chap. 14; Polanco, *Collectanea*, f. 26 (in the transcription of Hsü, pp. 108-109).
33   See MI FontNarr, I, 577.
34   See MI Regulae, 394-399.

encourage them with reminders and kindly admonitions; third, to care for them with such solicitude that all those who are in probation may love him, consult him in their temptations, and open themselves with confidence, hoping to receive from him in our Lord counsel and aid in everything ([263]).

There is also a certain ambiguity in the second part of [263], which deals with openness of conscience. At first sight, in addition to the account of conscience given to the superior spoken of in the Examen, and to perfect sincerity with the confessor ([278]), it seems that the novice would have to open his soul to the master of novices, for the Spanish text reads "to them" and not "to him" (*les sea*, and not *le sea*). The reason is that the legislator leaves the norm indefinite in order that it may be applied to particular cases with greater flexibility. It could happen, as we said, that the master of novices may be their confessor, and he may also be the superior (as was quite common in the early Society). The emphasis is on the novices' not desiring to be guided by their own judgment unless it agrees with the opinion of the one they have in place of Christ our Lord ([263]). It is the principle already inculcated in the Exercises:[35] the need for a spiritual guide in order to avoid being deceived by the enemy.

3. Practices

a. Treating Faults by their Opposites ([265])

It is not enough to instruct novices about the spiritual way; they must be required to exercise themselves in following it. For that purpose the first piece of advice given is to follow the classical medical remedy, applicable not only corporally but also spiritually: "opposite ills are treated by their contraries" (*contraria contrariis curantur*). But here it is proposed as a preventive remedy: "temptations ought to be anticipated by their opposites" ([265]).[36]

b. Religious Environment ([266-268])

One of the many misunderstandings of the thinking of Ignatius arises from the absence in the Society of monastic structure and stability. This is interpreted as a negation of all the normal elements and aspects of religious life and an assimilation to the life of the laity. Number [266] proves the opposite.

---

35   See *SpEx*, no. 326.
36   See St. Gregory, *Homilia 32 in Evangelia*.

When canon law did not yet have a law of cloister (introduced only in the time of Pius V), Ignatius prescribes that "for the sake of decorum and propriety" women should not enter our houses. To avoid any doubt about the meaning of the term "enter," he adds: "but only the churches" ([266]). He always leaves it to the discretion of the superior to dispense, but the conditions are significant: they are to be "persons of great charity or of high rank with charity" ([267]). This formula, written by Ignatius himself, was the outcome of a number of drafts. The important point is "charity," namely, the virtue of the person who is received; if on occasion consideration has to be given to the "high rank," it should be accompanied by charity. In the second place, they may only enter "to see" the house, "not to eat or sleep inside," as the first text explained.

But this "cloister" is not enough; the whole house must have a religious atmosphere. It should not contain arms or instruments for vain purposes ([266]).

We know from the declaration and from the source, the "Constitutions of the Colleges," what "instruments" the author had in mind.[37] The following are mentioned: (i) instruments used for games: chess, cards, dice, and so forth; (ii) musical instruments: guitar, clavichord, but not the church organ; (iii) profane books, "books about love and vanities," that is, novels and suchlike works. As these are only examples, "and similar things" is added.

On the other hand, the Constitutions give a positive picture of the aspect which the house should present. The things which ought to be found in it are those which are "helpful toward the end which the Society seeks, the divine service and praise" (266]).

c. Corrections ([269-270])

Some norms on corrections and penances come next. The legislation in other religious orders usually contained a kind of "penal code," with a classification of faults (slight, serious, very grave) and the penalties or penances corresponding to each.[38] Ignatius entrusted everything to the "discreet charity" of the superior and of those whom the superior puts in his place; "charity," holy zeal for God's glory and the sanctification of the

---

37 See MI Regulae, 225, no. 31.
38 See St. Benedict, Regula, chaps. 23-30; *Constitutiones O.P.*, Dist. I, chaps. 16-19; *Constitutiones O.F.M. Narbonenses*, Rubr. VII; Polanco, *Collectanea*, ff. 26v and 60v (in the transcription of Hsü, pp. 113-115 and 230-232); G. Oesterle, O.S.B., "De codice poenali in Regula S. P. Benedicti," in *Studia Anselmiana*, 18-19 (Città del Vaticano 1947), 173-193.

one at fault. But this charity was to be moderated by discretion, a discretion "coming from the Holy Spirit," taking into account all the circumstances: the general disedification which may have been caused by the fault, and the disposition of the individuals (their psychology, the concrete situation in which they find themselves, their maturity or spiritual preparedness), seeking always in everything "the divine glory" ([269]).

With regard to methods of correction, we referred earlier to the transformation through which declaration N passed at the hands of Ignatius. The source of this declaration is the commentary by Cardinal Torquemada on Benedict's Rule.[39] The cardinal's doctrine, inspired by John Chrysostom, had the offenders admonished with love the first time, brought to shame on the second occasion, and punished on the third. Ignatius modified the passage: inserting "love" three times, adding "gentleness" to the first step, and removing "punishment" from the last. It will be useful to put both texts together; the words written in Ignatius' own handwriting are in italics:

Those who commit a fault should be admonished the first time with love;	Those who commit a fault should be admonished the first time with love *and gentleness;*
the second time they should be humiliated with shame;	the second time *with love and also in such a way* that they feel humiliating shame;
the third time they should be punished with greater severity.	the third time *with love and in such a way that they have fear.*

No less perfection is asked of the corrected subject. He must accept correction "in a good spirit," willingly, "with a true desire of amendment and spiritual profit," seeing in it a providential means for correcting his ydefects and for advancing in spirit. This, "even when the reason for the correction is not that of some blameworthy defect" ([269]), that is, even though the fault committed would not have been morally culpable or even though actually there would have been no fault at all.[40]

---

39   See Polanco, *Collectanea,* f. 67 (in the transcription of Hsü, p. 255).
40   See Nadal, *Scholia,* on no. 269, "Culpa vacantem."

d. The Syndic ([271])

The task of the official known as the syndic ([271]) bears on the matter of corrections. It involved the supervision of the house and the church, noting irregularities in order to let the superior know of them, unless in some particular case he received authority to correct them on the spot.

In describing the duties of the syndic, the first text made use of Humbert of Romans's description of the office of the "circator" who among the Dominicans had a very similar function.[41] But this is another characteristic example of textual development: although the passage in the primitive text, a, was almost a transcription of the Dominican source, on passing to text A the details that had been borrowed were dropped and only the basic ideas retained, those which from the beginning were the original ones of the composer of our Constitutions.

In later times the syndic's functions were to be included in the offices of minister and subminister. Yet in one way or another, regular discipline requires such an office.

e. Illness ([272])

Illness is an incident, as it were a parenthesis, in ordinary life. It is not strange that here too, in the development of the thought, it enters in out of context.

The virtues to be encouraged in the sick are the same as those in the parallel passage of the Examen ([89]). Essentially it means edifying everyone in all circumstances. The Jesuit must always be an apostle, even while ill and, as we will see in Part VI, even on his deathbed ([595]). In the Examen only the edification given by obedience and patience is mentioned; here the following is added: "They should show that the sickness is accepted as a gift from the hand of our Creator and Lord, since it is a gift no less than health" ([272]). Ignatius used to say that a servant of God comes out of an illness with "half a doctorate" in the science of the spiritual life.[42]

4. Union ([273-275])

This first section of the first chapter concludes with an appeal for union. The subject is specially dealt with in Part VIII, but Ignatius judged it so important for the life and activity of the Society that he wants the novices to be working on it from the start.

Union is desirable above all in the field of ideas. Following the advice

---

41   *Liber de instructione officialium*, chap. 15.
42   MI Epp, I, 84-85.

of Paul, who exhorted everyone to feel and say the same,[43] the Constitutions urge members of the Society to avoid, as far as possible, diversity of doctrine. In its apostolic activity (preaching, books, and the like), the Society is not to introduce new doctrines differing from what is commonly held by the teaching Church ([273, 274]). The task of Jesuits is "to be good and faithful [note this adjective] sowers in the Lord's field and to preach His divine word" ([30]). "Those of the Society are not to be inventors of new things in the Church," as Nadal put it. Before proposing in public something new that comes to their minds, they should be sure of "ecclesiastical approval" either through common consent of authors or by the sanction of the magisterium.[44] Even with regard to doctrines about which Catholic teachers hold divergent opinions, Ignatius wanted to see an effort at uniformity in the Society ([274]).

Yet unity of doctrine in the speculative area does not suffice. Necessary too is a unity of criteria in the practical order, "in judgment about things to be done" ([273]).[45] We may note the principal reason given for this: diversity of criteria is generally the mother of discord and the enemy of union of wills ([273]); the union of wills, the union of hearts, desiring or not desiring in common—without these factors (as Cassian said) mutual love cannot endure.[46] This means that a great effort must be made "in order that, being united among themselves by the bond of fraternal charity, they may be able better and more efficaciously to apply themselves in the service of God and the aid of their fellowmen" ([273]). This union of hearts cannot be attained or preserved without the use of the same criteria "in judgment about things to be done." If there is a unity of criteria, then the other frictions which are unavoidable in human relations can easily be solved by means of the reconciliation mentioned in declaration P ([275]).

---

43 See Phil. 2:2; 1 Cor. 1:10; E. Rasco, S.J., "Idem sapiamus idem dicamus omnes: una cita de Pablo?" art. in *ArchHistSI*, 46 (1977), 184-190 (even though we do not subscribe to all the affirmations in this article). The first text and the first wording of text A were in the third person: "idem dicant omnes, idem sapiant."

44 MHSI Nadal, V, 460. A little earlier he leaves to other teachers in the Church the task of illuminating revealed truth, yet adding something new to make it clearer.

45 The "cosas agíbiles" of the Spanish text [154, 273, 423, 803] are those things which in medieval Latin were denominated "agibilia," that is, practical affairs. See Du Cange, *Glossarium mediae et infimae latinitatis*, s.v.

46 *Conlationes*, 16, 3.

III. SPIRITUAL PROGRESS ([276-291])

The rest of the chapter, as already indicated, deals with measures "toward progress for advancing in the virtues" ([276]). They can be summarized under the heads: the good example of the older members ([276]), spiritual instruction ([277-279]), spiritual exercise ([280-287]), the life of prayer ([288]). Finally, by way of an appendix, the studies of the novices are described ([289-290]) along with the ways of ensuring that they put them into practice ([291]).

We shall comment briefly on what we deem more important or significant concerning each of these points.

1. Good Example of the Older Members ([276])

The example of the older members is more effective than many words. As early as 1541[47] the first fathers established a norm by which from time to time they performed the duties of "those who serve," a norm to which Ignatius himself conformed so notably even after he became general.[48]

In the primitive text another means for advancing in virtue, the solicitude and vigilance of the superior, was in the first place. It was suppressed, perhaps because it belongs rather to Part IX than to Part III, although it is a pity it was omitted.

2. Instruction ([277-279])

In the second place, doctrinal and ascetical instruction is prescribed but always with the discretion and broadness of mind characteristic of Ignatius. It is to be accommodated to the capability of each one ([277]). On the other hand, those who "on their own part are acquainted with the Spiritual Exercises and have a plan for proceeding in them" may readily be dispensed from the "common rules" in this matter ([279]). "Superiors and prefects of prayer," Nadal writes, "are to use the moderation which we know was characteristic of Father Ignatius and which is proper to the Institute of the Society. If they judge in the Lord that someone is making good progress in prayer, they should neither prescribe anything nor make any objection; rather they should confirm and encourage him so that he may continue gently and strongly in the Lord."[49] The reason for this, as Nadal said on another occasion, is because "we are only cooperators with

---

47 MI Const, I, 47, no. 43.
48 See MI FontNarr, III, 373; PolCompl, II, 576, no. 600.
49 MHSI Nadal, V, 663.

God, and we ought not to prescribe for God how he is to help those whom he wishes to raise up by his grace and favor."[50]

Among the instructions that ought to be given the novices is advice on "striving to acquire as much devotion as divine grace imparts to them" ([277]). This is often understood merely as a recommendation about the way to practice the exercises of piety, that is, to make them with devotion. The history of the text shows that the author's intention goes much farther. Having spoken of the need for spiritual instruction and of practicing what was learned in it, he urges, in the third place and in general, the giving of oneself to devotion, seeking "the Lord's Spirit," as the primitive text said using a Franciscan term.[51] To give oneself to devotion means above all the frequent practice of exercises of piety through which the soul seeks God with "a pious and humble affection of the heart," as Bonaventure described devotion.[52] But Ignatius did not rest content with this; his desire was that members of the Society "if at all possible would not find less devotion in any work of charity and obedience than in prayer and meditation."[53] The novice, then, "ought to acquire devotion" not only in spiritual practices, but also in tasks that call for greater humility and charity ([282]), in fulfilling the orders of obedience, in fraternal interchange ([250]), and in all his activity.

The Spiritual Exercises, since they are an abundant wellspring of devotion, should be given to the novices if they have not made them before entry ([277]). The primitive text, a, had noted that the Spiritual Exercises help the novice to gain a clearer knowledge of Jesus Christ, move him more to love, and as a result make him more fervent in his practical day-to-day life.

3. Spiritual Exercise ([280-287])

Ignatius gave the title "Spiritual Exercises" to the one-month retreat of which we have just spoken. The term "spiritual exercises" also means the ascetical practices through which the virtues are exercised. We shall now discuss these. Significantly, great emphasis was placed on the exercise of preaching ([280-281]) and on the practice of the great virtues of humility ([282-283]), obedience ([284-286]), and poverty ([287]).

The exercise of preaching is in preparation for the principal ministry of the Society, "preaching the divine word" ([30]), the proper ministry of

---

50   *Pláticas de Coimbra*, 194-195, no. 29.
51   St. Francis, *Regula bullata*, chap. 10.
52   *Expositio in Regulam*, chap. 10.
53   MI Epp, III, 502.

the professed. So it is not surprising to find that, just as novices in other orders exercised themselves in the liturgical offices, those of the Society did so principally in preaching.

The three great virtues already mentioned are the same as those proposed to the candidate in the Examen as the fundamental Jesuit virtues (see [80-90]). For that reason, although the final number, on poverty ([287]), is an addition in the margin of the page of the definitive text, this addition was made not merely that poverty "be made a pendant to obedience, according to the classical perspective of the three vows," but it was also intended to complete the trio of the great virtues.

In the context of generosity towards the Lord, which requires the performance with all possible devotion of tasks in which humility and charity are practiced more ([282]), mention is made of the vows which the novices can spontaneously anticipate out of devotion (since none are obliged to do so before completion of the two-year novitiate). The novice can prove his generosity towards our Lord through these anticipated vows, binding himself more closely to Him and dedicating himself "completely and irrevocably" to His service ([283]). Perhaps these words are not pondered sufficiently by those who abandon religious life so lightly, as if it involved merely a change in the juridical and institutional order. To the generosity of the novice who binds himself irrevocably to Christ, the divine generosity will respond; and the more will the novice himself be disposed to receive graces and spiritual gifts which are greater each day ([282]).

4. For God and with God ([288])

We now come to [288], the most precious section of Part III. It deals with two topics, two spiritual principles which are closely related but not to be regarded as identical, as one author does:[54] right intention and seeking God in all things.

A right or pure intention "not mixed with human motives" ([180]) "about the state of life" is necessary. We saw this in Part I ([180]); here, however, Ignatius asks all to make diligent efforts to put this into practice "in all particular details," that is, in each of their daily activities.

To achieve this, it would be enough to act from a motive that is supernatural and not from a bad or merely natural motive. Furthermore,

---

54 See J. Stierli, S.J., "Das Ignatianische Gebet: Gott suchen in allen Dingen," in *Ignatius von Loyola, seine geistliche Gestalt und sein Vermacht* (Würzburg 1956), 152-182. English translation in *Woodstock Letters*, 90 (1961), 135-160. [Editor's note: Also in *Ignatius of Loyola: His Personality and Spiritual Heritage*, ed. F. Wulf (St. Louis 1977), 135-163.]

in the *Exercises* Ignatius noted that "not only is filial fear something pious and altogether holy, but servile fear too is a great help when someone attains to nothing else better or more useful."[55] But, in both the *Constitutions* and the *Exercises* he urges us to go forward with the most perfect motive of "pure love"; "to aim at serving and pleasing the Divine Goodness for its own sake and because of the incomparable love and benefits with which God has anticipated us, rather than for fear of punishments or hope of rewards" ([288]). Possibly there is an allusion here to St. John's words: "Love is not perfect in one who is afraid. We, for our part, love because He first loved us."[56]

This is not to deny that motives of fear and hope are also useful; anyone may be helped by such motives. "If because of my faults I forget the love of the Eternal Lord, at least the fear of punishments will keep me from falling."[57]

The second topic covered here is "seeking God in all things." We know that this is the formula Ignatius preferred for expressing the life of union with God proper to the Jesuit.[58]

To seek or to find God in all things (Ignatius used both terms) is above all to seek or find in all things the presence of God, as the saint explained to the scholastic Antonio Brandão, "for it is true that His Divine Majesty is in all things by presence, power, and essence." He added that this manner of meditating, finding God our Lord in all things, is very easy and that this exercise "can, by disposing us, bring about great visitations of the Lord, even though only in a brief prayer."[59] "All things therefore are charged with love, are charged with God," said the poet Gerard Manley Hopkins, "and if we know how to touch them give off sparks and take fire, yield drops and flow, ring and tell of him."[60]

However, this seeking of God in things is not to be reduced to the exercise of the presence of God. All the ways to God through creatures which the saints have discovered are ways of seeking him and finding him in them. When Ignatius—as Nadal tells us—was moved to sublime

55   *SpEx*, no. 370.
56   1 Jn. 4:18-19.
57   *SpEx*, no. 65.
58   See MHSI Nadal, V, 162. With regard to this formula, besides Stierli (cited in note 54), see M. Giuliani, S.J., "Trouver Dieu en toutes choses," art. in *Christus*, II (1955), 172-194. [Editor's note: An English translation is in W. J. Young, trans., *Finding God in All Things* (Chicago 1958), 3-24.]
59   MI Epp, III, 510.
60   *The Sermons and Devotional Writings of Gerard Manley Hopkins*, ed. Christopher Devlin (Oxford 1959), 195. It is a favorite subject of the poet.

thoughts about the Holy Trinity on seeing an orange leaf,[61] what was he doing but finding God in that orange leaf?

Ignatius also teaches us to find God in men; for example, he desires that by observing one another we should grow in devotion and praise God our Lord, "whom each one should endeavor to recognize in his neighbor as in His image" ([250]); he urges us to recognize Jesus Christ in superiors, reverencing Him in them as if He were present (see [551]).[62]

However, this last phrase shows us that the seeking or finding of God in things does not have to remain merely at a level of intellectual certainty; it should include the affection of the heart, for that is where union with God is really attained. John of the Cross gives this advice: "Regularly direct your affection towards God and your spirit will be divinely warmed."[63]

This demands an ever increasing purification of disorderly affections, "stripping off from oneself the love of creatures." Such a condition is indispensable for placing this love wholly "in the Creator of them." Then creatures will become so many motives for loving God. In them all, one will love "Him." For the person who is purified and inflamed with love for God will see in them only the Beloved whom he is seeking. However, he does not thereby lose his love of the creatures, but transforms it; he will love them all "in Him," with the love which comes down from Him ([671]). In this way no creature whatever, no matter how wretched and undesirable it may be in itself, or however hostile it may appear, can be separated from this love, because the soul loves it not in itself but "in Him" ([288]).

Nadal described such a life of prayer proper to a Jesuit by a formula that has now become classic: "contemplative in action."[64] This phrase had already appeared in a fourteenth-century book widely read by Jesuits in the time of Ignatius: *Stimulus divini amoris*.[65] One chapter of that book is devoted to teaching how one ought to enjoy contemplation in any action. The book also uses the expressions: not to seek anything else than to serve God and to please Him; also, to see God in all things. Likewise, it contains the advice which Ignatius used to give, that of imitating the angels who while

---

61 See Nadal, *Pláticas de Coimbra*, p. 71.
62 Form. Inst., no. 6.
63 *Avisos*, no. 79.
64 MHSI Nadal, V, 162.
65 There is more than one work with this title. We refer to the lengthiest treatise, divided into three parts, which begins with the words *Currite undique* and incorporates the shorter one written by Jacobus Mediolanensis. We think that this treatise, which had a wide circulation in Europe, is the one read in the early Society. Polanco also read it in Padua.

they are with us do not cease contemplating God.[66]

More directly we see in this constitution an echo (and perhaps more than an echo) of the "Contemplation to Attain the Love of God" in the *Exercises*. In that contemplation also Ignatius urges us to love and serve God not from fear of punishment or hope of reward but because of the love and outstanding benefits by which He anticipated us: blessings of creation, redemption, and special favors—pondering "how much God our Lord has done for me, and how much he has given me of what He possesses and finally, how the same Lord desires to give Himself to me. . . ."[67] There too he teaches us to seek God in all things, seeing how God dwells in creatures, . . . and in men, . . . and so in me, . . . making a temple of me, "since I am created in the likeness and image of His Divine Majesty."[68] Likewise Ignatius, by having us consider "how God works and labors for me in all creatures upon the face of the earth,"[69] rouses us to love Him in each one of them ("loving Him in all"); and through our seeing how "all blessings and gifts descend from above . . . as the rays of light descend from the sun, and as the waters from their fountains,"[70] he moves us to love all creatures in Him, the fullness of being.

5. Studies ([289-290])

By way of appendix, [289] deals with the studies of the novices. It might seem that academic studies are forbidden for novices during the whole time of probation, so that they may give themselves completely to self-denial and progress in virtue ([289]). But that is not the intent of this constitution; the concern here is with the distinction between houses and colleges. The houses, which in the Constitutions are intended at the same time for the professed and those in probation, are not to have classes or studies. This was a decision taken by our fathers as early as 1541[71] and made clearer later when it was confirmed in the Formula of the Institute of 1550: "The houses which the Lord will provide are to be dedicated to labors in His vineyard, and not to the pursuit of scholastic studies." Studies, and later on also lectures, will take place in the colleges. "For the colleges exist for the acquisition of learning, the houses that those who have acquired it may use it in practice [the formed religious], or those who must

---

66   See MI FontNarr, II, 476.
67   *SpEx*, no. 234.
68   *SpEx*, no. 235.
69   *SpEx*, no. 236.
70   *SpEx*, no. 237.
71   MI Const, I, 47.

still acquire it may lay a foundation of humility and virtue for it [the novices]" (289]). Mercurian said in the rules for the superior of a professed house: "The professed houses are not engaged as are the colleges in preparing the means for the end of the Society, but in the end itself and in the use of the means which contribute to this end."[72]

However, this does not mean that in the thinking of Ignatius novices had to spend two years without studying. They were not to study while in the houses, that is, during the first months or first year of the novitiate, but afterwards they could be sent to a college, there to complete the time of probation and at the same time continue their studies. This was the practice of Ignatius himself.[73]

It is interesting at any rate to note how Ignatius does not neglect the need for what nowadays would be called "ongoing formation." In declaration X he observes that, although in general studies are not pursued in the houses of the Society, "all those who attend to preaching and confessing may study what is helpful toward their purpose" ([290]).

6. Execution ([291])

This lengthy first chapter, the longest in all the Constitutions, concludes with a paragraph on execution. The 19th General Congregation (1758) declared: "The excellence of a religious institute does not consist in having a large number of the finest laws and statutes; but rather in this, that the lives of its members come close in practice to what these laws prescribe."[74]

Toward achieving this fidelity in observance two means are suggested. First, that superiors remind subjects of their duties: every week or at least every fifteen days an exhortation or instruction on "these reminders, or similar ones" ought to be given ([291]). In our terminology we would call it a community exhortation,[75] for which private reading could substitute. Second, the subjects should remind the superior of his obligation to urge observance. That is the meaning of the last part of [291], as can be seen from the source,[76] and from the first wordings of the text. The last of these drafts explicitly describes how subjects are to do this, by requesting penances from the superior for their negligence in keeping the rules. This will show the concern which is had (*se tiene*) to make progress in the service

---

72 *Regulae*, Reg. Praef. Dom. Prof., 31.
73 See MI FontNarr, I, 676, 696, 741; Epp III, 195.
74 C. G. XIX, d. 11. See *CollDecr*, d. 49.
75 See "Constitutions of the Colleges," I, no. 20 (MI Regulae, p. 223), which is the source here.
76 MI Const, I. 200, no. 8; see p. 229, no. 9.

of God ([291]). In the Spanish the concern "which is had" is written in an impersonal way; in other words, both subjects and superiors should have this concern, as in holy collaboration.

IV. HEALTH AND BODILY STRENGTH ([292-306])

1. Means of Preserving Health ([294-304])

The second chapter begins by laying down the basic principle of the whole chapter: just as an excessive preoccupation with the needs of the body is blameworthy (namely, exaggerated care to preserve health or exaggerated fear of losing it), so on the contrary "a proper concern about the preservation of one's health and bodily strength for the divine service is praiseworthy" ([292]). For, as the source, the "Constitutions of the Colleges," stated, physical strength is very necessary in our way of life, where the infirm need to be served instead of serving.[77] The situation of a sick person in a contemplative order is, of course, quite different.

Given this principle, concrete norms follow, means that will help in the preservation of health. Such are: informing the superior when something seems necessary ([292-293]), leading a regular life ([294-295]), using what is needed to sustain nature such as food, clothing, living quarters ([296-297]), moderating work and interrupting it with suitable relaxation ([298-299]), being discreet in corporal penances ([300-301]), assigning domestic tasks according to each one's strength ([302]), and finally having in the house someone who superintends what pertains to the preservation of health for those who have it and to its restoration for those who are ill ([303]).

The care of the sick is treated in a declaration (G, [304]), because it is more the concern of superiors: "Great care should be taken of the sick" —a phrase that recalls one in the Rule of Benedict: "Before and above all, have great care of the sick and serve them as Christ Himself."[78] Even more it recalls to us the maternal solicitude of Ignatius himself for them, as described with such delicacy by Ribadeneira in his treatise on the founder's government.[79] This care is to be shown in calling for a doctor and following his orders "as far as possible," and, if necessary, transferring the sick man to another place where he may have better bodily health ([304]).

---

77   See MI Regulae, 233-234.
78   Regula, chap. 36, 1.
79   See MI FontNarr, III, 617-618; J. A. de Laburu, *La salud corporal y san Ignacio de Loyola* (Bilbao 1956).

2. Indifference of the Subject ([292-293])

These are all prudential norms, although illumined and elevated by the end aimed at in them, the preservation of health and bodily strength for the divine service. With reference to them, [292] gives us an instruction on representation to superiors. The first requirement is prayerful recollection in order to find out in such an atmosphere if it is God's will that the representation be made. If after prayer it seems so, then the representation should be made verbally or briefly in writing if there is danger that the matter may be forgotten. Thirdly, once done there should be no argument or insistence that the request be granted ([292]). However, this "no argument" needs to be understood properly. For if the superior "is not yet fully aware," that is, has not understood the matter correctly, or if he himself requests further explanation, the subject can give a better explanation; and if the superior has forgotten, he can remind him ([293]). In an instruction written years later, Ignatius goes even farther. Even after receiving a negative answer, he makes allowance that, after some time has passed, a representation may be repeated, and this up to three times: "For experience makes new discoveries with the passage of time and furthermore changes occur in the things themselves."[80]

What is important is the interior disposition of the subject, a disposition of indifference and self-abandonment. When all representation and clarification has been done, the subject should leave all concern about the matter to the superior, whether he grants what is asked or not, "for he must persuade himself that what the superior decides after being informed is more suitable for the divine service and the subject's own greater good in our Lord" ([292]).

A like indifference is asked for further on: "to undertake whatever employment may be assigned to him" ([302]); and in order that in time of illness "without intruding himself in anything other than in exercising his patience and obedience" the sick man may leave the care of everything else to the superior and his ministers, "by means of whom Divine Providence directs him" ([304]). In this connection one recalls that our vocation is to travel and live in any part of the world and that therefore, although superiors will see whether a change of climate would be suitable for the sick man, he himself ought not to seek or show any inclination for such a change, leaving this concern to the superior ([304]). Always indifference, the fruit of self-denial.

80 MI Epp, IX, 90-91.

V. Preservation of Exterior Goods ([305-306])

The last part of the second chapter—as mentioned before-—deals briefly with the preservation of material goods (the building, furnishings, and the like) and with the provision of anything needed in this area. It is interesting to note that this topic of management is treated in the context of health, and not in Part VI along with poverty.

The means are: that all have consideration and concern for temporal goods; further, that someone should have special responsibility for them; and also that there ought to be a sufficient number of "officials," that is, of persons in charge of the various occupations ([305]).

Especially noteworthy here is the spiritual motivation: we may not abuse or waste material goods, for they are "the estate and property of Christ our Lord" ([305]). If we are consecrated to Christ, then all we have, just like ourselves, belongs to Christ. Benedict writes in his rule that all the objects of the monastery are to be regarded as if they are sacred vessels of the altar.[81]

VI. Final Observation

Part III speaks of the physical body. The dimension of the social body almost entirely disappears from view. It is presupposed rather than described. The house in which novices live, and which ought to have a religious atmosphere, is to be preserved as something belonging to Christ. The existence of a community is also presupposed, with novices, older members, a superior, a confessor, a master of novices, and officials. But no mention is made of any organic or juridical structure. Only the spiritual formation of the occupants in such a house is treated, and their preservation in spirit and health. We would say that rather than the constructing of the temple, we are dealing with the labor of preparing the stones which are to serve for its construction.

---

81   Regula, chap. 31, 10. It is interesting to note that the source, the Constitutions of the Colleges" (MI Regulae, p. 238, no. 9) said, "hacienda de pobres" (property of the poor).

Chapter VIII

FORMATION OF SCHOLASTICS
(Constitutions, Part IV)

I. PRELIMINARY REMARKS

1. Evolution of Part IV

Others more competent have described the origin and development of colleges in the Society, so there is no need to retrace the story here, particularly in view of the scope of this work. Nor is it necessary, since it is so well known, to dwell on the enormous importance which Jesuit colleges had for extern students in the Europe of the Counter Reformation. Besides, the Society itself has shown how highly it values this educational work, as General Congregation XXXI so strongly stressed.

As to the Constitutions, to which we restrict ourselves in the present work, the main objective of Part IV is stated in the title, which in the definitive text is worded: "The Instruction of Those Who Are Retained in the Society, in Learning and in Other Means of Helping Their Fellowmen." Having dealt with the admission of those who are apt (Part I), the dismissal of those who are not fit (Part II), and the spiritual progress of those remaining after this selection (Part III), Part IV describes how the last group can be helped to make progress in studies and in ways of helping their fellowmen—or, in other words, their intellectual and pastoral formation. Nevertheless, in chapter 7 and in chapters 11 through 17, of which we shall speak next, the Constitutions expressly permit the opening of our classrooms to non-Jesuit students as well; this is done from "a motive of charity" ([440]). At the end of this chapter we will deal with what concerns them alone.

In its present form Part IV comprises seventeen chapters, divided into two sections: the first (chapters 1 to 10) on colleges, and the second (chapters 11 to 17) on universities. When Nadal left Rome in 1553 to promulgate the Constitutions in Portugal and Spain, this Part had only nine chapters: 1-6 and 8-10. The seventh chapter was added between lines and in the margin, partly in the last years of Ignatius' life, partly afterward by the First General Congregation.[1] When was the second section (chapters 11-17), referring to the universities of the Society, added? Two quite distinct problems are to be distinguished here: when these chapters were composed or written, and when they were inserted in the book of the Constitutions.

It seems that this section (on universities) was composed at an early stage. In fact, a copy of these chapters is preserved in the hand of the young Neapolitan Pietro Vidal,[2] who left the Society in March of 1554.[3]

The second question is quite different. There is no doubt that from the beginning, from the introduction of the primitive text, a, Ignatius intended to write about universities in the Constitutions, for we read there: "First what concerns the colleges will be treated and afterwards what concerns the universities."[4] This explains why the copyist, in transcribing the definitive text B, left two blank leaves between chapter 10 of Part IV and the beginning of Part V, not only in the Constitutions but also in the Declarations.[5]

However, it seems that these chapters were not inserted into the book of the Constitutions during Ignatius' lifetime. We base this assertion on the following argument (though not exclusively). The manuscript of the Latin version of the Constitutions shows that when this translation was made these chapters did not as yet form part of the book. This is clear from the Declarations, for those of Part V were written immediately after those of chapter 10 of Part IV. When later the Declarations of these seven chapters had to be inserted, since there was no space they were added at the end of the codex.[6] A careful examination of the manuscript shows clearly that this is equally true for the Constitutions: these seven chapters are written on a quire of pages that are half a centimeter narrower and can be seen to be inserted between the pages of chapter 10 of Part IV and those of Part V.[7]

---

1   The fact that the listing of the chapters on universities was originally changed from 1-8 to 10-16 might seem to suggest that chapter 7 is later than the insertion of these seven chapters into the Constitutions.   But we think that this was due to the fact that when chapter 7 was inserted the numbering of the three following chapters, 7-9, was not immediately corrected to 8-10.

2   See MHSI MonPaed, I, 212 and 394.

3   See MI Epp, VI, 684. He was readmitted. But he was not received into the house at Rome, but sent instead to the college at Florence; from it he again left, "insalutato hospite."

4   MI Const, II, 170. Likewise in the Preamble of the definitive text.

5   In the Constitutions chapter 10 ends on folio 26, while Part V starts on folio 29. In the Declarations chapter 10 ends on folio 18, and Part V begins on folio 21.

6   After the Declarations of Part X there are still two blank folios (ff. 103-104v); those following contain the Declarations of the eleventh to the seventeenth chapters of Part IV (ff. 105-108v).

7   ARSI *Inst 7a*, ff. 23-28v. A blank folio comes next.

We already know that this Latin translation of all the Constitutions was certainly made after the death of Ignatius, "when the fathers were arriving for the general congregation," as Polanco specifically says.[8]

Efforts have been made to prove the opposite, namely, that these chapters were already in the Constitutions during the lifetime of Ignatius. As proof, allusion is made to an instruction supposedly given by Gonçalves da Câmara while visiting the colleges in Portugal in the spring of 1556. This instruction does indeed refer to "what is said in Part IV of the Constitutions, in the second section of it, dealing with the universities."[9] The only problem with this theory is that the attribution to Câmara and in those circumstances lacks foundation and sound probability. The author is without doubt Spanish, writing the language as he does with fluency and ease.[10] Although Câmara could write Spanish fairly correctly, he tended to introduce many Portuguese expressions, which do not appear here. It suffices to compare the letter he sent to Ignatius on May 22, 1556.[11] As to the circumstances, this instruction cannot be for the colleges of only one province. It is conceived and composed in a general and hypothetical tone, taking into account a diversity of situations in different provinces. For example, it speaks of taking men from the "houses of probation" (in the plural). In Portugal, in 1556, there was of course only one house of probation.[12]

More serious is another difficulty based on the silence of the First General Congregation. The force of the argument here is the fact that, while the acts of the Congregation do refer to other documents then existing apart from the Constitutions and about which the Congregation was deliberating as to their inclusion in the Constitutions,[13] nothing is said about these chapters. We do not want to deny the difficulty, although the force of the argument is not as great as would seem at first sight since the acts of the First General Congregation are incomplete. At any rate, as we know, an argument from silence is never very strong when there are other positive reasons to the contrary.[14]

---

8   Chron, VI, 55. See MI Const, III, p. lviii; M. Scaduto, *L'epoca di Laínez*, I (Rome 1964), p. 108.

9   MHSI MonPaed, I, 491.

10   We think of Polanco, in whose handwriting is the title, *Para las escuelas de los colegios.*

11   MHSI EppMixt, V, 330-334.

12   The reference itself to the Constitutions implies that they were available to everyone and that therefore they had already been printed and published.

13   See C. G. I, dd. 72-77.

14   So much the more since, as we shall say later (in note 17), we think that when the General Congregation was held these chapters had already been inserted in the

The following solution may perhaps be acceptable. Apart from the general Constitutions, particular constitutions were composed for the universities of the Society, as others had been composed for the colleges. In the general Constitutions also it was intended to say something about the universities, but more briefly. In the definitive text (text B), four leaves were left blank for this purpose (two in the Constitutions and two others in the Declarations). But Ignatius died without the project having been carried out. What was to be done? It was not possible to leave these pages blank, because it had been stated in the introduction to Part IV that the universities would he included. They had recourse then to this solution: the copies of these particular constitutions on the universities, and their declarations, were inserted in two fascicles. This would explain the disproportionate space devoted to the universities in Part IV (and even in the entire Constitutions): seven chapters on eight and a half leaves of text B[15]—although the intention had been to give less than half that space: only four leaves at most.[16]

This would also help to explain certain discrepancies. For instance, it is only here in these chapters that we find the statement that the general has to listen to the opinions of his assistants ([441, 442]). The norms for correspondence with the general given here in chapter 17 ([504]) do not agree with those of Part VIII, chapter 1 ([674]). The very style is different from that used in the rest of the Constitutions. To cite only one instance, the expression "in our Lord" (or its equivalent), so frequent in the rest of the Constitutions (we have found it in them 120 times), never appears in these seven chapters.[17]

book of the Constitutions.

15 Text B, ff. 60-64 (Constitutions) and 119-122v (Declarations).

16 It may be objected that in chapter 14, no. 1 [464], there is reference to the preceding chapter 5, no. 4 [358], with the phrase "as was stated in the treatise on the colleges." But this phrase was added by Polanco in the copy of Vidal (*Instit.* 7) and it is probable that he added it when this copy served as the original of what later was included in the book of the Constitutions.

17 There is perhaps a sign of the moment when the insertion of these chapters in the Constitutions was made. The copyist of text C, Giovanni Filippo Vito, at the end of the page closing the tenth chapter (f. 87v) wrote "Quinta pars" (fifth part), as indicating the beginning of the next page. Afterwards he erased these two words and wrote "De las," words which begin the section on the universities; and in the same group of folios in which he was writing chapters 8 to 10 he wrote the following chapters 11 to 17 and Part V. The only explanation seems to be that when he reached the end of the tenth chapter, these chapters were not yet in the original he was copying (text B); but Polanco, who directed the transcription, told him that he had to include them here. Now, the copy of text C was made after Ignatius' death (July 31, 1556) and before the General Congregation (June 1558). To the proofs brought out by Codina in MI Const, II, pp. xlvii-xlix, it may be

2. Structure

To understand the structure of the first section, and indeed the very institution of colleges in the Society, we should keep in mind the models which Ignatius and his companions had before their eyes, the university colleges of the time, especially those of the university of Paris, where all of them had lived. Those colleges were pious or charitable foundations (*causae piae*) established for the support of a limited number of poor students, *bursarii* (provided with a *bursa* or scholarship) as they were called in Paris —although rich students, *portionistae* (boarders, who paid their pension), were also admitted.[18] In charge of the college was a director (*principalis, magister*) who governed the house with his officials.

Hence we read, in Ignatius' own hand, in the document "For Founding a College" (*Para fundar colegio*)—of which we shall speak later—that the colleges of the Society are for "poor students"; and furthermore, that a founder should stipulate that "all the scholastics must be poor," being approved and destined to be united with and incorporated into the Society.[19]

The instituting of the colleges in the Society supposes, then, three main elements: the foundation, the students or scholastics on whose behalf the foundation is made, and the government. That triple division logically determines the structure of this first section. After an introduction or preamble on the need for colleges, there comes, firstly, the founding itself: the founder (chapter 1) and the acceptance and administration by the Society (chapter 2); secondly, the students: who they are to be (chapter 3), how their physical and spiritual welfare is to be cared for (chapter 4), their intellectual formation (chapters 5 and 6), their pastoral formation (chapter 8) and how they can be removed from a college even though beneficiaries of the foundation (chapter 9); and thirdly, the government of the college (chapter 10). Chapter 7, on the teaching in the colleges—a later addition, as we mentioned earlier—forms a sort of appendix to the chapters dealing with intellectual formation (chapters 5 and 6).

This character of being a special institution within the Society explains why "the constitutions which pertain to the colleges" ([439]) form a self-contained unit within the general Constitutions of the Society. They deal

---

added that Vito died on April 8, 1558.

18   Besides, there were the *camaristas* who rented some rooms in the college, where they lived with their tutors. We prescind from them to simplify the issue, for they are not related to our present discussion.

19   MI Const, I, 52-53.

with everything relative to the colleges: every aspect of the student's life (not merely intellectual and pastoral formation, as the title would lead us to expect), government (which in the Constitutions is treated in Part IX), and even spiritual ministries ([437]) (which pertain to Part VII) and they expressly state that "they could be kept apart and read publicly two or three times a year" ([439]).

The second section is also preceded by an introductory chapter on the reason for universities and the method of accepting them (chapter 11). The remaining material can be considered under three headings: first, pedagogical norms (the branches to be taught, the method of teaching them, textbooks, courses, and academic degrees—chapters 12-15); second, the religious and moral education of the students (chapter 16 [481-489]); third, the government of the university (chapter 17).

3. Sources

Contrary to the procedure in Part III, the sources of the first section of this Part IV are all internal, that is, documents of the Society itself. In general we may say that the preamble, on the necessity of colleges, and the first chapter, on founders and benefactors, derive from an older document first composed in 1540 or 1541. The first text was just a copy of a later revision of this document.[20] The chapters referring to intellectual formation (chapters 5 and 6) and to government (chapter 10) are based on the "Constitutions of the Colleges" (*Constituciones de los colegios*).[21] The chapter on pastoral formation (chapter 8) is taken from Polanco's sixth *Industria*. In the other chapters (2, 3, 4, 7, and 9) the Formula of the Institute is taken into account and also previous determinations or clarifications, but even more the practice of the Society.

In drawing up the section on the universities, Ignatius first wanted information about the constitutions or statutes of the universities at Paris, Cologne, Bologna, Padua, Salamanca, Alcalá, Coimbra, and Valencia.[22] We do not know the extent to which he was able to satisfy this desire. Points of contact have been found between these chapters and two treatises on the

---

20 The document *Para fundar colegio* (or *Fundación de colegio*), published in MI Const, I, 49-65. The first version, copied by Antonio Estrada, cannot be later than February of 1541, when Estrada left Rome to study in Paris. In the critical apparatus of the column on the right, reference is made to the copy of the second version made by Speg (d. Nov. 1548). This copy, transcribed by Botelho, was incorporated into the first text of the Constitutions.

21 The second and seventh sections, or parts, of these constitutions: MI Regulae, 227-235 and 241-247.

22 MI Epp, II, 550, 601.

studies of the Society, both of an uncertain date, one written by Nadal, the other attributed by the editor to Martín de Olave.[23] Perhaps this coincidence can be explained quite simply, since the three documents draw their inspiration from a common source, the method of Paris (*modus parisiensis*), which Nadal introduced in Messina and Olave in the Roman College and which the Society adopted as the most useful for its teaching. Nadal himself says: "Care should be taken to avoid abandoning the plan of studies of Paris, which our schools have made their very own, and which we should firmly retain."[24] In any case, these two documents cannot be considered as literary sources.

In the organization of the universities we can recognize some elements that seem to come from the Italian universities rather than Paris. It should be remembered that Polanco had made his theological studies at the University of Padua.

Since almost all the topics in the second section already appear in the first, we will present both sections together, adding to the comments on the various points of the first what would seem to be of special interest in the second. It would be tedious to treat the second section separately, especially in view of its rather academic character.

II. NECESSITY OF THE COLLEGES ([307-308])

Part IV is the only one preceded by a preamble. The author thought it necessary in order to explain the reason for studies and for colleges: they are a requirement of our vocation. The end of the Society—aiding our fellowmen spiritually—requires, "in addition to the example of one's life," "learning and a method of expounding it" ([307]). This had already been noted in the Examen ([109]). Therefore, after "the proper foundation of abnegation of themselves is seen to be present in those who were admitted and also the required progress in virtues," that is, after those who were admitted have achieved self-abnegation and progress in the virtues, which is the foundation or cement of religious life, it is necessary to construct on this the edifice of their learning and the manner of employing it. "Toward achieving this purpose the Society takes charge of colleges and also of some universities" ([307]).

---

23   See MHSI MonPaed, I, 25-26, 183-185.

24   *Scholia*, on no. 458, "More publicorum professorum." On the *modus parisiensis* and its relation to the teaching of the Society, see G. Codina, S.J., *Aux sources de la pédagogie des jésuites. Le "modus parisiensis"* (Rome 1968). However, it is restricted to a study of the humanities.

The same idea is more developed and better explained in the declaration. This reproduces, with retouches, the older document, "For Founding a College,"[25] in which Ignatius relates the reflections which our fathers made at the beginning about the manner of preserving and increasing the Society.

It begins by outlining our vocation to an apostolic or missionary life: "by traveling through the various regions of the world at the order of the vicar of Christ our Lord or of the superior of the Society itself, to preach, hear confessions, and use all the other means it can with the grace of God to help souls" ([308]). This is one of the passages in which this vocation is best described and it may be set alongside number [605] of Part VII and number [1] of the Formula of the Institute. This is an arduous vocation; the fathers noted as much in the Formula itself, saying that they knew it from experience.[26] It is arduous "because of the great labors and the great abnegation of oneself which are required in the Society" ([308]). On the other hand, virtue (a "good life") is not enough. Learning, adequate intellectual formation, is also needed. Now, reflected the fathers with some pessimism which was doubtless the fruit of experience, "those who are good and learned are few": men who have made their studies of philosophy and theology in universities (these were "the learned" referred to) and lead the life of "upright priests" are few, and even among these few there are fewer still who would desire to leave the world and embrace a life of poverty and apostolic abnegation; for most of them want to seek rest from the labor of their studies, and reap their fruits. So it would be difficult to preserve and increase the Society with such formed men, educated as they the first fathers were and as were some of the second generation (Araoz, Nadal, Olave, and others). Hence they "thought it wise to proceed by another path": to admit young men who give grounds for hope and have some education, and for their formation to "accept colleges under the conditions stated in the apostolic bull, whether these colleges are within universities or outside of them; and, if they are within universities, whether these universities are governed by the Society or not" ([308]).

An attempt has been made to dramatize this resolution of Ignatius and his companions by distinguishing a first time when they mistakenly thought they could build a community with men already formed, and a second time (said to be around 1541) when, having learned their mistake by experience,

---

25 Copied in the first text and omitted in text A, it was taken up again in text B (a unique case) with a title Polanco put on it: *Declaración sobre el proemio de la parte cuarta.* See MI Const, II, 169 (critical apparatus).
26 Form. Inst., nos. 4 and 9.

they adopted a different procedure, that of admitting young men.[27] It was not like that in reality. As early as 1537, at Vicenza, the fathers decided to disperse among the university cities of Italy "to see whether God our Lord would deign to call some student to enter our Institute."[28] In the first composition of the Formula of the Institute (1539) there is mention of supporting some young men in the universities who, after their studies, could be admitted into the Society. And in fact we find that in April of 1540 four scholastics left Rome with the intention of studying at the University of Paris. A few months later, in the bull *Regimini militantis*, we already find mention of colleges.

So the necessity of having young men for the preservation and increase of the Society was appreciated by Ignatius and his companions from the start, even before the Society was established as a religious order. What they could not see too clearly from the start, was how to support these youths; and it was at this point that Laínez intervened, although the nature of his intervention is not so clear.[29] But the decision itself to have colleges for this purpose is prior to September of 1540.

There are two expressions in the context here which ought not to be overlooked. First: "We shall accept colleges under the conditions stated in the apostolic bull" ([308]). This is a reference to the Formula of the Institute included in the bull *Exposcit debitum*.[30] This version of the Formula explains more precisely than the previous one the purpose and character of the colleges. The houses of the Society, it states, are not to be assigned to the pursuit of studies but are rather to be dedicated to labor in the vineyard of the Lord. On the other hand, it is necessary to prepare laborers for this vineyard so that they may form a "seedbed" of the Society. So, the

---

27 As proof the phrase is cited: "neither studies nor lectures in the Society." But this is taken precisely from the "Constitutions of 1541" (MI Const, I, 47), the document which, according to these authors, would mark the change of view on this matter. Furthermore, the ideas contained in this phrase remained in force later on also. For the word "Society" designates here the "houses" in contradistinction to the "colleges," which were institutions dependent on the Society. See Form. Inst., no. [8], and no. [269] in Part III.

28 Laínez, in MI FontNarr, I, 120.

29 See MI FontNarr, I, 610. The "colleges" do not appear in the first wording of the Formula, which speaks only of forming young men in the universities. "Colleges" appear in the Formula of 1540. It is one of the corrections made between the verbal approbation of Sept. 3, 1539, and the bull *Regimini* of Sept. 27, 1540. During this period Laínez was absent from Rome.

30 Clearly the reference is to this bull and not *Regimini*; for immediately afterwards it is said that colleges can be founded not only in the universities but also outside them. According to the bull *Regimini*, they could only be founded in the universities.

Society will be able, for the furtherance of studies, to have colleges of scholastics, wherever someone might be moved to found them. These colleges may have income, fixed revenues, and property, "for the use and needs of the students," the management and oversight remaining under the general and the Society. The students of these colleges ought to be such that on the completion of their studies and probation they can be received into the Society.[31] As one can see, among "the conditions stated in the bull" two are of clear interest to us now. First, the purpose of the colleges is to form youths who may form a seedbed or seminary for the Society. Second, the fixed incomes of these colleges are exclusively for paying the expenses of these scholastics, although it is understood that these expenses include the support of those who are looking after them (superiors and teachers).

The second clause deserving of notice runs: "whether [the colleges] are within universities or outside of them; whether they are governed by the Society or not" ([308]). And more clearly in the constitution: "Toward achieving this purpose" (that is to say, "to provide for the edifice of learning" necessary to this end), "the Society takes charge of colleges and also of some universities" ([307]). So then, not only the colleges but the universities themselves have as their purpose, at least their primary purpose, "the instruction of those who are retained in the Society, in learning and in other means of helping their fellowmen," as the title at the beginning of Part IV indicates.

This may seem not only surprising but even contrary to what the first number of chapter 11 states ([440]). Furthermore, it has been asserted that in that number Ignatius sanctions a class of college which is more for those outside the Society than for those of the Society: colleges of externs with a seminary for Jesuit scholastics. But if we read this number of chapter 11 without preconceptions, we will find not only that it does not contradict this preamble nor the Formula of the Institute, but that it explains how even the universities are also principally for the formation of the scholastics of the Society.

It should be remembered, above all, that the distinction between the concepts of "college" and of "university" was not as clear-cut in the time of Ignatius as it was to become later in the Society's history. At that time "college" simply meant a center for the study of humanities and "university" a center for higher studies. The university for Ignatius also covered studies in humanities, and in the colleges not only "humane letters" but also "some advanced subjects" could be taught ([392]). In fact, philosophy was taught in quite a few of the colleges at Paris and two of them (the

31   Form. Inst., no. 8.

Sorbonne and Navarre) had chairs of theology. These were the most important differences: a university was considered to be a *studium generale*, to which students came from various regions, while a college was considered to be a center for more local studies; a university also had some higher faculty (not necessarily several as would be required nowadays), which would have been rather exceptional in a college; most important of all, a university could confer academic degrees with the right to teach anywhere (*ius ubique docendi*), a privilege which a college lacked.

This supposed, the first number of chapter 11 ([440]) explains why the Society undertakes the government of some universities. Charity is the sole motive: zeal for the glory of God. The same charitable purpose inspiring the acceptance of colleges in order to increase the number of laborers in the Lord's vineyard, as we saw in the Formula of the Institute, led to the establishment within them of schools open to the public "for the improvement in learning and in living not only of our own members but even more of those from outside the Society." To put it in other words, so that not only our own scholastics may be edified and helped—as chapter 7 says ([392])—but those from outside the Society may also be benefited by the system.[32] But the ambit of charity continues to expand. The effectiveness of this edification in learning and life can be extended by accepting universities—for three reasons: because it is customary that more branches, especially higher ones, are taught in them; because more students come to them; and because they are able to grant academic degrees giving the right to teach elsewhere. Clearly the first and third reasons at least are of as much value for outsiders as for scholastics of the Society.[33]

So there is no contradiction between chapter 11 and the preamble. The Society takes charge of some universities, as it takes charge of colleges, in order to form young scholastics through whom it can be preserved and increased ([308]). But just as in the case of the colleges, the Society did not want to keep the fruits of teaching jealously restricted, and it shared them with the extern students who wanted to attend its classrooms. The idea was clearly expressed by Nadal after Ignatius' death, by which time the development of colleges had become quite notable: "There has never been more than *one class* of college, that in which the scholastics of the Society

---

32 Of course, it cannot mean that externs are supposed to be edified to a greater degree than the scholastics of the Society, but that this edification extends more widely, so that it reaches the outsiders.

33 This interpretation of no. 1 of chapter XI is not our invention. We found it in an anonymous document of the sixteeth century (ARSI *Inst 182*, p. 36) and in the manuscript commentary on the Constitutions by Nicasius Widmann (ARSI *Inst 8a*, p. 274). J. Granero thinks it is obvious (*Manresa*, 34 [1962], 90).

receive their intellectual formation and constitute as it were a seedbed of the professed Society. But from the very nature of things a way was easily opened, and offered the opportunity for a certain extension to those seeking the greater good. Therefore they were not content with colleges in which there were studies but no teaching; they instituted colleges in which they themselves would both exercise a role of teaching open to the public and where in addition they would undertake the government of universities with all the studies pertinent to theologians."[34] Ribadaneira wrote in the same sense in the third Spanish edition of his life of Ignatius when, on the general's orders, he corrected what he had written in the first edition.[35]

III. INSTITUTION OF COLLEGES ([309-332])

1. The Founder ([309-319])

A college supposes a founder, someone who—in the words of the Formula of the Institute—is moved by devotion to build and endow it; although, as a matter of fact, most of the colleges of the Society in the time of Ignatius, especially in Italy, started out poor, without a fixed foundation.

Ignatius considers founders and benefactors only from the point of view of the gratitude that is due to them. Gratitude was one of his most characteristic virtues.[36] In the context here, the point to note is the reason for this gratitude: "It is highly proper for us to do something on our part in return for the devotion and generosity shown toward the Society by those whom the Divine Goodness employs as his ministers to found and endow its colleges" ([309]). The gratitude returns to the Divine Goodness, of which the human benefactors are "ministers" or instruments; but it is also extended to these ministers because of their "devotion" to the Society and the "beneficence" they have toward it. The source, "Founding a College" (*Fundación de colegio*), added another point of view: the good and holy intention of the founders and benefactors in founding and endowing the colleges "out of love of God and for his service and for the salvation of souls."[37]

The Society matches the devotion and generosity of the founders and benefactors by spiritual works, celebrating Masses for them and offering other prayers ([309-317]).

---

34   MHSI Nadal, V, 772.
35   See MI FontNarr, IV, 23-29, 561, 961-962.
36   See Aicardo, *Comentario*, III, 35-68.
37   MI Const, I, 61.

Not satisfied with this, Ignatius declares that founders and benefactors share "in a special way" in all the good works of the Society ([317]). "In a special way" because (as was mentioned in the document granting the share in spiritual works) there is in the Church, the Mystical Body of Christ, a sharing of goods and services among members, in accordance with the grace which the Head shares with each individual; clearly this sharing will be easier and richer in proportion to the strength of the bond of charity.[38]

Furthermore, Ignatius wants some clear demonstration of this gratitude. For that purpose, each year on the anniversary of our taking possession of a college "a wax candle is to be presented to the founder, or to one of his closer relatives, and it should contain his coat of arms or emblems of his devotions" ([312]). The custom seems to be inspired by a privilege which was held by the patrons of some churches: a candle was presented to them as a sign of their right of patronage (*ius patronatus*).[39] This is the explanation for the declaration which explicitly notes that the candle is a sign of the gratitude owed to the founders, not of a *ius patronatus* or any claim against the college or its temporal goods ([314]).[40]

Concluding this matter, Ignatius still adds that the whole Society is especially obligated, out of charity and love, to show founders and benefactors and their families "whatever service it can according to our humble profession, for the divine glory" ([318]).

2. Acceptance of the Foundation ([320-325])

Although at first colleges were not considered to be houses of the Society[41] but merely institutions depending on it, they gradually became more integrated, until they came to be called, as here in [322], "members" of its body—a truly unusual expression, for in the rest of the Constitutions the members of the body of the Society are the individuals (see [511]) and not the dwellings.

At any rate, the colleges have always been something belonging to the Society, founded for the formation of its scholastics. Hence they could not be founded without the consent of the Society; in other words, it is for the Society to decide whether they are to be accepted or not.

In the context here, does Society mean the whole Society or the

---

38 See MI Epp, III, 234-236.
39 See *Summa Silvestrina*, which quotes Panormitanus as saying that the patrons have no right to receive this candle if it has not been expressly agreed upon in the contract of patronage.
40 St. Ignatius was quite familiar with the problems of the *jus patronatus,* for the Loyola family had the patronage of the church of Azpeitia. See MI FontDoc, 15 ff.
41 See Form. Inst., Julius III, no. 8.

general acting in its name? Clearly, it is as determined in the first numbers of the second chapter ([320-325]) in accordance with the norms of the Formula of the Institute.

Here we find the application of a very old principle according to which in this matter of the colleges it is the general's responsibility to preserve them and consequently to accept them, provide them with scholastics, superiors, and teachers, and the like; but should he wish to suppress or alienate them, he would have to have recourse to the Society.[42] This principle later on passed into the Formula of 1550.

In the first place, then, the general has "full authority in the name of the Society" to accept colleges, that is, to accept the foundations offered by benefactors for the purpose of supporting the scholastics of the Society ([320]; see [762]).

If the founder does not impose conditions, there would be no difficulty ([321]). If he wants to attach conditions "which are not *fully* in conformity with the order and manner of proceeding which the Society customarily uses," the general will see whether he can accept them, after having heard "the opinion of the others whom he will judge to have better understanding in these matters" ([321]) as well as the opinion of his assistants ([441]).

These conditions may be of a pastoral nature, for example, that the college should have a parish, or a chaplaincy with obligatory Masses ([324]), or confessors or preachers ([398]). They may be of an academic nature: that the college should have a certain number of teachers, particular subjects, and the like (see [325, 398-399, 441-442]). The norm given to the general points in two directions. First, he must keep in mind the gratuity of the spiritual ministry (see [565]) and also of the teaching ([478]). It is principally for this reason that "curacies of souls, obligations to celebrate Masses, and similar duties" should not be accepted in the colleges. Another reason is added in the case of houses: the freedom necessary for the "mission" (see [324, 588-589]). Therefore in the colleges, where residence is more stable than in the houses, some small obligation to say Masses may be accepted which is not proportioned to the assigned fixed revenue ([325]); the lack of proportion keeps it from being a recompense.

Since it is "so proper to our profession not to accept any temporal remuneration for the spiritual ministries in which we employ ourselves according to our Institute to aid our fellowmen" ([398]), gratuity is also the reason for not accepting obligations to supply a preacher or a confessor, or even a lecturer in theology, when founding colleges ([398]). Theology is expressly excluded, since its teaching is more appropriate to our Institute.

---

42   See MI Const, I, 215.

Ignatius sometimes agreed with regard to secular subjects, in the case of well-founded colleges where for this very reason the income had less the character of a salary.[43] In the universities it is clear that, upon taking charge of a faculty, the Society obliges itself to teach the appropriate subjects, including theology ([399]).[44]

The second point the general must keep in mind is not to accept these conditions too readily, but "consulting his assistants, he should take care that he does not burden the Society" ([442]). Furthermore, if the Society "should find itself burdened" with the conditions the general has accepted, "it can bring the matter up in a general congregation and decree that the college be abandoned, or that the burden should be lightened" ([321]).

For "closing" or "alienating" colleges or houses (here "alienate" does not mean specifically transferring the ownership but simply abandoning what was accepted),[45] the general needs the consent of the Society ([322]). However, he can obtain this consent in writing, without the need to convoke a general congregation ([323]).[46] In the Formula of the Institute this is considered to be a serious matter, and in order to underline its importance our text here speaks of its being like "severing a member" from the body of the Society ([322]).

3. Ownership, Administration, and Usufruct ([326-332]

Once the foundation of a college, or the building with its founded property, has been accepted, questions arise about the ownership of the property, its administration, use, and usufruct.

The question of ownership is discussed. Nadal always held that the subject of ownership of all the colleges of the Society was the whole Society or the "professed Society," the coadjutors being included in this expression.[47] Ignatius, in the documents prior to the Constitutions, and also in a later one, showed he had a contrary opinion, namely, that each college is the owner of its goods.[48] In the preparation of the final text of the

---

43   See MI Epp, XI, 296-297.

44   No. 3 of the seventh chapter [398] with its declaration [399], found outside the book of the Constitutions, was included here by G. C. I. Polanco would have preferred that they be included in the second chapter.

45   See Nadal, *Scholia*, on no. 322.

46   The Formula of the Institute says, "consilium necessario convocandum." But it adds, "iuxta Constitutionum nostrarum declarationem."

47   See, for example, *Scholia*, on nos. 326, 561 and 554, 562.

48   It is very clear in *Para fundar colegio* (MI Const, I, 52) and in the Formula of the Institute. We said, "also in a later one." He sought to obtain, in the brief *Sacrae religiones* of 1552, that there should be no need for the scholastics in a college to meet in chapter for decisions on contracts about its properties. This would have

Constitutions an effort was made to introduce Nadal's viewpoint. But the sentence which appeared to introduce it was not copied down in the definitive text (intentionally or due to the misunderstanding of the copyist?). Actually nothing is said on this point (see [326]).

The administration, on the other hand, is clear from the beginning, from the Formula of the Institute of 1540. It is in the hands of the Society, which exercises it remotely through the general ([327]) and immediately through the rector ([326]). This administration will be so much the more disinterested insofar as the Society can take nothing of the goods of the college for its own use ([326]).

In fact, the sole users and beneficiaries of the goods of the colleges are the scholastics. In the Formula of the Institute it is formally stated that it is permitted to have stable income "for studies," for the use and needs of the students, "to provide for the needs of the students." We find this repeated in the Constitutions: "for the use of its scholastics" ([327]), "for the benefit of the students" ([740]).

However, the Constitutions declare that among these "necessities" of the scholastics are included not only the personal support of the scholastics themselves but also that of those others who are necessary for their spiritual and intellectual formation. Those listed are: the rector ([560]), the confessors ([330, 558]), the lecturers or professors ([330, 558, 560]), the administrators ([330]), even some who hold the more burdensome domestic duties ([330, 334, 364]), those who minister in the church by hearing confessions and preaching ([330, 365, 368]), and finally those who look after the external affairs of the colleges ([326]), such as procurators or business agents. Included in a general way are all those who, like the minister and other officals [430], "further the welfare of these colleges" [330].

Furthermore, the Constitutions permit giving food for a day or some little travel money to a Jesuit passing through a college. This is expressly stated in order to remove any scruples one might have, on the one hand, of "acting contrary to the intention of the Apostolic See," which prohibits the Society's use of the fixed income of a college for its own purposes and, on the other hand, of "acting in an inhuman manner" by denying to a brother what would be given to a stranger.

However, Ignatius was very strict on the observance of the Formula of the Institute in this matter. On taking over a college, he would have wanted the scholastics to oblige themselves on oath not to give anything to

no meaning if the goods belonged not to the college but to the Society.

the Society.[49] He used to require that this oath be taken by the rectors of the Roman College and of the Germanicum. He even ordered the community of the Roman house not to dine in these colleges so that their rectors could with greater ease of conscience swear that no one of the house was taking advantage of the goods of the college.[50]

The second chapter concludes with a later constitution (after 1553) which is a cause of surprise. Ignatius, who chose living on alms (see [557]) as the type of "evangelical poverty" for the Society, does not want the colleges to receive or ask for alms, except in special circumstances. The reason is "for the greater edification of the people" ([331]). The situation of the houses of the Society, which have no fixed income whatsoever, is quite different from that of the colleges which are endowed with revenues. In the latter, seeking alms could give the impression of avarice. Besides, if the college has schools open to students who are not members of the Society, the alms might appear as a certain recompense for the teaching given them.[51]

IV. THE SCHOLASTICS

1. *Requisite Qualifications ([333-338])*

We said that the colleges in the universities of that time, as in Paris for example, were charitable or pious foundations for the support of poor students, those receiving a scholarship, although some rich students who paid for their board were also accepted. Something similar may be said of the colleges of the Society.

The students or scholastics for whose support and instruction the Society accepts colleges must have these qualifications ([333]):

(1) They ought to be without the impediments mentioned in Part I and be "such subjects that they give reasonable hope that they will turn out to be fit laborers in the vineyard of Christ our Lord" ([334]).[52]

(2) They should have "the promise or intention of serving God our Lord in the Society" ([338]). However, after taking into account the endowment of the college, if there is not a sufficient number of scholastics who have made this promise or proposal, it would not be against our Institute to admit—with permission from the general and for the time that

---

49 See MI Const, I, 327.
50 MI FontNarr, I, 870.
51 See MI Epp, IV, 99; V, 111.
52 See MI Const, I, 188, no. 9.

seems good to him—other poor students who do not have this intention of entering the Society and even an occasional rich student able to pay his own expenses (as with the boarders [*portionistae*]) of the colleges of Paris) ([338]).[53]

(3) Those who wanted to enter the Society could be either candidates who are admitted to probation in the same college (see [71]), or novices sent from the houses to the colleges before finishing their novitiate and probations ([337]), or approved scholastics who have already taken their first vows with the promise or vow of entering the Society in order to be professed or formed coadjutors ([121, 336]).

2. Preservation of their Health and Spiritual Welfare ([339-350])

Once a college has been established, the young scholastics who have entered it have to be formed. However, prior to formation and as its foundation comes the preservation of bodily health and spiritual welfare; the fourth chapter treats of this preservation.

a. Health

As regards health and external matters, the reader is referred to the second chapter of Part III. Only three points are emphasized here, as more appropriate for the time of studies: abstaining from study when it could be harmful to health (for example, immediately after meals), sufficient sleep, and moderation in mental labor ([339]).

b. Spiritual Welfare: General Principles

The treatment of spiritual welfare begins by making a distinction between two classes of students. As we saw ([337]), some of them are still novices who either have been admitted into the Society in the same college or have been sent to the college before finishing their novitiate. For the latter, also with regard to spiritual matters, we simply refer again to Part III: "The same order of procedure will be used with those who are received in the colleges, as long as they are still going through probations, as that which is observed with those who are received in the houses" ([340]).

For the others, the approved scholastics, before everything else a general principle is laid down: two extremes are to be avoided. On the one hand, "care must be taken that through fervor in study they do not grow cool in their love of true virtues and of religious life" ([340]). Ignatius was deeply concerned about this point. As Polanco put it—in a way that brings

---

53   See ibid., 188-191, no. 22.

out the contrast—when Ignatius saw that a scholastic was suited for studies but studies were not suited for him, because he advanced in learning but not in spirit, he would pull him out of studies to do other work.[54]

On the other hand, "during that time [of studies] there will not be much place for mortifications and long prayers and meditations." The reason is simply this: since the demands of intellectual and pastoral training "in a certain way require the whole man," the scholastic who "with a pure intention of the divine service" commits himself to this work of his formation makes of himself a total sacrifice which "will be not less but rather more pleasing to God our Lord" than the mortifications, prayers, and long meditations already mentioned ([340]), "since it results from a more vehement and forceful charity."[55]

c. Duration and Manner of Prayer ([342-345])

Having established this principle, the author now gets down to the practical application, whereupon it comes as a surprise to us that Ignatius, who has undoubtedly been one of the most outstanding teachers of prayer in modern times, and especially of mental prayer through his *Spiritual Exercises*, prescribes only one hour of prayer for scholastics, apart from weekly confession and communion and daily Mass. This hour includes the two examinations of conscience, at noon and at night, thereby reducing the time to half an hour. This half hour is not for mental prayer but devoted to the recitation of the "Hours of Our Lady" (the Little Office) "and other prayers according to the devotion of each individual, until the hour is completed" ([342]). It is only in the Declaration that we find a concession that "at times" some of the scholastics who are not obliged to recite the Divine Office may substitute for the recitation of the Office of Our Lady "meditations and other spiritual exercises" ([343], see [345]).

Our perplexity will increase if we examine the way in which this norm was formulated. In the source, the "Constitutions of the Colleges," Polanco —perhaps in an effort to find a *via media* among the differing customs of the various colleges[56]—had assigned two times a day for prayer: one for

---

54 See MI Epp, III, 503.
55 MI Epp, IV, 127. However, it may be noted that in text A St. Ignatius removed the comparison. He erased "más" (more) and wrote "mucho grato" (very pleasing). Later on Polanco restored the comparison, strengthening it by the expression "no menos antes más" (not less but rather more). No doubt he would not have done this without reference to St. Ignatius, who, of course, later approved the composition.
56 See MHSI MonPaed, 1st edit., pp. 78-79, nos. 2, 3, 5 (with the notes); Leturia, *Estudios ignacianos*, II, 198-199 (although not all the statements or conclusions do

oral prayer, during which the scholastics, according to the days of the week, would recite the office either of the Virgin or of the dead or of the Holy Cross, and another for mental prayer for "those capable," which would last for three quarters of an hour or an hour.[57] One or two examinations of conscience were added.[58] This resulted in a total of an hour and a half or two hours, while Ignatius had always taught that an hour was enough for the scholastics.[59] So the first texts of the Constitutions reduced all to an hour, which could be spent in vocal or mental prayer, or in spiritual reading, in the measure helpful to each individual and according to the advice of the confessor.[60]

Ignatius, after having corrected with his own hand these norms in text A, erased them in order to write what we now have. He did not want to leave the question undecided. As a general rule the hour was to be spent in reciting the Office of Our Lady and in making the two examinations of conscience and, if time remained, in other prayers according to each one's devotion. However, he added that "they will do all this according to the arrangements and judgment of their superiors, whom they oblige themselves to obey in place of Christ our Lord" ([342]). Those who were unable to read, as was then the case with some of the temporal coadjutors, were to recite the rosary or chaplet of our Lady instead of her office ([344]). This is the general norm for everybody. In particular cases it may be permitted that this time assigned for oral prayer could be spent in mental prayer, having regard to greater spiritual progress and keeping in view the devotion of the scholastic and also that of the founder, and circumstances of persons, times, and places ([344, 345]).[61]

To understand this attitude of Ignatius, we need above all to keep in mind—as Nadal observes[62]—that there is question here only of scholastics "who are in studies," or in a period of intellectual formation, not of novices nor of formed religious to whom reference is made in Part VI ([582]).

---

seem legitimate to us).

57   MI Regulae, 221-222, nos. 14-15.

58   Ibid., 220-221, no. 12.

59   See MI FontNarr, I, 676-677, no. 256; Epp, II, 585.

60   See MI Const, II, 178 and 410 (critical apparatus).

61   A sentence in no. 343 is obscure in the definitive text due to the omission of an "etc." and to a change in punctuation and the substitution of the word *pero* (but) for the word *para* (for). Text A (written by St. Ignatius) said: "La hora determinada tomándose, poco más o menos, para las Horas de nuestra Señora, *etc., para* los escolares . . . se podría mudar" (Taking the determined hour, a little more or less, for the recitation of the Hours of our Lady, etc., in the case of scholastics it could be changed).

62   *Scholia*, on no. 342.

Secondly, there are two distinct problems here: the time, and the method of prayer of the scholastics.

The duration of one hour, or of one half hour if we subtract the two examinations of conscience, seems short to us now. At that time it seemed even shorter, especially in Spain where we find Granada, for instance, writing: "Less than an hour and a half, or two hours, is but a short time for prayer, because more than a half hour is spent tuning the guitar and calming the imagination and all the rest of the time is needed to enjoy the fruit of prayer."[63]

It should be noted that Ignatius fixed this norm for the approved scholastics who had passed through the "experiences" of the novitiate, during which time they laid down "the proper foundation of abnegation in themselves" ([307]). He was profoundly convinced that a person of mortification and self-abnegation could pray better in a quarter of an hour than an unmortified person could in two hours. Hence, in a conversation on this very point which took place on November 22, 1554, with Nadal and Câmara, the latter says that Ignatius "put all the stress on the supposition that this mortification and abnegation was present." Câmara added: "Thus we see that Father sets great store by all the elements of the Society, such as the indifference which is presupposed, the examination following the probations through which they pass, and the testimony of approval which ought to remain after them; and no store by prayer unless it springs which proceeds from these things."[64]

One may add Nadal's observation that the scholastics had made the month of the Exercises and one supposed that they had emerged from them so inclined to prayer and devotion that there is more need for restraint than exhortation.[65]

With regard to the method of prayer: as we saw, apart from the examinations of conscience, the daily prayer is as a general norm reduced to oral prayer (recitation of our Lady's office or rosary, with other prayers according to personal devotion); first of all we may note that this is an indication of the esteem in which Ignatius, along with St. Teresa of Avila, held this form of prayer.[66] Of course, like Teresa, he meant what Nadal calls "perfect oral prayer," that is, oral prayer which also involves mental

---

63   L. de Granada, *Libro de la oración y meditación*, chap. 10, 30.

64   *Memorial*, no. 256; MI FontNarr, I, 677. Here, unless we are mistaken, one must seek the origin of the need to increase time for prayer which the Society felt later on. Once the fervor of the first enthusiasm ceased, this fruit of prayer did not spontaneously arise as in the beginning.

65   See MHSI Nadal, V, 95 and 455; *Pláticas de Coimbra*, 185; MI Regulae, 490-491.

66   See St. Teresa of Avila, *The Way of Perfection*, chap. 30.

prayer.[67] As proof of this we may cite his advice on the recitation of the rosary: "They should be instructed how to *think* or *meditate* about the mysteries which it contains, so that they may take part in this exercise with greater attention and devotion" ([345]).[68] It may be that the second and third methods of prayer in the Exercises are aimed at preparing for this perfect oral prayer rather than at teaching mental prayer.[69] Nadal came to prefer this form to simple mental prayer because God receives through it a fuller worship of mind and body; in support he quotes Psalm 83 (84): "My heart and my flesh cry out for the living God."[70] We may note as well that Francis Borgia, another contemplative and mystic, did not want anyone to oblige himself to spend all the time of prayer in mental prayer.[71]

Our intellectual formation at times puts us in danger of falling into intellectualism, even in our dealings with God. The great advice of Teresa of Avila was: "The important thing is not thinking a lot but loving a lot; so, do whatever moves you more to love."[72] Let us keep in mind that prayer in the deepest sense—what the praying heart is seeking, "that which I want," to use the Ignatian expression which is indeterminate because indescribable[73]—does not consist in reflection or discourse, just as it does not consist in reciting a psalm or liturgical text. Both of these forms of prayer are just means for disposing oneself interiorly for the divine communication. In that sense Ignatius wrote to Francis Borgia that "that part"—or rather, that method of prayer—is "much better for any individual, where God our Lord *communicates Himself the more* through His holiest gifts and spiritual graces."[74]

The second thing we should note is the realism of Ignatius. Not everybody is capable of reflection or speculative discourse, due either to natural temperament or physical infirmity and debility. In one of his letters to the nun Teresa Rejadell, Ignatius told her: "Every meditation in which the intellect labors, wearies the body. There are other meditations, orderly and restful, which are soothing for the intellect and not tiring for inferior areas of the mind; they do not have either an exterior or interior drive, and neither do they tire the body but rather give it repose."[75] Calveras,

---

67 MHSI Nadal, V, 478.
68 This first part of declaration C is also wholly in the hand of St. Ignatius.
69 *SpEx*, nos. 251-260.
70 MHSI Nadal, V, 478; see IV, 323; *Pláticas de Coimbra*, 189.
71 See MHSI Nadal, III, 487. Partly for accommodation to the Constitutions, but partly also because it is more in accord with reason.
72 *Interior Castle*, IV, chap. 1.
73 *SpEx*, no. 76.
74 MI Epp, II, 236.
75 MI Epp, I, 108.

when editing this letter, refers to the three methods of prayer in the Spiritual Exercises.[76]

We have noted the realism of Ignatius. It was during the conversation with Nadal and Câmara about the prayer of the scholastics that he made the well-known comment: "In spiritual matters there is no greater error than the desire to govern others by the yardstick of one's own experience." Câmara adds that Ignatius said this on account of the long hours that he himself had given to mental prayer.[77] In fact, he was spending up to seven hours in prayer at Manresa and, even with that, according to Câmara's testimony, he spent at least two consecutive hours in mental prayer after Mass.[78]

The quotation—from the passage of Câmara's *Memorial*—closes with the following words: "In that way Father greatly praised prayer, as I have many times observed, especially that prayer made by having God continually before one's eyes."[79]

This last sentence leads us into the third reflection that ought to be made on this question. Ignatius assumed that the scholastics would be living the life of prayer as taught in Part III, ([288]), as they were taught in the novitiate: "seeking God in all things." Or better, that they would be living the life of prayer as taught in the Contemplation to Attain Love, and that in response to the love of God as present they would also be living constantly in the spirit of the oblation: "Take, Lord, and receive." The reply that Ignatius gave to the scholastic Antonio Brandão in June of 1551 is enlightening. Brandão had asked: "In what way could one exercise himself the better in meditation so that it would be in accordance with our vocation?" Ignatius replied: "Bearing in mind the purpose of studies, which prevent the scholastics from spending long periods in meditation (see [340]), beyond the exercises they already have for making progress in virtue— daily Mass, an hour for reciting the Office of Our Lady and so on, examinations of conscience, and confession and communion every eight days (see [342])—they can exercise themselves in seeking the presence of our Lord in all things: conversing, walking, seeing, tasting, hearing,

---

76   *Ejercicios espirituales, Directorio y Documentos* (Barcelona 1958), p. 285. Note the different usage of Valencia, before the Constitutions were promulgated. There the norm was mental prayer in the morning on a mystery of the life of Christ, and in the evening on the divine benefits or the Passion. Anyone who was not capable of meditating was told to recite the rosary. See EppMixt, I, 415; MonPaed, 1st edit., 78-79, nos. 2-3.

77   *Memorial*, no. 256; MI FontNarr, I, 677.

78   *Memorial*, no. 179; MI FontNarr, I, 637.

79   *Memorial*, no. 256; MI Font Narr, 677.

understanding, and all activity; for it is indeed true that His Divine Majesty is in all things, by presence and power and essence. And this manner of meditating, finding our Lord in all things, is easier than raising ourselves up to abstract divine truths, making ourselves present to them with difficulty. This good exercise—by disposing us—will bring about great visitations from the Lord, even within a short prayer. Moreover, the scholastics can exercise themselves by offering very often to our Lord their studies and tasks, recalling that we accept them out of love for Him, putting aside our own tastes so that we may serve His Majesty in some way, helping those for whom he died. We should examine ourselves about these two exercises."[80]

d. Renewal of Vows ([346-347])

Another very effective means of preserving the spiritual life of the scholastics is the renewal of their vows. Originally the main purpose of this practice was so that they could recall their obligation to serve God in the Society and "confirm themselves more solidly in their vocation" ([346]), and so that at the same time the Society would have a greater guarantee of their perseverance. The novelty of the simple vows made this especially necessary at the time, all the more so since during the period when the Constitutions were being composed scholastics were not obliged to take more than the vow of entering the Society.[81]

In his *Industrias* Polanco shows that he was not unaware that there was question here of a new institution, not customary in other religious orders. But he adds that it was also a novelty to have young students in this manner with only simple vows.[82] However, Ignatius did not introduce this practice without seeking advice. This is clear from the extant account of the consultation with Egidio Foscarari, O.P., Master of the Sacred Palace and later bishop of Modena; with Robert Wauchop, archbishop of Armagh and formerly professor of theology at Paris; and with the canonist James del Pozzo, then dean of the Rota and later a cardinal. The response was affirmative. Foscarari found a basis for the practice in the Lord's renewal of His alliances and covenants with the people of Israel.[83]

Fostering devotion became another objective of the renewal of vows: "for greater devotion" ([346]).[84] Hence the choice of occasions "in which

---

80   MI Epp, III, 510; see 502.
81   See MHSI Nadal, IV, 97; MI Regulae, 218, no. 4.
82   See MHSI PolCompl, II, 738-739.
83   MHSI Nadal, IV, 97.
84   These words were added by Polanco in the rough draft of the definitive text.

men are more disposed toward God,"[85] such as Easter and Christmas or the days preceding and following these feasts ([346, 347]).[86]

Later on, a triduum of preparation was introduced as a means of further increasing devotion. The first time this seems to have been done was at the beginning of 1557 in the Roman College. At that time Nadal gave three fine talks which made a great impression on the scholastics.[87] However, this triduum was not established by law until 1608.[88]

e. Outside the House ([349-350])

The fourth chapter concludes with some norms for preserving the spirit of the scholastics outside the house. While they must leave the house, in particular to attend classes in the university, they should not go alone but with the companion designated by the rector ([349]), so that they can mutually support each other ([350]). Outwardly their bearing should be modest, while interiorly recollected ([349]), as in the norm stated in [250]. We would say, in the words of a contemporary regulation of the Roman residence, that they are "to show devotion within and modesty without."[89] Of necessity they will have to converse with other students of the university, but it should only be about academic matters or spirituality. Ignatius indicated the apostolic motive in his own hand by the closing words: "that thereby they may find help in everything toward greater divine glory" ([349]).

3. Intellectual Formation ([351-391])

The central theme of Part IV is the intellectual and pastoral formation of the scholastics. Two chapters deal with intellectual formation, one (the fifth) on the subjects which ought to be studied ([351-359]) and another (the sixth) on the means to be used for making progress in studies ([360-391]).

In the constitutions on the universities the corresponding chapters are 12, 13, 14, and 15, dealing with subject matter, teaching methods, textbooks, courses and degrees ([446-480]).

---

85 *Industrias*: PolCompl, II, 739.
86 See Nadal, *Scholia*, on no. 347.
87 See MHSI PolCompl, II, 593-594 (diary of the scholastic Geeraerts); MI FontNarr, II, 1-10. On the rite of renewal, see MHSI Nadal, IV, 611.
88 We shall speak of declaration E [348] in Part V, to which it properly belongs.
89 MI Reg, 162, no. 12.

a. What They Should Study

Subjects

Before everything else the directive principle of the whole treatise is laid down; as always it is drawn from the objective:

The purpose of studies in the Society is not the acquisition of learning itself, nor theological reflection, nor, much less, scholarly research. "The end of the learning which is acquired in this Society is with God's favor to help the souls of its own members and those of their fellowmen" ([351]).

It was in order "to be able to help souls" that Ignatius decided to study;[90] as he explained later in the Examen, "to fulfill the function of sowing and dispensing the divine word and of attending to the spiritual aid of the neighbors, it is expedient to possess a sufficiency of sound learning" ([109]).

But what is most remarkable is that this directive norm is applied not only to the schools of the scholastics of the Society but equally to its universities. In these also the purpose of studies is "to aid our fellowmen to the knowledge and love of God and to the salvation of their souls" ([446]).

This purpose gives us the criterion for determining the subjects which the scholastics of the Society are to study. Those listed in [351] constitute the general norm. It can be summed up as a formation at once humanistic, philosophical, and theological.

Everything is aimed at forming a priest apostle. We shall find this confirmed more explicitly further on. In this context the following paragraph by Nadal is enlightening: "Imitating the apostles, to whom the Lord gave the gift of tongues and prophecy and the teaching function (or *magisterium*) of the Church, and this by gift and miracle, we hope in the Lord that He will give us a similar grace: that we will be prophets, that is, interpreters of the Scriptures, and will know languages in order to be able to do so well; and so make such progress in philosophy and theology that we may be able to teach others and rescue them from darkness, to the greater glory of the Lord."[91]

This being supposed, the constitution notices in its usual flexible way that greater importance should be given to whatever helps more to the end in view, namely, spiritual help to our neighbor "with circumstances of times, places, persons, and other such factors taken into account, according to what seems expedient in our Lord to him who holds the principal

---

90   *Autobiog*, no. 50.
91   *Pláticas de Coimbra*, p. 128, no. 14.

charge," namely, the general.

Nowadays it is common to give great importance to changes in the "circumstances of the times." Ignatius too was aware of that need. When dealing with humanistic studies, for instance, he always tended to emphasize their special importance for his age (see [447]). Writing to the young Gerard van Werden, he told him: "Humanistic literature is very important for helping souls in our times, especially in the northern regions. For ourselves theology could be enough, without so much Cicero or Demosthenes. Nevertheless, as Paul made himself all to all, in order to win all, so our Society, in the desire to help souls, picks up these spoils of Egypt ([see 359]) to convert them to the honor and service of God."[92] However, a distinction needs to be made. Obviously, the study of Greco-Roman authors does not now have the importance it had in the time of the Renaissance. Nevertheless, knowledge of the classical languages, especially Latin, continues and will always continue to be an indispensable instrument for a serious study of the sources of revelation and of patristic literature and medieval theology.

As to the "circumstances of persons," the principle of specialization mentioned in declaration C of the fifth chapter is worth noting. Not every scholastic could be eminent in all the subjects mentioned. Some way then has to be found so that, while general formation is assured, a man who cannot distinguish himself in all subjects ought to try to do so in one of them—taking into account age, ability, the man's own inclination, and the common good hoped for from him, that is, the apostolate for which he is being considered ([355]).[93]

In detail, what each scholastic of the Society ought to study is left to the discretion of superiors ([355]). Even before entering they are asked "whether they will allow themselves to be directed in regard to what they should study, and how, and how long" ([124]). The only addition here as a norm for superiors is that when someone has aptitude, the more complete his humanistic, philosophical, and theological formation, the better ([355]).

All this is said with reference to the colleges for the scholastics of the Society. Moving on to the universities, we might expect to find a wider gamut of subjects and branches. But this is not so. What we find in chapter twelve, on "the branches to be taught in the universities of the Society," is exactly the same.

---

92   MI Epp, VIII, 618.
93   Nadal, in the corresponding scholion, does not understand this declaration as about specialization but as the exclusive study of one subject, leaving aside the others. But the motivation adduced proves our interpretation.

Theology dominates. This is what is mainly insisted on, for it is "the means most suitable" for the end of the studies in the Society—which is, as already mentioned, "to aid our fellowmen to the knowledge and love of God and to the salvation of their souls" ([446]).

All the other branches have a relative value. They are taught and studied in view of their relation to theology—humanistic literature, for example, because "it is required for the learning and use of theology (especially in these times)" ([447]). As to practice, we have already spoken of the "circumstances of the times," but the constitution also takes into account adaptation to local conditions in the apostolate. It adds that, according to the regions, it will be possible to teach Chaldaean or Aramaic, Arabic, Indian, and so forth ([447]).

The study of philosophy also is related to theology, since it "disposes the intellectual powers" for theology and is "useful for its perfect under-standing and use" ([450]).

On the other hand, there is a prohibition in the universities of the Society against "the study of medicine and law, since they are more remote from our Institute." Or at least, if a university governed by the Society has to include these branches of learning, "the Society will not undertake this teaching through its own members" ([452]); it will be in charge of others.

To understand the background here we must remember that the universities at that time had four faculties: one, arts (comprising grammar and philosophy), which was considered "lower"; and three "higher" faculties: theology, medicine, and law. Almost all the universities had these four faculties, though Bologna was famous for its faculty of law, Salerno for that of medicine, Paris for theology. The law faculty trained lawyers; that of medicine, doctors; that of theology, churchmen-theologians.

Apart from the faculty of arts—always required, at least theoretically, with the preparatory character of our intermediate studies—the Society chose theology alone for its universities from the three superior faculties and expressly rejected the other two. It is worth quoting the words of both Nadal and Olave on this point. Nadal: "[The Jesuits] took on the govern-ment of some universities with all the studies which correspond to a theologian."[94] Olave: "In all the universities which the Society will found, the disciplines which can help and perfect a theologian will be taught. . . . The teaching of civil law and of medicine will not be permitted in these universities. This is because of the end in view: to instruct and form suitable ministers of the Church, not only religious but also seculars."[95] It

94   MHSI Nadal, V, 772, no. 186; see 194, no. 171.
95   MHSI MonPaed, 165-166, nos. 1 and 7.

should be noted that what is said here about the universities was extended by Nadal to the colleges, although theology was not taught in them: in all of them "learning which can serve theology" (*litteras quae ad theologiam conferre valeant*) was to be taught.[96]

Plan of Studies

We will not delay on the curriculum or the courses; enough to say that Jesuit universities followed the procedure of the university of Paris: three and a half years of philosophy ([473]) and six years of theology ([476]).[97] We have already seen that the Society wished to follow in its teaching the method of Paris (*modus parisiensis*), which—in the words of Nadal—was "most exact and fruitful."[98] However, there is here a notable difference. At the university of Paris, after the six years of theology only the degree of bachelor (*baccalaureus*) was granted; to become a master or doctor in theology the new "baccalaureus" had to continue at the university for another six or eight years, teaching, debating, and preaching. In the universities of the Society, according to chapter 16, the doctorate was granted immediately after the six years of study and academic trials ([476]).

For the scholastics of the Society, the time to be given to each one of these branches is not fixed nor when they are to move on from one to another. All is left to the discretion of the rector, "who will consider and decide it by means of a suitable examination" ([357]); that is to say, when the different examinations continued to show that a scholastic had obtained the result intended in each branch and could pass on to another, without —as Polanco said in the *Industrias*—letting him "strain or spend too long a time in studies."[99] It is clear that if someone is to receive a degree (see [390]), then he will have to take the courses required for it by the university. In Part V we shall also see that for the profession of four vows, among other things "the study of theology for four years" is required ([518]).

---

96   MHSI Nadal, V, 193, no. 170; see 194, no. 171.
97   See H. Rashdall, *The Universities of Europe in the Middle Ages* (London 1936), I, 404, 474-486; Ch. Thurot, *L'organisation de l'enseignement dans l'université de Paris au Moyen-Age* (Besançon 1850), pp. 15-159.
98   MHSI Nadal, V, 738.
99   *Industria* 4ª, no. 25

Doctrine

"The doctrine which they ought to follow in each branch should be that which is safer and more approved, as also the authors who teach it" ([358]).

This norm has given rise to a good deal of question and not a few legislative provisions. To understand the norm, it is helpful to remember —as the historian Charles Thurot remarks—that at that time science was not taught directly in itself but by way of the explanation of books which drew their authority from their authors. Roger Bacon formulated the principle in this way: "When the textbook is known, all that pertains to the branch of study, the object of which is this textbook, is known." One did not speak of "giving a course" or "taking a course," but rather of "reading a book" or "hearing a book read or expounded."[100] We can see the same usage in the Constitutions, in the parallel place of the second section, for the title of chapter 14 is: "The books which should be expounded."

So, the word "doctrine" in the passage of the fifth chapter to which reference has been made does not mean the different philosophical or theological opinions or propositions as, for instance, the principle of individuation or the distinction between essence and existence, but the book which is proposed as a base for the lecture (*praelectio*). For that reason the phrase "and authors who teach it" is added in explanation ([358]).

Presupposing this principle, we may note the following applications. For the *praelectio* in theology, along with Sacred Scripture, we find "the scholastic doctrine of St. Thomas," that is, the *Summa Theologica*, proposed. This is not as obvious as might be thought, for throughout the Middle Ages the textbook in the schools of theology had been the *Liber Sententiarum* of Peter Lombard.[101] Ignatius and his companions studied in the Dominican convent of St.-Jacques at Paris where, from the time of Pierre Crockaert, Thomas Aquinas was taught.[102] There they had learned to love the Angelic Doctor and had found that his "doctrine" was "safer," of an orthodoxy free from all suspicion, for it was "approved by the Apostolic See."[103]

The books of Greco-Roman classical literature, as we said, were thought to be indispensable for an education in the humanities during that epoch of the Renaissance. The norm given here is that "nothing immoral should

---

100 Ch. Thurot, op. cit. in note 97, pp. 65-66.
101 On the introduction of the *Summa* of St. Thomas as a textbook, see R. García Villoslada, *La universidad de París* (Rome 1938), pp. 279-319.
102 See ibid., pp. 261 and 276-277; Schurhammer, *Franz Xaver*, I, 235-238; MHSI Nadal, V, 280 (critical apparatus).
103 Polanco, *Industria* 4ª no. 15. It seems that for this statement Polanco bases himself on the Dominican Constitutions, Dist. II, chap. 14, dcl. b.

be lectured on" ([359]), no book "which contains matters harmful to good habits of conduct, unless previously expurgated of objectionable matters and words" ([468]); and if some books, such as Terence, cannot be expurgated at all, it is better they not be lectured on, "in order that the nature of the contents may not injure the purity of minds" ([469]).

The example of Terence is significant because the humanists of that time gave this author a great importance, greater than he merits. But when Ignatius saw the difficulty of expurgation, as explained by de Freux, he decided that the author should simply be omitted.[104] The Society has been criticized for these editions of expurgated, and consequently mutilated, classics. But this procedure was also advised by the humanist Luis Vives[105] and, in general, Christian humanists were against putting these books in the hands of the young except on a selective basis.

The norm for other books is, if possible, even more severe: it excludes not only books which are bad from the point of view of orthodoxy or morality, but also "those which are suspect" ([464]); even further, works of authors who are bad or suspect, even though a particular book might in itself be good ([359, 464]). Two reasons are given for the norm: "lest attachment to the author be acquired" ([359, 465]) and because "it rarely occurs that some poison is not mixed into what comes forth from a heart full of it" ([465]).

Since the French Revolution, modern liberties have accustomed us to look at everything, hear everything, read everything. Consequently, these norms may seem almost childish to us. But how many falls, how many desertions would be avoided, if there were greater control over reading! And also, how many doctrinal errors and lapses in moral judgments!

The objection will be made that, in following these norms for safeguarding the most sound and approved doctrine, scholarly research will be impeded. But the purpose of the studies of the Society, including its universities, is—as we have seen—not the progress of scholarly research but "to help our fellowmen" or, in the phrase of Olave already quoted, is "to instruct and form suitable ministers of the Church."

---

104 See MHSI Chron, II, 214, no. 103.
105 See G. Codina, op. cit. in note 24, pp. 98-99.

b. How They Should Study

Obstacles

The Constitutions do not merely indicate the subject matter and the doctrine to be followed; they also propose in the sixth chapter ([360-391]) "the means by which the scholastics will progress toward learning the aforementioned branches well."

It is remarkable that the first means is not of an intellectual and pedagogical character, but spiritual: "to keep their souls pure and their intention in studying right, by seeking in their studies nothing except the glory of God and the good of souls" and "to beg in prayer for grace to make progress in learning for the sake of this end" ([360]). The source and the first text cited as basis the words of Scripture: "Wisdom will not enter a deceitful soul" and "a holy and disciplined spirit will flee from deceit."[106]

It is not a question of seeking to obtain an infused knowledge, nor is there a confusion between the natural and the supernatural orders; the object is the removal of impediments of a moral order. There is no doubt that sin and passions obscure the mind and incapacitate it even for finding out natural truth, much more for the truths of faith, the object of theology. Furthermore, from a psychological point of view, insincerity and a self-centered intention lead to disquiet and a lack of balance, both of which are a hindrance to work, especially work of an intellectual nature.

To this must be added application to study: "They should keep their resolution firm to be thoroughly genuine and earnest students"; this will not come about unless they "persuade themselves that they cannot do anything more pleasing to God our Lord than to study with the intention mentioned above" ([361]). The reason for this was indicated in the source and in the first text: The act of studying takes its inspiration from obedience and charity.

Other obstacles to study which must be avoided are: (a) excessive devotions and mortifications (we know that Ignatius, early on in his new life, found that spiritual fervor was an impediment to study);[107] (b) "burdensome" household tasks; (c) spiritual ministries with neighbors: in order to help them better later on, the Constitutions say, "it is wise to postpone exercises such as these until after the years of study" ([362]).

The first text had this addition: "neither the one nor the other will they do well, and it is better to do the first well in order to do the other later."

---

106 Wis. 1:4-5.
107 See *Autobiog*, nos. 54-55.

Order

With these obstacles removed, the second means for progress is to preserve the proper order in studies. Not having done this at Barcelona and Alcalá, Ignatius had to repeat his studies on arrival at Paris.[108] And it was precisely the college of Montaigu where he went that was the first or among the first to divide students into "classes" according to the each one's level of learning.[109]

For the scholastics of the Society, it is considered essential that they acquire a good foundation in Latin before attending lectures on philosophy, in philosophy before moving on to theology, and in scholastic theology before beginning the study of positive theology ([366]).

This last element may seem surprising but, as Nadal points out,[110] without a theological method the reading of the positive doctors may lead to errors. Once a theological framework has been acquired through the study of scholastic theology, it will be easier to discern the doctrine of other authors.

This too explains the difficulties which were raised about the study of "the languages in which Scripture was written or into which it was translated," namely, Hebrew, Greek, and Aramaic. The matter is left to the discretion of the superior. One of the aims in such study must be the defense of the Vulgate ([367]). "It would be good for [those who learn these languages] to have their degrees in theology or at least to be fairly well versed in it; however, if some are seen to be so humble and firm in their faith that in their cases nothing harmful is to be feared from the study of languages, the superior may grant a dispensation" ([368]).

This all springs from an early determination or clarification (*antigua determinación*)[111] and originally has even deeper roots in Ignatius' own experience at Paris. Nadal says: "Father Ignatius had seen that the majority in Paris, and had heard that many in Germany, lacking theology, were lost during their study of Greek and gave up the faith to embrace new doctrines."[112] Schurhammer confirms this by reference to many specific examples of members of the humanist party in conflict with the traditional approach defended by the faculty of theology.[113]

---

108 See *Autobiog* no. 73.
109 See G. Codina, op. cit. in note 24, pp. 99-109.
110 *Scholia*, on [366].
111 MI Const, I, 191; see 203, 293-294.
112 *Scholia*, on no. 367.
113 See Schurhammer, *Franz Xaver*, Bk. II, chap. 3, no. 5; G. Codina, op. cit. in note 24, p. 79.

This explains why this norm has been preserved despite seeming to be counter to what is said in the fifth chapter, that the scholastics are to study "the humane letters of different languages" ([351]);[114] and explicitly in the twelfth chapter: "Both the learning of theology and the use of it require knowledge of the Latin, Greek, and Hebrew languages" ([447]).

Of importance here, then, is the principle, and it is of wide and lasting application. The reading of books which may constitute a danger for the faith is not to be permitted except for those who have finished their studies of theology, if they are "moderately" trained in it and know "the interpretations of the holy doctors and of the Church," unless in some particular case it is believed that this reading would not cause any problem because the subject is "humble and firm in the faith."

Pedagogical Methods

Most characteristic of the method of Paris was its pedagogical practice. One author suggests that it could be defined as "an indefatigable activity, an exercise and a practice, a sort of incessant gymnastics of the mind which brings into play in the process of education all the resources and all the faculties of the human person."[115] Polanco summed it up briefly: "in the manner of Paris, with much exercise."[116]

In the sixth chapter we meet all the exercises: after the professor's *lectio* ([369, 374]) there are the repetitions ([374, 375, 459]), disputations ([378-380]), compositions in prose or in verse ([380]), speaking in Latin ([381]), orations ([381]). There is particular stress on the disputations, which were considered as most important. In those days they attracted as much interest as the sporting events of our day and were followed with equal enthusiasm. This explains why our scholastics are advised "to distinguish themselves" not only "by their learning" but also "by their modesty" ([378]).

In the description of these pedagogical methods, the sixth chapter goes into details which are perhaps too concrete. Polanco had already noted this in 1565. The parallel text of the thirteenth chapter treats this subject in a more general way. It only calls for a "method and order" and a certain uniformity in the midst of the varied local conditions; for further particulars

---

114 Perhaps because the contradiction was too blatant, the words "debajo las lenguas se entiende la latina, griega y hebrea" (under the name of languages, Latin, Greek, and Hebrew are understood) in declaration A were erased at the last moment, after 1552.

115 G. Codina, op. cit. in note 24, p. 109.

116 MI Epp, IV, 7.

it refers to the future Plan of Studies (*Ratio Studiorum*) ([453-455]). For that reason, and because it is of less interest for our purpose here, we will not delay further on the question. The principle of lasting value here, and in the method of Paris, can be stated thus: The student ought not to be merely "a listener," a passive recipient of the words and ideas flowing from the lips of the "lecturer"; he must actively take part in his own formation "with much exercise."

In addition to attendance at the disputations and repetitions, the Constitutions add "private and undisturbed study, that the students may better and more profoundly understand the matters treated" ([384-385]). This may be taken perhaps as a correction of the method of Paris. In the timetables of the Paris colleges, such private study was almost impossible. Only by special permission could some students continue studying for one or two hours during the night.[117]

Among the remaining aids to greater progress in studies, it is worth-while to note the following recommendations. Teachers are told that they are not only to be "learned, diligent, and assiduous" but they are also to ensure the proficiency of each one of the students ([369, 450]). If the number of students hinders the teacher from giving this individual care to each one, it is preferable to divide the classes and increase the number of teachers ([457]). The scholastics are to be "regular in going to the lectures, diligent in preparing for them beforehand, in repeating them afterwards, in asking about points they do not understand, and in jotting down what they hear or anything which strikes them as noteworthy" ([374, 376, 389]). Making such extracts was a favorite work method of Polanco. The rector will see to it that everyone does what he ought ([367]): those running too rapidly should be restrained, the negligent stimulated, and the fainthearted encouraged. Furthermore, "if someone is wasting his time, either because he does not care to advance or cannot, it is better to remove him from studies and to let someone else who will make better progress take his place" ([386]).

Finally, the Constitutions deal with examinations and degrees ([390, 478-480]). Not every scholastic is required to graduate. They may do so "for the sole purpose of being better able to help their fellowmen for glory to God" ([390]). But it certainly is required that the three following conditions be fulfilled on the occasion of the conferring of degrees, both in colleges and universities: (1) degrees are to be granted only to "those who after careful examination are found to deserve them"; (2) the door to ambition should be closed by giving no special places to those who receive

---

117 See G. Villoslada, op. cit. in note 101, pp. 44-45 and note 38.

the degrees; (3) poverty should be safeguarded, with the degrees being conferred gratis, banquets and other costly celebrations not being permitted nor money nor gifts accepted; the constitution says: "for according to our institute, our reward should be only Christ our Lord, who is our reward exceedingly great"[118] ([390, 478-480]). Ignatius had experience of the abuses prevalent in his time, particularly in regard to the third point. The excessive expenditures at graduation time in Paris were proverbial: rights demanded by the faculty, gifts to teachers and other professors, splendid banquets. As a result, some of those receiving degrees were in debt for the rest of their lives.[119]

4. Pastoral Formation ([400-414])

Part IV has as its title: "The Instruction of Those Who Are Retained in the Society, in Learning and in Other Means of Helping Their Fellowmen." Intellectual formation was covered in the fifth and sixth chapters; the eighth chapter deals with instruction in the means of helping our fellowmen—what we would nowadays call pastoral formation.

After an introduction on the need for this pastoral formation ([400]), this chapter lists the means of helping their fellowmen in which the scholastics should be instructed. It is to be noted that in all the texts except the last, the order of treatment is the same as in the fourth chapter of Part VII: first, Mass and the sacraments; then preaching, with the Exercises and the teaching of catechism; finally, assisting the dying. But in the last text preaching was put before the administration of the sacraments, immediately after Mass. It does not seem to be a mistake on the part of the copyist because the same order is seen in the Declarations. Perhaps it was intended to indicate the preeminent place which the ministry of preaching has. But it was not suitable to separate it from the other forms of ministry of the word (the Spiritual Exercises and the teaching of catechism), just as Communion ought not to be separated from Mass.

The necessity of this pastoral formation is deduced, as always, from the purpose of studies in the Society, which is—as mentioned several times already—to aid our fellowmen ([351, 446]), "to instruct and form ministers of the Church." Intellectual formation, then, is not enough. The soldier, before entering into combat, has to know how to handle his weapons. Thus the new soldier of Christ, at the end of his studies, must "begin to accustom himself to the spiritual arms he must employ in aiding his fellowmen"

---

118 See Gen. 15:1
119 Thurot, op. cit. in note 97, pp. 62-64 and 156-158; Rashdall, op. cit. in note 97, I, pp. 487-489.

([400]).

We shall not delay too long on each of these means of helping one's fellowmen, as we will be dealing with them in Part VII.

The dominant note here is the practical character which is evident in this concept of pastoral formation.

In the celebration of Mass the scholastics must attend not only to interior understanding and devotion but also to the exterior manner, celebrating in a way that will edify those who attend. From among the variety of ceremonies—in those days before the promulgation of Pius V's Missal—the Roman usage was chosen for the Society. This was done for two reasons: it was more universal, and it was approved in a special way by the Apostolic See ([401]). This is a guide for us when some doubt arises in liturgical celebrations: the usage adopted (or approved) by the Apostolic See.

Preaching.—In the first place, an effort should be made to "learn well the vernacular language" ([402]). In the intellectual formation of that time no attention was paid to the vernacular language; the humanists had no use for it. They were so taken up with Latin that, as a French pedagogue said, the vernacular language served only for conversation with one's mother and with servants.[120] Ignatius, on the contrary, considered the vernacular very important for the apostolic purpose of the Society, for communicating with one's fellowmen through "a pleasing manner of speech" ([157], see [814]) resulting from a good knowledge and use of the language of the region.

In the second place, the scholastic should prepare the subject matter for preaching. Everything is conceived from the practical point of view of a life of mission, without any stable residence. Hence the advice "to have, as matters previously studied and ready at hand, the means which are most useful for this ministry" ([402]), and preferably in summary form "to avoid the need for books" ([404]). The first text added: "to be prepared wherever one finds oneself."

The "useful means" are listed as: (a) the Sunday gospels (in our day they have been tripled); (b) some book of Sacred Scripture (a Gospel or an epistle of Saint Paul) for a series of sacred lectures; (c) material for sermons on morality, that which pertains to vices and their abhorrence, and to the virtues and ways to acquire them ([404]). The primitive text added: "especially what moves men to approach Christ by means of the sacraments of confession and communion, and through prayer."

Moreover, they ought to use every suitable means to perform this office of preaching better and with greater fruit for souls ([402]); for example,

---

120 Mathurin Cordier, cited by G. Codina, op. cit. in note 24, p. 81.

learning the theory, "listening to good preachers," and also reading the speeches of famous orators. Ignatius approved of the scholastics reading Cicero and Demosthenes for this purpose.[121] At the same time they were to practice in the presence of someone capable of correcting them. He also had them declaim out in the open among the ruins of ancient Rome, where Cicero had delivered his famous orations.[122]

With regard to the sacraments, only confession and communion are mentioned; the others—as noted in the sixth *Industria*—"are not so much a part of our profession." Here again, speculative or scholastic knowledge is presumed and this section concentrates on practice, whether it concerns minister or penitent or communicant. This explains the reference to the usefulness of having at hand a list of reserved cases and a brief questionnaire on sins and their remedies ([407]).

For the formation of a director of the Exercises, the path pointed out is first that he have had "experience of them in himself." It does not state that he has to have made them himself but to have experienced personally their value and efficacy. After that he should "acquire experience in giving them," beginning with "some in whose case less is risked" and consulting about the method of procedure with someone more experienced ([408-409]). This is what Câmara did with Ignatius when he, Câmara, was giving the Exercises to Abbot Martinengo, and Vitoria when he gave them to Lorenzo Maggio.[123] But the constitution also demands a speculative knowledge of the Exercises: "each one should know how to give an explanation of them" ([408]). This sentence is of scriptural inspiration, an accommodation of Peter's exhortation to be ever ready to reply to those who ask the reason for our hope, but speaking gently and respectfully.[124] In a somewhat similar manner we must be ready to give information about "this spiritual weapon, which God our Lord has made so effective for his service" ([408]), to all who sincerely desire to know, whether friend or foe. This information has a double purpose: apologetic, since "it gives satisfaction to others"; and apostolic, since "it moves them to desire to be helped by the Exercises" ([409]).

Turning to the teaching of catechism, we shall only note the pedagogical advice given to the scholastics "to adapt themselves to the capacities of children or simple persons" ([410]).

As to the assistance to be given to the dying, this is the only place in

---

121 MI FontNarr, II, 315.
122 Unless Nadal, who gives us the information (V, 827), alludes rather to the Baths of Caracalla, which were near the villa of the Roman College.
123 See Iparraguirre, *Historia de los Ejercicios*, I, p. 150.
124 1 Pet. 3:15.

the Constitutions that deals with the matter ([412]). The practical advice is given in the Declaration, which says: "It is good to have a compendium on the method of helping someone to die well, to refresh the memory when this holy ministry must be exercised" ([413]).

The eighth chapter concludes with a kind of epilogue on the manner of dealing with our neighbors in general ([414]). It is one of the most notable passages in the Constitutions.

The concrete circumstances are noted first. "A member of the Society in his life of mission" has to go to "various parts of the world" and to meet with "a great variety of people." The scholastics need to be prepared for the "inconveniences" or dangers they will encounter under such circumstances, as well as the "opportunities" to be grasped for the greater service of God and the "means" to be used in taking advantage of them.

However, Ignatius does not mean to propose some kind of general formula covering every situation in which they find themselves. That would be neither necessary nor possible, for with such a variety of places, times, and persons "only the unction of the Holy Spirit" and "the prudence which God our Lord communicates to those who trust in His Divine Majesty" can teach the right way of acting in each concrete case.

However, "the gentle arrangement of Divine Providence requires cooperation from his creatures" ([134]). This action of the Holy Spirit does not prevent the scholastics from being given some "suggestions" or counsels which will serve to "open the way." In what manner? A correction made in successive texts of this passage is more enlightening than many commentaries. The primitive text had: "to assist and supply what of itself discretion could not achieve." To these "suggestions" is added the supplementary character of discretion. This phrase was not carried over into the subsequent text. Instead, in the definitive text Polanco wrote: "suggestions which aid and dispose one for the effect which must be produced by divine grace." So there is question of disposing the subject for divine grace, in order that the Holy Spirit may find less hindrance to his action and can more easily act in the Jesuit apostle and guide him.

Polanco composed the "compendium" alluded to here as a help for these varied ministries or means of assisting fellowmen. He wrote a *Brief Directory on the Proper Procedure of the Confessor and the Penitent* (*Breve directorium ad confessarii et confitentis munus rite obeundum*), a directory on the Exercises, a *Method of Helping the Dying* (*Methodus ad eos adiuvandos qui moriuntur*), and "Practical Notes on the Way a Member of the Society of Jesus Can Better Attain its Ends" (*Industrias con que uno de la Compañía de Jesús mejor conseguirá sus fines*)—all of these aimed at being those "suggestions which aid and dispose for the effect which must be produced by divine grace" mentioned in [414].[125]

V. GOVERNMENT OF THE COLLEGES

One of the indications that in Ignatius' mind, at least at the beginning, the colleges were rather institutions constituted in themselves and distinct from the Society proper, although dependent on it, is the fact that he deals with their government in Part IV, chapter ten, instead of leaving the matter for Part IX, the Part concerned with the government of the Society.

The source of this tenth chapter is, as already mentioned, the "Constitutions of the Colleges."[126] The division is clear: who will govern the colleges ([419-422]), what qualities the rector must have ([423]), how he is to perform his function ([424-427]), and with what help ([428-438]). A paragraph is added by way of appendix on the spiritual ministries of the college, the distribution of which depends on the rector ([437-438]).

Apropos of the first and third points, we shall point out what the constitutions of the universities add on particular points in the seventeenth chapter ([490-509]).

1. Those Who Have the Authority ([419-420])

At the university of Paris and in other medieval universities, each college had a director or president in charge; the title varied and he was normally chosen democratically by the members of the college itself.[127] Nevertheless, the founders of the colleges of Paris tended rather to reserve to themselves and their successors the administration of the property and even of the scholarships, or to subject them to a certain patronage. Thus, for instance, the college of Montaigu was subject to the "authority and discretion" (*potestati et discretioni*) of the Carthusian prior;[128] the college of Navarre was under the patronage of the confessor of the king, whose agents

---

125 On these writings of Polanco see J. F. Gilmont, *Les écrits spirituels des premiers jésuites* (Rome 1961), pp. 201-207, nos. 220, 221, 224ᵃ, 225. The Directory of the Exercises was published in MHSI Direct, 274-316; the second *Industrias* in MHSI PolCompl, II, 776-807, and in *Imagen Ignaciana del Jesuita en los escritos de Polanco* (Rome, CIS, Subsidia, 9), pp. 77-122. That there is reference to these "Industrias" in no. 414 by the expression "algunos avisos" (some suggestions) is clear from the source of that number (the first series of *Industrias*), which explicitly refers to them.

126 Part seven, nos. 3-5, 9-12; and for the last number of this chapter, part six: see MHSI Regulae, 239-245.

127 See G. Codina, op. cit. in note 24, pp. 62 and 63.

128 See M. Godet, *La Congrégation de Montaigu* (Paris 1912), p. 162.

administered the revenues.[129] In the Italian universities, however, the colleges had a more independent regime internally.[130]

Ignatius had the problem in mind from the beginning, from the time that the idea of the colleges first appeared in the Formula of the Institute of 1540. Although the colleges were institutions distinct from the Society, they were not to have autonomy. The Society and its general will be fully in charge of their government, superintendence, and administration, in such a way that neither can the scholastics misuse the property nor the Society apply it to its own use.[131] And the almost contemporary document "On Founding a College" prescribed that the founder would leave to the Society the power "to remove or appoint all officials and governors and other persons of such a college."[132]

The idea is repeated here, explicitly by reference to the bulls of the Society, namely, *Regimini militantis* and *Exposcit debitum*, which contain and approve the Formula of the Institute ([419]).

2. *The Rector ([420-427])*

"The administration and in general the execution of this superintendency will be vested in the superior general" ([420]), and the general, by himself or through another such as the provincial, will appoint in each college a rector "who is to have the principal charge of it" ([421]).

We see, then, that the rector is not elected by the members of the college, as in those of Paris, Bologna, and Padua, but appointed by the general. We know of only one occasion, in 1547, when Ignatius allowed the first rectors of the colleges of Gandía and of Valencia to be elected.[133]

As to the title of the one who is to "have the principal charge" in a college, various forms were used in the colleges at Paris: *primarius*, *principalis*, *magister*. In the early documents of the Society we find a certain vacillation. Later on, the title "rector," the most common in the colleges of the Italian universities, prevailed.[134] Properly speaking this means "guide" or "director"; it was used in the Roman empire to designate the governor of a province. The use of this title by universities came from the corporations or guilds which, in turn, had taken it from civic administration.[135]

In the universities of the Society the one responsible for the overall

---

129 See Rashdall, op. cit. in note 97, I, p. 183.
130 Ibid., p. 201.
131 Form. Inst., no. 8.
132 MI Const, I, 53.
133 See MI Epp, I, 551-562; EppMixt, I, 411-412; Chron, I, 212, no. 174.
134 See G. Codina, op. cit. in note 24, p. 62.
135 See Rashdall, op. cit. in note 97, I, pp. 162-163.

government was also called "rector," which was and still is the most common title since the Middle Ages;[136] and "he may be the same person who governs the principal college of the Society" ([490]). The university is viewed, as were those of that time, as composed of various colleges, one of them at least belonging to the Society. At any rate, the rector of the university will not be elected but appointed, either directly or indirectly, by the general ([490]).

The rectors of the colleges must be coadjutors; they may not be professed. The basic reason for this prohibition is that the fixed incomes of the colleges are exclusively for the use and benefit of the students, and the Society—above all the professed Society, the Society in its most proper meaning—cannot licitly utilize them for itself. Therefore the professed may only reside in the colleges and have some function of government or teaching when some special need demands this or some special advantage accrues to the college itself ([557]; see [422, 588]). In such a case, effectively, their residing in the college would redound to the advantage of the students, not to that of the Society.

We neither can nor desire to enter into the difficulties that this principle was to cause later on when the colleges of the Society multiplied and those for externs were separated from those for scholastics.

a. Requisite Qualities

The qualities of the rector described in [423] are very similar to those listed in Part IX as required for the general. In fact, it seems that both lists have their origin in the same source: the eleventh *Industria* of Polanco.[137]

The list begins with the virtues required. The rector must be "a man of great example and edification" (see [725]) and "of great mortification of all his evil inclinations" (see [726]). He must be "especially approved in obedience and humility," the fundamental virtues of a Jesuit (see [102]), in which he should give an example to his subjects (see [434, 659]).

But natural gifts and experience ought to be joined to virtue: "he ought to be discreet and fit for governing." Polanco commented: "Some, although virtuous, devout, and intelligent, are not suited to this; they are more fitted to be soldiers than captains."[138] He ought to be "experienced

---

136 Formally, not only in Paris but also in other universities, such as that of Padua, he was *rector* of the Faculty of Arts. But in fact his jurisdiction extended to the whole university.

137 The second chapter of Part IX directly, this number by way of the *Constituciones de los Colegios*, P. VII, no. 9.

138 *Industria* 11ª, no. 4.

both in matters of business and of the spiritual life" so that "he may be able to discern the various spirits and to give counsel and remedies to so many who will have spiritual necessities" ([729]). Moreover, "he should know how to mingle severity with kindness at the proper times," "to such an extent that he neither allows himself to swerve from what he judges to be more pleasing to God our Lord nor ceases to have proper sympathy for his sons" ([727]). He should be "solicitous" in undertaking enterprises as well as energetic in carrying them out (see [730]). He is to be "stalwart under work," patient and strong in suffering. Finally—what will be surprising in one who is supposed to be a coadjutor and not professed— he is to be "a man of learning" ([423]). This proves that in the mind of Ignatius the spiritual coadjutors of the Society were not necessarily men of but little culture, as some suppose.

Finally, a general norm is given: the rector must be one to whom higher superiors (the general and the provincial) can delegate their authority with confidence. It is fundamental in the government of the Society that immediate superiors have much authority over their subjects (see [206, 820]), and on the other hand that the subordination of some superiors in regard to others be observed (see [662]). This is necessary so that the general, from whom all authority descends as from the head ([666]), may have full confidence in subordinate superiors, so that he can "give them much authority" ([791]).

b. His Function

In [424] the function of the rector is considered, not only from the point of view of the duties of the rector himself but also from that of the subjects towards him. In the source, the "Constitutions of the Colleges," separate paragraphs cover each aspect.[139]

The rector's primary obligation is to prayer and holy desires, "prayer which is assiduous and full of desires" ([790]). In that way he is "to sustain the whole college" ([424]). His second obligation is "to bring it about that the Constitutions are observed" ([424]). He will also be able to grant dispensations from them "with authority from his own superiors" ([425]). Does this refer to the Constitutions of the Society or only those of the colleges? The fact that the colleges are institutions distinct from the Society, and that at the close of the chapter it is stated that "the constitutions which pertain to the colleges could be kept apart" ([439]), inclines us to the second opinion. So there would be no contradiction between this declara-

---

139 See MI Reg, 243-245, nos. 10 and 12.

tion ([425]) and declaration D of the third chapter of Part IX, which prohibits the general from delegating authority to dispense from the Constitutions of the Society, except in extraordinary cases or "to someone in whom he has confidence as in himself" ([747]).

Another very important duty of the rector is vigilance: "to watch over all his subjects with great care, and guard them against difficulties from within or without the house," by anticipating difficulties, remedying them if they have occurred, in a way that seems conducive to the good of individuals, even dismissing those causing the difficulties if the universal good requires it.

But besides all that, the rector has the responsibility for the direct implementation of all the norms mentioned in the previous chapters of Part IV: to see that the scholastics "make progress in virtues and learning" and keep up their health, and also to ensure the preservation of the temporal goods "both stable and movable" ([424]). In all this he will be helped by officials, about whom we shall be speaking next.

To these duties towards his subjects one must add that of subordination to the general and to the provincial, keeping them informed and having recourse to them in matters of greater moment ([424]).

The duties of the members of the college toward their rector are reduced to two principal attitudes. The first is "respect and reverence" as to one who holds the place of Christ our Lord. It is notable that we find here, with reference to the rector, this binomial or two-word phrase "respect and reverence," which Ignatius uses four times in the *Exercises* and sixteen times in the *Spiritual Diary*, always with reference to God.[140] This is an indication of the vivid realism with which the Constitutions assume that we are to consider Christ as present in the superior.

The second attitude is "true obedience," an obedience which is not merely doing what the superior commands but a complete surrender into his hands, letting him dispose freely of the subject and all he has, not keeping anything closed to him, not even one's own conscience, and following his judgment "without showing any repugnance or any manifestations of contrary opinion."[141] This will bring about that union of criteria and feelings which so greatly helps a community to preserve itself and to

---

140 See *SpEx*, nos. 39 and 114; A. Nebreda, in *Manresa*, 32 (1960), 48. A. Hsü found the same binomial in *Amadís de Gaula*. See *Dominican Presence in the Constitutions of the Society of Jesus*, p. 163.

141 As the source shows, this last phrase refers not only to not keeping anything closed, but to the whole paragraph: "without showing any repugnance or any manifestations of contrary opinion." Of course, the possibility of representation is supposed.

"make greater progress in the divine service" ([424, 427]).

3. *Aids toward Good Government ([428-436])*

In order to be able to govern a college well, a rector needs to be helped in two ways: by persons and by organization—some individuals with whom he can share his responsibility, and a certain stable organization in the life of the institution.

The individuals with whom the rector shares his responsibility in government, and who are known by the originally academic title of "officials," are likewise of two classes. In the tenth chapter, apropos of the colleges, only the officials "for the good government of the house" are mentioned ([428]). It is clear that the term "house" here does not have the ordinary meaning as opposed to "college" (see [289]); it means—as correctly interpreted by Nadal—"the domestic government of the college,"[142] or rather, the government of the college in its domestic and religious aspects. The second class of officials is the one responsible for "carefully organizing the studies" (see [493]). These are mentioned only in the seventeenth chapter, in the context of universities, because the colleges, before the late seventh chapter was written, were thought of as residences for students, not as centers of instruction.

So that these officials may be a real help for good government, the following is desired of them: They ought to be as many as are necessary ([428, 431]) and as far as possible fit for their offices ([428, 429]), taking into account not only their personal talents but also their occupations and their experience ([428, 429]). They ought to be well instructed in their offices by means of proper rules ([428, 430]). No one should interfere in the business of another ([428]), since work is done in a more orderly and beneficial way if each one takes his own proper share of responsibility. Finally, the constitution foresees that in the distribution of common tasks some may be overburdened while others have but little to do. So the rector is advised that "just as he ought to have help given to them when they need it, so when time is left over he ought to see to it that they employ it fruitfully in the service of God our Lord" ([428]). This norm of paternal solicitude, which has such relevance for community life, seems to be inspired by a comment in the Benedictine Rule which says with reference to the kitchen for guests: "In all the functions of the monastery, care should be had to provide assistants for those who need them; at the same time, when somebody is free, let him obey what is ordered."[143]

---

142 *Scholia*, on no. 428.
143 Regula, chap. 53, 19-20.

We shall not delay in listing the officials. By this term the Constitutions understand anyone who fulfills an office, from the minister to the cook ([431-433]) and from the chancellor or prefect of studies to the beadles of the university ([490-509]. What is important is the observance of the subordination so desired by Ignatius (see [662, 666]). Those living in a college must observe full obedience to the officials, to each one in his own office (see [87, 286]), and the officials are to obey the minister, who is the universal instrument of the rector, and the rector himself. And all this in order that—as the "Constitutions of the Colleges" said—"the rector may know about all things in the house, and manage and run them through these officials."[144] It is the principle of subsidiarity.

We conclude by referring to the academic meetings ([502]). Besides the rector and the chancellor or prefect of studies, the deans and "representatives" of the faculties take part in them, though how many and who these representatives are to be is not stated. The rector may summon others from within or without the Society to these meetings. The vote is advisory. The rector is given this norm: he should take account, not of the opinion of the majority, but of the opinion of those who are more cognizant; however, if all have one and the same opinion it would be imprudent to go against it without consulting the provincial about the matter ([503]). Although this refers to meetings of an academic character, these norms could serve as guidelines for other meetings and consultations, especially if we compare them with the practice in the universities at that time. At Paris, for instance, all masters in theology actually teaching took part, and in the theological faculty at Padua the masters in theology. In both cases the vote was deliberative.[145] The Society, partly profiting from the usage in the universities, adjusted the system in favor of the authority of the superior. Only some teachers participate as representatives, and those whom the rector would invite; their votes have no more value than those of advisors to the rector, without decision-making power.

The second help is more for the general efficient running of the house or college than for the rector himself. It consists of "a suitable order of time" ([435]) or in other words a proper distribution of occupations during the day. A fixed timetable—as General Congregation XXXI said—is "a very apt means for making more efficacious both individual and community work, for making mutual interchange among members easier, and for creating those exterior and interior conditions of silence, recollection, and

144 MI Regulae, 212, no. 4.
145 See Rashdall, op. cit. in note 97, I, p. 408-416; G. Brotto and G. Zonta, *La facoltà theologica dell'università di Padova* (Padua 1922), p. 280.

peace of mind which are so useful for personal study, reflection, and especially prayer. In addition, it is a complement of charity itself and its realistic expression, as well as a sign of religious consecration and union in the service of Christ."[146]

4. Ministries of the Colleges ([437])

The final number of chapter 10 treats of apostolic ministries: "dealing with their neighbors inside or outside the house" ([437]). At times teaching in our colleges has been called a ministry; but in the Constitutions it is not so considered. As we have already seen, the purpose of the colleges and universities is to form "ministers." The ministries of the colleges, the means by which the neighbor is helped in the colleges, both here ([437]) and in Part VII ([636-649]), are those listed in the first number of the Formula of the Institute and those we have also seen in the eighth chapter of this Part: spiritual conversations, the Exercises, confessions, preaching, sacred lectures, teaching catechism. As a help in understanding the history both of the text here and of the teaching of catechism, we may add that the obligation imposed on the rector to teach catechism for forty days is a much later addition, later than 1553; this is an indication of the importance Ignatius continued to give to this ministry up to the end of his life.

VI. EXTERN STUDENTS ([392-397, 481-489])

Chapters 7 and 16 cover what is of importance for extern students, those from outside the Society. It consists in this: "that along with knowledge, they acquire good and Christian moral habits" ([481], see [395]). To achieve this, three principal means are indicated, as follows.

(1) They should be well instructed in catechism ([395], see [483]). Moreover, "the masters should make it their special aim, both in their lectures when occasion is offered and outside of them too, to inspire the students to the love and service of God our Lord, and to a love of the virtues by which they will please Him, and they should urge their students to direct all their studies to this end" ([486]).

The exercises of declamation by the students themselves "about matters which edify the hearers and lead them to desire to grow in all purity and virtue" have the same purpose ([484]; see [485]). Ignatius had a high regard for these declamations and saw in them a means of fostering

---

146 C. G. XXXI, d. 19, no. 15, f.

vocations to the Society.[147]

(2) They should practice exercises of piety. Those suggested are: confession and communion at least once a month, daily Mass and sermons on feast days ([481]).[148] The teachers, who in the Constitutions are not considered as simply lecturers but real tutors interested also in the good of each one of their students, will take care that they are faithful to the practices mentioned ([481]). The discretion shown in declaration A of this sixteenth chapter, on the way to secure this fidelity of the students, is remarkable. The same method is not to be applied to every student: moral pressure could and should be employed with some (perhaps the youngest); better that others be "gently persuaded"; nobody is to be forced, nor should anyone be expelled from the university (or college) for not assisting at these exercises of piety, provided he is morally sound and not an occasion of scandal to others ([482]).

(3) Bad language and immorality are not to be permitted ([486]). When kind words and admonitions alone are insufficient in such cases, a student should be corrected and punished, and even be dismissed ([395, 488]), though an effort should be made to proceed "in a spirit of leniency and to maintain peace and charity with all" ([489]).

For this purpose of maintaining discipline a special office was established (that of "corrector"), in imitation perhaps of the practice in the college of Montaigu at Paris,[149] but with the strict prohibition that no member of the Society exercise the function. On this point Ignatius was very strict.[150]

VII. FINAL OBSERVATION

We have seen in Part IV that the very existence of scholastics in the Society was due to the difficulties and demands of the "apostolic or missionary life." The intellectual formation of these scholastics leads logically to their preparation for this apostolic life. This is what provides the criterion for the subjects they are to study; even the manner of instruction is inspired by the method of Paris because it is more suited to attaining a sound theological formation in a few years than the lecture system of the Italian universities, where a whole scholastic year might be spent on a

---

147 See MI Epp, III, 485-486; IV, 7, no. 4.
148 In the seventh chapter, only the monthly confession and the frequent sermon are mentioned.
149 See M. Godet, *La Congrégation de Montaigu*, p. 49.
150 See MI Epp, II, 442, 498; III, 668; IV, 10-11, 601.

single question of Thomas Aquinas. The Constitutions do not deal merely with this intellectual formation; they also cover pastoral formation, concentrating on the spiritual ministries of the apostolic life.

After 1540, however, it was decided that scholastics should receive both their intellectual and pastoral formation in "colleges," institutions dependent on the Society. Part IV therefore considers the institutional dimension under this aspect and treats of the founder, the supervision of the foundation by the Society, and the government of the college. Nevertheless, with respect to this institutional dimension, a difference is to be noted between the other Parts and this one. In the other Parts the institution is the Society itself, as an organized body in which the ideal or charism takes on flesh; in Part IV the institution is the college itself, with the fixed income from its foundation, its scholastics benefiting from these stable revenues, and the rector who guides them (although dependent on the Society, which exercises the supervision by means of the general).

Chapter IX

INCORPORATION INTO THE SOCIETY
(Constitutions, Part V)

I. PRELIMINARY REMARKS

Incorporation or admission into the body.—In a social body we find a process that cannot take place in a physical body, namely, that the members are formed first and brought together afterwards. The preceding Parts dealt with formation; now we move on to aggregation and its diverse circumstances and modalities. Using another image, we could say that it is the placing of previously carved stones into the fabric of the temple.[1]

1. Structure and Evolution

The structure of Part V did not change in the successive texts. First laying down that there are different ways of being incorporated into the Society according to the more or less intimate grade of belonging to it ([510-511]), there follows the order of factors involved in this incorporation: (a) who has the authority to incorporate ([512-513]), (b) when he can do so ([514-515]), (c) who can be incorporated ([516-523]), and (d) how the incorporation is carried out ([524-541]). A paragraph on change from one grade to another is added by way of appendix ([542-543]), and a further paragraph on the vows of religious in formation who are not scholastics ([544-546]).

The primitive text, a, was not divided into numbered chapters but consisted of a series of paragraphs grouped under eight internal titles.[2] Text A divided these paragraphs into seven chapters; the definitive text reduced them to four, joining the first three into one and the last two into another.

More important than the distribution of paragraphs into a greater or lesser number of chapters is the re-elaboration they underwent in passing from text A to the definitive text. Polanco, after having had text A copied

---

1   See 1 Kings 6:7.
2   In the first edition there were nine titles. Later Polanco crossed out the second, "What it means to be incorporated into this Society."

and correcting it,[3] made a new arrangement of all the matter and this took the place of the previous texts.[4] This re-elaboration was certainly necessary, for the first texts were very meager and almost purely juridical.

2. Sources

Along with Part II, Part V is the one with the fewest sources. It is clear that the contents, the norms prescribed in it, are based on the Formula of the Institute or on other previous decisions. But as to literary sources properly so called, we can only indicate an echo of the fifth *Industria* of Polanco in the paragraph dealing with the third probation ([516]) and, for the formula of profession ([527]), the one which Ignatius and his companions used at the basilica of St. Paul on April 22, 1541.

II. WHAT INCORPORATION IS ([510-511])

In order to understand the meaning of incorporation or admission into the body of the Society, it is necessary to know what the word "Society" means from the juridical or social point of view, and of what members its body is composed.

What does "Society" mean, juridically or socially considered? This question is not answered as easily as might appear at first sight, for the concept of "Society" is not univocal. Declaration A of the first chapter ([511]) presents the Society through a geometrical figure, with a center and a series of concentric circles or spheres.

The central nucleus is formed by the professed of four vows. It is of them that the Formula of the Institute speaks almost exclusively, referring to the others only briefly at the end. This "professed Society," as it is often called (see [4, 5, 7, 111, 324], and passim), is the Society in the first and strictest sense of the word.

Next to the professed of four vows we find their auxiliaries (see [815]), the formed coadjutors, spiritual and temporal (some of whom have solemn vows). All, professed and coadjutors, constitute what we might call the formed Society. This is the Society into which the scholastics take the vow of "entering," and it is the second accepted sense of "Society," less strict

---

3   This copy is the one which the editor of the Monumenta calls text *V*, thinking it is the work of Father Gian Filippo Vito, although it is probably by Father Romei.

4   The rough drafts are preserved in the codex *Instit.* 7, ff. 163-164 (for chapters 1-2 and the first four numbers of chapter 3), in *Codex A*, fol. 151 (for numbers 5 and 6 of chapter 3 and all of chapter 4), and in codex *Instit.* 7, ff. 113-114 (for the declarations).

than the previous one.

In the third place, those who are not yet formed (approved scholastics) are added to the previous categories in order to constitute with them (the professed and the coadjutors) *the body of the Society*. That is a third accepted sense of "Society," still broader: all those who belong to its body.

Finally, there are others in the Society "who live under obedience to its superior general" but do not yet "belong to the body of the Society," being neither professed nor formed coadjutors nor approved scholastics. Such are the novices and "persons who, desiring to live and die in the Society," are still in probation. These, along with the others already mentioned, form the Society in the widest sense of the word.

According to this multiple concept of "Society," not only being "admitted" into it but even being "incorporated" can have different meanings. One who is accepted for probation is already admitted into the Society. Such admission is not dealt with here since it was the subject matter of Part I. Also admitted into the Society is one who, having completed probation, is "incorporated" or admitted as a member of the body of the Society. But just as among these members there is a gradation with reference to the concept of the Society, so also there can be a greater or lesser incorporation, more or less internal. Approved scholastics are incorporated, for they form part of the body; but more intimate is the incorporation of the formed coadjutors, and much more so that of the professed of four vows (see [510]).

Dumeige observes that "it can be said that these differences arise from the development of a human group which fairly quickly had to think about its recruitment and found itself faced with the need to seek help in various spiritual and temporal works under the pain of compromising its apostolic contribution and restricting the field of work which had been proposed for the greater glory of God."[5]

On their arrival from Paris, the first fathers were all educated men, masters of arts who had studied for some years. Others, equally "learned," joined them in Italy, for instance the bachelor Hoces, who was to die soon, the bachelor Araoz, and others who did not persevere.[6] But we saw—when speaking of the need for colleges in the preamble to Part IV—how they very soon realized that they could not ensure the preservation and growth of the Society with learned men because "those who are both good and learned are few" ([308]). We also saw how, as early as 1537 in Vicenza,

---

5   "L'incorporazione dei membri della Compagnia," conference published in *Le Constituzioni della Compagnia di Gesù* (CIS, Subsidia, 7), p. 76.
6   Antonio Arias, Lorenzo García, Miguel Landívar, and Diego Cáceres.

they thought of recruiting youths,[7] for whose formation they established colleges.

Further, the preservation and growth of the Society by recruiting young men was not something novel. All the religious orders did likewise from the beginning. What was new was that, whereas in other orders youths made solemn profession on completion of the novitiate and were professed as were their elders, in the Society during its earliest years they were merely candidates. Subsequently they were more and more integrated until they came to be considered part of its body, as we see here. But they never came to be "professed." Why? Due to the conviction, expressed as early as the first Formula, that none may be admitted to profession except those who are very well tested and approved and seen to be prudent in Christ and distinguished for their doctrine and purity of life.

Along with this concern about the recruitment of youths who share the same ideal and can continue carrying on the undertaking for the glory of God, another phenomenon is soon apparent, from 1538—that of some men, laymen and priests, who came with desires not "to be of the Society," not to form part of the number of companions, but "to serve" the Society or someone belonging to it.[8]

No doubt Ignatius saw in the spontaneous offering of these men (which we could perhaps qualify as "charismatic") a new intervention of Providence in the progressive realization of the Institute. On the one hand, it would not be necessary to require these auxiliaries to have the qualities seen to be needed in the professed,[9] and on the other hand, besides service in the house, they could be entrusted with some of the offices that called for more stability, as in the colleges, thus leaving greater freedom to the professed for their missionary vocation.[10]

Ignatius sought to formalize this situation, obtaining from the pope in 1546 the brief *Exponi nobis*, which granted authority for the admission of spiritual and temporal coadjutors. However, as these were only auxiliaries of the professed and not required to have the qualities of the professed, logically they did not have to make profession. Furthermore, at the beginning they were not considered as formally belonging to the Society.[11]

Up to the end of 1548 or the beginning of 1549, by the word "Society"

---

7   See Laínez, MI FontNarr, I, 120.
8   See A. M. de Aldama, S.J., "De coadiutoribus Societatis Iesu in mente et in praxi sancti Ignatii," art. in *ArchHistSI*, 38 (1969), 392-393.
9   So it is expressly stated in the documents (*litterae patentes*) by which some were made coadjutors. See MI Epp, I, 641; DocInd, I, 195.
10   See Aldama, art. cit. in note 8, pp. 420-421.
11   See MI Const, I, 274, no. 25.

was understood only the professed of four vows.[12] The extension of the meaning of this term by which it is understood more or less strictly appears for the first time in a letter of October 8, 1549.[13] Probably by that time the first text was being composed, and the necessity of clarifying the meaning of the various modes of being admitted into the Society led to this solution.

III. WHO CAN INCORPORATE ([512-513])

We will not delay here on the question as to who has authority to incorporate; it will be treated in the commentary on Part IX. The legislator considers it obvious that this authority "will be vested in him who is head" of the Society, "as reason requires." This is obvious in a hierarchically organized body such as the Society where the entire influence is to proceed from the head to the members (see [666]). It would not be obvious in other social bodies where the head merely has a function of presiding; in such bodies the admission of members would concern the whole group acting in a collegial or corporate manner.

IV. WHO CAN BE INCORPORATED

1. General Principle ([516])

With regard to the qualifications of those who are to be incorporated, the general principle is "that no one should be admitted into any of the aforementioned categories unless he has been judged fit in our Lord" ([516]). Basically this is a repetition of the prevailing reason: that one enters the Society not only to be converted himself, to "help himself," but also to convert and help his fellowmen. Those who have no ability for this "reveal that they have not been called by His Divine Wisdom" ([243]).

This requires a lengthy probation, a probation which is at the same time a test and a training.

As early as the first Formula of the Institute (1539), great care was taken not to admit anyone to profession until he had been tested "for a long time and very diligently." When the grade of coadjutors was introduced in the new Formula of 1550, there was also an addition to the effect that they too, like the scholastics, would have to pass adequate tests and a diligent examination and should not be admitted unless they are

---

12 See ibid., 307-308 and 328, no. 43.
13 See MI Epp, II, 553.

found to be suited to the end of the Society.

2. Length of Probation ([514-515])

The determination of the minimum time for probation came about gradually. Canon law at the time did not lay down any general rule for religious. Benedict's Rule prescribed a year of novitiate;[14] Boniface VIII had also prescribed a year for the mendicant orders.[15] Ignatius and his companions accepted this norm at the beginning.[16] But to this year they added a prior three-month period of special experiences or tests: the month of the Exercises, a pilgrimage, and a hospital trial.[17] When at the end of 1540 or the beginning of 1541 special legislation was drawn up for scholastics, it prescribed for them, besides these three months of tests or trials and the year of probation (which they could make along with their studies), another year of probation at the end of their studies.[18] Around 1545 or 1546 this second year was extended by another three-month period of tests in humble exercises and in spiritual ministries.[19] In the first text of the Examen the tests are increased even more, with six months at the beginning and six months at the end, reaching a total of three years: a year and a half before studies and another year and a half afterwards.[20] Finally, in the texts of 1550 the time was redistributed according to a new arrangement: two years at the beginning for all and a year after studies for the scholastics ([514]). However, the superior general was given power to lengthen or shorten the time ([515]). The Council of Trent confirmed the authority to prolong the probation in the Society and on the same occasion approved its Institute.[21]

---

14   Chap. 58, 5-10.
15   Chap. 2 and chap. 3, III, 14, in Sexto.
16   On the other hand, they did not accept the norm of the original Constitutions of the Theatines, which established a probation of two or three years. See I. Silos, *Historia Clericorum Regularium*, I, 74.
17   MI Const, I, 12.
18   Ibid., I, 33-60.
19   Ibid., I, 56, col. 2.
20   See MI Const, II, 56-58, 108-110.
21   Sess. 25 (Dec. 3, 1563), *De reformatione*. That in those words the Council "approved" the Society was explicitly affirmed by the reigning pope, Pius IV, in four letters sent on May 29, 1565, to the king and queen of France, to the parliament of Paris, and to the Cardinal of Bourbon. See Sacchini, *Historia*, Part III, bk. 1, nos. 18-19. See also MHSI Nadal, V, 253, 255, 680.

3. Third Probation ([516b])

In these probations the two elements most characteristic and proper to the Society, not found in the older orders, are the six "experiences" (trials or tests, often translated in English by "experiments") and the third year of probation. The six "experiences" were covered when we dealt with the fourth chapter of the Examen; we may now turn to the third probation.

What is the reason for the existence of this practice? All scholastics, and they alone, have to make this third probation, after finishing their studies and before making profession or taking the vows of a formed coadjutor (see [16, 71, 119, 514]). Why? It is not improbable that—as with the six "experiences" of the novitiate and other points of the Institute—Ignatius and his companions wanted the Society's new members to profit from the advantages they themselves had derived from their own experience (see [81]). After their studies and ordination to the priesthood, the first companions spent some three months in various parts of the Venetian dominions, giving the time partly to prayer and partly to an experience of the apostolic life.[22]

However, this does not explain everything. In the Constitutions this year is called by two terms, (1) *probación*, "probation," and (2) *escuela del afecto*, "school of the affections," or "of the heart." Some tend to stress this second denomination, obscuring or denying the aspect of probation. They cannot understand how after so many years of consecrated life the vocation or suitability of a religious must or can still be put to the test.

Nevertheless, it is evident in the Constitutions that this third year is considered as a time of genuine probation. It is mentioned in the same line as, and without distinction from, the two years of the novitiate: "two complete years of probation; the scholastics will have an additional year" ([16]); "in the case of scholastics, when their studies have been finished, in addition to the time of probation required to become an approved scholastic, another year" ([71]); "two years of experiences and probations, and one more year if they have been scholastics" ([119]). More explicitly in the first chapter of this Part V: "He will have another year . . . to become still better known, before pronouncing it [the profession]" ([514]).

There is no doubt that to the extent that the scholastics have been more integrated into the body of the Society it is harder to understand this new probation after studies, especially from the point of view of a proof or test. But let us remember that this integration of members in the Society

---

22 See *Autobiog*, nos. 94-95; MI FontNarr, I, 41, 118-120, 193; II, 83-84, 580; III, 82-85. Laínez asserted that the preaching was a "trial," ("more for self-mortification than for anything else"); Nadal said the same (ibid., I, 120; II, 84).

is always differentiated and gradual and that therefore so too is the incorporation into the body. There is a double incorporation. Through the first incorporation one comes to be only partly a member of the body of the Society; through the second there is a more intimate "entering" into the formed, and perhaps into the professed, Society. Consequently, there are also two periods of probation which precede and prepare for each one of these incorporations. In other words, we would say that the two years of novitiate are for the scholastics the probation required for their provisional incorporation, and the third year the probation required for definitive incorporation into the Society, which they make a vow to "enter."[23]

In [516b] the third probation is treated under its aspect of a school of the heart. This second paragraph is inspired by Polanco's fifth *Industria*, of which it is almost a compact résumé.[24] This Latin expression *schola affectus*, often cited, is generally poorly interpreted. Modern versions translate it "school of the heart," understanding this term in the sense of the formation of the interior man. Anthony Ruhan relates it to what some modern psychologists call "involvement," that is, the affective maturity which is achieved through contact with others in intensely emotional circumstances.[25] But these authors base their views on an incorrect understanding of the Latin word *affectus*. In the terminology of not a few scholastic theologians such as Bonaventure, *affectus* means merely the affective or appetitive

---

23   See J. B. Janssens, in *ActRom*, 13, 782.

24   See MHSI PolCompl, II, 744-748; A. M. de Aldama, S.J., *Imagen Ignaciana del jesuita en los escritos de Polanco*, (CIS, Subsidia, 9), pp. 56-65. [Editor's note: In the present paragraph, the author discusses a subtle problem about the meaning of *escuela del afecto*. The following background is perhaps necessary to understand his discussion. In the current vernacular translations of *Cons* [516], Ignatius' Spanish phrase *del afecto* is translated respectively by *du coeur*, *del affetto*, *des Herzens*, and "of the heart." Modern Spanish dictionaries list affection, passion, and the like among the meanings of *afecto*, thus making it a synonym for *corazón*; and the dictionary closest to Ignatius' day, Covarrubias (1611), defined *afecto* as "passion of the soul" which overflows into the body and "moves us" to compassion, mercy, joy, sorrow, and the like—emotions important for an orator. Some pertinent considerations were found in Mario Gioia's note on *Cons*, [516] in his *Scritti di Ignazio di Loyola* (Turin 1977), p. 547. He points out that in Ignatius' anthropological vision, *afecto* takes in not merely the area of the senses but also the interiority of the human person, the ego, on a level so profound that it is similar to the word "heart" understood in its biblical meaning: the whole person, with his intellect, will, and affections. Hence the training in Ignatius' tertianship involves all the young Jesuit's faculties, natural and supernatural, bodily and spiritual, so that his knowledge and his affections contribute to increased union with the person of Christ.]

25   "The Origins of the Jesuit Tertianship," in *Jesuit Spirit in a Time of Change*, ed. R. A. Schroth (Westminster 1967), pp. 107-108.

faculty of the soul, that is, the will.[26] The Latin expression *schola affectus* seems to be taken from Gerson, who uses it in opposition to the term "school of the understanding," as is done here also in the first texts.[27]

It is clear, on the other hand, that neither is this "school" of the affections or of the will to be understood in a modern psychological sense of education of the will. That would be anachronistic. The will is regarded as the seat of moral virtues. *Schola affectus* is therefore, in our final opinion, a school of virtues.

The virtues indicated in this constitution are "greater humility, abnegation of all sensual love and will and judgment of their own, and also greater knowledge and love of God our Lord" ([516]).

The principal means for obtaining these virtues is exercise: "exercising themselves in spiritual and corporal pursuits," that is, in practices of prayer and devotion and in exercises of humility and mortification. Hence we find it stated in the Examen that this third year must be spent in passing through various probations and trials, and especially through the six "experiences" of the novitiate if they did not have them previously, and through some of them even if they had ([71]). An excellent development of these ideas will be found in the fifth *Industria* of Polanco, to which we have already referred.

The reason given for all this "schooling" of the *affectus* or will is that "when they themselves have made progress they can better help others to progress for glory to God our Lord" ([516]). Polanco says that in order to help our fellowmen spiritually we must ourselves be spiritual men. He defines spiritual as "knowing and loving spiritual things and doing works in conformity with this love; hence follows contempt for temporal things and the abnegation of the old man."

Probation in the Society is also a time of training. This training is included in the *schola affectus* and in the "experiences" previously mentioned. But Polanco insists even more on the point, proposing that the fathers in third probation be trained not only in spiritual ministries of the Society, but also in administrative functions such as those of minister or subminister in order to test their prudence.

26 See F. Sirovic, *Der Begriff "Affectus" und die Willenslehre beim hl. Bonaventura* (Rome 1945).

27 In the Spanish text the words "diligencia y cuidado de instruir" are due to a correction by St. Ignatius himself, as a substitute for "escuela de."

4. Spiritual Qualities ([516a])

Moral or spiritual qualities are required, and intellectual qualities as well.

It was not so at the beginning. In the first deliberations of 1539 it was decided that not only those who had talent for helping their fellowmen but also those less capable should take the vow of obedience to the pope.[28] In the first editions of the Formula of the Institute it was laid down that the professed should be "distinguished" either for learning *or* for holiness of life. But it must soon have become apparent that "learning" was a necessity for papal missions ([109]); and as early as 1541 Ignatius and his companions decided that "the learned" ought to constitute at least two thirds, and that the lack of intellectual formation of those not learned was to be supplied by other natural or supernatural gifts.[29] Finally, after the grade of coadjutor had been introduced, when Ignatius was asked whether all the professed had to be learned, he replied that they should, "although there is latitude in the sufficiency of learning."[30]

What moral or spiritual qualities are required? At times an effort has been made to establish for the professed a degree of virtue superior to that for the nonprofessed. But, prescinding from many other difficulties with this criterion, is it possible to measure degrees of virtue? The Constitutions do not give grounds for such a way of thinking.

The Formula of the Institute speaks of "the integrity of Christian life" (*vitae christianae puritate*) or of an irreproachable life. And the first edition probably intended to mean no more than that by using the phrase "holiness of life" (*vitae sanctitate*). This is based on the necessity that the evangelical man has of leading a unblemished life "because of the ordinary and common weakness of many persons" ([30]).

Besides that negative aspect, both the Formula and the Constitutions insist that those admitted to profession be very well known and approved: "They should be tested at length in their life and habits" ([12]); "persons whose life is well-known through long and thorough probations and is approved by the superior general" ([516]); "thoroughly and lengthily tested, and known with edification and satisfaction to all after various proofs of virtue and abnegation of themselves" ([819]). The reason given in the

---

28   See MI Const, I, 10.
29   Ibid., pp. 47-48, nos. 46 and 48.
30   Ibid., pp. 310, 330. Before this, in the account given to Charles V which we will cite later (text corresponding to note 34), it had been said that only "persons who are well tested and learned" ("personas bien examinadas y letradas") are to be admitted to profession.

Formula is that our Institute requires men who are "humble and prudent in Christ." One thinks, perhaps, of "the faithful and wise servant whom his master has set over his household,"[31] or rather of the serpent's prudence which our Lord commends to his apostles on sending them to preach "like sheep among wolves."[32] Imitating the apostles, a professed must go out to preach in the world. His life has to be well tested and approved so that the Society may have confidence in him that he will proceed with supernatural prudence and thus be able to be placed at the disposal of the pope. Making use of a term much used nowadays, we would say that what is mainly desired in the virtue of the professed is authenticity, soundness; and this is obtained by making him pass through the crucible of tests and trials.

5. Intellectual Qualities ([518-521])

We said that, although it was not so at the beginning, Ignatius soon came to the conclusion that all the professed had to be "learned." A man who had done superior or higher studies was "learned" (*letrado*); for a priest, this meant in practice one who had done university studies, for before Trent there were no seminaries. The Formula of the Institute says that the professed must be "conspicuous in learning" (*conspicui in doctrina*) and this word "conspicuous," which already Polanco thought could seem pretentious, gave rise to false interpretations. Other Ignatian writings show that in the mind of the founder to be "conspicuous in learning" is equivalent to being learned, being well versed or adequate in learning. And he added that this sufficiency in learning could have latitude, that is, could be more or less.[33]

The word "sufficient" is the most used in the Constitutions (see [12, 308, 518]). It is a relative term. Later on, the Society was to require a sufficiency or capability for "teaching" philosophy and theology. In the Ignatian documents the sufficiency mentioned is always for exercising the sacerdotal ministries proper to the Society. In this context, some information that was sent on to Charles V in 1547 is noteworthy. Polanco had written in rough draft that the Society admits to profession only persons who are well examined and learned, so that they have some talent for helping the neighbor. Ignatius erased the last words and in their place wrote "for preaching and hearing confessions."[34]

In [518] this sufficiency in learning is spelled out more clearly with

31   Mt. 24:45.
32   Mt. 10:16.
33   See MI Const, I, 310, 330, nos. 54 and 55.
34   MI Const, I, 242.

regard to both the kind of learning or doctrine and the standard required. The learning or studies which the professed should have are those we saw in Part IV: humanities, philosophy, theology—or rather, theological formation which supposes as preparation a humanist and philosophical formation (see [351, 446-451]).

Two concrete norms are laid down for establishing the standard. First, a certain number of years of study: the theological quadrennium, "four complete years" ([518]). This norm is very old in the Society; it appears as early as 1541.[35] We may note that in the universities of the Society four years of theology constitute the ordinary course, two others being added for "the public trials customary for a doctorate" ([476]). This confirms what has been said: the knowledge of a licentiate or of a doctorate in theology is not required but that of one who had followed a full ordinary course in theology in which "all the matter which must be lectured on will be expounded" ([476]).

The second concrete norm prescribes a final examination before four examiners who judge the "sufficiency" in learning of the candidate, an examination which is to be repeated if on the first occasion "the subjects are found not to have enough learning" ([518]).

After this presentation of intellectual qualities in general, a long-standing exception appears, in two ways. Some with a lesser degree of theological knowledge could be admitted to profession of three solemn vows if other titles such as knowledge of canon law or other relevant qualities make up for the lack. Others, referring to "outstanding persons," will also be able to be admitted to the profession of four vows. It is noted, however, that this second exception "ought not be extended" ([519]).

The professed of three vows appear unexpectedly for the first time (without earlier documentation) in the Formula of the Institute of 1550. But it could be asked: Are they an exception in the grade of professed of four vows ("professed" lacking the fourth vow) or rather an exception in the grade of coadjutors (coadjutors with solemn vows)? In the Constitutions ([520 and 531]), perhaps for juridical reasons, they are placed next to the professed of four vows; but in the Formula of the Institute it seems clear that they form part of the coadjutors. We would say that they are coadjutors of special caliber to whom is granted—because of their devotion (their desire for more intimate union with the Society), their merits and qualities, or for other reasons—the privilege of taking solemn vows and not just simple vows like the other coadjutors. Only the case of priests is considered in the Constitutions (see [521]), but the sense of the words in

---

35 See MI Const, I, 57.

the Formula is wider; and it is notable that on at least one occasion Ignatius granted profession of three vows to a brother coadjutor.

V. MANNER OF INCORPORATION

"Religious congregations, like all human societies," as Dumeige aptly comments, "need ceremonies and public commitments, feasts and celebrations, in which the individual can profess the determination to form part of the group, and the group, for its part, can declare its acceptance of the individual."[36]

The first monks publicly declared their intention to abandon the world and profess the monastic life by taking the monastic habit; clergy entered the clerical state by means of ecclesiastical tonsure, and virgins the state of virginal consecration by taking the veil. Later on—in the fourth century —we find the requirement of an explicit declaration of submission to a superior and to the prescriptions of a rule.

Confining ourselves to the West, we see that rites varied at different periods and in differing religious institutes. But the two most important rites were those entitled "profession on the altar" (*professio super altare*) and "profession into the hands" (*professio in manus*).

The "profession on the altar" is the monastic rite, later on also adopted by the canons regular. The ceremony took place in the church and during Mass celebrated by the abbot (although Benedict's Rule does not as yet make mention of Mass). During the offertory the novice first pronounced orally his "promise" (*promissio*), by which he committed himself to monastic stability, to "reform of life" (*conversatio morum*), and to the observance of obedience; then he placed on the altar his "request" (*petitio*), a document written in his own hand which would serve as proof of his promise and of his desire to enter and form part of that community. Immediately he began to recite the versicle: "Receive me, Lord, according to thy promise" (*Suscipe me, Domine, secundum eloquium tuum* [Ps. 118:116]). At the end of Mass the abbot picked up the "request" (*petitio*) from the altar and carried it away with him. Some authors see a connection between this rite and certain customs in Roman law.[37]

---

36 Conference cited in note 5, p. 89.
37 See I. Zeiger, S.J., "Professio super altare," art. in *AnnGreg*, 8 (1935), 166-170; A. H. Thomas, O.P., "La profession religieuse des dominicains," art. in *ArchFFPraed*, 39 (1969), 23-24.

The "profession into the hands" (*professio in manus*) was inspired by the offering of homage (*homagium* or *hominium*), the principal act of the contract of vassalage in feudal society from Carolingian times. In the twelfth century some canons regular adopted the ceremony as a rite of religious incorporation for the admission of novices, and the Cistercians used it for the profession of the *conversi* (applicants) though not for that of the monks, and it seems that the Dominicans took it from them. The ceremony took place in the chapter hall, not in the church. Kneeling before the superior, the novice joined his hands and the superior took them between his own (*immixtio manuum*). In this posture of submission he pronounced the words of profession, and then the superior gave him the kiss of peace.[38]

When Ignatius and his companions made their profession in the basilica of St. Paul on April 22, 1541,[39] they used a completely different rite which later passed into the Constitutions. Suárez, who knew about the legislation and customs of other religious orders, says that this rite is "peculiar" to the Society.[40]

We shall deal first with the solemn profession of four vows, which is, so to speak, "the prime analogue," and then note briefly the differences in the ceremonies of the other grades.

1. Rite ([524, 530])

The profession takes place "in the church publicly," before the members of the house and the others who may be in the church, and during Mass celebrated by the general or his representative. It might seem from the wording of the constitution ([525]) that the profession is made after the celebration of Mass, and at one time some held that interpretation. However, in the light of the source, which is the profession of the first fathers in the basilica of St. Paul Outside the Walls, the passage has to be understood as meaning that the vows are taken just after the communion of the celebrant.[41] He then turns round with the Blessed Sacrament in his hands, and the one who is making profession pronounces the vow formula and then receives Communion from the celebrant ([525, 530]). That is all the Constitutions say; the only addition is a declaration for determining

---

38   See R. Creyteus, O.P., "Le Directoire du Codex Ruthenensis," in *ArchFFPraed*, 26 (1956), 119; Thomas, art. cit. in previous note, 25-33, 39-42.
39   See MI FontNarr, I, 21.
40   *De Soc.*, no. 746. See also the passage in the Franciscan Constitutions of 1331, referred to by Zeiger in the article we will later cite (in note 51), p. 178. Furthermore, these ritual symbols introduced by the innovating minister general Gerard of Aquitaine did not remain in later Franciscan Constitutions.
41   See MI FontNarr, I, 21.

what constitutes the essence of the act juridically ([526]). Afterwards the names of the newly professed and of the one who received the vows are registered in the appropriate book ([530]).[42]

If we now compare this rite with the two others already mentioned, we will find that in the monastic rite the central element is the church and the altar on which the newly-professed places his request or *petitio*. By this gesture he shows publicly that he is consecrating himself in that church and that particular monastery in order to observe monastic stability (*stabilitas monastica*). It was for that reason that the rite was abandoned by an apostolic order like the Dominicans. In their rite the central element is the joining of the subject's hands between the superior's (*immixtio manuum*), which signifies a commitment of personal submission to the master general of the order.[43] In the Society of Jesus the central element is the Blessed Sacrament. In describing the profession on April 22, 1541, at the basilica of St. Paul, Ignatius says: "Iñigo, saying the Mass, at the time of Communion, holding with one hand the Body of Christ our Lord over the paten and with the other hand a paper on which was written the vow formula and with his face turned to the kneeling companions, said in a loud voice: 'I, Ignatius, . . .' After these words had been said, he received the Body of Christ our Lord."[44]

What is the significance of this rite?

Some have thought of it as a mutual giving: the one making profession gives himself to Jesus Christ, and Jesus Christ in Communion gives Himself to him. But we find no basis in Ignatian spirituality for such an explanation. We might think of the "Take, Lord, and receive" in the Contemplation to Attain Love, which is a response to "how much God our Lord has done for me and how much he has given me of what he has . . ."; but that is an inverse rhythm, which would be quite appropriate if the profession followed Holy Communion, while here it precedes it.

If we retrace the earlier life of Ignatius after Montserrat and Manresa, we will see how its most important acts culminate in eucharistic Communion. He ended the nocturnal watch of spiritual arms at Montserrat with Communion. And it was with Communion, in a ceremony very like that of religious profession, that on August 15 of 1534 he and his companions ratified the first vows at Montmartre.[45] Similarly, in 1539, before receiving

---

42 This last is inspired by the *Constit. O.P.*, Dist. I, chap. 15, decl. b, which reproduces a decision of the general chapter held in Paris in 1246. See *Acta Cap. Gen. O.P.*, I, p. 36.

43 See Thomas, art. cit. in note 37, pp. 51-52.

44 MI FontNarr, I, 20-21. The profession of the companions follows in the same way.

45 See Simão Rodrigues, in MI FontNarr, III, 24-27.

Holy Communion from Favre's hands, each of the companions declared his agreement to the decision taken to convert the Society into a religious order, committing themselves to enter it if the pope approved. In this last action the significant words are: "in memory of which decision . . . I now approach Holy Communion" (*ad cujus deliberationis . . . memoriam, nunc ad sacratissimam communionem . . . accedo*).[46]

From a mystical or spiritual point of view, two principal elements emerge here: first, the real presence of Jesus Christ in the Eucharist and, second, Holy Communion. Christ really present is the omnipotent God to whom the professed commits himself, to whom he "binds" himself (see [17, 283, 544]). Ignatius writes in his *Spiritual Journal*: "As I held the Blessed Sacrament in my hands, a word came to me with an intense interior movement never to leave him for all heaven and earth, and so forth."[47] Christ is, at the same time, witness of the commitment undertaken.[48] Communion follows with the value of a confirmation, a ratification, a sacred seal set by Jesus Christ on the commitment the professed has made to him.

Guided by reasons which are merely speculative and not historical, Suárez wrote: "With this Communion a sort of covenant is made between God, the Society, and the professed. For by administering the Eucharist to the professed the celebrating priest shows that he accepts his profession and receives him into communion with himself. By the gift of himself Jesus Christ tacitly promises the professed His help so that he may keep the faith he has sworn to him, and grants him the pledge of a special reward if he does not separate himself from Him. Receiving Christ, the professed presents and offers the Eucharist to God the Father as a warranty of the faith he has sworn."[49]

We said that the Constitutions reduce the rite to these very simple but meaning-laden features. After the time of Ignatius—although quite soon, since Nadal already mentions it in his *Scholia*—additional ceremonies were introduced. After reading the words of profession, the professed hands the paper over to the celebrant, who places it on the altar and at the end of Mass picks it up and takes it away with him. Nadal adds that it was necessary to introduce this custom in order to show that the profession is received into the hands.[50] We know that the rite of "profession into the hands" (*professio in manus*) is a very distinct one; and in the Society "the

---

46 MI Const, I, 8; see MHSI Bobadilla, 617.
47 Feb. 23, 1544.
48 See MI Epp, I, 225. Ignatius takes his oath in the Pantheon at Rome "before the Blessed Sacrament."
49 *De Soc.*, no. 746.
50 *Scholia*, on no. 525.

vows are said to be made in the hands when they are made into the presence of the recipient who has authority for this" ([534]). However, the placing of the paper with the formula of profession on the altar and its being picked up by the celebrant at the end of Mass is evidently connected with the Benedictine rite—a practice that is all the more strange since, as we saw, in that rite it signifies monastic *stability*, quite contrary to the mobility proper to the missionary charism of the Society.

In 1940 Ivo Zeiger published an article on the juridico-liturgical form of our profession. The article attracted a good deal of attention. He calls the rite of the Society "profession over the host" (*professio super hostiam*) and he relates it to the rite, used during the Middle Ages, of confirming oaths with eucharistic Communion, and to the form used in making private vows.[51] The basic defect of this article is that in the rite of the Society he does not distinguish between the ceremonies in the Constitutions and those added later on. He considers them all primitive and Ignatian rites. It is even more strange because Zeiger does not know about the passage in Nadal's *Scholia* (at least, he does not quote it). Apart from the Constitutions, the only document on which he bases his argument is a twentieth-century German custom book dating from 1913! It is possible that Zeiger is right in seeing an influence on the Ignatian form of profession in the medieval tendency of confirming commitments by eucharistic Communion; for example, the case he cites on page 185 of Paschal II giving Communion to Henry V is interesting. The pope said to the emperor: "This Body of our Lord Jesus Christ must be the confirmation of peace and concord between the two of us." However, when Zeiger cites the gesture of placing the document of profession between the fingers of the one receiving it while the latter is holding the Blessed Sacrament, in order to link the rite with some "body oaths" (*juramentos corporales*) in the Middle Ages which were performed by placing the hand "over the Body of the Lord, over the Eucharist of the Lord, the right hand placed over the sacrament of the Eucharist" (*super Corpus Domini, super Eucharistiam Domini, dextera supra Eucharistiae sacramentum posita*), he is not convincing. For, apart from its not being Ignatian, it is a very different gesture. Furthermore, according to Nadal the gesture signifies that the profession is received into the hands. Neither is the expression "profession over the host" (*professio super hostiam*), coined by Zeiger, a happy one. In the first place, the word *hostia* is not Ignatian; Ignatius always speaks of the "Most Blessed Sacrament" or of the "Body of Christ." Nor does it appear even in the medieval texts which

---

51   I. Zeiger, "Professio super Hostiam: Ursprung und Sinngehalt der Profeßform in der Gesellschaft Jesu," *ArchHistSI*, 9 (1940), 172-188.

Zeiger thinks are its source. In the second place, *super* does not have any meaning here, for the one making profession does not put his hand "over" the Body of Christ, as in the medieval oaths.[52]

The difference between the rite of profession and that of admission to other grades is centered mainly in the external publicity. While the profession (of four as well as of three vows) is to be made "in the church publicly before the members of the house and the externs who happen to be present" ([525], see [531]), the vows of the formed coadjutor may be made "in the church or the chapel of the house or in another fitting place, in the presence of the residents of the house and all the other externs who happen to be present" ([533]), and those of the approved scholastic "in the presence of some residents of the house" ([537]).

2. *Formula of Profession ([527-529])*

Here also the direct literary source is the formula used by Ignatius and his companions at the basilica of St. Paul on April 22, 1541.[53] Furthermore, in the first text of the Constitutions this form of vows was copied verbatim, omitting only the vow of teaching catechism. Later minor corrections were made.

The three elements of the formula concern: the one making the profession and devoting himself to the service of God, the person he makes the commitments to, and what he commits himself to.

The first correction was the addition—at the beginning—of the phrase "I make profession" (*professionem facio*). This was probably taken from the Dominican Constitutions.[54] The phrase "religious profession" (*professio religiosa*), which originally meant only the practice of religious life inasmuch as it is distinct from that of other Christians (*professio christiana*), from the seventh and eight centuries took on the specific meaning of a formal commitment to embrace the religious state with all its obligations.[55] However, we believe that the reason why this phrase has been added here is seen in a declaration of the Dominican Constitutions which says: "We declare that *professio* is the solemn vow, which makes the person a religious

---

52 We prescind from the fact that it is scarcely probable that St. Ignatius knew about those Germanic oaths. In Spain the manner of taking oaths was by placing the hand over the Gospels or on the cross or over the altar. See *Partidas*, P^a 3^a, tit. 11, leg. 19. The military orders also took their vows by putting their hands over the Gospels.

53 See MI Const, I, 67-68.

54 Dist. I, chap. 15.

55 See Thomas, art. cit. in note 37, pp. 17-19.

and establishes him in the state of perfection."[56] Perhaps it was thought that in order to distinguish the formula of the solemn vows from that of the simple vows it was necessary to add the phrase "I make profession" (*professionem facio*). In fact, up to the middle of the nineteenth century the words "profession" and "professed" referred only to solemn vows.[57]

The one making the vow addresses God: "to Almighty God, in the presence of His Virgin Mother, the whole heavenly court, and all those here present, and to you, Reverend Father . . . holding the place of God" (*omnipotenti Deo, coram eius Virgine Matre et universa caelesti curia ac omnibus circumstantibus, et tibi Patri Reverendo . . . locum Dei tenenti*) ([527]).

The sequence of God, Mary, the saints, the superior, is found in the formula of profession of both Dominicans and Franciscans. But we may note some interesting differences which recall the oblation in the meditation on the Kingdom.[58] God is here considered under the attribute of omnipotence; the promise is made trusting in His "omnipotent hand" ([812]). This God is the Word Incarnate, Jesus Christ; for immediately afterwards mention is made of His Mother: "in the presence of His Virgin Mother" (*coram ejus Virgine Matre*). The promise is made to Jesus Christ as God and not to the Blessed Virgin or the saints as in the other formulas. Our Lady and the saints are witnesses, as in the meditation on the Kingdom. Witnesses, too, are "those present" from within as well as from outside the house, representing the Society and the Church.[59] The promise is also made to the general or his delegate, "and to you Father" (*et tibi Patri*), because of the social dimension which every religious profession has: a promise to the order in the person of the general. But there is emphasis on the fact that the general acts in the place of the Jesus Christ himself as God—"holding the place of God"—and this is another trait characteristic of the Society.

Next comes the content of the promise. First come what we are accustomed to call the substantial vows of religion: the three evangelical counsels of poverty, chastity, and obedience.

We mentioned before that the early monks did not make a formal promise; putting on the monastic habit was a clear indication of their intention to embrace the religious life. When a formal promise began to be required, it was not at first, as we might expect, a promise to observe the

---

56   Dist. I, chap. 15, decl. a.
57   See E. Bergh, *Éléments et nature de la profession religieuse* (Louvain 1937), p. 9.
58   See *SpEx*, no. 98.
59   See Nadal, *Scholia*, on no. 527. At the Basilica of St. Paul, St. Ignatius and his companions said "in praesentia Societatis."

three evangelical counsels. Confining ourselves to the West, we find that Benedict's Rule has the monk promise "stability, reform of life, and obedience" (*stabilitas, conversatio morum et obedientia*). The "reform of life" (*conversatio morum*, later called *conversio morum*) included the whole life of perfection and consequently, with the other practices and austerities of the Rule, the observance of chastity and poverty as well. The Dominicans promised only obedience according to the Rule and Constitutions, and as late as 1524 we find that the first Theatines made their profession in the same manner.[60] But as early as the twelfth century the three evangelical counsels began to appear, not only in the new orders of an active character like the military orders and those devoted to the redemption of captives but also among some of the canons regular. Hertling suggests that this development was due to the influence of ascetical considerations about renouncing the triple concupiscence (1 John 2:16).[61] The formula prescribed for the Franciscans in St. Bonaventure's Constitutions of Narbonne, using words inspired by the Rule of Francis, expressed the three counsels in this way: "I promise to observe the Rule of the Friars Minor . . . living in obedience, without possessions, and in chastity" (*promitto servare Regulam Fratrum Minorum . . . vivendo in obedientia, sine proprio et in castitate*).[62] By the time of Ignatius it was common doctrine, well established by Thomas Aquinas, that the religious state consisted essentially in the three vows of poverty, chastity, and obedience.[63]

The extent and manner in which the professed of the Society are obliged to observe these evangelical counsels are determined in the following words: "according to the manner of living contained in the apostolic letters of the Society of Jesus and in its Constitutions." The "manner of living" (*forma vivendi*) contained in the apostolic letters is the Formula of the Institute, which is the *Rule* of the Society. The Constitutions are added because they are the explanation and interpretation of the Formula.

Besides the three evangelical counsels, the teaching of catechism is expressly mentioned. But there is no question of a special vow here (as some modern translators seem to have understood it); otherwise, there would be five vows and not four. As explained in declaration B ([528]), this is merely a special mention of something already contained in the vow of obedience, a special mention because of the importance of this ministry and

---

60   See A. Veny Ballester, *San Cayetano de Thiene* (Saragossa 1950), pp. 764-765.
61   L. von Hertling, "Die professio der Kleriker und die Entstehung der drei Gelübde," art. in *ZschrKathTheol*, 56 (1932), 170-173; See J. G. Gerhartz, *Insuper promitto* (Rome 1966), p. 195; Thomas, op. cit. in note 37, p. 14.
62   See *ArchFrancHist*, 34 (1941), 40.
63   See St. Thomas. 2-2, q. 186, art. 7.

the danger that it might be forgotten.[64]

"I further promise" (*Insuper promitto*): the formula ends with the fourth vow of special obedience to the pope "in regard to missions" (*circa missiones*).

Recently the scope of this fourth vow has been the object of controversy. We shall treat of it more thoroughly in Part VII; yet we cannot do less than present some ideas now in advance.

A distinction must be made, above all, between the promise or vow which Ignatius and his companions made in 1534 at Montmartre, of offering themselves to the pope if their projected pilgrimage to the Holy Land was not successful, and the fourth vow of special obedience which they made for the first time on April 22, 1541, at the basilica of St. Paul. The early promise may have been the germ of this fourth vow but is not identified with it.

The concrete object of the vow of Montmartre, especially what refers to the so-called "papal clause," is not wholly clear. This is so because the formula used by the fathers has not been preserved, and although contemporary testimonies coincide in substance they differ on numerous important points.[65] But that promise is not our present concern.

The fourth vow of special obedience to the pope is the one which, at the meeting on May 3, 1539, our fathers decided should be taken by those who would enter the new institute of the Society.[66] Afterwards they included it in the second chapter of the Formula of the Institute.

The wording of the Formula remains obscure, and precisely for that reason, in order to avoid false interpretations, Ignatius added here declaration C of the third chapter of Part V. It is an authentic interpretation of the Formula and leaves no room for doubt: "The entire meaning of this fourth vow of obedience to the pope was and is in regard to missions." And quoting in Spanish translation the words of the Formula, he adds: "In this manner too should be understood the bulls [that is, the Formula of the Institute included and approved in the bulls *Regimini* and *Exposcit*] in which this obedience is treated: in everything which the sovereign pontiff commands, and wheresoever he sends one" ([529]).[67] Nadal notes with good reason that the Formula of the Institute is to be

---

64 We have studied the history of the reference to the teaching of catechism in the formula of profession in the article "Peculiarem curam circa puerorum eruditionem," published in *Recherches Ignatiennes* (Rome, CIS), vol. 4 (1977), no. 5.

65 See P. Leturia, S.J., *Estudios Ignacianos*, I, 188-195.

66 See MI Const, I, 10.

67 "Quidquid modernus et alii Romani Pontifices . . . iusserint . . . et ad quascumque provincias nos mittere voluerint." See also the parallel text in Part VII, chap. I, no. 1, and decl. B [603, 605].

understood in this way, although it may seem that in it the vow refers not only to missions but also to other things. He adds the reason: "The Society can, with apostolic authority, interpret the words of the Formula of the Institute, composed and presented by the Society itself to the Apostolic See. So it is not strange that the Society explains its words which were confirmed by the Church. It interprets them with the authority of the supreme pontiff, who in the bull confers upon the Society the right to clarify anything that might be uncertain in our Institute as contained in the confirmed Formula."[68]

3. Other Grades ([531-541])

The formula of profession of the professed of four solemn vows is the model for the other definitive grades. The formula of the professed of three solemn vows lacks only the last phrase containing the fourth vow: "I further promise . . . (*Insuper promitto* . . .) (see [532]). In the formula of the spiritual coadjutors the words "I make profession" (*professionem facio*)—which, as we explained, means the solemnity of the vows—are also suppressed (see [535]). Finally, in that of the formed temporal coadjutors, the reference to the teaching of catechism to children is also omitted (see [537]).

On the other hand, the vow formula of the scholastics is completely different. In a letter to Araoz in July 1549, Polanco relates its origin: "Someone first used it, and, since it seemed good to our Father, others followed him."[69] Who was the person who first used this formula? It has been thought that it was Antonio Rión. The only thing that can be certain is that the oldest vow document preserved in the archives written according to this formula is his. (It is dated March 11, 1549).[70]

This formula does not have the sobriety of the vow of the professed. It begins with an invocation followed by three phrases which express the unworthiness of the one making the vow, reliance on the divine goodness and mercy, and desire to serve God. Finally, an offering of the act as a "fragrant holocaust" is added, and a petition for grace to fulfill it. The most notable difference is that it is not addressed to Jesus Christ but the

---

68 *Scholia*, on no. 529. On the meaning of the word "mission" and its semantics we have written in *Repartiéndose en la viña de Cristo*, pp. 9-14.

69 MI Epp, II, 471.

70 See E. Olivares, S.J., *Los votos de los escolares de la Compañía de Jesús* (Rome 1961), pp. 28-29 and 229. On the other hand, the document is not written by Rión. Only the signature is in his hand. The text, as that of others in 1549 written according to the same formula, is in the hand of a copyist. This leaves us to suppose a distinct original.

"Almighty and eternal God," whose grace is sought "through the blood of Jesus Christ."[71] In a conference on "The Christology of the Constitutions," Jesús Solano notes that this is the only passage of the Constitutions in which there is an appeal to Christ's mediation.[72]

The vows are four: of poverty, chastity, and obedience and "entrance into the Society." They are conditional vows, at least to some degree, although the condition is not expressed in the formula itself: they only oblige "if the Society will desire to retain" the men taking them ([539]).

The vows are not made "into the hands of anyone" ([537, 539]). We have already met the expression "profession into the hands" understood as a special rite of profession. Here the characteristic ceremony of that rite, the placing of the subject's joined hands between the superior's (*immixtio manuum*) has no place. The making of vows "into the hands" of someone has a meaning which is only juridical, not ceremonial. Therefore everything is reduced to the necessary presence of someone legitimately designated to receive the vows in the name of the Society and of the Church (see [534]).[73] Thus, the vows of scholastics are not received by anyone; consequently they are not made "into the hands" of anyone. The reason is because they are "made to God alone" ([539]). They lack the social element which the vows of the professed and of the formed coadjutors have, and also in general every religious profession in the cenobitic life, as we indicated above. Since there was no promise to the Society on the part of the one making the vows, the Society or the superior cannot accept his vows; God accepts them, God, to Whom alone they are directed.

The result is that these vows do not incorporate one into the Society. The scholastics, even in the time of Ignatius—as we have seen—belonged to the "body" of the Society, but the incorporation was not made by means of these vows but by a different and independent juridical act.[74]

The law in the Constitutions says nothing else. Nevertheless, the explicit declaration of Gregory XIII in the bull *Ascendente Domino* states that by these vows the scholastic dedicates and hands himself over to the Society, and the Holy See accepts these vows as substantial vows of religion. This

---

71 The words *Omnipotens sempiterne Deus* are due to a correction in the hand of St. Ignatius. The reference to God the Father was clearer before this correction was made: *Creator meus et Deus ac Pater sempiterne*. On the other hand, instead of the clause *per Iesu Christi sanguinem*, one reads in the formulas used in 1549 "per la sua solita et infinita clemenzia." See Olivares, op. cit. in the previous note, p. 229. (See pp. 28-29, note 23.)

72 See *Ejercicios-Constituciones: Unidad vital* (Bilbao 1975), p. 214.

73 See CIC, can. 572, §1, 6°.

74 See Olivares, op. cit. in note 70, pp. 46-49, 99-103; Nadal, *Scholia*, on no. 336.

supposes an evolution in the concept of these vows; perhaps the linkage in a single act of taking vows and of being accepted as a formed scholastic contributed to this.[75] Now there is no doubt that the vows called biennial are public vows, accepted by the legitimate superior in the name of the Church.

We conclude this discussion by quoting the words of Benedict XV to a Father Nalbone at an audience on January 25, 1918: "How beautiful are your simple vows! How pleasing and satisfying they are to me! They deserve to be kept in the Church and I will not permit the Society to be deprived of so fine an ornament, so noble a privilege. I want it to be preserved. Assure the general that we shall leave this privilege intact."[76]

4. Passage from One Grade to Another ([542-543])

The teaching already inculcated in the Examen is repeated as an appendix: "After anyone has been incorporated into the Society in one grade, he should not seek to pass to another, but should strive to perfect himself in the first one and to serve and glorify God our Lord in it" ([542]).

Clearly there is question here only of passing from the grade of formed coadjutor to that of professed or of passing from that of temporal coadjutor to that of scholastic or spiritual coadjutor (see [116 and 117]). For the scholastic makes a vow "to enter the Society" by passing from his provisional grade to a definitive one, and the professed of solemn vows cannot pass to a condition of simple vows.

If one has been "incorporated into the Society in one grade" ([542]), it is clearly God's will and "call" that he serve Him in the Society in that grade, and so he must not "inaugurate or attempt some change from his vocation to another" but "proceed to make his way along the same path which was shown to him by Him who knows no change and to whom no change is possible" ([116]).

However, there can be exceptions. At the suggestion of Salmerón,[77] a declaration was added in the Examen ([131]), and another parallel one in this Part V, which says that "to represent his thoughts and what occurs to him is permissible. Nevertheless, he should be ready in everything to hold as better that which appears to be so to his superior" ([543]). In fact, God

75   See Olivares, op. cit. in note 70, pp. 126-130.
76   ARSI *Codif. Inst.*, A², no. 17. It was a privilege in the sense that these vows were not envisaged in the Code of Canon Law.
77   See MI Const, I, 393.

our Lord can also manifest His will through interior movements, the authenticity of which the superior is to judge.

VI. FINAL OBSERVATION

It may be said that Part V is one of the most juridical of them all; for that reason we have made many comparisons with other religious orders. The whole purpose of this Part is due to the institutional dimension of the Society. We saw how it deals with incorporation, which supposes that the Society constitutes an organic body, into which members are "incorporated." It belongs to the same dimension to determine who has the authority to make this incorporation, logically the "head" of this body, and the manner of making it through a juridico-liturgical act.

Nevertheless, the other dimension, the charismatic, is not absent and indeed is clearly present. The fact that there are different ways of belonging to the body and consequently of being incorporated into it; that (contrary to what happens in other religious orders) only some make solemn profession while others take simple conditioned vows; that profession is not necessarily made at the end of novitiate, but after prolonged probation— all these features are demanded by the apostolic life of mission. Such a life, in fact, requires that the solemn profession of four vows be granted only to men who are very proven and approved in virtue and with a sound theological formation, "men fully humble and prudent in Christ and distinguished in purity of Christian life and learning."

One significant detail is the inclusion of the teaching of catechism in the formula of profession, a point desired by Ignatius even though it was not necessary, since it was implied in the vow of obedience.

Chapter X

RELIGIOUS LIFE
OF THE INCORPORATED MEMBERS
(Constitutions, Part VI)

I. PRELIMINARY REMARKS[1]

1. Historical Background

In 1539 Ignatius and his companions decided to add to the vows of poverty and chastity which they already had a vow of obedience to one of their number whom they would choose as superior. This does not mean that it was only at that time that they began to practice the virtue of obedience; they had practiced it while traveling from Venice, each of the group in turn holding the office of superior. The decision consisted in embracing the *state* of obedience (*status pendens ab obedientia*), as the Vulgate version of the *Exercises* defines religious life.[2] In this way they added the religious dimension to the apostolic or missionary dimension and converted the Society into a religious institute. Bobadilla expressed it well when he said that the institute of the Society was "a pilgrimage in the religious state" (*peregrinación en religión*).[3]

As the previous Parts dealt with the admission, formation, and incorporation of the members of the Society, the present task is to develop the two following aspects of the life of the incorporated or formed Jesuit: the religious aspect (Part VI) and the apostolic aspect (Part VII).

2. Sources, Evolution, and Structure

The textual evolution of Part VI presents some unusual characteristics.

The first numbers of chapter 3 and the whole of chapter 4 do not appear until the final text. The remainder, in the primitive text, a, consisted of twenty paragraphs, numbered marginally; Polanco later divided these into three chapters. They had subtitles written between the lines

---

1   For a fuller treatment of Part VI, see our *La vida religiosa de la Compañía de Jesús* (Rome: CIS, 1989).
2   *SpEx*, no. 135.
3   MHSI Bobadilla, p. 602 (letter to Aquaviva, 1589).

which more or less designated the matter of each.

These twenty paragraphs were not written by Polanco but by an Italian copyist, who seems to have written them as dictated. They reproduce norms which were previously established either in the Formula of the Institute, the Constitutions of 1541, the *Determinaciones antiguas*, or in replies which Ignatius gave to doubts expressed by Polanco. An early clarification (*antigua determinación*) on religious observance and obedience was copied literally but with the notable change that the second half (on obedience) was placed first while the first half (on observance) was placed three paragraphs later.

In the definitive text, text B, besides the addition of some new paragraphs (as already noted), everything relative to obedience was separated from the paragraph on observance and placed at the beginning of the Part. The author does not indicate a reason for this rearrangement of the material, and this has given rise to various more or less apriori interpretations of the change. If we compare the new order with that followed in the Formula of the Institute and recall that in other places in the Constitutions the order followed is determined by the greater or lesser importance of the material, we can conjecture that quite probably here too the guideline was the relative importance of the themes.

Preeminent among the obligations of the religious life is the observance of the evangelical counsels. The first two chapters deal with them and after brief mention of chastity treat first of obedience, the characteristic virtue of the Society (chapter 1), and then of poverty (chapter 2). Other obligations follow: first, those of the spiritual and religious life; second, those of occupations to be avoided (chapter 3); and finally those of the last hours of life (chapter 4). The fifth chapter, on the observance of the Constitutions, is conclusive or summarizing, for in this observance all the obligations of a religious are included; for that reason it comes last.

II. THE EVANGELICAL COUNSELS

1. *Chastity ([547])*

There are only some brief remarks in the Constitutions on the vow of chastity: "What pertains to the vow of chastity does not require explanation, since it is evident how perfectly it should be preserved through the endeavor in this matter to imitate the angelic purity by the purity of the body and mind" ([547]).

"Does not require explanation"—since the Society has no manner of its own for observing the vow of chastity, as it has of observing the vows of obedience and poverty.

The question has been raised as to why Ignatius is so sparing in his treatment of this subject. It cannot be attributed to lack of experience of life, even of worldly life, nor to any idea that the moral climate of the sixteenth century—so influenced by neo-pagan humanism—was any less dangerous than that of the twentieth century.[4] Rather we think that for Ignatius the step of embracing perfect chastity coincides with that of abandoning the world and giving oneself over completely to God (unless indeed it is identified with it). So chastity is something taken for granted, not a matter of discussion, just as the decision to "serve God totally" ([53]). In his lectures on the Examen, Laínez commented: "Chastity is presupposed; it is necessary for all religious, under pain of losing their character as religious."[5] Ignatius himself received the gift of chastity in the first days of his conversion, while still at Loyola; during the journey from Loyola to Montserrat shortly afterwards he confirmed it with a vow, the first time in his life that he took a vow to surrender himself to God.[6]

However, these phrases say a good deal despite their brevity. As Nadal observed, "There is no perfection of chastity which Ignatius did not encompass within these few words."[7]

The phrase "imitating angelic purity" puts Ignatius in the mainstream of the full patristic and medieval tradition; the Fathers and other spiritual writers often liken Christian life, particularly religious life, to the state of the angels. Indeed, "angelic life" is precisely one of the ways used to designate religious life. Monks were thought to imitate the angels especially by their practice of perfect chastity.[8] Bernard even said that chastity converted men into angels[9] and John Chrysostom held that chastity set humans higher than the angels for, while connatural in an angel, chastity in a human is the fruit of personal self-dominion.[10]

This manner of speaking is due not to a fleshless and unreal "angelism," but to a profound sense of the eschatological nature of the Church. The Lord says: "When people rise from the dead, they neither marry nor are given in marriage, but live like angels in heaven."[11] We Christians are on the threshold of heaven; even now we share eternal life. The state of abnegation and consecration to God which religious profess is

4   See Pecchiai, *Roma nel cinquecento* (Bologna 1948), pp. 297-320.
5   *Esortazioni sull'Examen Constitutionum*, ed. C. de Dalmases, in *ArchHistSI*, 35 (1966), 15.
6   *Autobiog*, no. 10 (MI FontNarr, I, 76).
7   *Scholia*, on no. 547, "Enitendo angelicam puritatem."
8   See J. C. Didier, "Angélisme ou perspective eschatologique?" in *Mélanges de Science Religieuse*, 11 (1954), 31-42; Jean Leclercq, *La vita perfetta* (Milan 1961), pp. 19-55.
9   *De moribus et officiis episcoporum*, III, 8.
10 *De virginibus*, chap. 10.
11 Mt. 22:30; see Conc. Vat. II, *LG*, no. 48.

a testimony in the Church to this new and eternal life attained through the redemption of Jesus Christ; it is a foretelling of the future resurrection and the glory of the heavenly kingdom.[12]

But the angels are also the ones who show the way to achieve this "angelic purity." Inspired by the Lord's saying that the angels are contemplating the face of the heavenly Father,[13] Basil observes that they are unable to withdraw their gaze to look at any other beauty than that of the divine countenance.[14] It is interesting to note how this observation coincides with that of Ignatius. He says that we should imitate the angels who, since they are always contemplating the face of God, preserve peace without any movement of passion.[15]

2. Regarding Obedience ([547-552])

The first chapter is entitled "What pertains to obedience" (or, what regards obedience), for it does not treat exclusively of the third vow. Prescinding from the introductory sentences and from the reference to chastity which we have just seen, the chapter contains a small treatise on the relations between subjects and superiors: obedience ([547-550]), reverence and love ([551]), and dependence ([552]).

a. Obedience

What kind of obedience is being treated here? We may ask because it has rightly been observed that there are two "lines" of obedience in the Society.[16] The purpose of this first section of Part VI is to state the obligations of the three vows of religion. So it is to corporative obedience that this chapter refers, as does the third in the Formula of the Institute. Part VII of the Constitutions deals with the other "line," obedience for mission, as does the second chapter of the Formula. In other words, the obedience examined here is that which must be observed in virtue of the third vow, whereas the fourth vow and the obligations it implies are considered in Part VII.

In the first number ([547]), the lengthy paragraph on obedience is the

---

12   Ibid., no. 44.
13   Mt. 18:10.
14   St. Basil, *Sermo asceticus*, 2 (cited by Leclercq in op. et loc. cit., note 7).
15   See MI FontNarr, II, 476. The idea is already found in the *Stimulus divini amoris*, P. II, chap. 7, a book widely read in the early Society.
16   See I. Iturrioz, S.J., "Dos líneas de obediencia en la Compañía de Jesús," art. in *Manresa*, 43 (1971), 59-78. The idea had already been pointed out by L. Mendizábal, S.J., in the same review, vol. 37 (1965), pp. 53-76, and implicitly also by P. Blet, S.J., in *ArchHistSI*, 25 (1956), 514-530.

result of three stages of composition. The oldest stage is the central section beginning with the words "They should keep in view God" and going as far as the phrase "in which some species of sin cannot be judged to be present" ([547]). With some slight variations, this reproduces an "early determination" of 1546.[17] In the course of being transcribed into the first text of the Constitutions, some phrases on the necessity of obedience ("Everyone must be ready to observe," and so forth) were placed before that section, but with a certain repetition of concepts. Finally, in the second draft of the Constitutions (text A), the two comparisons of the dead body and of the staff were added, together with the succeeding sentences up to the end of the number.

We will concentrate mainly on what we have stated to be the oldest stage because it expresses the first inspiration or intuition of Ignatius about obedience, containing in short compass the essential elements of his doctrine on this virtue. We shall distinguish four ideas in the section: (i) the fundamental principle of obedience, (ii) the spirit with which it ought to be observed, (iii) its field of extension, and (iv) the manner of observing the virtue.

The fundamental principle is that the superior stands in the place of Christ. "The Abbot is considered to take the place of Christ in the monastery" (*Abbas Christi agere vices in monasterio creditur*), Benedict wrote in his Rule.[18] This principle was enuntiated, and hence formally approved, in the Formula of the Institute: They should "recognize and properly venerate Christ as present in him." This idea is perhaps the one most often repeated in the Constitutions; and it is developed especially in the Examen ([84-85]).

Here, in short but pregnant phrases, the whole doctrine is given. In obeying, a Jesuit "should keep in view (or before his eyes) God our Creator and Lord, for whom such obedience is practiced," and "should be ready to receive its command just as if it were coming from Christ our Savior." The reason is that he obeys the one who is "in his place and because of love and reverence for him"; not just out of love and reverence for Christ, who wishes us to obey the human superior, but also because this human superior is in his place, substitutes for him, is his representative. Effectively he governs by virtue of the authority received from Christ.[19]

---

17   See MI Const, I, 216-217.

18   Chap. 2, 2. See chap. 5, 4-6; chap. 63, 13. The idea is also found in other religious legislation. See L. Mendizábal, "Riqueza eclesial y teológica de la obediencia ignaciana," art. in *Manresa*, 36 (1964), 283-302 (summary on p. 301).

19   The Letter on Obedience says, "From whom all ordered authority comes down." It is also the reason adduced by Suárez (*De Soc.*, Bk. 4, chap. 15, no. 14).

The spirit with which one ought to obey is that of love "and not as men troubled by fear" ([547]). This is a logical consequence of seeing Christ in the superior and of obeying out of love and reverence for Christ. Fear brings trouble and disquiet. Ignatius wants us to obey out of love, desiring "to please the Divine Goodness for its own sake" ([288]), led by "the interior law of charity and love" ([134]) which impels us "not to miss any point of perfection which we can with God's grace attain in the observance of all the Constitutions and in our manner of proceeding in our Lord, by applying all our energies with very special care to the virtue of obedience" ([547]), the special virtue of the Society, for it is the virtue most proper for the apostle, the one sent by Christ.[20]

The field of obedience: The spirit of love for Christ present in the superior determines also the field into which obedience is extended, not only in regard to persons who are to be obeyed but also to things in which one ought to obey.

"Things": At the beginning of the paragraph Ignatius stated that everyone is to be ready to observe obedience and be distinguished in its observance "not only in matters of obligation but also in other things, even though nothing else is perceived except the indication of the superior's will without an express command." He now adds that we must be alert to the voice of obedience "in all the things into which obedience can with charity be extended" ([547]). Thus he distinguished between things of obligation and others which are not so, but in which charity also impels us to obey.

The obligatory things are those which—as the Formula of the Institute says—"pertain to the Institute of the Society,"[21] that is, everything which the superior orders "according to the rule" (*secundum regulam*).

To understand what those other things are "into which obedience can with charity be extended," it is well to recall that the Fathers and medieval writers, basing themselves on some words of Peter[22] about obedience in obligatory things, which they call an "obedience of necessity" (*obedientia necessitatis*), contrast it with an "obedience of charity" (*obedientia caritatis*) which is extended to everything, even to the impossible: "One should obey out of charity" (*ex caritate . . . oboediat*), Benedict said in a famous passage of his Rule.[23] According to Bernard, the only limit is death in imitation of

---

20 See Letter to Miró, Dec. 17, 1552, in MHSI, MI Epp, IV, 560.
21 "In omnibus ad institutum Societatis pertinentibus parere semper teneantur" (chap. II, no. 6).
22 See 1 Pet. 1:22.
23 Chap. 68, 5.

Jesus Christ, who was obedient to death and even to death on the cross.[24]

However, charity does not permit obedience to be extended to those things "in which some sin is manifest" ([549]), where the subject "decides" or comes to the conclusion that some species of sin is involved in what the superior commands ([547]), namely, that it is a sin, a defect, or a positive imperfection. How the subject is to proceed when sin is not obvious, when he is in doubt and unable to settle whether what is commanded certainly involves some kind of sinfulness, Ignatius explained in the points on obedience dictated to Gianfilippo Vito.[25]

The persons to whom this obedience is given are: "first to the sovereign pontiff, and then to the superiors of the Society" ([547]).

"First to the sovereign pontiff." Let us recall that we are not dealing here with the fourth vow of the professed, of the special obedience to the pope "with regard to missions" (*circa missiones*), but with the third vow of obedience common to all Jesuits. For that reason the explicit and emphatic mention of the pope as "first" is surprising; it is all the more strange since at that time the stipulation in canon law about religious being obliged to obey the pope as supreme superior in virtue of the vow of obedience had not been made (it came much later).[26] It is possible that someone may prefer to say that this mention of the pope alludes to the special obligation of the fourth vow. In any case, it is clear that everything stated about the extension of obedience, and everything mentioned later about the manner of obeying, Ignatius understood not only of obedience to the superiors of the Society but "first" of obedience to the pope.

The manner of obeying embraces first of all the prompt execution of what is commanded: "We should be ready to receive [the] command [of obedience] just as if it were coming from Christ our Savior, . . . ready to leave unfinished any letter" ([547]).[27]

But Ignatius was not satisfied with prompt execution. He wants us to "apply our whole mind [or, intensity][28] and all the energy we have in the Lord of all that our obedience may be perfect in every detail, in regard to the execution, the willing, and the understanding" ([547]). This is one of the most original and characteristic points of his doctrine on obedience.

Declaration C says: "The command of obedience is fulfilled in regard to the willing when the one who obeys wills the same thing as the one who

---

24   *De perfectione oboedientiae*. The same doctrine is found in William of St. Thierry, in Humbert of Romans, and in other authors.
25   See MI FontNarr, I, 595, no. 6.
26   See CIC, can. 499.
27   See MI Epp, III, 156; St. Benedict, *Regula*, chap. 5, 1-13.
28   "Intensión" (intensity), not "intención" (intention), the source says.

commands" ([550]). These words require an explanation, for it may also be asserted of obedience of mere execution that the one obeying wishes the same thing as the one who commands. If this were not so he would not do what is commanded, or his action would not be a human act. The "will to do the same" in obedience of the will is—as we find in the parallel place of Part III—"bringing their wills wholly into conformity with what the superior wills" ([284]), or in more concrete terms, as the Letter on Obedience says, "to make his own the will of the superior, despoil himself of his own beforehand, and clothe himself with the divine will as interpreted by him." That is, it does not suffice to resign oneself passively to do what is commanded because nothing can be done about it. In order to have true obedience of the will, the subject must make a positive effort to make the will of the superior his own, relinquishing his own will. This he is to do in such a way that he wills what the superior commands with the same desire as he would have willed it if it had been the object of his own spontaneous choice—and this with an integral will, "totally" ([284]), discarding all contrary desire. This he is to do, not as in the classic example of the merchant who casts his riches into the sea to save his life yet clings to the wish to save those riches also if it were possible.

The expressions used in the Ignatian writings to define obedience of judgment are: "in regard to the understanding, when he forms the same judgment as the one commanding and regards what is commanded as good" ([550]); "persuading ourselves that everything is just" ([547]); "bringing their judgments wholly into conformity with what the superior judges" ([284]); "having the same feeling as his superior, subjecting his own judgment to his" (Letter on Obedience). Here too is the teaching that the subject should make the superior's judgment his own, giving up the one he perhaps has himself. While I prepare myself to preach, thinking that is best for the glory of God and the good of souls, the superior orders me to hear confessions because he judges it better under present circumstances. I must judge that hearing confessions in the present circumstances is better than preaching. Obedience of judgment is docility of mind, the fruit of humility. As such it will not be possible when there is clear evidence to the contrary. But cases where there is such evidence are rare. The great majority of cases are those in which there is probability on both sides, and in such circumstances true humility considers that the opinion of another is more probable than one's own; as the Letter on Obedience states, this is much the more so if this opinion of another is that of the superior, whom God has given him as a guide.

This Ignatian doctrine about the way we ought to obey may seem excessively severe. Is it not enough to do what the superior orders, even though difficult and repugnant to nature? What need is there to conform the will and intellect as well? Ignatius certainly requires "genuine resignation and true abnegation of our own wills and judgments" ([284]) and "renouncing with blind obedience any contrary opinion and judgment of our own" ([547]), a resignation and abnegation which the Letter on Obedience does not hesitate to label "sacrifice" and "holocaust." But, having this resignation and abnegation, obedience of the will and judgment makes us obey with greater peace and serenity of mind, with greater ease "in a spirit of love" and "with spiritual joy" ([547]), even perhaps with enthusiastic expectation, the hopeful anticipation of one who does something because he personally thinks it is an excellent means for God's glory and consequently loves and desires it by his own choice. This is very much the opposite of the way of acting of one who grudgingly supports the imposition of obedience, judging it to be folly; he will perhaps do what is asked, but with interior rebellion, like a slave.

Besides, blind obedience—as much calumniated as it is little understood —is only "blind" in order to escape the pretexts against obedience stirred up by our self-love.[29] Nadal links blind obedience to the fundamental principle of Christ's presence in the superior: "We embrace a blind obedience," he says "to deprive ourselves of our own judgment through the splendor of holy obedience and the contemplation of Jesus Christ present in our superiors; why should we be surprised that the presence of the divine light dissipates our darkness and takes over our will and judgment in such a way that we will and judge in Christ and through Christ?"[30]

Section [547] ends with two comparisons which have become celebrated: the lifeless body and the old man's staff. The phrase "like a lifeless body" (*perinde ac cadaver*) is often quoted as the special and even sole norm of Ignatian obedience, to the scandal and annoyance of many. In truth, there is no reason for such amazement. Let us note that it is only a question of comparisons, added as second thoughts (in the second composition) to illustrate the doctrine set forth in the previous paragraphs; and we know that every comparison limps. It does not mean that we have to obey like automatons or robots; in such circumstances, obedience of the will and judgment would not be present. The only intention here is to stress the indifference and availability of the truly obedient person, who does not

29   See H.-A. Parenteau, "La notion d'obéissance aveugle," art. in *RevAscMyst*, 38 (1962), 31-51 and 170-195 (esp. 35-44).

30   MHSI, Nadal, V, 161; see pp. 430-431, 799; *Pláticas de Coimbra*, p. 170; *Scholia*, on no. 547, "Caeca quadam oboedientia."

resist but "allows himself to be carried and directed by Divine Providence through the agency of the superior" ([547]). Besides, these comparisons or similar ones were used by other spiritual writers before the time of Ignatius without anyone being scandalized. We specifically find "the lifeless body" in the writings of Sts. Nilus and Francis of Assisi.[31]

b. Reverence, Love, and Dependence

Obedience does not include all the duties of subjects toward superiors. In the second number, ([551]), two other duties are mentioned and very specially recommended: reverence (especially interior, which does not exclude but rather presupposes exterior reverence) and love. Both are based on the fundamental principle of Christ's presence in superiors. The subject will hold them in "great reverence" if he considers and venerates Jesus Christ in them. This idea has already been inculcated in the Formula of the Institute: Christ is recognized as present in the superior and given due veneration.

The love also has to be "in Him," in Christ, through the love which the subject has for Christ, whom the superior represents; with a love "very much from the heart," as that to one's very father: "It was I who begot you in Christ Jesus through my preaching of the Gospel," Paul wrote.[32] This is the only place in the Constitutions where the name of father is given to the superior. This is all the more remarkable if—as is probable—Ignatius learned from Benedict the doctrine that the superior is in the place of Christ; because for Benedict this is precisely the reason for being called "abbot" or father.[33]

This love, this "spirit of charity," will bring the subject to trust fully in the superior and not to keep anything back from him, "exterior or interior." Hence the readiness to give an account of conscience "with great charity," as the Examen says ([93]).

The same love and trust will move subjects "to have recourse to the superior for the things which they happen to desire" ([552]). It is not "infantilism" or lack of emotional maturity; it simply means maintaining oneself within the special order of Divine Providence through which God

---

31 See St. Nilus, *De monastica exercitatione*, chap. 47 (PG 79, 771); St. Bonaventure, *Legenda maior*, chap. 8.

32 1 Cor 4:15.

33 See *Regula*, chap. 2, 2; chap. 63, 13. J. F. Gilmont notes that in the ten most important letters of St. Ignatius on government and obedience, the term *pater spiritualis* does not appear more than twice, both times in quotes from St. Bernard; and that in another text, attributed to St. Gregory, the word *patres* has been replaced by *praepositi*. "Paternité et médiation," art. in *RevAscMyst*, 40 (1964), 407.

guides by means of the superior.

The last sentence of this third number, [552], may appear to impede free recourse to the Apostolic See. But it ought to be noted that there is only question here of not seeking favors or privileges without the consent of the superior. The Franciscans had a similar norm, at least from 1260, the year in which the Constitutions of Narbonne—as composed by Bonaventure—were approved.[34] Furthermore, Nadal assures us that the pope approved this norm of our Constitutions.[35] More recently, in the eighteenth century, it was expressly confirmed by Clement XII.[36] As to the recourse, it is known that the older religious orders had a privilege which impeded recourse "in suspensivo" (a formal appeal against the corrections of superiors).

3. Regarding Poverty ([553-581])

a. Preserving It Intact

The Jesuit is to distinguish himself in obedience ([547]), but he is to love poverty with solicitous love, preserving it "in its integrity," without "altering" what has been laid down by the founder ([553]). The reason is that poverty is a "wall" of defense, the rampart which will protect the Society against the assaults of the enemy of human nature and the other adversaries of perfection.

Ignatius knew that the laxity of religious orders was to a great extent, even chiefly, due to the alterations in "what was well ordered by their first founders, by means of interpretations and innovations not in conformity with those founders' spirit" ([553]).[37] Thus, this solicitude for poverty is motivated by love for the Society and the desire to preserve it in its being and spirit (see [816]).

The Formula of the Institute, which the Constitutions presuppose and explain, puts forward other values of poverty, each of which is a fresh motive for loving it and preserving it intact. The more life is separated from avarice and the more it comes close to "evangelical" poverty (as the first fathers state in the Formula and affirm that they know from spiritual experience), the more joyful it is and the more free from care about riches. It is a purer life and more removed from the occasions of sin, more apt for the edification of the neighbor: in effect, it makes our apostolic work more

---

34 See *ArchHistSI*, 34 (1941), 64.
35 *Scholia*, on no. 552, "Ne privatus quisquam."
36 See *Epist. Select.*, ed. 1951, pp. 75-76.
37 See G. Switek, S.J., *In Armut predigen* (Würzburg 1972), pp. 21-22.

credible and more convincing .[38] Another value of poverty is added, one
that was much esteemed by Ignatius: trust in our Lord Jesus Christ. He will
give all that is needed to feed and clothe his servants who seek only the
kingdom of God.[39] Switek rightly comments that this last reason brings us
to the theological basis of poverty: only this trust in God actualizes the basic
relationship of man to Him, namely, his insecurity, his total dependence
on the only One who can give him security.[40]

The absence of the Christological motives so prominent in the
Exercises, and to which Ignatius gave such importance in the Deliberation
on Poverty, will cause surprise.[41] But as we shall soon see, they are included
in the expression "evangelical poverty."

First of all, what is poverty? Of course, we are speaking of voluntary
poverty. Sometimes one hears it said that poverty is the use of temporal
goods with moderation or using them in conformity with the purpose of
divine service, which the wealthy also should do. At other times poverty is
understood to mean not making use of things without the authorization of
obedience; this may be the consequence of one's being poor but is not
poverty itself. Various types of poverty are also discussed, such as the
poverty of the beggar who lives on alms (and would be the ideal figure of
the voluntary poor man in the Middle Ages) or the poverty of the worker
who lives by his labor (which would be the model preferred nowadays). But
neither living on alms nor living by one's own labor is poverty; they are
rather different ways of supporting oneself which a poor person has: what
Thomas Aquinas calls "manners of living" (*modi vivendi*).[42]

In the whole religious tradition from the time of Abbot Anthony,
poverty has been understood to mean nonpossession, not owning temporal
goods: "One lives without possessions" (*ut aliquis absque proprietate vivat*), in
the words of Aquinas.[43] This is also the thought which Ignatius reveals in
the Deliberation on Poverty.[44] The first fathers understood poverty in this
sense from the beginning when in 1539 they decided that anyone entering
the Society, before being accepted, ought to be "poor in fact" (*actu pauper*),
that is, ought to relinquish the ownership of his goods.[45]

---

38 These ideas have been developed by St. Bonaventure in *Apologia pauperum*, chap.
    9, nos. 14-22.
39 Form. Inst., chap. 4, no. 7. See Mt. 6:33.
40 Op. cit. in note 36, p. 246.
41 Ibid., pp. 204-207, 242-244.
42 *Summa contra gentiles*, III, chaps. 31 and 35.
43 St. Thomas, 2-2, q. 186, art. 3.
44 See Switek, op. cit. in note 36, pp. 202-204. We do not except Part VI, chap 2,
    no. 1 [553-554], nor Part X, no. 5 [816].
45 MI Const, I, 12.

One can live without ownership in two ways: without possessing individually (while the community to which one belongs is able to do so) and without possessing collectively (neither the individual nor the community). The first form was the one practiced by the monks of cenobitical life in imitation of the primitive church of Jerusalem.[46] The second is the form adopted by Dominic and Francis.

This second form of poverty is also the one that the Formula of the Institute intends to be understood when it treats of "evangelical poverty." We know this from the Deliberation on Poverty written by Ignatius in 1544. One of the reasons given there for adopting strict poverty, without any kind of fixed income, is that this was the poverty that Jesus Christ practiced and which He taught His apostles when He sent them out to preach.[47] Bonaventure says: "The example and form of the second kind of poverty is the life of the apostles as Christ the teacher of perfection taught them when He sent them out to preach; St. Matthew tells us so [chapter 10]. This form of poverty, worthy of preference in the order of perfection, Christ Himself observed, taught to the apostles, and recommended to those who desire to follow in their footsteps."[48]

This "evangelical poverty" taught by the Lord to his apostles when He sent them out to preach consists of three elements: (i) non possession: "take no gold nor silver"; (ii) not receiving remuneration: "give freely what you have freely received"; (iii) living on alms: "the laborer is worthy of his hire."[49]

To preserve this poverty "in its integrity" against the attacks of "the enemy of the human race and other adversaries of perfection," Ignatius saw that papal approval alone—even if given in a specific form—was insufficient because history showed that in such cases one pope, at the request of a religious order, could alter what another pope had approved. He therefore devised this method of a personal commitment to Christ: the professed, who are almost the only ones in the Society with power to legislate, were obliged to "promise not to take part in altering what pertains

---

46   See St. Bonaventure, *Apologia pauperum*, chap. 7, no. 4.

47   See MI Const, I, 80, no. 14. See *SpDiar*, Feb. 11 and 23, 1544.

48   *Apologia pauperum*, chap 7, no. 5. In the following paragraphs he shows, through quotations from many authorities, that this was the poverty of Jesus Christ.

49   Mt. 10:8-10. We are not so much interested here in the correct exegesis of this gospel passage but rather in how it was understood by the legislators of what is known as "mendicant poverty"—how such as St. Dominic, St. Francis, St. Bonaventure, St. Ignatius understood it, . . . all of whom were inspired precisely by these words of the Lord. See A. M. de Aldama, S.J., "La misión, centro focal de las Constituciones," art. in *Ejercicios-Constituciones* (Bilbao 1975), pp. 263-265, 267-268.

to poverty in the Constitutions, unless it be in some manner to make it more strict, according to the circumstances in the Lord" ([553]).

In a report on the Society and its Institute written by Polanco at the end of 1564, we read: "The strictness of poverty in the Society is greater than many think or understand; for neither the houses of the professed nor their churches or sacristies can have any fixed income in common or individually (see [555]), but should live on alms alone (see [557]), alms which they neither request nor accept for Masses or confessions or sermons or any of their other ministries (see [565]); not even the houses or colleges will be able to inherit through their individual members (see [572]); all take a particular vow not to try to slacken *this poverty.*"[50]

b. Neither Fixed Revenues nor Possessions

Ignatius was guided by the ideal of "evangelical poverty" not only in his personal life (at least from the time that he learned during the Exercises about the manner of following Christ to which he was called) but also in his legislative work. It is not surprising that he looked to the experience of his predecessors (such as the founders of the mendicant orders)[51] when determining the particular details of this ideal of evangelical poverty.

It was at the general chapter of 1220, held in Bologna under the presidency of their founder, that the Dominicans found the appropriate formula: neither income nor property.[52]

From the beginning, from the first Formula of the Institute, it was laid down in the Society that no civil right (that is, no right to property under the protection of civil law) could be acquired to yield any fixed revenues (*"ad proventus seu introitus aliquos"*). Nevertheless, a little later, in 1541, it was thought that a distinction could be made between two subjects of ownership:

---

50   MHSI PolCompl, I, 503.
51   See Switek, op. cit. in note 36. There are some positive indications that St. Ignatius took St. Dominic and St. Francis as special models. In the first days of his conversion these are the two saints who, according to the *Autobiography*, no. 7, stirred him by their example to embrace the service of Christ. Later, in the famous letter to Giam Pietro Carafa, he confirms his view on the manner in which a founder should conduct himself, with the examples of how Dominic and Francis proceeded "at the time they instituted and gave order and example to their orders" (MI Epp, I, 116).
52   *Possessiones seu reditus nullo modo recipiantur.* It seems they were inspired by a general chapter of the Cistercians, although understanding the formula in a stricter sense. See A. H. Thomas, O.P., *De oudste constituties van de dominicanen* (Louvain 1965), pp. 197-198, note 312; p. 240, note 22; p. 360. Later, the Second Council of Lyons (1274), d. 23, used the expression while defining as "mendicants" those religious whose rule or constitutions forbid having *reditus aut possessiones* for appropriate sustenance, and who live from *incerta mendicitas.*

the professed or community (there were as yet no coadjutors) and the house or church (the sacristy). The community would continue without any right to fixed income the house or the church could have some fixed revenues not only for worship and the building or construction of the church (which the mendicants commonly allowed) but also for other purposes such as furniture, the library, medicines, postage, and the like, but with sustenance—food and clothing—always excluded.[53]

Ignatius must not have been satisfied with this solution. Three years later, when he got down to composing the Constitutions, he took this as the first point to be considered. During the well-known forty days of divine communications, he rejected this solution, to return to the original concept of poverty. This explains why the new Formula of the Institute (1550) stresses that neither the professed (or community) nor any of their houses or churches can have fixed revenues (*"professi vel ulla eorum domus aut ecclesia"*).[54]

We read the same here in [555]: "In the houses or churches which the Society accepts to aid souls" (in contrast to the colleges, which can accept fixed income for the formation of the scholastics; see [308]), "it should not be licit to have any fixed revenue, even for the sacristy or building [as the mendicant orders allowed] *or for anything else*, in such a manner that any administration of this revenue is in the control of the Society."

The last phrase leaves the door open for the sole exception: perpetual alms. These are allowed (as they also were among the mendicants) but under the following conditions: (i) "No civil right should be acquired by the Society which makes it possible to claim these alms through a court of law" ([564]); (ii) "This revenue is not at the disposition of the Society and the Society is not in charge of this revenue" ([556]), that is, it can neither dispose of the revenue freely nor administer it; (iii) "No one of the Society ought to or may induce any person to establish perpetual alms" ([564]).[55]

---

53 This solution cannot be explained by the practice or theory of the mendicants, as Codina seems to think (MI Const, I, 35, note 3). The document *Fundación de casa*, which is prior to the *Constituciones de 1541* and probably served as a basis for discussion, expressly speaks of taking something from the mendicant orders and also something from the monastic orders (ibid., pp. 62-63).

54 The word *eorum* is added to distinguish from the colleges, which can have fixed incomes for the scholastics.

55 As we already noted in the preface, we comment on the Ignatian Constitutions and restrict ourselves to constitutional law. Later on, G. C. XXXII (1975), "the better to meet the new demands of our poverty" (d. 12, no. 11), stated that the "apostolic institutes" established in the houses of the Society may possess endowments and needful revenue (ibid.). They cannot have stable revenues from

"Not only fixed revenue, but also stable goods (*possessiones*) of any kind, should not be possessed" ([561]). In the strict sense the Spanish word, *posesiones* means stable goods that are productive. But here, as in the Formula of the Institute, the term has the meaning of any immovable goods.[56]

At first even the building in which they lived was not excluded. Later, for practical reasons, the Formula of 1550 made an exception of the stable goods which were essential for personal use and habitation. The Constitutions interpret this exception to include also "some place apart from the common habitation" where the sick may spend the time of convalescence and the healthy "withdraw to devote themselves to spiritual matters" ([561]). This second reason or purpose for the country house is interesting because it reveals that in Ignatius' mind Jesuits may at times interrupt their apostolic work to devote themselves for a time to a purely contemplative life. And this is what the Society later made more practical by prescribing the annual Spiritual Exercises.[57]

c. Living on Alms

With stable revenues and property excluded, only alms remained as a means of livelihood. The professed should live on alms ([557]), and the coadjutors as well ([560]). Consequently, they will live in houses which subsist on alms, not in the colleges, which are able to have a fixed income and properties for the benefit of the students. The coadjutors, and with more difficulty the professed, will only be able to live in a college when that is necessary or expedient for the good of the college ([557-560]); this would in effect redound to the benefit of the scholastics.[58]

A professed could also live in a college if necessary or expedient for the general good; for instance, "if someone with an explicit commission from the superior general retires there for a time for the purpose of writing" ([558]). But the tone of these expressions ("someone," "for a time,"

---

capital (ibid.). However, the community can be the juridical subject of all goods and rights pertaining to the apostolic institutions which depend on it (ibid., no. 22); and the goods and incomes of such institutions can be used "for a suitable remuneration for work in such institutes or for services rendered" in them by the members of the community (ibid., no. 21).

56   The Formula of the Institute approved by Julius III (1550) distinguishes better than the former one: *ad reditus, possessiones sed nec ad ulla alia bona stabilia.*

57   The wording of the first text was clearer: "for those who are convalescing and for those who have need of seclusion in order to attend to spiritual matters." The annual Spiritual Exercises were prescribed by General Congregation VI (1608), d. 20, no. 2, as a means for spiritual renewal.

58   Form. Inst. of 1550, no. 8.

"with an explicit commission") shows that this is exceptional, not to be converted into a rule under pain of violating the very serious condition in the Formula of the Institute: "nor may the professed Society be able to convert [the goods of the colleges] to its own uses."[59]

However, these alms are to be "pure alms," as Polanco calls them, given "ex caritate,"[60] not in compensation or remuneration for some ministry. Indeed it is forbidden to "demand or accept any stipend or alms in recompense for Masses or confessions or preaching or lecturing or visiting or *any other ministry* among those which the Society may exercise according to our Institute" ([565]).

Ignatius may have learned the distinction between "pure alms" and stipends, or alms in remuneration, from the passage in Matthew 10 already quoted: there the Lord tells the apostles that, on the one hand, they should give freely what they have freely received and, on the other, that the laborer is worthy of his hire. Thus, although gratuity of ministries has other values as well, such as "greater liberty and greater edification of the neighbor" (see [565]), it is principally based on the poverty which Christ assumed for himself and taught his apostles when he sent them out to preach. It is "how they should go" in preaching what Christ gave them, as Ignatius says in the *Exercises*.[61]

Ignatius carries this "purity" of alms to such an extent that he does not want any poorboxes to be placed in our churches ([567]), nor should Jesuits make small gifts to "important persons" nor visit them except for apostolic purposes ([568]).

There is no basis for making a contrast between living on alms and living from one's own labor. Anyone thinking that to live on alms means to live without working, like vagabonds or professional beggars, would perhaps be justified in asserting (as some have done) that living on alms is today unacceptable since it is an sign of incompetence or inability— although what religious should give testimony to is not precisely skill in worldly business or getting along in life. In the mind of Ignatius, living on alms does not mean to live without work but to live by working disinterestedly, without asking or accepting remuneration for one's labor: "without asking for or expecting any reward in this present and transitory life" ([82]), "for our reward should be only Christ our Lord, who is our reward exceedingly great" ([478]).

---

59 Ibid. Declaration D [559], in the cases it enumerates, is treating of a reasonable application of the general norm so as to avoid scruples, rather than of exceptions.
60 Form. Inst., no. 7.
61 *SpEx*, no. 281, 3°.

Further, far from thinking that living on alms would be equivalent to living without working, living on alms was positively linked to this labor. We see this for instance in the famous letter he wrote to Gian Pietro Carafa, where he outlined in a number of points the concept of religious life which was later to become a reality with the founding of the Society. In that letter Ignatius indicates his belief that it would be very difficult to maintain a religious group who neither produced goods (as the monks had), nor sought alms (as some mendicants did), nor labored "in the sight of the people" by preaching or charitable work; on the other hand, he thought that even if those who devoted themselves to such apostolic and charitable activity did not seek alms, "people are more moved to support them and with much greater charity."[62] Later on, in the Deliberation on Poverty, one of the reasons he adduces in favor of complete poverty is that in this way Jesuits would be more diligent and more disposed to travel and undergo hardships.[63]

There is no doubt that it will be necessary at times to seek alms; this way of life entails such uncertainty. Hence the exhortation that "members should be ready to beg from door to door when obedience or necessity requires it" ([569]).

If we understand living on alms in this way, it obviously is not a sign of incompetence or inability but rather a witness to disinterestedness and indifference and to one's trust and abandonment to Divine Providence. Such a witness is very much needed in our materialistic age, in which everything is bought and sold and people, in the fullness of their pride in technical progress, are easily led to think that they can do without God.[64]

---

62 MI Epp, I, 117.
63 MI Const, I, 79, no. 1; 80, nos. 8 and 10.
64 As already mentioned, we do not intend to present here more than the constitutional law. Having considered the circumstances of our times, G. C. XXXI (1965) stated that "in addition to the alms and income admitted by the Constitutions, gain from or remuneration for work done according to the Institute is a legitimate source of material goods which are necessary for the life and apostolate of Jesuits" (d. 18, no. 15); that "this gratuity is not opposed to the acceptance of Mass stipends or alms" (ibid., no. 16, b); that "Jesuits may *demand* no stipend for their work in spiritual ministries; they may *accept* those which are offered to them" (ibid., no. 16, c); and that they may also legitimately receive gifts which are considered to be the fruit of the talents and industry of Jesuits (ibid., no. 16, d); to which G. C. XXXII (1974-1975) added, "so also the remunerations attached to certain stable ministries, such as those of hospital chaplains, catechists, and the like" (d. 12, H).

d. Poverty of Individuals

After speaking of collective dispossession, which characterized the poverty of the mendicant orders, our Constitutions deal with individual dispossession, common to all religious:[65] "No personal possessions may be held; each one should be content with what is given to him from the common supply" ([570]).

At this point the incapacity to inherit is considered. Religious with solemn vows were always incapable of inheriting personally; but in other orders, instead of the individual religious, his order (or province or house, according to the constitutions) could inherit.[66] The poverty of the Society is stricter on two points: first, not only the professed of solemn vows in the Society, but also the formed coadjutors who have only simple vows, are incapable of inheriting personally; and second, the order (or its houses or churches) cannot inherit "through those individual members" or in their place ([572]).

The last numbers of the chapter ([573-580]) define some aspects of the practice of poverty in the Society. Indeed, it would help but little if, neither individually nor collectively possessing any property, the members were able to enjoy from the alms they receive all the comforts of the rich.[67]

When one is sent on an apostolic mission, it is the responsibility of the one sending, be it the pope ([609-610]) or the superior of the Society ([625]), to determine how one is to go, "whether on foot and without money, or with better facilities." But on papal missions, for greater availability, the one sent "may not demand any provision for the journey" ([573]).

The "facilities" of those days were above all a horse or a mule. But this also might show ostentation or luxury, for the poor went on foot. Hence the norm, antiquated only in its expression, that for reasons of poverty and humility "no mount will ordinarily be kept in the houses of the Society for the use of any member of the Society itself, either superior or subject" ([575]), "unless it should be because of constant infirmities or of urgent necessities in regard to public business" ([576]).[68]

---

65 See, for instance, St. Benedict, *Regula*, chap. 33.

66 See CIC, can. 582.

67 This was a subject of ardent discussion among the Franciscans of the Middle Ages. They all agreed that poverty included not only property but also the use of necessary things. They differed as to the definition of this "usus pauper."

68 St. Ignatius' thinking is expressly stated in a letter to Nadal dated June 1553 (MI Epp, V, 151-152). We said "antiquated only in its expression," because evidently the spirit of the norm can well be applied to modern means of transportation. This W. Ledóchowski did in 1925 (*ActRom*, V, 375). See also J. B. Janssens (ibid.,

Clothing will be "proper," that is, in accord with "clerical propriety," not monastic and much less worldly, but priestly.[69] More than that, it ought to be "conformed to the usage" of "upright" priests in the region where one is living ([577]).[70]

Something similar is said in regard to food, furniture, and the other things necessary or expedient for life. All will be "ordinary," but not ordinary as among people of the world but as among "upright priests,"[71] taking medical advice into account as well ([580]).

However, one condition is mentioned in both cases. Not only in the matter of dress but in other necessary things as well, concern for "humility, poverty, and spiritual edification" should be maintained ([577, 580]): they ought to be "what is characteristic of the poor" ([81]). This proves that the norm of "the manner of living in regard to what is exterior" ([8]) or of "the common and approved usage of upright priests" is not seeking to determine the level of poverty but the style of life. The style of life of the Society is not singular like that of John the Baptist, but ordinary like that of Jesus Christ, who "ate and drank."[72] If it was intended to determine the level of poverty, the phrase would be tautological or redundant. It would be the equivalent of saying: "The *poverty* of the Society is that of upright priests; but let there be consideration for *poverty*." However, the meaning is that the style of life is not singular, but the ordinary lifestyle of exemplary priests; but it should also be poor, humble, and edifying— though the style could be different if the occasion makes it desirable. The use of things necessary for life, although it is to be ordinary (without a penitential habit and fasting or austerities prescribed by rule), has to be poor and consisting of things characteristic of poor people.[73] The history of this norm would lead us to the same conclusion.[74]

XII, 120-121; XIV, 314).

69 See M. Dortel-Claudot, S.J., *Le genre de vie extérieur de la Compagnie de Jésus* (Rome 1971), pp. 37-39 (esp. pp. 41-42). Nadal expressly wrote in his annotations to the *Examen*: "We understand that our life is externally ordinary; not ordinary in the sense that it is accommodated to the secular lifestyle, which is alien to our religious institute, nor ordinary in the sense that it is accommodated to the life of monks" (MHSI Nadal, V, 156).

70 See Form. Inst. of 1550, chap. V, no. 8; MI Const, I, 317 and 333.

71 See loc. cit. in previous note.

72 See Mt. 11:18-19.

73 Dortel-Claudot has a different interpretation, in *Mode de vie, niveau de vie et pauvreté de la Compagnie de Jésus* (CIS, Recherches), IV, 53-66 (esp. 57-60). Still, it seems to us that we agree on substantials.

74 See first Form. Inst. (also called "Five Chapters"), chap. V, and the citations above, note 69.

III. OTHER OBLIGATIONS

What has principally to be observed by the formed Jesuits is "reduced to their vows which they offer to God our Creator and Lord" ([547]). However, religious consecration and the special manner of living it in the Institute of the Society also involves other obligations. Some of them are considered in the last three chapters of Part VI: those referring to individual spiritual life ([582-583]), frequentation of the sacraments ([584]), regular discipline ([585]), unsuitable occupations which are to be avoided ([586-594]), helping dying members and suffrages for them after death ([595-601]), and observance of the Constitutions ([602]).

1. Practices of the Spiritual Life ([582-583])

By his special call to perfection, a religious is particularly obliged to seek union with God through exercises of the interior life such as "prayer" and "meditation" and to exercise himself in the practices of the ascetical life such as "fasts, vigils, and other austerities and penances" ([582]). The constitution considers this as something generally admitted, not requiring proof. It surprises us, then, to find that study is added. What kind of study, we may ask. Doubtless, it is the only kind permitted in the "houses," the updating needed by preachers and confessors to keep on top of their work (see [290]). For that reason the text previously had the addition "sacred"; later on, the adjective was erased, perhaps to avoid giving the impression that it was referring exclusively to the study of Sacred Scripture.

Despite the obligations imposed by these practices, the formed religious are not given any other rule or norm in their regard except "that which discreet charity dictates to them" ([582]).

Some find in this expression "discreet charity" the most extraordinarily recondite and mysterious meanings. The reality is simpler although more fruitful.

The expression already appears in Polanco's *Industrias* (1548)[75] and in the original text of the Constitutions. In the definitive text of the Constitutions we find the expression five times,[76] always in passages composed by Polanco and never from the hand of Ignatius himself.

The adjectival form of the first word, "discreet," might lead to its being

---

75 *Industrias*, 2nd series, 1st *Industria*, no. 10.
76 Once in the first text, under the form of "prudent charity" [754], three times added in text A [209, 237, 269], and once more in text B [582]. We could also add the equivalent term, "discreet zeal" [211].

interpreted as qualifying the second, "charity," as if there were one charity which due to its special nature or intensity is discreet, and another charity which lacks this quality. This is not so. The adjectival form is simply a literary figure indicating—as Polanco says elsewhere—that charity is to be "joined to discretion,"[77] ought to be "ordered" or "moderated" by discretion.[78] So Polanco can speak, negatively, of "indiscreet charity" ([217]) and of "zeal not ordered by proper discretion,"[79] and he can equally apply the adjective "discreet" to other virtues, speaking of "discreet humility"[80] and "discreet freedom,"[81] that is, of a humility or freedom maintained within the limits of discretion.

It will be said that discretion or prudence, guide of the moral virtues, cannot regulate or moderate charity because the measure of the love of God is to love Him without measure. That is true if the phrase refers to charity considered in itself, but it is not true if it is applied to the manifestations of charity. Nadal writes: "Discretion prevents the love of charity from going astray along paths differing from those demanded by true charity."[82] Love is the force; discretion keeps that force within proper bounds. In the actual case under consideration, charity, the love of God and the neighbor, is the driving force for spiritual activity (prayer, meditation, study, penances). It likewise inspires the apostolic work of the spiritual aid of souls. The "discretion" regulates these manifestations of the "charity" in such a way that excessive use of the practices of the spiritual life "may not weaken the bodily energies and consume time to such an extent that these energies are insufficient for the spiritual help of one's fellowmen according to our Institute"; and furthermore, on the contrary, in such a way that "these practices may not be relaxed to such an extent that the spirit grows cold and the human and lower passions grow warm" ([582]).

The reason for not giving to formed religious any rules than those dictated to them by discreet charity is that "it is presupposed that they will be men who are spiritual" ([582]), that is, that they will be men of ardent charity who consequently have no need of exterior impulses on the path of perfection and at the same time are men illuminated by supernatural discretion and accustomed to hear and discern the interior voice of the Spirit and to be docile to it. They are *theodidactoi* as Nadal, using a Pauline

77   MI Epp, VI, 364.
78   See Polanco, *Industrias*, 2nd series, 4th *Industria*, no. 41; MI Epp, III, 485.
79   MI Epp, I, 717. The same expression is found in Form. Inst., no. 2: *ne quis zelo utatur, sed non secundum scientiam.*
80   *Industrias*, 2nd series, 5th *Industria*, no. 34.
81   Ibid., no. 17.
82   *Scholia*, on no. 209, "Prudens caritas."

word, calls them—instructed by God.[83]

However, even spiritual persons can err, either because the fire of charity is not always alive in them or because they do not habitually maintain such a quiet and docile soul that they know how to perceive and follow the gentle whisper of divine invitations. Wisely therefore Ignatius wants the confessor or spiritual director to be informed always, and in case of doubt the superior too—this evidently in order that one or the other may intervene if it should be necessary. Furthermore, the sufficiency of the rule of discreet charity is a general norm; as such it can have exceptions. Ignatius does not forget this and treats of it in the declaration. The superior could fix the time of spiritual exercises for some, to prevent them from being either excessive or deficient, and prescribe other means of perfection for them as well ([583]). According to Gil González Dávila, it was on this declaration and on a parallel passage in Part IV ([343]) that in later years the Society based the prescription of a daily hour of prayer.[84]

2. *Reception of the Sacraments and Regular Observance ([584-585])*

In dealing with reception of the sacraments and regular discipline, it is likewise presupposed that the formed religious are spiritual men. Thus the legislator contented himself with recommending this frequentation and with indicating that, without legitimate excuse, eucharistic communion and celebration of Mass should not be deferred beyond eight days ([584]). Obviously this has to be understood in the historical context in which it was written; the same goes for the item immediately following about the confessor "assigned by the superior" ([584]). We may note nevertheless that even in our day canon law obliges a superior to ensure that religious receive the sacrament of reconciliation frequently.[85]

The extension of the norm to cover the observance of local rules is more unusual. The formed religious are not obliged to observe all the particular rules "which are employed in the houses where they happen to be." They are told only that "it is proper that they should endeavor to observe that part [of the local rules] which is expedient either for their own progress and edification or for [the progress and edification] of the others among whom they find themselves." Clearly, all this is dependent on the judgment of the superior ([585]). This will not be understood if one does not recall—as Nadal notes—that during the lifetime of Ignatius the house in Rome was at one and the same time a house of professed and of

---

83 *Scholia*, on no. 582, "Non videtur in eis"; see 1 Thess. 4:9.
84 *Pláticas sobre las reglas* (Barcelona 1964), p. 292.
85 See CIC, can. 595, §1, 3°.

novices.[86] Furthermore, such was the situation of the "houses" considered in the Constitutions (see [289]). In similar houses it is obvious that local rules are framed chiefly with the novices in mind and that some of these rules are not appropriate for formed religious, supposing always that they are spiritual men.

3. Unsuitable Occupations ([586-594])

The last numbers of the third chapter ([586-594]) are concerned with occupations which should not be undertaken by members of the Society, such as holding choir for the canonical hours, singing Masses and offices ([586-587]), undertaking the office of pastor or parish priest, the care of religious women in community, chaplaincies ([588-590]), and secular employments ([591-594]).

Some will ask why this topic has been included in Part VI and not in Part VII, since it does not concern the "personal spiritual life" of members of the Society but rather their apostolic work "for their fellowmen."[87] Perhaps the explanation is that these items are considered from the point of view of being occupations or offices implying a certain personal responsibility, rather than as apostolic ministries for the help of souls.

The precise reason why members of the Society are not to engage in such labors is because they impede or may impede the spiritual help of our fellowmen which is in conformity with the Institute of the Society and calls for freedom and mobility in the task of evangelization.

The ritual or cultic aspect of the priestly ministry (choir, solemn Masses, other sung offices), which makes up the essential occupation of canons and to a certain extent also of monks,[88] does not form part of the means of evangelization properly so called[89] and would lessen the energy and time needed for such evangelization (see [586]).

The curacy of souls in parishes, and even the spiritual responsibility for religious women, would not have the same problem. But the solemn liturgy in the churches, the office of a pastor or of a regular confessor of religious women, and chaplaincies with Mass foundations are an impediment to the missionary character of the Society's apostolate, with its mobility and availability. In both cases the Constitutions note that our

---

86 *Scholia*, on no. 585, "Ut eam partem."
87 In fact, the first compositions treated of the charge or care of women in Part VII, and of secular business matters in both Parts VI and VII.
88 See A. de Vogüé, O.S.B., "Les sens de l'Office Divin d'après la Règle de S. Benedict," art. in *RevAscMyst*, 42 (1966), 389-404.
89 See Paul VI, *Evangelii nuntiandi*, Dec. 8, 1975; Form. Inst., no. 1; Constit., nos. 400-414, 636-653.

residence "in one place or another" is very "uncertain" ([586]) and that "the members of the Society ought to be ready at any hour to go to some or other parts of the world where they may be sent by the sovereign pontiff or their own superiors" ([588]).

More alien to our vocation of evangelizing and "to the spiritual pursuits pertaining to our profession" ([591]) are "secular employments." To what does this refer? The constitution gives some examples: being "executors of testaments or mandates, or procurators of civil affairs." But obviously these are only examples, to which the norm cannot be restricted. The expression "secular employment" was a technical one used in former church legislation. One title in the Decretals prohibits them for priests and religious: "Neither clerics nor monks ought to be involved in secular employments" (*Ne clerici vel monachi saecularibus negotiis se immisceant*).[90] "Secular" in this context meant occupations or offices which, although licit in themselves, were proscribed for ecclesiastics since they are more appropriate for the laity; examples would be merchants, doctors, civil governors, and the like. The teaching of Vatican II follows the same line of thought. According to it, the secular (occupation with worldly business, management of temporal affairs, involvement with technology, secular culture, and sociopolitical action—which develop created goods and distribute them more equitably) is proper to and characteristic of the laity. On the contrary, although those who have received sacred orders may occasionally (*aliquando*) deal with temporal affairs and even practice a secular profession, they are principally and formally (*praecipue et ex professo*) destined for the sacred ministry by their particular vocation.[91]

4. On the Occasion of Death ([595-601])

The fourth chapter, which did not exist in the first texts, gives norms for the time of death: how the Jesuit who is dying and the others in the house, especially the superior, are to conduct themselves. The entire chapter is notable for its supernatural spirit and the evidence of fraternal charity.

Death is defined as the moment in which "the soul, now freed from the body, is received by Him who redeemed it by that price so high, His blood and life" ([596]). In that moment, as throughout his life and indeed even "much more," the Jesuit "ought to strive earnestly that through him God our Lord may be glorified and served and his fellowmen may be edified" ([595]). Perhaps he will not be able to do so by words, but he

---

90   *Decretales Gregorii IX,* bk. III, tit. 50.
91   Conc. Vat. II, *LG,* no. 31.

should ensure it at least by the example of his virtues: patience and fortitude in supporting the pains and anguish of infirmity, along with faith, a "living" faith in the eternal blessings of future life, the hope of attaining those eternal goods along with desire for them, a faith, hope, and love which are not founded on the merits of his own life, but on Jesus Christ our Lord, who merited and acquired them for us "by those altogether incomparable sufferings of His temporal life and death" ([595]). Let us note that the words "altogether incomparable" were added by Ignatius himself.

The "fraternal charity" of all the residents of the house will be shown by ensuring that their dying companion receives the holy sacraments in due time and "fortifies himself for the passage from this temporal life to that which is eternal by means of the arms which the divine liberality of Christ our Lord offers" ([595]) They are to help him by "special prayers," keeping him company and recalling to his mind helpful thoughts which are appropriate at that moment ([596]); and after his death, with suffrages for his soul "so that charity be shown in our Lord toward the departed no less than toward the living" ([598-601]).

A trait of delicate charity is expressed in declaration A, which says: "When some sick persons fall into delirium . . . or when someone does not give as much edification as he ought to in his infirmity, those assisting could be few and chosen from among those in whom more confidence is placed" ([597]).

5. Observance of the Constitutions ([602])

Some might think that the Preamble to the Constitutions is the proper place to deal with the question of obligation rather than at this point. In fact both passages are inspired by the same thought. Perhaps the stress here is more precisely on the point that formed religious have to give an example by their observance (see [276]). We noted at the start of the chapter that historically this paragraph comes from an early "determination" dealing with obedience as well as observance, and that for that reason the editor of the primitive text included it in Part VI.

The Society desires "that all the Constitutions and Declarations and its regime of living should be observed in every regard according to our Institute, without deviation in anything" ([602]). The assertion could not be more explicit. Nor is this the only place in the Constitutions where it is found. At the beginning of Part VI we saw that Ignatius urged us "not to miss any point of perfection which we can with God's grace attain in the observance of all the Constitutions and in our manner of proceeding" ([547]). In Part IX the general is reminded that it depends on him "to see to it that the Constitutions of the Society are observed in all places" ([746]), and this norm is given to him as a means for governing the Society well ([790]). And in Part X it is noted, as a means of preserving and developing the body of the Society, that "all should apply themselves to the observance of the Constitutions" ([826]).

Ignatius does not want to impose this observance under pain of either mortal or venial sin because he wants the members of the Society to be "free from anxiety and aided against falling into any snare of sin." If all the prescriptions of the Rule were to oblige under pain of sin, then—as Thomas Aquinas comments—the religious state, which ought to be more secure than the secular, would be the most dangerous.[92]

The extent to which rules or constitutions are obligatory was a subject much debated in the Middle Ages.[93] On this question as on other points of religious legislation, the Dominicans adopted a radical and unequivocal position: the constitutions do not oblige "under sin but under penalty, unless by a commandment or because of contempt" (*ad culpam sed ad poenam, nisi propter praeceptum vel contemptum*).[94] Ignatius followed on the same line; however, we may observe a notable difference. The Dominicans said that the constitutions do not oblige under sin but under penalty, unless by a commandment or because of contempt; Ignatius said that they do not oblige under pain of sin, mortal or venial, if the superior does not order in the name of Christ or in virtue of obedience ([602]). As among the Dominicans, the obligation under pain of sin is removed; but, differing from them, the obligation of penalty is omitted as well. The reason is that the Dominican constitutions, like those of other religious orders, including the Rule of Benedict, contained a penal code.[95] In the Society there is no penal code; even the word "punishment" was erased by Ignatius when speaking of corrections ([270]). It is only on those who attempt to disturb the election of a general that some censures are to be imposed ([695, 696, 700]).[96]

If the Constitutions do not oblige under pain of sin or penalty (which does not prevent a superior from imposing penances because of faults—see [269, 270, 291, 754]), how is their observance to be enforced? Ignatius has recourse to the evangelical law of charity which the Holy Spirit writes

---

92   S. Th., 2-2, q. 186, art. 9, Sed contra.

93   See C. Mazón, S.J., *Las reglas de los religiosos* (Rome 1940), pp. 183 ff.

94   See *Constitutiones O.P.*, Prolog., §4. The resolution was taken at the general chapter in Paris in 1236, under the presidency of Bl. Jordan of Saxony. See *MonOPHist*, III, 8.

95   See *Constitutiones O.P.*, dist. I, chaps 16-19; St. Benedict, *Regula*, chaps. 23-30.

96   The word "chastisement" appears only once in the definitive text, in reference to extern students of the universities [488]. Neither is contempt (*contemptus*) mentioned in the constitution; probably because sinning *propter contemptum* is a moral norm which applies to every law.

upon hearts ([134]): "In place of the fear of giving offense [or of the penalty] there should arise a love and desire of all perfection, and a desire that greater glory and praise of Christ our Creator and Lord may follow" ([602]). The interior law of charity and love, stronger than any fear of fault or punishment, will inspire us not to lose any point of perfection which we can attain by fulfilling the Constitutions.

Despite all this, one of the anti-Jesuit legends—which we mention merely as a curiosity—uses this chapter as a basis for the argument that superiors in the Society can oblige subjects to commit sin. They interpret it like this: the Constitutions do not oblige one to *commit* a sin unless the superior orders it in the name of Christ or in virtue of obedience. There is no need to refute this enormous bit of nonsense. Prescinding from history, from the context, and from the explicit affirmations that we find in other passages (see [284, 547, 549]), how is it possible that one can be ordered to commit a sin *in the name of Christ*? Nevertheless, not a few writers have made that assertion.[97] To take but one example, here is what the historian Jules Michelet has written, in a tone of empty rhetoric: "In this militant order, under its pacific garb, to what point will obedience come? This is the capital point. And it is here that the Basque captain was really original. The founders of the older orders had said: 'Unto death.' Loyola goes much further and says: 'Unto sin.' Venial? No, even further still. He includes mortal sin as well under obedience: 'Our considered opinion in our Lord is that no constitutions can oblige under mortal or venial sin unless the superior orders (in the name of Jesus Christ or in virtue of obedience).' 'No rule can impose mortal sin unless the superior orders it.' So, if it is ordered, one has to sin, sin mortally. This is new, audacious, fecund."[98]

IV. A FINAL OBSERVATION

Part VI takes for granted, as always, a constituted Society, having its own houses and churches, a community which aids its dying members with fraternal charity and recites the office of the dead for one who has just died and which has local superiors. It was precisely the decision to have an

---

97 See B. Duhr, S.J., *Jesuiten-Fabeln*, chap. 17.
98 Quoted by G. Monod in the introduction to the French translation of the work of H. Boehmer, *Les Jésuites* (Paris 1910), p. xiii-xiv. The Protestant Gabriel Monod (pp. xiv-xvi) refutes what he calls "the monstrous error" in the interpretation of a chapter which he qualifies as not only "irreproachable" but "touching." [Editor's note: Michelet has omitted essential words from the rest of Ignatius' statement, which show that a superior may order only things which are licit.]

internal superior whom all are obliged by vow to obey that determined in 1539 the constitution of the Society as a religious order.

That supposed, it is the life of apostolic mission that gives its specific character to the norms in this Part.

The superior himself is not, as in some other orders, a mere agent of the community. Even in treating here of "corporative" obedience, not of "missionary" obedience, the superior is the one who substitutes for Christ, in whose place he guides each one of his subjects. It might be said that, as during the years in Paris when he was looking for a master to serve and obey,[99] Ignatius always has present the image of Jesus Christ surrounded by His apostles. From this presence of Christ in the superior follow the remaining qualities of Ignatian obedience: the spirit of love, promptitude in execution, submission of the will and judgment, the dazzling light of "blind obedience," reverence for the superior, and so on.

The poverty is clearly that which, according to Matthew, Jesus Christ taught the apostles on sending them out to preach: poverty in the giving up of all property; poverty in living from pure alms; poverty even in the use of necessities; although the style of living is not austere, like that of John the Baptist, but ordinary, like that of Jesus Christ and His Apostles.

As to unsuitable occupations, we already noted that they are so because they are contrary to the mobility and availability of evangelization. Such are even spiritual occupations if they have a more ritual or cultic than evangelizing character and above all if they bind to a place. But secular occupations conflict even more with that mobility and availability.

---

99   See *Autobiog,* no. 78.

Chapter XI

APOSTOLIC LIFE
OF THE INCORPORATED MEMBERS
(Constitutions, Part VII)

I. PRELIMINARY REMARKS

1. Structure and Evolution

The treatment begun in Part VI, concerning those already incorporated into the Society, now continues. In Part VI the members were considered under the religious aspect: "In Regard to Themselves"; now, in Part VII, we look at the apostolic aspect: "The Distribution of the Incorporated Members in Christ's Vineyard and Their Relations with Their Fellowmen."[1]

This "distribution" is done in two ways: either by the members' being sent to evangelize in various parts of the world in imitation of the Apostles or by their residing at a fixed place in expectation of being sent. For the life of the Jesuit is "missionary" but not nomadic. Jesus Christ Himself left Capernaum to preach "in the synagogues, towns, and villages," but also returned to Capernaum, which Matthew calls "His own town."[2] Our first fathers decided from the beginning, from 1539, to have not only houses where they resided but also churches where they exercised spiritual ministries on behalf of their fellowmen.[3]

Thus, the four chapters which go to make up this Part can be divided into two sections: the first dealing with missions (being sent) and the second with apostolic activity in the place of residence. With regard to missions, the following distinctions are made: one may be sent to a definite spot by the pope (chapter 1) or by the superior of the Society (chapter 2) or to a larger region without specification of place or activity (chapter 3).[4]

This scheme has been preserved in all the texts. The most important

---

1 Fuller references will be found in our extensive commentary on Part VII published under the title *Repartiéndose en la viña de Cristo* (Rome: CIS, 1973).
2 See Mt. 4:13; 9:1; 11:1; Mk. 1:35; 2:1.
3 MI Const, I, 13, no. 15.
4 This content and division are indicated in the introductory paragraph [603a]. It was enuntiated more explicitly in the earliest text, which we shall quote later on.

change was that a great deal of the second chapter passed from the Constitutions properly so called into the Declarations. This change was doubtless influenced by a suggestion from Salmerón, but there is also the fact that the norms contained in these declarations are more the concern of superiors than subjects.

2. Sources

In a certain sense Part VII is the oldest of all. Ignatius had hardly solved the serious question of poverty when the first subject he began to develop in writing was that of "missions" from the pope and from the superior of the Society. This work he entitled "Constitutions Regarding Missions" (*Constitutiones circa missiones*). The notebook containing these writings was inserted in the first text in order that—along with some paragraphs added by Polanco—they would form Part VII.

Generally speaking, the first chapter reproduces the "Constitutions Regarding Missions" and the second chapter the declarations to these constitutions. The present declarations of the second chapter, and the third chapter, derive from Polanco's seventh *Industria*. The fourth chapter, also added by Polanco, seems original although evidently based on the first Formula of the Institute.

First Section: On Missions

II. Missions from the Pope

Missions from the pope are treated in the first chapter. After a paragraph introductory to the entire Seventh Part ([603a]), the chapter deals with the meaning of the vow of obedience to the pope "in regard to missions" (*circa missiones*) ([603b-605]), the manner of its execution [606-616]), and the obligation of informing the pope about this vow of special obedience ([617]).

1. Meaning of the Fourth Vow ([603-605])
    a. Object of the Vow

In commenting on the formula of profession in Part V, we noted that there has been some debate in recent decades on the meaning of this vow. The controversy has been centered on this point: Whether the object of the vow covers the entire scope of religious obedience or is limited to "missions."

As we also mentioned there, we do not intend to examine the content of the so-called "papal clause" of the vow at Montmartre.[5] Nor are we speaking here of the obligation to obey the pope in view of his universal jurisdiction as supreme pastor of the Church; nor of the obligation of the professed, along with the nonprofessed and all religious, to obey him by virtue of the third vow, the ordinary vow of obedience, as the supreme superior of religious. We are speaking solely of the obligation incumbent on the professed of the Society by virtue of the fourth vow of special obedience.

The fact that Ignatius did not treat of this fourth vow in Part VI along with the other three, but reserved it for Part VII, is already an indication to us of the object of the vow. But we have in addition the very words in which the vow is formulated in the formula of profession: "I further promise a special obedience to the sovereign pontiff in regard to missions" (*insuper promitto specialem oboedientiam Summo Pontifici circa missiones*) ([527]).

It will be objected that the Formula of the Institute seems to give the vow a greater extension when it states: "We are to be obliged to carry out whatever the present and future Roman Pontiffs may order which pertains to the progress of souls and the propagation of the faith and to go to whatsoever provinces they may choose to send us" (*ut quidquid modernus et alii Romani Pontifices pro tempore existentes iusserint ad profectum animarum et fidei propagationem pertinens, et ad quascumque provincias nos mittere voluerint . . . exsequi teneamur*). It could be said that two distinct objects or two elements of the same object are indicated: first, "whatever they may order" (*quidquid iusserint*); second, "to whatever provinces they may choose to send us" (*ad quascumque provincias nos mittere voluerint*). The first element is very extensive, although somewhat restricted by the words "which pertains to the progress of souls and the propagation of the faith" (*ad profectum animarum et fidei propagationem pertinens*). It refers to what the pope may order in line with the objective of the Society expressed in the first number of the Formula itself: the spiritual progress of souls and the propagation of the faith.[6]

But we ask ourselves: Since the first element is so wide, for what purpose is a second added? Is not the phrase "to whatever provinces they may choose to send us" (*ad quascumque provincias nos mittere voluerint*) included in the phrase "whatever they may order" (*quidquid iusserint*)? And

5   Personally, however, we think that the vow of Montmartre referred only to the destination or field of the apostolate.

6   So it is stated in the Formula in 1539 and 1540. In 1550 the defense of the faith was added in no. 1; but the corresponding correction which ought to have been made in this place was disregarded.

note that the second element was not contained in the first composition of the Formula or "Five Chapters"; it was introduced into the Formula of 1540, and thus deliberately. This addition cannot be explained if it was not made with the intention of explaining and defining the first element, precisely because its formulation was too extensive. This interpretation is not something we have discovered; we find it expressly stated by Nadal in his commentaries on the Formula; he says that, in the phrase "and to whatever provinces" (*et ad quascumque provincias*), "the *et* is explanatory; for this vow is understood only in regard to missions."[7]

This explains how, when the Formula itself wanted to give concrete examples of the object of the vow, it did not say "whether they order" (*sive iusserint*) but "whether they send us among the Turks" (*sive miserint nos ad Turcas*, etc.); and this right from the first composition of the "Five Chapters." In the whole of the following context, mention is made only of missions: that there is to be neither ambition for nor refusal of "these missions" (*missionum ac provinciarum huiusmodi*) nor efforts to make arrangements with the pope about "these missions" (*de huiusmodi missionibus*), nor is the general to try to arrange to be sent or not sent (*de sui ipsius missione in alterutram partem*).

Therefore, when a short time later Ignatius and his companions made their profession in the basilica of St. Paul, they expressed the fourth vow by saying: "I further promise a special obedience to the sovereign pontiff in regard to the missions as contained in the bull" (*insuper promitto specialem oboedientiam Summo Pontifici circa missiones in bulla contentas*); not "in regard to everything he may order" (*circa omne id quod iusserit*)—a sign that what the bull (that is, the Formula approved in the bull) contained as the object of the vow was only the missions, not all religious obedience.

But the most important argument, and to our mind the decisive one, is the authentic interpretation given by Ignatius in declaration C in the third chapter of Part V, already quoted. Citing the very words of the Formula, he formally declares that they are to be understood of obedience "in regard to missions" and that this "was and is" the intention of the vow ([529]). Nadal notes that the vow has to be understood in that way even though the Formula seems to refer it not only to missions but to everything else. This is so because the Society has the papally granted power of interpreting the Formula.[8] In other places he expressly asserts that the

---

7   M. Ruiz Jurado, S.J., "Nadal y Polanco sobre la Fórmula del Instituto de la Compañia de Jesús," art. in *ArchHistSI*, XLVII (1978), 237 ("et ad quascumque provincias," etc.).

8   *Scholia*, on no. 529, "Et sic intellegi opportet."

obligation of the fourth vow refers only to missions.[9]

b. Meaning of "Mission"

We believe then that there is no doubt that the sole object of the special vow of obedience to the pope is the missions. The only possible doubt concerns what is meant by missions; for this word had, and still has, various meanings. The most common, mainly in our times (with no slight danger of confusion), is that of commission, charge, or mandate and, in a derived sense, that of destination or vocation. In this sense General Congregation XXXII could speak of "our mission today." From the end of the sixteenth century, apostolic expeditions began to be called "missions" in the Society and afterwards in the Church too. Thus the *Epitome of the Institute* expressly defines them.[10] But in the Constitutions and in some of his other writings Ignatius uses the term "mission" in the original Latin sense of "sending."[11] As early as 1539, when the first fathers decided that the members of the Society should make the vow of obedience to the pope "in regard to missions" (*circa missiones*), they stated it by saying that by the vow each one has to offer *to go* to any region whatever (*se offerat iturum*). Ignatius entitled the first chapter of the "Constitutions Regarding Missions": "On the Promise and Vow *to Travel* through Any Part of the World."[12] Likewise in the Examen he says that the professed "make a vow to the pope *to go* anywhere His Holiness will order" ([7]). The same concept is supposed throughout the first chapter and even in the remainder of Part VII: No one is to seek "to reside in or to be sent to one place rather than to another" ([606]); "he who has been designated to go to some region should offer his person generously" ([609]); the pope, without designating the person, could order that "one or more should go to one region or another" ([611]); "it is highly expedient that the mission should be entirely explained to the one who is sent" ([612]); "being sent" without determination of time means that the residence should last three months ([615]); if this is prolonged in some determined place, it will not be improper for the one on the mission to make some excursions to aid the souls in the

9   *Scholia*, on no. 605, "Ad locum aliquem particularem"; *Orationis observationes*, p. 132, no. 351. See Ruiz Jurado, art. cit. in note 7, p. 234, no. 14, where Nadal proposes that the phrase in the Formula be corrected so that it not seem to contradict the interpretation of the Constitutions. The reference "2° cap. 7 par.," perhaps through a copyist's mistake, is obviously wrong. It ought to read: "1° cap. 7 par." or "3° cap. 5 par."

10   *Epitome Instituti*, no. 612, §1.

11   A. Codina had already noted this: MI Const, II, p. lxxiv.

12   MI Const, I, 159.

neighboring regions ([616]); and so forth.

But most important of all is the first number of chapter 1 ([603b]), for it is there that Ignatius states what was his and his companions' "intention" or mind when they decided that this vow was to be made in the Society, that is: not for all to be sent together by the pope to a particular place, such as a city or diocese, but to be *"distributed* into diverse regions and places throughout the world," "leaving the distribution of its members to the sovereign pontiff" (the first text had: "our distribution and mission"). And the reason was their desire "to travel throughout the world . . . ever intent on seeking the greater glory of God our Lord and the greater aid of souls," and not to know "into which regions they were to go, whether among the faithful or the unbelievers" ([603, 605]). Nadal understood this well; he comments: "The obligation of the vow refers only to the missions themselves precisely as such; as if we would say, to the distribution of the workers in the vineyard of the Lord."[13]

The difference between the apostolic work which is done by being "sent" and that which is done by "residing" is indicated in the first half of the same number ([603a]), especially in the first wording of the primitive, *a,* text. There the distinction is made between the missions through various places where the Society does not establish any residence and the places where it normally is present, and it is explained that the missions are of three types: first, "being *sent* by the Holy Father to a determined place"; second, "being *sent* by the general"; third, "each one choosing where to work in the vineyard of Christ, having been given a commission for this, as one who is *sent* to the Indies."

It is clear that such missions or "sendings" have an apostolic purpose. They have as their objective "to exercise any ministry of those the Society uses for helping the neighbor" ([743]; see [308]). It is also clear that if the pope sends anyone *in order* to exercise a ministry or carry out a definite task belonging to the specific end of the Society, this ministry or task is inseparable from the mission itself and so enters into the obligation of the vow. Therefore Ignatius desires that "the mission should be entirely explained to the one who is thus sent, as well as the intention of His Holiness and the result in hope of which he is sent . . . so that he may be better able to accomplish what is entrusted to him" ([612]). From this, Suárez deduces that as the pope can order one to exercise a ministry in the place of the mission to which he is sent, so he can also order him to exercise it in the place of residence; because, if he did not reside in that

<hr />

13   *Scholia*, on no. 605, "Ad locum aliquem particularem."

place, the pope could send him to it.[14] For this reason some designated as a "pontifical mission" any apostolic work or ministry exercised in any place by order of the pope.

Of course, it is certain the pope can order a professed member of the Society to undertake a particular ministry in the place where he resides and that the professed member has an obligation to obey him. The question is whether in such a case there is a "mission" and consequently whether the obligation to obey is then by virtue of the fourth vow. For in such a case, according to the obvious and commonly accepted meaning of the words used, there would be no sending, no "division" or "distribution" of the members of the Society; nor would they be "spread" throughout various regions and places ([603, 605]). From the fact that when a professed Jesuit is residing *away* from his usual place of residence he may have been sent there by the pope, it by no means follows that when residing *in* his usual place of residence he has been sent or could be sent there by the pope.

Ignatius always had in mind the mission and dispersion of the apostles, whom the Lord "sent through all the world, spreading His sacred doctrine through all states and conditions of persons."[15] On February 11, 1544, Ignatius wrote in his *Spiritual Journal*: "At this moment other lights came to me, namely, how the Son first sent the apostles to preach in poverty and afterwards the Holy Spirit, giving His spirit and the gift of tongues, confirmed them and thus, the Father and the Son sending the Holy Spirit, all Three Persons confirmed the mission."[16] It is not surprising that Favre had a special devotion to the feast of the distribution or dispersion of the apostles, which was then celebrated in some dioceses on July 15.[17]

2. Manner of Fulfilling This Vow ([606-612])

After explaining the meaning of the fourth vow, Ignatius moves on to explain the best way of fulfilling the obligation it imposes.

The first requirement is indifference. Papal missions may not be rejected nor sought ([606]). The Formula of the Institute had already stated as much. There too the attitude of constant preparation and availability was underlined: "being day and night clad for traveling, prompt in carrying out this obligation." Here that attitude of availability is more interiorized. In

---

14   *De Soc.*, no. 706.
15   *SpEx*, no. 145.
16   MI Const, I, 90-91. Note the words "sent to preach in poverty." To preach in poverty, sent by the Vicar of Christ, is the vocation of the Society. The Spanish gerundive "enviando" is causal, equivalent to the Latin "cum mitteret."
17   MHSI Faber, 514, no. 46.

[606] it is stated: "In this matter" (that is, in this area or in this field of pontifical missions), our "judgment and desire," our understanding and will are wholly subjected to Christ our Lord and to His vicar, through whom Christ sends us. To the pope and to the general, who will be able to treat of it with the pope, is to be left all concern about one's own destination and that of others of the Society.[18]

The Formula of the Institute also advised the one chosen for a mission that he should leave "without subterfuge or excuses."[19] Here the same idea of promptitude and effective indifference is developed, touching also on affective and positive readiness. He is to offer his person liberally, that is, he is to make an unconditional offering of himself, without seeking "anything corporal," not even traveling expenses or provision for the journey—leaving it up to the pope to determine whether he should make the trip and live in the place of mission begging for alms or in another manner, as His Holiness judges to be for the greater service of God and of the Apostolic See; further, without the pope's paying attention to anything else in the one sent, that is, without the pope's having any consideration or regard for his person apart from this service of God and of the Holy See ([609, 610]).

Other similar prescriptions follow ([611-617]), which reveal the effort of Ignatius to ensure the faithful, though not scrupulous, observance of the fourth vow. We will not delay on them as we judge they are not of such great interest spiritually.

III. MISSIONS FROM THE SUPERIOR GENERAL

The second chapter has an internal structure which, because of its genesis and the fact that the greater part passed on into the Declarations, makes it difficult to understand at a first reading.

Four topics can be distinguished: (a) the reason for missions from the superior ([618a, 619-621]); (b) how the superior should proceed when sending subjects ([618b, 618c, 622-626]); (c) the attitude of the subject ([618d, 627-628]); (d) help given by the superior to the one sent ([629-632]).

---

18   Compare "reside in or be sent" with "going or remaining" of no. 618c.
19   The Latin word *tergiversatio* does not have the meaning of falsification, alteration of meaning, but rather that of subterfuge or evasion.

1. Reason for These Missions ([618a, 619-621])

The chapter begins with a reference to a faculty granted by the pope for the superior general of the Society to have authority "to send any of the Society's members whomsoever to whatsoever place he thinks it more convenient to send them." It states the reason which moved Ignatius to ask for this faculty ([618a]).[20]

We think it rather strange that Ignatius should have needed to ask for and obtain such a faculty, for we conceive of the fourth vow only as an obligation which the Jesuit undertakes to obey the pope, *in case* the pope should happen to send him. But the intention of the first fathers was that, "to avoid erring in the path of the Lord," the pope was to be the one who makes the division or distribution of the subjects of the Society (see [603, 605]). Ignatius considered it as something ordinary and exclusive to the vicar of Christ to send the professed—to such an extent that without a special faculty from the pope himself the general could not do so. It follows from this that when the general of the Society, by himself or by means of other superiors (see [620]), sends some professed on an apostolic mission, he does not act of himself by reason of his office as general, but "in place of the pope" (according to the expression of Ignatius himself in the Examen [82]) by virtue of a special faculty or delegation granted by the pope. A more serious consequence is that in this field of the missions, when obeying the general or superior of the Society who sends him, the professed is observing the fourth vow.

It is also logical that this special faculty—granted by the pope to the general of the Society—of having authority to send the professed in his place should not create an impediment to missions which the pope himself personally wants to arrange. The constitution states that the members of the Society "wherever they are" (in their place of residence or sent by the general) "will be at the disposition of His Holiness" ([618a]). Under the same condition the faculty was requested and granted: "in such a manner that those who are sent should always be ready to go wherever His Holiness would wish to transfer them, according to the vow made to His Holiness from the beginning."[21] Even more expressly the bull *Licet debitum* states that "wherever they should be, on receiving notice from the Roman Pontiff, they will have to come to the Apostolic See or go wherever it is expedient and where the same Apostolic See should order, in conformity with the profession of the Society."[22]

---

20   See MI FontDoc, 657-658.
21   Ibid.
22   MI Const, I, 358.

2. Procedure of the Superior ([618bc])

The superior who makes use of this faculty of sending is to ensure above all that he is quite clear about the mission itself, that is, about the different aspects and circumstances of the assignment. Once the assignment has been decided, he is to assist the one sent by instructions, counsel, prayer, and "all other aids he can," such as letters patent, ministerial privileges, and so forth ([629-633]). Of these two points, the one presenting some difficulty and more developed in the Constitutions is the first, and we will delay on it alone.

That the superior may succeed better in his missions, norms or criteria are given which he ought to apply ([618b, 622-626]); and he is then shown how to apply them ([618c]).

(a) The norms or criteria are reduced to a basic principle: The one who sends "ought to bestow much careful thought . . . in order that . . . that procedure may always be used which is conducive to the greater service of God and the universal good" ([618b]). Here we come across the double phrase which is often repeated in the Constitutions: service (glory, praise) of God and the good (help, edification, spiritual benefit) of souls. It is a double phrase which is summed up in a single concept: "the service given to God by aiding the souls which belong to Him" ([528]), because the service of God which is sought consists in helping men to know and love Him and thereby to save their souls ([446]).

The second element of the double phrase is conceived here under the aspect of "universal good," because precisely this universality, proper to the vocation or charism of the Society, is what led to the making in it of the vow of obedience to the pope "in regard to missions" (*circa missiones*) (see [603, 605]). Therefore the superior "ought to bestow much careful thought" so as not to yield readily to pressures from those who are seeking rather the particular good of a town or diocese ([618b]); and a saying of Thomas Aquinas (based on Aristotle) is quoted: "The more universal the good, the more divine" ([622]).[23]

It is to be noted, however, that this universality does not refer to the "comprehension" of the concept of good but to its "extension." In other words, it is a good which reaches all kinds of people (see [163]) and places (see [603, 605]), not a good which comprises a particular aspect of good (material, cultural, or spiritual). Missions of the pope and consequently

---

23   "Quanto aliquod bonum est communius, tanto divinius" (St. Thomas, in IV Sent., dist. 49, art. 1). See Aristotle, *Nicomachean Ethics*, chap. 1, 2. We owe the reference to J. M. Fernández-Cueto, CPCR.

those of the superior of the Society, who acts in his place, are for things which "pertain to the benefit of souls and to the defense and propagation of the faith."[24] From the way in which the double phrase is formed in other contexts, we also deduce that Ignatius thought only of the spiritual good of souls. In fact in the "Constitutions Regarding Missions," which is the source of this passage, he had written "the greater and more universal benefit of souls." Furthermore, as Nadal notes, basing himself on a reply which Ignatius gave to Dr. Ortiz, not just any spiritual good whatever of souls but that which is in accordance with our Institute.[25]

This basic norm is the one which the superior has to apply in judging the different circumstances of a mission: where to send, for what purpose, who is to be sent, in what manner, for how long ([618b]). Declarations D to H ([622-626]) indicate some more particular deductions from this principle which will help the superior to apply it better. They are clear and need no commentary.

(b) Application: How are these norms to be applied to a concrete case? The third paragraph of the constitution ([618c]) instructs the superior in a method along the same lines as the one indicated in Part II for dismissals ([220-222]), the method used by Ignatius himself and the one he advised other superiors to use.[26] The "right and pure intention" of the greater service of God and the universal good being supposed, this method can be summarized in three elements or acts:

Prayer: "He will commend the matter to His Divine Majesty and cause it to be commended to the prayers and Masses of the house."

Consultation: "He will discuss it with one or more members of the Society who happen to be present and whom he thinks suitable."

Decision: "He himself will decide."

Prayer is necessary because "the supreme providence and direction of the Holy Spirit" is what "efficaciously must guide us to bring deliberations to a right conclusion" ([624]).[27] Consultation, as Ignatius had written in the "Constitutions Regarding Missions," "can often help so that the superior, listening to diverse views and reasons, can decide with greater facility." The decision is exclusively the superior's: "He himself will decide"; the decision —the same constitutions add—should always remain with the superior, although he consults with others (see [810]).

---

24 *Form. Inst.*, chap. II, no. 3. See Examen, no. [7].
25 *Scholia*, in no. 618, "Et bonum universale."
26 See MI Const, I, 217-219; Epp I, 621; IX, 215 and 226; FontNarr, I, 732.
27 The words "in everything" (*en todo*) were added by St. Ignatius himself (in text A) to bring out that the assertion is not restricted only to the subject treated in that declaration.

3. Attitude of the Subject ([618d, 627, 628])

As in pontifical missions ([606-609]), so also in those given by the superior of the Society, the attitude of the subject is to be one of indifference and availability, an attitude so fundamental in Ignatian spirituality: "The part of him who is sent will be, without interposing himself in favor of going or remaining in one place rather than another, to leave the disposition of himself completely and freely to the superior who, in the place of Christ our Lord, directs him in the path of His greater service and praise" ([618d]; see [304]).

This availability does not, however, prevent the subject from "representing" to the superior "the motions or thoughts which occur to him contrary to an order received" ([627]). These terms have also an almost technical value for Ignatius.

The *Exercises* assume that "interior motions" and "thoughts" can result from the activity of various spirits and can be a means of discovering the will of God for a soul.[28] "Representing"—something far different from what is nowadays called "confrontation"—has no suggestion of opposition or contrast. It simply means sharing humbly with the superior "the reasons or inconveniences which appear to the subject, not inclining him one way or another, so that afterwards he can follow the way that will be shown to him with peace of mind"[29] and "submitting his entire judgment and will to that of his superior," who is "in the place of Christ" ([627]). One of the reasons, and perhaps the main one, given in the Examen for the necessity of the account of conscience is that the superior will be able to decide better about missions through his knowledge of these interior motions and inclinations ([92]).

Once in the place of the mission, it is the duty of the one sent, as the Constitutions indicate indirectly, to inform the superior "about the entire outcome" ([629]).

There is no need to speak about the third chapter ([633-635]). Some have marveled at the broad-mindedness of Ignatius in holding that "members may themselves choose where and in what work they will labor" ([603]). They do not notice that this refers only to the case in which someone is sent, not to exercise some ministry in a city or a definite place, but to evangelize "an extensive region" ([633])—as, for example, Francis Xavier in the mission of India. Even then it is stated that the superior

28   See *SpEx*, nos. 17, 32, 313, 316, 317, 333 . . .
29   St. Ignatius to the young J. B. Viola in 1542 (MI Epp, I, 288).

could intervene and "direct a member to one place rather than another" ([633]) and that "it will always be safer for him [the one sent] to confer with his nearest superior about the means to be used" ([635]).

Second Section: In the Place of Residence

IV. WAYS OF HELPING THE NEIGHBOR

The principal and most perfect residence of the Society—Nadal wrote —is the journeys or missions of the professed.[30] However, as we pointed out at the beginning, "mission" (sending) implies a place from which one is sent and to which one returns on completion of the time for which one is sent. Nadal considers houses of the Society to be like army encampments from which soldiers make forays to attack the enemy and to which they return to restore themselves in body and spirit.[31]

The fourth chapter lists means of helping the neighbor which are to be used in the colleges and houses of the Society. They are no different from those employed on mission (see [633]). But they are placed here because on missions it belongs to the one who sends to determine the ministry which the one sent is to exercise or the task he has to accomplish (see [612, 616, 623]).

Ignatius composed three lists of ministries proper to the Society: one is in the first number of the Formula of the Institute, another in the eighth chapter of Part IV, and the third here in Part VII. These lists coincide in content, in the ministries enumerated, but they differ in the order of listing, which depends on the purpose intended in each case. The intention in the Formula is to define the specific ministries of the Society; hence the order proceeds from the most to the least appropriate. In Part IV the objective is pedagogical, to teach the scholastics how they are to prepare themselves to exercise the ministries of the Society; so the list is ordered according to the intrinsic dignity of the ministries (although this order is somewhat altered in the final text). Here in Part VII the purpose is to indicate the means for helping the neighbor in the houses and colleges of the Society. Presupposing the general division between spiritual ministries and works of mercy, the ministries are ordered according to greater or lesser frequency: going from those which everyone can exercise at all times to those exercised only occasionally and by selected persons.

---

30 See MHSI Nadal, V, 195, 364-365.
31 Ibid., 195, 470, 773.

How these ministries are to be practiced in the particular circumstances of our times is not for us to determine but for those who are charged with directing the Society in its apostolate. We wish only to draw attention to the surprising coincidence of these Ignatian lists with the Apostolic Exhortation *Evangelii Nuntiandi* of Paul VI (December 8, 1975).[32] Excepting perhaps prayer, the means listed in the Constitutions for helping the neighbor spiritually are the same as those which the pope indicates as means of evangelization.

1. Good Example and Prayer ([637-641])

The first two means for helping the neighbor, good example and prayer, are universal: every member of the Society can and should use them.

The Apostolic Exhortation *Evangelii Nuntiandi* gives first place among the means of evangelization to "the witness of an authentically Christian life, given over to God in a communion that nothing should destroy and at the same time given to one's neighbor with limitless zeal."[33]

The constitution adds to prayers "desires in the presence of God our Lord" ([638]). These are desires for greater divine service and glory: that men may know and love God more and more and save their souls; desires which make prayer itself more fervent and, if they animate other activities, convert them into an enduring apostolic prayer.[34]

Mass, the celebration of the Eucharist, is prayer in the highest degree since it is the prayer of Christ, who offers the sacrifice of his body and blood to the Father, and also the prayer of the Church. This is the point of view from which Ignatius considers it both here ([640]) and elsewhere in the Constitutions. He considers the Mass not so much from the aspect of liturgical worship, which is less special to our Institute (see [586]), as from its value as prayer of petition. He prescribes and counsels that Mass be celebrated for benefactors ([309-316, 640]), for fathers sent on a mission ([631]), for a general congregation ([693, 711]), for the election of a general ([692-697]), for the preservation and increase of the Society ([790, 803, 812]), and so forth. He only observes that, in accordance with the gratuitous character of our apostolic service (see [82]), Masses "are to be celebrated without accepting any alms" ([640]; see also [4, 565, 810]).

---

32 *AAS*, 68 (1976), 5-76.
33 *Evang. nunt.*, no. 41.
34 MI Epp, I, 509. The last two means of helping the neighbor indicated in that letter as accessible also to scholastics are precisely good example and also desires and prayers.

2. Administration of the Sacraments ([642-644])

The sacraments, instituted for our sanctification and the building up of the Body of Christ, nourish and strengthen the faith; they not only confer grace but prepare the faithful to receive this grace fruitfully, to worship God and practice charity.[35] They are, therefore, fully part of the work of evangelization. The Apostolic Exhortation *Evangelii Nuntiandi* stresses their intimate connection with the ministry of the word, from which they must not be separated.[36]

From the beginning our first fathers administered the sacrament of reconciliation[37] and included it in the Formula of the Institute of 1540 among the proper ministries of the Society under this aspect of evangelization: "for . . . the spiritual consolation of Christ's faithful through hearing confessions" (*per . . . christifidelium in confessionibus audiendis consolationem*).[38] In the Formula of 1550 the other sacraments were added: "and administering the other sacraments" (*ac ceteris sacramentis administrandis*) according to the grant made by the pope to the Society in 1544.[39] But it is evident that the episcopal sacraments (confirmation and ordination) and ordinarily also the parochial sacraments (baptism, matrimony, anointing of the sick) are to be excluded. Nadal called attention to this.[40] For that reason the constitution states: "especially the hearing of confessions and administering Holy Communion" ([642]). The exception in regard to administering sacraments at Easter time ([642, 644]) refers, of course, to former Church discipline.

3. Ministry of the Word ([645-649])

The ministry of the word occupies the first place in the Formula of the Institute in order to indicate that it is the ministry most proper to the Society. Actually the Examen, alluding to the parable of the sower,[41] says that men enter the Society "in order to be good and faithful sowers in the

---

35 Vatican II, *SC*, no. 59.
36 *Evang. nunt.*, nos. 20 and 47.
37 MI Const, I, 15, lines 18-19.
38 We understand consoling in the sense it has in the Exercises, "to give courage and strength . . . by making all easy, by removing all obstacles so that the soul goes forward in doing good" (*SpEx*, no. 315; see no. 316).
39 We think that the rest of the sacraments were added with the object of confirming the favors previously granted by the Holy See. This was partly what motivated the new bull of confirmation of the Society. See MI Const, I, 375.
40 See *Scholia*, on no. 642, "Praecipue in audiendis confessionibus"; MHSI Nadal, V, 850-851; Ruiz Jurado, art. cit. in note 7, p. 233, no. 5; p. 237, "coeteris sacramentis administrandis."
41 Mt. 13:1-23.

Lord's service and to preach His divine word" ([30]). "Preaching in poverty" was the apt expression used by Ignatius in 1536 to formulate his ideal of the apostolic life.[42] After the Society had been founded, he declared that our "profession" or charism is to travel under the banner of Christ in order "to preach and exhort."[43] Consequently this is also the ministry most proper to the professed and the one that particularly demands "learning and ability in preaching" ([521]).

We may easily be inclined to think that this no longer applies in our civilization where the image is so important. The Apostolic Exhortation disabuses us of that notion: "The fatigue produced these days by so much empty talk and the relevance of many other forms of communication must not, however, diminish the permanent power of the word or cause a loss of confidence in it. The word remains ever relevant, especially when it is the bearer of the power of God. This is why St. Paul's axiom, 'Faith comes from what is heard,' also retains its relevance: It is the word that is heard which leads to belief."[44]

In view of the limits we have set to the present work, we need only deal with the forms of preaching the divine word as listed in the Constitutions. They are three: sermons, sacred lectures, teaching of catechism ([645]), following the three steps of evangelization: initiation into the faith (catechesis), instruction in the faith (sacred lectures), and exhortation to live it (sermons). The parallel place in Part IV shows us that homiletic or liturgical preaching (also possible apart from the Eucharistic celebration)[45] is considered as included in the sacred lectures (see [404]).

Ignatius gave such great importance to catechesis that even after it ceased to be the object of a special vow he wanted it to continue being mentioned in the formula of profession.[46]

Spiritual conversations are included in the concept of the preaching of the word ([648]). Besides that proclamation of the gospel which we could think of as general and public, the gospel can be proclaimed in another way which is always effective and highly important, namely, by interpersonal contact. Our Lord used this method, as his conversations with Nicodemus, Zacchaeus, the Samaritan woman, Simon the Pharisee, and others show. The Apostles too used the same method.[47]

---

42 To Jaime Cazador, Feb. 12, 1536 (MI Epp, I, 96).
43 "Deliberation on Poverty," MI Const, I, 80, no. 13.
44 *Evang. nunt.*, no. 42; see Rom. 10:17.
45 See ibid., no. 43.
46 See A. M. de Aldama, S.J., "Peculiarem curam circa puerorum eruditionem," art. in *Recherches Ignatiennes*, 4 (1977), no. 5.
47 *Evang. nunt.*, no. 46.

The Spiritual Exercises are linked to "spiritual conversations" ([648]). We might perhaps find this strange at a first reading; it shows us what the function of one giving the Exercises ought to be: he should create a person-to-person relationship with the retreatant in order the better to help him in his response to the divine call, as Jesus Christ did in the examples mentioned.

4. Works of Mercy ([650-651])

Finally, the "corporal works of mercy" are mentioned ([650]). This appellation should not be given too much importance. One could argue as to the place a particular work has in the classical division of the works of mercy, spiritual and corporal. The meaning here is any office of charity towards the neighbor which does not specifically belong to the spiritual ministry (preaching and the administration of the sacraments).

These works of mercy are not alien to the Institute of the Society; we also find them mentioned in the first number of the Formula of the Institute. The Apostles were sent by the Lord so that, following His example, they would heal the sick besides preaching the coming of the Kingdom.[48] To accomplish this they had the charism of miracles, the Society the charism of mercy.[49]

However, these works of mercy occupy a secondary place. Jesuits will occupy themselves in them "to the extent that the more important spiritual activities permit and their energies allow" ([650]); in other words, if after carrying out the spiritual ministries—which are always to be preferred as much more important for the purpose of helping souls—time and strength still remain. In the Formula of the Institute of 1550 this secondary character had already been defined. It is noted there that the Society was founded especially (*potissimum*) in order that it apply itself mainly and preferably (*praecipue*) to the defense and propagation of the faith and the welfare of souls in Christian life and doctrine, through the ministry of the divine word and the administration of the sacraments; and that "nevertheless" (*nihilominus*) each one must show himself ready to work for the pacification of discords, to help and serve the imprisoned and the sick, and to practice the other works of charity insofar as it is expedient for the glory of God and the common good. Nadal stressed strongly the difference between the two types of activity: "The *potissimum*" he said "is contrasted with the *nihilominus*, which follows somewhat later. By *potissimum* it is intended to indicate that we should embrace the spiritual activities of the

48   See Mt. 9:35—10:8.
49   See 1 Cor. 12:10; Rom. 12:8.

Society with principal intensity, in the first place, with much greater diligence than the others added later, which belong rather to the corporal works of mercy. These we should undertake in the second place, when we have time left from the first, unless we can undertake both."[50] The Apostles also left the care of alms to others and did so in order to dedicate themselves to prayer and the ministry of the word.[51]

5. In Colleges ([652-653])

There is a brief treatment of the way our neighbor can be helped in the colleges. It states that what was previously explained about the houses in this matter is also applicable to them and to their churches; special mention is made of the activity of writing books. On the other hand, no reference is made to "scholarly lectures," which make up the main occupation of a college. This was not due to an oversight, for Polanco had mentioned them in the first wording of the first text and later on they were erased. The only plausible explanation we find is that the Constitutions do not consider scholarly lectures to be means of "helping the neighbor" but as means of instructing and forming those who will later do so (see [308]).

As to the activity of writing, it is surprising that it is only mentioned indirectly in the final text: "one who has talent to write books useful for the common good and who has written them."[52] The only direct reference is the stipulation that nobody "ought to publish any writing unless the superior general sees it first and has it read and examined." What kind of writings? This is apparent from the expressions "books useful for the common good" and "something which will edify" ([653]). In practice, the books published on the initiative of Ignatius or with his approval confirm this. They must be books which contribute to the progress of souls in Christian life and doctrine: almost a complement of the ministry of the word.

The last number forms a conclusion to the whole of Part VII and perhaps even to Part VI as well. The manner of regulating the life and discipline of each house is left to the rules; rules which—as were those of the Roman house in the time of Ignatius—are of two kinds: general or common for all in the house and particular for different offices (see [136]).

---

50   Ruiz Jurado, art. cit. in note 7, p. 237, "Ad hoc potissimum."
51   Act. 6:1-4.
52   "Los hiciese" in text B; but the "s" was later erased in this text. The copyist of text C did not see this and rewrote "los." Thus it passed on to text D.

V. FINAL OBSERVATION

It is in Part VII that Ignatius has set out most clearly the primitive ideal, what he calls his and his companions' "intention." It was "to travel throughout the world" and, when they could not find the desired spiritual fruit in one region, to pass on to another and yet another, ever intent on seeking the greater glory of God our Lord and the help of souls ([605]). In a word: "apostolic life." He also tells how this original idea or apostolic life acquired a "missionary" character: the first fathers, not knowing the regions to which they ought to go, made a vow of obedience to the pope in order that the Vicar of Christ be the one who sent them out and determined their distribution ([603, 605]).

From this point of view, Part VII is the most important of all the Parts and the one which sheds light on the others and even on the entire Institute of the Society.

It is always understood that this ideal has to be lived in an organized social body. For that reason we find mention of an internal superior and of houses where communities reside. But even so, this internal superior appears only as an active subject of the mission, the one who can send in place of the pope. The houses are conceived of only as centers of evangelization, where those not actually on a mission help the neighbor by means proper to the Society. The disciplinary side is consigned to the rules ([654]).

Chapter XII

UNION AMONG THE MEMBERS

(Constitutions, Part VIII)

I. PRELIMINARY REMARKS

1. Reason for the Existence of Part VIII

Part VIII seeks to solve the problem arising from the Society's specific way of life, an "apostolic life," the mode of life led by those sent on mission.[1] This kind of life involves both the dispersal of the subjects (see [603, 605]) and the absence of many of the means of union found in other religious institutes, such as monastic stability, living together under the same roof, choral or communal prayer, conventual chapter, and the like. But the greater its difficulty, all the more is union in the Society needed. The Society, in fact, must have union "for preserving itself," for without union and cohesion it would completely disintegrate. It needs union "for governing itself," so that the authority of the head can influence and animate the members. "Consequently" it also needs unity to attain its objective, "the spiritual help of souls" ([655-657]).

Historically, this problem was felt by our first fathers from the beginning. Indeed, it may be said that it was out of this need that the Society was born as a religious order. Up to 1539 they had been united by bonds of spiritual friendship ("friends in the Lord"), in a union based on their shared ideal of evangelizing the world in imitation of Christ and the apostles (see [605]). "They had no head among themselves nor any other superior than Jesus Christ."[2] They made their decisions collectively. But when, in accordance with the vow of Montmartre, they presented themselves to the pope and Paul III began to disperse them on various "missions," this gave rise to a disconcerting dilemma: union or dispersion. The solution reached in the deliberations of 1539 was to sacrifice neither union for dispersion nor dispersion for union, but to reinforce union so that it

---

1   For Part VIII we may also refer to our more extensive commentary published under the title *Unir a los repartidos* (Rome: CIS, 1976).
2   Polanco in MI FontNarr, I, 204.

would remain firm in dispersion: founding a spiritual community based on apostolic dispersion.[3]

2. Structure and Sources

This Part is clearly divided into two sections, according to two possible modes of union. The first corresponds to "union of hearts" (*unión de los ánimos*). In the Spanish text the word *ánimo*, corresponding to the Latin *animus*, means the principle and seat of thoughts and feelings. The phrase refers, then, to an interior or spiritual union, which must be constant even in dispersion. The second kind of union is that of physical presence: the meeting together of the dispersed, which cannot be constant or permanent and which has no place in the Society except rarely and for serious reasons.

The first section consists of a single chapter, the first. This chapter and the third chapter of Part II are the two most methodically organized in the Constitutions. Chapter I has a tripartite division: means for union on the part of subjects ([656-665]), on the part of superiors ([666-670]), and on the part of both ([671-676]). Each of those divisions has likewise a triple division of the means of union. Given that we do not now intend to make a commentary on this Part VIII but only to suggest some ideas for further study, we will here ignore this division, which is in any case somewhat artificial.[4]

The remaining chapters (the second to the seventh) make up the second section. They follow the order which we saw in the more juridical Parts (such as I, II, and V): when a general congregation is to be convoked (chapter 2), who are to attend (chapter 3), who convokes the congregation (chapter 4), the time and place of meeting (chapter 5), the procedure when a general is to be elected (chapter 6), and other matters apart from the election of a general (chapter 7).

The most notable change in Part VIII was that the definitive text joined into a single chapter the three into which the first section had been divided in the earlier texts.

The source of the first chapter (that is, the first section), is Polanco's eighth *Industria*; that of the sixth chapter is the Dominican Constitutions, and some other norms drawn from common law or from particular laws in other orders. The remaining chapters are based on the Formula of the

---

3   See L. Renard, S.J., "Un type d'appartenence communautaire dans la vie consacrée apostolique," art. in *NouvRevTheol*, 95 (1974), 61-88.

4   For instance, the first division ("on the part of subjects") actually deals not with the means to be used by the subjects, but rather with those to be used by superiors in the government of their subjects.

Institute and on replies given by Ignatius to queries about it.

II. First Section: Union of Minds and Hearts

1. Social Union in One Body ([659-670])

The solution which Ignatius and his companions found in 1539 was to strengthen their union—until then only a union of spiritual friendship—by incorporating it into a social body (*reducendo nos in unum corpus*), a body which, after lengthy and laborious deliberation, they decided would be that of a religious order, with its own internal superior to whom all would render obedience. This is also the basic idea here. The social body, like the physical body which is its image, "receives nourishment and coherence from the head by way of joints and ligaments."[5] This supposes, first, that the members subject themselves to the head, which is brought about by obedience; second, that the head actually performs the function of head and influences the members; and third, that in both movements (ascending and descending) a procedure is followed according to the organic articulation of members with each other. We shall have a word to say on each of these points.

a. Obedience

"This union is produced in great part by the bond of obedience" ([659]). Obedience "binds all the members of the Society into a single spiritual body, wherever they are found."[6]

But let us note that we are dealing with the interior union of hearts, not a merely exterior and juridical union. Therefore obedience of execution is not enough; it must be extended to that of the will and judgment, to conform the will and judgment of the subject totally to what his superior wills and judges ([284]). It is necessary to obey "promptly, humbly, and devoutly" ([659]), "recognizing the superior as being in the place of Christ our Lord and maintaining interior reverence and love for him" ([284]).

Ignatius gives such importance to this bond of obedience that—always in the perspective of missions—he does not want anyone to be sent from the houses to labor in the field of the Lord except "persons practiced in this virtue" ([659]), and if, after they have been sent, "experience reveals that some of those sent are not proceeding correctly in regard to obedi-

---

5   Col. 2:19.
6   Polanco *ex commissione* to the scholastic Francesco Mancini, April 7, 1554 (MI Epp, VI, 586).

ence," that is, show signs of independence, "they ought to be recalled" ([660]). If circumstances require that someone less exercised in obedience should be sent, or should not be withdrawn, "a companion advanced in it ought to be sent" ([660]) "because in general a companion more advanced in obedience will help one who is less so, with the divine favor" ([659]). Ignatius certainly granted great freedom of action to those who were sent on an apostolic mission, but he always assumed that the bond of obedience was firmly maintained.

There is greater need of a remedy when someone not only loosens the bond of his own obedience, but is also "a cause of division" among those who live together. Ignatius does not hesitate to compare such a case to plague, that is, to a highly contagious disease. The remedy is that used to avoid contagion in time of pestilence: to remove the one infected from the place of residence and, if necessary, even from the Society ([665]), "so that a sick sheep may not contaminate the whole flock," as Benedict says in a classical comparison.[7]

b. Authority

Obedience and authority are correlative. The subject will not be able to exercise obedience unless the superior orders with authority. For this reason Ignatius includes in his listing of the means for union that the general carry out his office, which is "to be a head for all the members the Society" ([666]). This he will do if he has the qualities for so doing and if in fact the vital influence of the body flows down from him to the members.

The qualities which the general ought to have are described in detail in the second chapter of Part IX ([723-735]). Here, in the context of union, emphasis is placed on two qualities: a good reputation and the ability to rule.

Reputation or moral authority is necessary so that subjects will have confidence in those who govern them, being convinced that the general (and other superiors according to their rank) "has the knowledge, desire, and ability to rule them well in our Lord" ([667a]). When such confidence or conviction is lacking, when there is a crisis of authority, it is impossible for the head to influence the members, with the consequent danger that each individual will tend to govern himself, with serious harm to union. It will be helpful to the credit and moral authority of the superior to have with him "persons able to give good counsel" ([667a]), for often the defects of a less efficient or less prudent government are attributed to those who

---

7   Regula, chap. 28, 8.

advise the one governing.

The paragraph about the manner of commanding ([667b]) is very remarkable because, besides other reasons, it was written almost completely by Ignatius himself and gives one of the clearest indications of his spirit of meekness.[8] In the first place it is stated that the manner of commanding should be "well thought out and ordered"; "ordered," doubtless, according to the meaning of this word in the *Exercises*: not influenced by any disordered affection. The superior should "endeavor to maintain obedience in the subjects" not in an authoritarian manner but humbly and benignly, "using all the love and modesty and charity possible in our Lord." The relations between subjects and superiors ought to be animated by "a spirit of love" (see [547, 551]), "so that the subjects[9] can dispose themselves to have always toward their superiors greater love than fear." Ignatius realistically adds: ". . . even though both [love and fear] are useful at times." But in the kindness of his heart he goes further still; he advises the superior that he can "refer some matters" to the subjects "when it appears probable that they will be helped by that." He himself did so frequently, using a well-known expression: "You who are on the scene of the work will see better what should be done" (*vos que estáis al pie de la obra, veréis mejor lo que se debe hacer*), and even giving blank sheets with his signature.[10] Further, he thinks that at times one may show condescension to subjects "by going along with them to some extent and sympathizing with them when it seems this could be more expedient" ([667b]). No doubt this refers to cases where a subject, either because of his spiritual immaturity or some spiritual or even psychic crisis, or for some other reason, lacks adequate dispositions for accepting a difficult order.

This Ignatian page has not been read or considered by those authors who want to present us with an Ignatius who is rigid, somber, insensitive to every human feeling and even impenetrable to those living with him, to whom (they imagine) he responded in an impassive and administrative tone when they came to him with their troubles.[11]

However, it is not enough that the general has the qualities proper to his office. He must actually fulfill his office, which is to be a head for all the members; this means that the impulse necessary for the end which the Society seeks must descend to all of them from him ([666]). Thus it is that

8   It can be connected with the declaration on corrections in Part III [270].
9   The Spanish text says *subiectos* (individuals). But this is probably a mistake by the copyist; St. Ignatius had written *súbdictos* (subordinates).
10   See MI FontNarr, III, 619.
11   See L. Marcuse, *Ignatius von Loyola, ein Soldat der Kirche* (Hamburg 1956), p. 177.

from the general as head flow all the juridical authority of the other superiors, the apostolic movement of all Jesuits, and the granting of ministerial favors or faculties.

"Juridical Authority."—The superiors of other religious orders were ordinarily elected by their subjects and remained subject with them to provincial or conventual chapters. In the Society it is the general who "appoints them" and who "gives them the power he judges wise" ([757]), being able to extend, restrict, and even revoke such authority ([759]).

"Apostolic Movement."—The missions or "sendings" of subjects to work in this or that part of the Lord's vineyard also are to come from the general (who then takes the place of the pope) or at least "by the general's mandate and approval" ([666]), since the general can send either by himself or through other persons ([620]).

In other orders "ministerial faculties" and other grants from the Holy See are made directly to provinces, convents, or particular individuals. In the Society the case is different. They are considered as granted to the general, who, as may seem proper to him, will communicate them to others.[12]

The influence of the head on the members is also the factor that determines the ordinary place of residence of the general and by analogy that of a provincial. It will be "the location favorable for communication between the head and the members." The residence of the general will be in Rome, "where communications with all regions can more easily be maintained." Provincials, for the greater part of the time, "should be in places where they can communicate with their subjects and the superior general" ([668]).

c. Subordination

However, to obtain the genuine union which is desirable, it is furthermore necessary, in regard to the submission of obedience as well as the influence of the head on the members, to take into account the differences between members and the dependence which some have on others in every social body just as in a physical body. This is what the Constitutions mean by the word "subordination," namely, ordered and hierarchical submission (see [206, 422, 662, 663, 791, 821]). Here subordination is considered from a twofold aspect: that of obedience ([662]) and that of the influence of the head ([666]).

The bond of obedience, mentioned earlier ([659]), is made up of

---

12 See Gregory XIII, *Decet Romanum,* May 5, 1575.

numerous ligatures or interdependencies "of some superiors with others and of subjects with the superiors." Normally individuals will have recourse to the local superior and will be ruled in everything by him. The local superiors will communicate with the provincial and will likewise be ruled by him in all things. In like manner the provincials will be ruled by the general ([552]). This does not prevent direct relations with mediate superiors (see [671]), nor does it prevent there being some exceptions. By way of exception a provincial can exempt someone from obedience to a local superior, and the general from obedience to a provincial, when it is more expedient for the divine service ([663]).

The most notable of these exceptions is constituted by the office of "collateral" to a superior, whether local or provincial ([661]). The one holding this office is not subjected to the obedience of the one of whom he is the collateral. He is given him rather as a companion, friend, and confidant; as a consultor and admonitor; as a secretary and executor of his orders; and even as an angel of peace when difficulties could arise between the superior and the subjects. Ignatius conceived of this office principally as an aid to those superiors who, having the best desires and an approved life, lack experience in governing; though there can be other reasons for the arrangement, even on the part of the one who exercises it. In fact, according to Polanco's testimony, practice showed that it was very useful and even necessary;[13] and a few months before his death Ignatius manifested a desire that each provincial and rector have a "collateral," "even though not all of them had need of it."[14] In conceiving of this quite original office of collateral, Ignatius revealed his profound intuition concerning the loneliness which the office of superior entails. It is not enough for the superior to have someone or several individuals to advise him in dubious cases; such advisors can readily be found among his subjects. He needs to have at his side a confidant to whom he can open his heart, overburdened perhaps by the weight of his office, a friend from whom he can receive not only light and counsel but also relief and fraternal help and eventually admonition, not to speak of his pacifying action in moments of trouble. All this he will best find in one who is not a subject, but a friend and companion.

As for the influence of the head on the members, subordination requires the general to communicate authority directly to the provincials, through the provincials to local superiors, and through the latter to particular individuals. The same is said of "missions" or apostolic assign-

13   MI Epp, V, 164-165.
14   MI Epp, X, 129.

ments and of the communication of privileges and faculties. The constitution says: "For the more the subjects are dependent on their superiors, the better will the love, obedience, and union among them be preserved" ([666], see [206]).

2. Spiritual Union in Christ ([671-676])

a. The Principal Bond

Although the means considered up to now have been grouped under the title "social union in a body," we do not intend to mean that they bring about a merely external or juridical aggregation; union of "hearts" is always under consideration too. However, if this union is to become really intimate, close, and firm, it must be founded on Christ, on union with Christ. This is the basic concept in the first paragraph of [671].[15] It is one of the most inspiring passages in the Constitutions although not so easy to interpret as might appear on a first reading. Normally the first phrases only are cited, leaving the development of the idea incomplete, at the risk of falsifying the meaning. A study of the genesis of the paragraph, as well as the parallel passages, has led us to the following interpretation.[16]

The paragraph begins with the fundamental affirmation that the principal bond of union for the members among themselves and with their head is "the love of God our Lord" ([671a]).[17]

On hearing the expression God our Lord, we think right away of God the Father or of the divine nature, abstracting from the distinction of persons. Ignatius—as has been shown—had in mind the Incarnate Word, Jesus Christ our Lord.[18] In the present instance this is confirmed by Polanco's Latin translation of the Constitutions, which reads *Amor Dei ac Domini nostri Iesu Christi*. So it is the love of Christ which constitutes the principal bond of union.

But to what love of Christ is reference being made? Not to a mere affective feeling of the human heart toward the Savior, nor simply to

---

15   In the numbering of the paragraphs of each chapter done for the first Latin edition of the Constitutions, these two paragraphs were grouped together under a single number. As can be seen from the Spanish texts and even the very structure of the chapter, they are distinct and deal with two different means of union.

16   The source is the 8th *Industria* of Polanco, nos. 2 and 15; parallel texts are nos. 2 and 9 of Part X [813 and 821].

17   The first Spanish text said "el *del* amor," that is to say, the bond of love. The present reading is probably due to a mistake made by the copyist of text A. However, there is no substantial change in the meaning.

18   See J. Solano, S.J., "Cristología de las Constituciones," in *Ejercicios-Constituciones* (Bilbao 1975), pp. 207-208.

familiarity with Him in prayer, but to something more fundamental and permanent: the love of the heart of Christ for the faithful soul, whom the divine life which he merited for us continues to sanctify more and more each day. It is the love of which Jesus Christ spoke to his disciples at the Last Supper: "As the Father has loved me, so I have loved you; live on in my love. You will live in my love if you keep my commandments, even as I have kept my Father's commandments, and live in his love."[19]

Hence, growth in holiness helps to tighten the bond of union; on the other hand, whatever hinders this growth is an obstacle to union. "Thus" (for this reason)—the constitution says—"charity" (in the perfection of which Christian holiness substantially consists) "and in general all goodness and virtues" (everything which makes one better and more virtuous and disposes him to progress in conformity with the Spirit) "will come to further this union between superiors and subjects." On the contrary, as regards the obstacles, union will be helped by a "total contempt for temporal things," that is, complete renunciation and separation from them, not because they are judged to be lacking in true values but precisely because of the seductive power which these values have for men: "In regard to them, self-love, the chief enemy of this union and universal good, frequently induces disorder" ([671a]).

This is basically the reason why we find listed at the beginning of the chapter among the means of union "not to admit a large crowd of persons to profession, nor to retain any other than select persons even as formed coadjutors or scholastics," "for a large number of persons whose vices are not well mortified is an obstruction to order and to union" ([657]).

Still, it will be asked why the love of Christ for those who keep his commandments, and in that way continually grow in goodness and virtue, particularly charity, and in mortifying their self-love, should be a bond of union for members of the Society among themselves and with their head. Paul says: "The love of God has been poured out in our hearts through the Holy Spirit who has been given to us."[20] Echoing these words of Paul, Ignatius teaches that the love which comes down to us from the Divine and Supreme Goodness not only comes to be in us a reciprocal love of friendship with Christ but will overflow from our hearts and, turning into fraternal love, will "spread to all other persons, and particularly into the body of the Society" ([671a]). It would be hard to express in a more precise and enlightened way the unity of charity, in its twofold aspect of love of God and love of neighbor, and its divine origin, the effect of the love with

19 Jn. 15:9-10.
20 Rom. 5:5.

which God loves us. "Love, then, consists in this: not that we have loved God, but that He has first loved us."[21]

b. Ways of Fostering Fraternal Love

Holiness of life, which makes us persevere in the love of Christ and grounds in Him our love for our brothers, is then in summary the principal bond of union of hearts. But there are other ways of fostering this same fraternal love; such are uniformity ([671b-672]) and mutual communication ([673-676]).[22]

Uniformity is above all interior, that is, unity in doctrine, judgments, and wills ([671b]). The union of wills, the *idem velle idem nolle*, is at once effect and cause of love and, especially, an efficacious means of keeping the love alive. Cassian says: "Love is not preserved except between those who have identical aims and wills. Where there is diversity of wills, peace is not preserved intact."[23] But the union of wills requires union of minds in doctrine and above all in practical criteria; there is no true union of hearts without union of minds. Ignatius points this out clearly in the parallel text in Part III, where he says that diversity in judgments about things which are to be done "is generally the mother of discord and the enemy of union of wills" ([273]). Even in speculative matters—as Polanco told Urbano Fernandes—Ignatius did not want, as far as possible, differences of opinion among those of the Society.[24] However, he was well aware of possible difficulties in this area, especially for those who did studies before entering. But he exhorts even these men to endeavor "to prevent any diversity from damaging the union of charity" and "to accommodate oneself in what is possible to the doctrine which is more common in the Society" ([672]).

As to exterior uniformity, "in respect to clothing, ceremonies of the Mass, and other such matters to the extent that the different qualities of persons, places, and the like permit" ([671b]),[25] we may feel inclined to underrate it as something accidental. However, such uniformity helps greatly in uniting those whom it distinguishes from others, over and above

---

21 1 Jn. 4:10.
22 As aids to love and fraternal charity, these two means are considered in the parallel text in Part X [821].
23 *Conlationes*, 16, 3. In the parallel text in Part III [285], fraternal charity appears as identified with union of wills; at least it is considered as intimately dependent on it.
24 June 7, 1551 (MI Epp, III, 502-503).
25 There was much variety in the ceremonies of the Mass until the publication of the missal of Pius V (1570).

the fact that the exterior attitude is usually a manifestation of the interior while at the same time influencing it.

In other religious institutes, living together, working together, and praying together are a source and nourishment of mutual love. In the Society (as we recalled at the beginning) dispersal hinders all this. Our community is a community in dispersion. Nadal said that "the most important habitation and the one most proper to the Society is the apostolic journey."[26] So it is necessary to make up for this lack of living together by other means, which bring close those who are far from each other and must so remain. Such means are social communication: exchange of letters between subjects and superiors "through which they learn about one another frequently and hear the news and reports which come from the various regions" ([673-676]).

Moreover, uniformity and continued mutual contact have another more important and more profound purpose in the Society. The communitarian life of religious is like a sacrament (a sign and fulfillment) of the communion of love which Christ merited for us and communicated to us by the outpouring of His Spirit, through whom we are all children of the same Father in Christ. From the time of Pachomius down to our day, religious have felt themselves moved with a supernatural instinct (the work of the Holy Spirit) to give this testimony of fraternal communion, and it has come to be regarded as one of the characteristics of religious life.[27] Is the Society of Jesus, because of its apostolic dispersion, to be deprived of these quasi-sacramental values of the religious life? By no means. It will not be able to give this testimony of communion in the same way as other religious, but in its own particular way instead: through mutual interest, sharing information about each other's activity, rejoicing in their apostolic successes, emulating their zeal, praying for them and for their work. And the motivation for such activity will come not just from esprit de corps but from the desire to share more intimately the mutual love uniting them in Christ. Likewise, uniformity in doctrine and judgments, union of intentions and wills, and even external uniformity will all demonstrate to the world that in the midst of dispersion a single community is formed which is both sign and fulfillment of the *koinonia* of love and reconciliation which all the redeemed share in Christ.

---

26   See MHSI Nadal, V, 195, nos. 174-175.
27   See Conc. Vat. II, *PC*, no. 15; J. Beyer S.J., *De vita per consilia evangelica consecrata* (Rome 1969), pp. 163-181.

III. Second Section: Meeting Together of the Dispersed ([677-718])

The last six chapters of Part VIII deal with the meeting together of the dispersed in a general congregation. Only indirectly is anything said about provincial congregations, which prepare the general congregation and are in a certain sense modeled on it ([662b, 692]).

1. Meaning of the General Congregation

The first problem presented to us is the very name "general congregation." Why is this name given to what other religious orders for centuries have called and continue to call "general chapter"? The word chapter also appears in our Constitutions, even in Ignatius' handwriting, so that we cannot say that it was rejected as something foreign to the nature of the Institute. But there is no doubt that the term congregation predominates, used in a proportion of three to one (forty times to thirteen).

In the Constitutions the term congregation means a gathering of persons, whether a provisional or occasional reunion or meeting (see [502, 712]) or a permanent and stable reunion, community, or association (see [184, 651, 719, 817]). In this second sense, the Society already is, and is called, a congregation (see [1,119,655]). The general congregation is then only the temporary reunion or concentration of this permanent congregation, which is the Society normally dispersed throughout various parts of the world (see [603, 605]). To use some expressions in the Constitutions, we would say that a general congregation is "the congregation assembled from the entire Society" ([554]), "the general congregation" of the Society ([719]; see [682, 689, 698]), in which all the Society "is assembled"; and that to convoke the general congregation is "to assemble all the Society" ([679, 689]). In clearcut terms, we might say that the general congregation is simply the Society: the Society joined together or concentrated for a period of time in one place.

It is usually said that the supreme authority of the Society resides in the general congregation. This is true, but it needs to be properly understood. It does not mean that the fathers who form the general congregation constitute within the Society a governing body, a kind of oligarchy or collective superior vested with supreme authority over the individuals of the Society. The general congregation has the fullness of authority granted to the Society because it is the Society itself, the whole Society.

We hear the reader's objection. In a general congregation the *whole* Society is not assembled but only the provincials, with two professed members from each province elected at a provincial congregation. The professed impeded by physical indisposition, distance, or the importance of the apostolic work in which they are engaged are excluded. Scholastics, too, are excluded. Of the formed coadjutors only some are admitted, not by reason of grade but because of the office they hold ([682-683]). The fact that, apart from these coadjutors, only unimpeded professed members attend offers no major difficulty since the Formula of the Institute speaks of "the greater part of the entire *professed* Society which can be summoned *without grave inconvenience* by the superior general." After all, the professed of four vows constitute the Society in its most precise meaning ([511]). But can it be truly said that the provincials and two professed chosen in each province are the whole Society? No, if they are considered as particular individuals; yes, if they are representatives of the rest.

That they are to be considered as representatives the following norm proves: "Those who remain behind [in the province] will rely on these three and on the general chapter" ([682]). Polanco translated this into Latin with a paraphrase: *his tribus suas vices tota provincia committet, et quidquid a conventu generali cui ipsi interfuerint constitutum fuerit, ratum habebit,* "the whole province transfers its own rights to these three representatives and will ratify whatever has been decided in a general congregation at which they were present."[28] He was correct; for the Spanish word *remitirse,* or trust to the judgment of another what is to be decided in a particular case, supposes a certain cession of rights in favor of this other and includes the anticipated acceptance of what the other decides. In the paraphrase Polanco separates these two concepts: those who remain in the province (or the province as a whole) transfer their own rights to these three representatives (*vices suas committit*), and they approve or accept beforehand (*ratum habet*) not what the three representatives determine—for they alone can determine nothing— but what the general congregation determines.[29]

In declaration C of the third chapter we have a confirmation that those sent from each province to the general congregation are the representatives of the others. In fact, they are the ones who will report to the congregation the opinion or judgment of those who remain in the province ([685]).[30] It is to be noted that these words are due to an autograph correction by Ignatius.

---

28 See MI Const, III, 229, lines 28-29 in critical apparatus.

29 In fact the words *y al Capítulo general* ("and to the general chapter") were added during a revision. In order to accommodate the Latin translation more to the Spanish text, the second Latin edition of the Constitutions (1570) changed Polanco's paraphrase to read, "his tribus et Congregationi generali quicumque in provincia remanent, suas vices delegabunt."

30 "Quid et alii sentiat," Polanco translated into Latin.

On the other hand, the head of the Society is obviously included in "the whole Society," and in an essential manner. We must not conceive of the general congregation as something distinct from the superior general (much less as something opposed to him). In the Formula of the Institute the general congregation is only the council of the superior general for the most important matters; and it is to the superior general—with the vote of this council—that legislative authority is given.[31] In the Constitutions the superior general is also the one who convokes the congregation in the cases, place, and time he judges opportune (with the sole exception, obviously, of a case in which the congregation is convoked for the election of a new general or for something that touches his person) ([687-691, 782]). Once the congregation is in session, the superior general is the one who "directs those who attend and who dismisses them when the agenda have been concluded" ([755]). The superior general is no less the head of the assembled Society than of the dispersed Society. In an extreme situation the Society will be able to judge and depose him ([782]). But this is not because he is not the head of the congregation, but because the healthy body is enabled, in the case of the sickness of the head, to react and prevent this sickness from corrupting the whole organism. The correction made by Ignatius in number 8 of Part X is significant: Instead of saying that the Society has authority "over" (*sobre*) the general, the founder wrote "in regard to (*cerca*) the general, as is explained in Part IX" ([820]).[32]

2. Work and Distraction

General congregations are necessary at times. They are, of course, necessary when a new superior general is to be elected ([677]). The Formula of the Institute also prescribes that the general convoke a congregation to make or change constitutions and for other matters of importance such as the suppression or transference of houses or colleges,[33] and, as the Constitutions say, "when matters arise which are very difficult pertaining to the whole body of the Society or its manner of proceeding" ([680]). Furthermore there can be cases of such seriousness that if the general does not spontaneously convoke a congregation "the assistants to the general, the provincials, and the local superiors" could oblige him to do so by a majority of votes ([681]).

However, the general congregation is considered as a "work and

---

31 Form. Inst., chap. I, no. 2.
32 Not taking this difference into account, the Latin version reads "Societas *in* Generalem."
33 Form. Inst., Julius III, chap. I, no. 2.

distraction" from which the Society must be spared as far as possible ([677]). Effectively it "distracts" the Society, depriving it of the time and attention which, in conformity with its Institute, it ought to give to the apostolic ministry.

Hence, "it does not seem good in our Lord that such a congregation should be held at definite intervals" ([677])—that is, periodically, as is prescribed in other religious orders—but when circumstances demand it. One of the reasons for the lifelong term of office of the general is that "thus the Society, being universally occupied with important matters in the divine service, will be less disturbed and distracted by general congregations" ([719]; see [722]).

Neither shall a congregation be convoked "very often" ([677]), "many times" ([689]). When it convenes for the election of a general it "could take up other matters" ([689]).

The advantage which could be gained by more frequent congregations, "either through the greater information which it possesses or through some more distinguished persons who express their opinion," can be had by other means—such as the communication the general can have not only by way of the exchange of letters mentioned in the first chapter ([673-676]), but also by the innovative provision of "procurators" who should come to Rome every three or four years for this purpose. By this twofold communication, epistolary and oral, and with the help of those who ordinarily assist in government, the general will obtain, without the need of convoking a congregation, not only the desired information but also the evaluation of it. For by means of this communication he will be able to understand the opinion of "those from the whole Society whom he considers to have better judgment," when necessary ([677, 679)]).

The same concern to avoid as much as possible hindering the apostolic labor of the Society appears when dealing with the makeup of the congregation. Not only are those who are "physically ill" and those who are "in far places" excluded, but also those "who have in their hands some undertakings of grave importance which cannot be omitted without great inconvenience" ([682]). Furthermore, the provincial congregations are given the norm that they should choose to go to a general congregation those "who will cause less harm through their absence" ([692]).

Once the congregation has been assembled, one notes in the legislation an effort to ensure that the meeting lasts only as long as necessary. In keeping with this is the stipulation about "locking [the electors] within the place of the congregation, . . . in such a manner that they may not leave nor have any other food except bread and water until they have elected a general" ([698])—a method taken from what the Dominicans had established in the thirteenth century for the same purpose. A like concern is evident when a congregation is reaching a decision about other matters than the election of a general: "Although" the locked enclosure will not be necessary, "an effort should be made to finish as soon as possible everything requiring discussion" ([711]). For this purpose, apparently, the election of four definitors is provided for; these, along with the general, conclude or define what is presented and discussed by the congregation ([715-719]).[34]

3. In a Spiritual Atmosphere

Because of the nature of the topic, the six chapters of this second section are rather dispositive and juridical. However, everything is conceived in a spiritual, prayerful climate.

When a congregation is convoked, instructions should be given "that all those under obedience to the Society (including even the novices—see [511]) should offer prayers daily, be mindful in their Masses to commend earnestly to God our Lord those who are going to the congregation, and beg that whatever matters will be treated in it may all turn out as is expedient for His greater service, praise, and glory" ([693]; see [692]). Likewise, when the congregation is only about other important matters than the election of a general, these prayers are required. Then the supernatural motivation is stated: "Since the light to perceive what can best be decided upon must come down from the First and Supreme Wisdom, Masses and prayer will be offered in the place where the congregation is held as well as in the other regions of the Society; this should be done throughout the time the congregation lasts and the matters which should be settled within that time are being discussed, to obtain grace to conclude them in a manner conducive to greater glory to God our Lord" ([711]).[35]

The election of a general is to be done prayerfully and in complete docility to the action of the Holy Spirit. In order to avoid any human influence which may hinder this supernatural action, rigorous measures are taken against ambition ([695-696]). Moreover, the method of *tractatio* or *tractatus*, common in the ecclesiastical elections of the time, is discarded; according to this method the electors proposed candidates, discussed their relative merits, even carried on campaigns in favor of one or other, and perhaps came to agree on the one whom they should elect. Ignatius replaced this method by that of the four-day period of prayer, personal

---

34   With regard to the first sentences of no. 715, our interpretation can be seen in the work cited in note 1, pp. 259-260.
35   See *SpEx*, no. 237.

reflection, and information. The most notable and significant point is that during this four-day period, while the elector seeks information, reflects, and commends himself to God, he must not make any decision; in order, as Nadal puts it, to follow and not go ahead of Christ, he will leave the decision "until he enters the place of election" ([694]). Then, after the Mass of the Holy Spirit and the hymn *Veni Creator* ([698]), "each one should pray privately," and in that prayer, "without speaking with anyone else, he will come to his decision in the presence of his Creator and Lord. Then he will write on a paper the name of the person whom he chooses for superior general" ([701]). All this is original and comes from Ignatius himself; we have not found it in any other religious or ecclesiastical legislation.

We will not delay on the possibility, supposed by Ignatius, of "common inspiration." The three forms of election (common inspiration, ballot, and compromise) were known in canon law and expressly approved by the Fourth Lateran Council. The distinctive trait is the added supernatural motivation: "For the Holy Spirit, who has moved to such an election, supplies for all methods and arrangements" ([700]).

Various other details reveal this spiritual atmosphere in which the whole procedure of the congregation is conceived. Let us point some out:

The electors of the general swear that they will elect the one whom they judge most suitable for the office, using the formula: "With all reverence, I call upon Jesus Christ, who is the Eternal Wisdom, to witness . . ." (*Testem invoco cum omni reverentia Iesum Christum qui Sapientia est aeterna* . . .) ([705]). The most interesting point to note here is that the words "cum omni reverentia" were added by Ignatius himself and reflect the characteristic trait of his mysticism of "respect and reverence."

Once the general has been elected, the electors pay him reverence by kissing his hand. The constitution adds: "The one elected should not have the right to refuse either the election or the reverence, being mindful in whose name he ought to accept it" ([701]).

In the discussion of problems, the members of the congregation "will propose the matters which they think should be discussed . . . after each one has seriously pondered his opinion and commended it to God our Lord" ([712]).

The norm given for voting—inspired by the Dominican Constitutions —is that [in case of a tie] the vote of the provincials and of the general prevails. But again an original supernatural motivation is added: "For, just as the divine aid is more necessary to them because of the charge they hold, so it is to be hoped that God our Lord will give that grace to them more copiously that they may perceive and state what is conducive to His service" ([686]).

Generally speaking, we could say that when Ignatius finds inspiration in other legislation he takes external and juridical dispositions from it; it is the additional matter, of a supernatural order, which is most characteristic and original.

IV. FINAL OBSERVATION

In the whole of Part VIII one senses a certain dialectical tension between mission and body, between charism and institution.

Mission involves dispersal (see [603]) and has consequently a tendency towards separation. Our first fathers decided to form themselves into a body precisely in order to avoid such separation. Here the means are sought for reinforcing that union of the body in the midst of the dispersal of its members.

But dispersal prevents, on the one hand, the use of the means for strengthening union as traditionally employed in religious orders and, on the other hand, determines those means which are to be used in this body of the Society. Dispersion, in fact, requires a union which is vertically oriented: obedience, influence of the head on the members, subordination —all founded on the holiness of a life in union with Christ. It calls for the uniformity of the dispersed and their maintaining contact, through interpersonal relations, with those members who are far away.

The dispersed members of the body need to meet together at times; it is a requirement of the institution, of constituting a social body. But even then "apostolic life" demands that these reunions be neither periodic nor frequent, and last as briefly as possible, so that they will not distract the Society from its evangelizing endeavor.

Chapter XIII

GOVERNMENT

(Constitutions, Part IX)

I. PRELIMINARY REMARKS[1]

1. Presentation of Part IX

The eight preceding Parts dealt with the members of the body of the Society: their admission and possible dismissal, their spiritual and intellectual formation, their incorporation or integration into the body, their religious and apostolic life, their union with each other and with their head. The subject matter of Part IX is simply the head of the body.

The head of the body of the Society is the superior general. One might ask: Is it not Jesus Christ who is the head of the Society? An easy reply to such a question would be that the general holds the place of Jesus Christ ([765]). However, we do not think that this is the correct answer here. Jesus Christ and the general are the head of the Society under two different aspects. Ignatius calls Jesus Christ "head" of the Society, inasmuch as he is its chief, its leader and supreme captain, around whom it is assembled.[2] The general is the head of the Society in the sense that, as in a biological body—in the image of which the structure of the Society is conceived (see [135])—he is the principal member, whose influence and authority descends to all the other members ([666]). That Jesus Christ is the head of the Society in the sense mentioned belongs to its charism; precisely for this reason it is called the Society of Jesus.[3] That the general is the head of the body of the Society is due to its juridical structure. The very title of Part IX indicates that fact: "The Society's Head, and the Government Descending from Him."

Government.—There is no human form of government which is perfect. All have their advantages and disadvantages. Besides, depending on

---

1   For a fuller treatment of Part IX see our *El General de la Compañía de Jesús: su persona y su gobierno* (Rome: CIS, 1982).
2   See "Deliberation on Poverty," III, 13 (MI Const, I, 80); *SpDiar*, Feb. 23, 1544 (ibid., p. 104); Letter to Teresa Rejadell, Oct. 1547 (MI Epp, I, 628).
3   See Polanco in MI FontNarr, I, 204.

the varied natures of the collectivities governed, one form is more adapted for some, a different one for others. Ignatius was not unaware of the capitular and elective form of government in other religious orders, and for the election of the general of the Society he was inspired by the eminently democratic constitutions of the Dominican Order.[4] Yet he saw that the Society, dispersed throughout various parts of the world ([603, 605]), needed a centralized government, of "monarchical" form,[5] in the hands of one person, with a lifelong term of office and endowed with full powers— one from whom all authority would descend. This does not imply that the risks and inconveniences to which such a system is exposed were unknown to him; taking everything into account, he preferred this system to others while providing for all appropriate correctives and safeguards.

2. Structure and Sources

The structure is clear: we can distinguish two ideas or topics which correspond logically. In the first place, assuming that there has to be a superior general in the Society, one individual holding office for life (chapter 1), the qualities he must have are described (chapter 2) and the authority he must enjoy (chapter 3). In the second place, since such a form of government—lifelong and centralized—has its disadvantages, safeguards are proposed not only to avoid abuses and deficiencies in the person of the general himself (chapters 4 and 5) but also to help him the better in bearing the burden of office (chapter 6).

This structure has been preserved unchanged in each successive text. The only difference is that the final text has joined into one chapter (the sixth) material that was divided into two in the previous texts.

The source of the second chapter is the eleventh *Industria* of Polanco. The other chapters reproduce norms previously fixed in the Formula of the Institute and other papal approbations, in the Constitutions of 1541 and other determinations of the Society, and in an autograph document of Ignatius on the "provident care" of the Society in regard to the general and other decisions and responses of the founder. However, these documents cannot be regarded as true literary sources. Here and there some echoes of the Dominican Constitutions can be heard, as also of Humbert of Romans' work "The Instruction of Officials"(*De instructione officialium*).

---

4   See L. Moulin, *Le monde vivant des Religieux* (Paris 1964), pp. 131-132.
5   "Gubernatio monarchica" Gregory XIV expressly called it in *Ecclesiae catholicae*, on approving it *in forma specifica*.

II. IMAGE OF THE SUPERIOR GENERAL

It is primarily the superior general who is under consideration here; nevertheless, we are informed in the last declaration of the sixth chapter that it will be possible to infer from what has been said about the general all that is applicable to provincial and local superiors, leaving more concrete applications to the rules of each one ([811]).

As a basic principle it is laid down that there must be a superior general who is one person and *ad vitam*, "with a lifelong term of office" (chapter 1).

There is stress on the fact that he is to be *one person* and in charge of the whole body of the Society ([719]); excluding, therefore, any capitular or collegial government such as was then normal in other religious orders like the mendicants. There will have to be collaborators, as we shall see, but the power to decide will always and solely be the general's ([761]; see [222, 810]). This is a point in the Institute on which Ignatius and his companions were clear from the beginning: "He will decide and define, he alone making judgment" (*determinabit et definiet, ipse solus iudicans*), they wrote emphatically in the "Determinations of 1539."[6]

"Lifelong" (*ad vitam*).—This too was already established at the same time.[7] The Constitutions multiply the reasons here in an unusual way; we must admit, however, that the greater number of them show the advantages rather of a lengthy generalate than of a lifelong tenure of office.

1. Qualities of the General ([723-735])

This subject might also be treated in the second section of the two into which we divided Part IX; however, since one of the safeguards against the dangers of monarchical government is for the one exercising it to have suitable qualities (see [666, 820]), we deal with it here so as not to disturb the order of the Constitutions and because it contributes greatly to a portrayal of the person of the general.

Some contemporaries and confidants of Ignatius (Ribadeneira, Nadal, Câmara, and others) testify that we have in this second chapter of Part IX a description of the virtues and qualities of the founder himself.[8] Moreover,

---

6   MI Const, I, 13-14, no. 16.
7   MI Const, I, 13, no. 14.
8   See Ribadeneira, *Vida de san Ignacio*, Bk. 5, Introduction (MI FontNarr, IV, 735); da Câmara, *Memorial*, nos. 98 and 226 (MI FontNarr, I, 584 and 659); MHSI Nadal, *Scholia*, on no. 723.

the chapter is interesting in another respect: it concludes in a summary manner by saying that the general must be "one of those who are most outstanding in every virtue" and most deserving in the Society ([735]). This seems to indicate that the present chapter presents the ideal image of the Jesuit, to which, consequently, we must endeavor to bring ourselves as close as possible.

This chapter divides the qualities of the general into six groups and arranges them in their order of importance.[9] Keeping to the same order of importance, we could perhaps make a simpler division: into personal qualities of a supernatural order, personal qualities of a natural order, and external gifts or circumstances. (To forestall confusion, we merely want to note with regard to the Spanish word *afecto* that neither here ([724]) nor on the other occasion that it occurs in the Constitutions ([516]) does it refer to feeling or affection in the modern sense; it means the affective faculty of the soul, that is, the will, which is perfected by moral virtues.)

The qualities of a supernatural order can be considered under a twofold aspect, frequently intermixed in the second chapter of Part IX: first, the qualities which one must possess to be able to be elected to the office of general and, second, proof of those qualities which the elected person must give in his exercise of government. Here we will only give some brief indications about the first aspect, leaving the second for treatment later. The person who is elected as general is to be above all a man of prayer ([723]) and a man of great virtue ([725, 735]). He must have controlled and mortified all his passions so that interiorly they do not disturb him in the right judgment of affairs and outwardly permit him to be very composed and self-controlled in speaking ([726]). Among the virtues particularly indicated are humility, charity, and love for the Society ([725, 735]), meekness and kindness, along with rectitude and holy zeal for the divine will and service ([727, 728]), magnanimity in initiating great undertakings, constancy in persevering in them, and fortitude and patience to bear "the weaknesses of many" and contradictions even from persons of high rank and power ([728]).

As a natural foundation, Ignatius wants the general to be endowed with great understanding and practical judgment, learning or theological formation, experience of the spiritual life, discretion in the handling of business matters, a good manner in dealing and conversing with many different persons from within and without the Society ([729]), diligence and solicitude in work and in the effort to bring things to their completion and

---

9   Note the explicit statement by the author. At least in this case there is no need to search for the order he follows.

perfection ([730]), and, finally, health and physical energies, "appearance" and suitable age ([731]).

If to these qualities are added some external gifts or circumstances (nobility, renown, wealth which was left in the world, and the like), these will help toward edification and the service of God because they can increase moral authority with outsiders and even with those of the Society. We think of Francis Borgia. Therefore, "everything else being equal, these external circumstances come into some consideration," but they are not sufficient if the others are lacking ([734], see [161]).

Ignatius was very realistic in realizing that it would not be easy to find an individual in whom all these qualities would be joined and balanced. It is an ideal picture. So the chapter concludes by delimiting the qualities to the required minimum: "great probity, and love for the Society, and good judgment accompanied by sound learning" ([735]). Two points ought to be noted here. The first is that the Spanish word *bondad* (probity) is to be understood in the sense in which it is constantly used in the Constitutions, in the sense of moral perfection, being virtuous, not in the sense of gentleness or mildness of temperament or being kind, as it has been interpreted at times.[10] That is why Polanco rightly translated "bondad" by the Latin word *probitas*, which does not have the cold and moralizing tone of its derivatives in the Romance languages. The second point to be noted is that the insert "accompanied by sound learning" was added by Ignatius himself and reveals how necessary he regarded this theological formation for satisfying the demands of our vocation.

2. Authority of the General ([736-765])

The point on which our Institute has perhaps been most criticized and attacked, outside and inside the Society, is that of the authority of the general. It has come to be presented as a spiritual despotism and as a wild beast that destroys everything.

Ignatius shows us its purpose when, in the first number of the third chapter, alluding to a saying of Paul, he writes: "It is judged altogether proper for the good government of the Society that the superior general should have complete authority over it, *in order to build it up*" ([736]).[11]

---

10 Sometimes it is compared to intellectual gifts: *letras y bondad* (learning and goodness) [48, 256], *discreción y bondad* (discretion and goodness) [431], to designate someone who is *bueno y docto* (good and learned), *de buena vida y letras suficientes* (of good life and sufficient learning) [308]; at other times the meaning is stated by adding the word "virtue" or "virtues" [671, 813].

11 See 2 Cor. 10:8.

Faithful to his principle of means adjusted to end, he was convinced that it was of the greatest importance for the conservation and growth of the body of the Society that the general have power to act with full authority (see [820]).

However, the fact that the general has "complete authority" is not to be understood in an exclusive sense, as if all authority is to be concentrated in his hands (we shall see shortly how the principle of subsidiarity is established), but rather that all authority in the Society must proceed from him as from the head ([666]). It dwells in him as in its source and consequently in fullness; in the others it is as derived or communicated.

The general, therefore, not only "appoints" provincials and local superiors ([757]) but gives them the authority which he judges wise, being able to increase, restrict, and even revoke it entirely ([757, 759]) and likewise approve or cancel what they did ([765]). This is very different from other religious orders, in which provincials and local superiors are elected by the subjects and by the mere fact of election receive the authority proper to their offices.

The third chapter gives a detailed list of the main objectives of this authority of the general, following the order of execution observed in the ten Parts of the Constitutions from admission up to government (see [135]): admission into the Society and vows ([736]; see also [168]); possible dismissal ([736]; see [206]); the colleges (sending of scholastics, government and administration) ([739-745]; see [420]); regular observance (with opportune corrections and exemptions) ([746-748, 754]); missions and distribution of apostolic offices and functions ([749-752]; see [618, 620]); grants or faculties from the Holy See ([753]; see [666]); convocation and direction of a general congregation ([755]; see [689]); everything referring to government: acceptance of dignities ([756]), appointment of superiors and officials ([757-761]), foundation of houses and colleges ([762]; see [321, 441]), reception of account of conscience ([764]). Authority is limited only, according to the norm in the Formula of the Institute, for abandoning, or transferring houses and colleges already founded ([765]; see [322, 680]).

Let us now see how the general should use this authority.

3. Office of the General

We read at the beginning of the third chapter that from its description of the authority of the general "his functions also become manifest" ([736]). However, for a complete picture of the general's office according to the mind of Ignatius, it would be necessary to examine the entire Constitutions and even other Ignatian writings. We do not intend to do so now. We will content ourselves with picking up some traits which are found here and there throughout this Part IX, mainly in the second, third, and sixth chapters.

In general terms, the functions of the general are defined by saying that he must have charge of the Society as his "proper duty" ([719]), "in such a manner that through the divine grace it may be preserved and developed in its well-being and manner of proceeding for glory to God our Lord, by employing his authority as is expedient for that end" ([789]).[12] Therefore, although as a private person he will be able to exercise some spiritual ministry of preaching or confessions, it is not proper to his office ([789]); and neither is it proper that he occupy himself in particular affairs, for instance, the government or administration of a house or college ([795], see [792]). It is his function to organize the procedure to be followed ([796]), leaving to others its execution.

Much less is he to engage himself in "secular" employments, alien to our Institute (see [591]), and not even in spiritual works which do not belong to the Society "in such a way that time and energies fail him for what is proper to his office, which requires more than the whole man" ([793]).

In order to fulfill his office properly, he must first of all be closely united with God our Lord and intimate with Him, not only in prayer but also "in all his actions" or occupations. God is the source of all goodness.[13] Like another Moses, the general ought to be on the mountain of prayer, imploring for the whole Society divine gifts and graces and also great power and efficacy for all the means used by the Society to help souls ([723, 790, 812]). Indeed, it is not a question here of efficacy in the natural order, calculated by numbers and statistics, but of supernatural efficacy, that is, the fecundity of the divine works, which is the fruit of the interior action of grace (see [813]).

Following the advice of Peter, the general is to be "an example to the flock."[14] By his example in all virtues he is to help the rest of the Society ([725], see [790]), and they should regard him as "a mirror and a model" ([726]).

"In all virtues."—However, Ignatius wants this splendor of virtues to have a special coloration and tone: of love and of humility; of love and

---

12 In the Spanish text this number [789] is the protasis of a periodic sentence which lacks an apodosis. Actually, the apodosis was the following number [790], which in the final wording passed on to form part of the Declarations. In doing this, the composer did not notice that the meaning of the first half of the sentence remained in suspense.

13 See James 1:17; *SpEx*, no. 237.

14 1 Pet. 5:3.

charity for all one's neighbors, but especially for the Society ([725, 735]), for which the general must be ready to give his life if necessary ([728]); and of genuine humility. This love and humility will make him very lovable to God and men ([725])—in this respect also like Moses,[15] or rather, like the One who described Himself as "gentle and humble of heart."[16]

However, meekness is not a synonym for permissiveness. Sometimes the general will have to give corrections and impose penances ([754]). Yet he has to know how to mingle the "necessary severity" with kindness and gentleness and not swerve from what he judges "more pleasing to God our Lord nor cease to have proper sympathy for his sons. Thus, although they are being reprimanded or punished, they will recognize that in what he does he is proceeding rightly in our Lord and with charity, even though it is against their liking according to the lower man" ([727]).[17]

Another means of preserving and increasing the well-being and manner of proceeding of the Society is solicitude to maintain observance of the Constitutions ([790], see [746, 826]). Although he can dispense from them according to circumstances, he will do so using only the discretion which the eternal light gives him, in cases where he judges that this is the intention of the Constitutions, keeping in mind their purpose: the greater divine service and the good of those who live in this Institute; and generally he will exercise such authority personally ([746, 747]).

To ensure this regular observance, he will keep himself informed of what is occurring in the provinces, through the provincials and even other superiors and individual Jesuits ([790-792]). Next, he will make "provision" ([790]) by applying the principle of subsidiarity, that is, "by sharing his labor" with subordinate superiors who are to be "men worthy of great confidence," to whom he can give much authority ([790, 797]). Thus "he will have more time left to himself to comprehend the matters of universal import which he alone can handle. He will also have more light to see what is expedient in connection with them, since his mind does not lose a portion of the light it has (as so easily happens) through being much absorbed with particular matters and details in which it becomes oppressed and less fit for matters of universal importance" ([797]).

Nevertheless, he will not cease to help these subordinate superiors "with counsel, reprimand, and correction, if necessary" ([791]), "for he knows that the good government of the Society depends in great part on

15 See Eccli. 45:1.
16 Mt. 11:29.
17 The Spanish word "flectar" is a Latinism or neologism not found in the dictionaries. Polanco later changed it to "declinar," but this correction was not picked up in text C and consequently neither in text D, which is the official text.

them" ([797]) and that "it pertains to him to supply for the defects of the lower superiors and, with divine favor and aid, to bring toward perfection what has been imperfect in them" ([791]).[18]

Assuming then that the government of the Society is interior (see [91-92]), Ignatius desires that the general "should know the consciences, as far as possible, of those whom he has in his charge, especially of the provincial superiors and others to whom he entrusts charges of importance" ([764]).

Finally, he should not lose courage in the face of contradictions even though they come from persons of high rank and power; and he should not allow himself to be moved by their entreaties or threats from what reason and the divine service require, being superior to all eventualities, without letting himself be exalted by those which succeed or depressed by those which go poorly ([728]).

He will employ the time which his health and energies allow him— partly with God, partly with his officials and ministers, and partly with himself—"in thinking out and deciding what should be done with the help and favor of God our Lord" ([809]).

III. REMEDIES FOR DISADVANTAGES ([766-809])

We said at the beginning that Ignatius was not unaware of the dangers and inconveniences which this lifelong and centralized government of the general involved. Hence, he devised opportune safeguards.

The inconveniences are of two classes: some inhere in the functions of the general, others can regard the person exercising the office. The remedies will be different in each case.

1. In Regard to the General's Person ([766-788])

Personal circumstances, voluntary or involuntary, may obtrude which can make difficult or impede the good government of the general. To surmount these inconveniences Ignatius laid it down that the Society should have authority or "provident care" (*providencia*) "in regard to the general" (*cerca el Prepósito General*).

We ought to pay particular attention to these two words, *providencia* and *cerca*, both written by Ignatius. Originally the title of the fourth chapter read: "On the Authority of the Society *over* the General" (*De la autoridad*

---

18 The principle of subsidiarity was clearly explained by St. Ignatius in a letter to Miró of Dec. 17, 1552 (MI Epp, IV, 558-559).

de la Compañía sobre *el Prepósito General*). Ignatius corrected this by writing "in regard to" (*cerca*) instead of "over" (*sobre*) and by adding to "authority" (*autoridad*) the explanatory phrase "or providence" (*o providencia*). The change from *sobre* to *cerca* was later also made in the first number of the chapter ([766]) and in the parallel passage of Part X ([820]).[19] The authority which the Society has "in regard to" the general is "a provident care" inasmuch as in certain cases which refer to him the Society is authorized to "provide" or take suitable measures.[20]

The responsibility for this "provident care" rests above all with the provincials, who are not to limit themselves to ensuring the particular good of their own provinces. They are obliged before God our Lord "to consider and to do what they ought to do for the universal good of the Society" ([778]).

Speaking more concretely, among the circumstances which can affect the person of the general with damage to good government, the Constitutions distinguish some less important, which create inconveniences but do not prevent the general from exercising his functions, and others more serious, which do prevent him from doing so.

The first set of circumstances refers to the externals of his life (such as his clothing and food) ([768]), the care of his body that he may not go beyond measure in labors or excessive severity ([769]), his spiritual life and his manner of exercising his functions ([770]). In order that he be properly "cared for" should it be necessary in such cases, there will be no need to convoke a general congregation. The very congregation which elects a general will also elect four subjects ([781]) who "in the sight of their Creator and Lord should be under obligation to say and do everything they think to be for the greater glory of God" ([779]). Ignatius first called them "laterals" or "collaterals" and later on "assistants." They are to be "persons of discretion and zeal for the good of the Society" ([779]), and "professed fathers if this is conveniently possible" ([780]),[21] and "should remain close

---

19   In Part X the correction is also by St. Ignatius, whose intention there is clearer; for while it is said that particular superiors have authority *sobre* (over) subjects, and the general *sobre* superiors, as to the Society it is only asserted that it has authority *cerca* (in regard to) the general. The Latin translation did not take into account this difference, and all three times used the preposition *in* without any distinctions.

20   There are two documents, apart from the Constitutions, in which St. Ignatius revealed what he thought on this point: a *determinación antigua* (early clarification) and a later document in his own hand (MI Const, I, 215 and 385).

21   In order to measure the force of this requirement, it is well to note the limitation in the previous text: "personas professas." St. Ignatius erased the word "professed" in the constitution, and wrote in the declaration the sentence we now read: "They should be professed fathers if this is conveniently possible" [780].

to the general" ([778]), which does not necessarily mean in the same house.

Besides these assistants, the Constitutions speak (although only in relation to the third more delicate case) of the admonitor, who is obliged, after having had recourse to God in prayer, to advise the general, with due modesty and humility, as to what he judges would be conducive to the greater service and glory of God ([770]).

More important are the circumstances which can hinder the general in exercising his functions. The Constitutions enumerate three. A dignity (for instance, a bishopric) which is offered to or even imposed on him, though not under pain of sin ([771-772]); lack of physical strength for government, due to illness or old age ([773]); seriously irregular conduct of the general himself which would make him unworthy of his office ([774-777]).

In the first of these three cases, neither can the general accept such a dignity without the consent of the Society, nor can the Society ever give its consent ([771-772]); there is therefore no reason to convoke a general congregation ([786b]).

The second case can be more or less serious according to whether it involves greater or lesser incapacity in exercising his office. In less serious circumstances it will suffice to give the general some further assistance. In others, it will be necessary to elect a vicar to perform the functions of general even though without the title. We shall not go into juridical details; we will only say that there does not seem to be a perfect agreement between the fourth and fifth chapters concerning the manner of proceeding in this case.[22]

The third case, evil conduct of a general in the moral order, is the most serious and the most delicate case. Ignatius hoped in the Divine Goodness that it would never occur ([774]) and up to now his hope has been fulfilled. Nevertheless, given its gravity, the situation cannot continue without a remedy provided for in law. The remedy is to convoke a general congregation. The four previously mentioned assistants will convoke it. But if the case has become public knowledge, the provincials do not have to wait for this convocation but will come spontaneously to Rome, "with some provincials summoning the others." After the case has been investigated, and the general found guilty, he will be deposed and someone else will be

---

22 In the fifth chapter, the convocation of the general congregation is supposed [786a]; in the fourth, the necessity of convoking it is expressly excluded [773]. This inconsistency is due to a correction which Polanco introduced in the fourth chapter, after the definitive text had been written, forgetting to make the appropriate correction in the parallel place in the fifth chapter. In the latter, the possibility of the resignation of the general was admitted. But the clause was erased in text B.

elected in his place ([782]).

Ignatius is careful to give two warnings. The first is that the evidence be full and truly conclusive, "because," he says, "those who hold offices, and especially one so universal, can be calumniated by many persons for various reasons" ([777]). Thus, a qualified majority of votes is required for the deposition of a general: more than two thirds. Secondly, as far as possible, concern should be had for the reputation of an accused general. The matter in its entirety should be kept as secret as possible ([783]). If it transpires that there is no reason for deposing the general, other matters should be taken up "to give the appearance that the congregation was called to discuss them" ([785]). If deposition is decided, there should be secret discussion with the general about resigning his office, "that this can be published and by it his sin can be concealed" ([785]). The universal good of the Society and the particular good of the general are thus secured with equal charity.

2. In Regard to the General's Office ([789-809])

The functions of the general of the Society "require more than the whole man" ([793]). Hence the inconveniences which surround them; not only because the one who exercises them can succumb under such a burden, but also because the very efficacy of government can suffer. Although of itself the monarchical form is more efficacious than others, it can turn out to be less effective because of the impossibility of one man attending to everything.

The remedy is that the general share his responsibility with others. The Constitutions distinguish two classes of "ministers" who help the general in his government: those who help him in particular matters and those who help him in universal ones.

For the particular matters of each province and of each house, there will be provincial and lower superiors. The first Formula of the Institute does not mention them. In 1546, with the brief *Exponi nobis*, Paul III granted Ignatius the right to have "some superiors or vicars of yourself, both provincial and local" (*alios praepositos seu vicarios tuos, tam provinciales quam locales*). We already saw how Ignatius instructs the general to apply the principle of subsidiarity, "sharing with them his labor" ([797]).

But the general also needs "ministers" or helpers in order to carry out "smoothly and well" his functions with regard to universal affairs ([798]). Following the classical plan of the powers of the soul (memory, intellect, and executive will), the Constitutions divide these helpers into three categories: one who helps the general "by reminders connected with his solicitude to attend to the numerous affairs of his office," one who helps him "with counsel" for ordering them, and one who helps him "with diligence and effort to carry them out" ([798]). We will see that this scheme is too artificial and forced.

The first help is that which the secretary of the Society gives the general. But his office, described later, is not limited to recalling to the general the things he must attend to or drawing his attention to them. He is the general's "memory" but also his "hands." Even further, he must "take on the general's own person" and imagine that, apart from his authority, he carries on his own shoulders the general's whole burden ([800]). More than that of a simple secretary, his office is presented as that of an intimate collaborator, although without authority.

To the second category Ignatius again gives the name of "assistants" and declares that they can be the same as those designated by this title in the fifth chapter ([805]). They can be the same, but not necessarily. In fact the juridical image of each category is different. These assistants are to be "persons of prominence in learning and all good qualities" ([803]). In the others (the four assistants mentioned earlier), only discretion and zeal for the good of the Society is sought ([779]); on the other hand, they ought to be professed members if possible ([780]), while the grade of this second category of assistants is not mentioned. But most important, the responsibilities of each category are different. The assistants mentioned in the fifth chapter exercise the authority or provident care of the Society in regard to the general; the role of the assistants named in this sixth chapter is to study the universal affairs of the Society with reference to both doctrine and practice, whether they "spontaneously" study affairs and "represent them" to the general or he entrusts them with the examination of business in order that they may be more "simplified" or clarified for his final decision.

In order to ensure a deeper understanding of affairs, the Constitutions propose that care for the different regions of the Society be divided among the assistants of this second category. Hence, in the course of time, the term "assistancy" began to be used to signify a region or group of provinces.[23] There is no question in the Constitutions of a territorial division of the Society but rather of the distribution of labor among the assistants.

We leave to a more extensive commentary an explanation of the evolution which this office has undergone in our institute, an evolution due principally to the growth of the Society and the multiplication and

23   See *CollDecr*, d. 264.

complexity of affairs.[24]

The third help given to the general is that of the procurator general. His office also is not adequately described by the words "diligence and effort to carry out" the business ordered by the general ([798]); carrying out or executing the decisions of the general pertains to a great extent to the office of the secretary (see [801]). The responsibility of the procurator is to take charge of the dispatch of papal grants needed for houses and colleges, the "defense" of the rights of these houses and colleges, and "generally . . . all the temporal business of the Society" ([806]; see [591]). Nevertheless, Ignatius regards "secular" business, even if it concerns necessary affairs, as so alien to the Institute of the Society that he does not want the procurator to be a professed member or even to live in a professed house except in special circumstances, temporarily, "when he is not handling lawsuits" ([807]).

Since the 1917 Code of Canon Law, this office has been divided in two: that of procurator general and that of treasurer general.

To summarize the entire sixth chapter in such a way that it is also applicable to other superiors (see [809]), we can keep in mind the idea that these "ministers" and helpers are given to the general so that he can carry out the duties of his office "smoothly and well" ([798]).

IV. FINAL OBSERVATION

Because of its subject matter, Part IX considers the Society mainly as an institution, a company. The first words of the first chapter show this when, in mentioning as an element common to "all communities or congregations," it speaks of someone having charge of "the whole body," "whose duty is the good government, preservation, and development of the whole body" ([719]).

Certainly we are dealing here with a spiritual company, a body animated by a supernatural spirit. So the one who is to govern it must not only have natural gifts but be united with God and lead a virtuous life; and he is given directives to aid him in spiritual and religious government. But the norms on the length of his office, on the extension of his authority, on safeguards against abuses and other inconveniences, and on aids towards the better exercise of responsibility are consequences and concrete

---

24 See our *El General de la Compañía de Jesús*, pp. 167-173. General congregations later clarified and completed the norms contained in the Constitutions. See *CollDecr*, dd. 259-261; G. C. XXXI, d. 41.

determinations of the institutional nature of the Society. None of this would have any meaning if the Society did not form an organized body. For that reason, in our exposition we were content to indicate some general ideas.

Nevertheless, the foundation is always the charism, the life of apostolic mission. For instance, we do not see any other explanation for the extremely centralized monarchical form of government which Ignatius thought necessary for the Society: all the authority, and all the activity of the members, should descend from the head. The reason is given in a passage of the first text which did not pass on to the following ones: it is necessary—it said—that one person have charge of the whole body of the Society, "which is distributed throughout the world, and will be distributed more and more every day by divine grace." The "distribution" or dispersion which the apostolic mission entails (see [603]) on the one hand makes imposssible the capitular and democratic regime of other religious orders and, on the other, requires the convergence of all lines of action on the center.

The bull *Ecclesiae Catholicae* of Gregory XIV (1591), in specifically approving this monarchical form of government in the Society, related it to the vow of obedience to the pope "in regard to missions" (*circa missiones*). According to the bull, from this monarchical government follows, among other advantages, this one: that the members of the Society, "distributed throughout the whole world, united with their head by means of this total subordination, can more promptly and easily be directed and moved to various missions by the supreme head, the vicar of Christ on earth, in conformity with their own proper vocation and special vow."

Chapter XIV

PRESERVATION AND GROWTH
OF THE SOCIETY
(Constitutions, Part X)

I. PRELIMINARY REMARKS

1. Importance of Part X

Part X is the briefest of all, having only a single chapter with thirteen numbers and three declarations. However, it is no less important for that. Its importance is due to the purpose of the chapter, which is, as the title indicates, to present the means of preserving and developing the body of the Society in its well-being. Up to this point the Constitutions have shown how the body of the Society needs to be continually built up; the body (members and head) having been constituted in accordance with these norms, we now want to see how it is to be preserved and developed in its well-being.

"In its well-being."—It is not enough to preserve the body of the Society in its being, in its existence. It is necessary that this existence be according to the demands of the religious state and of the institute or "way of proceeding" of the Society. Equally, it is not enough to develop the body or make it grow in number of subjects or variety of activities. The growth must be made in harmony with the nature of the body itself; otherwise it would be an abnormal growth.

In the history of the Church we have heard of religious orders which were not preserved, or became lax, or ceased to be animated by the founder's spirit. The Society itself was suppressed for some time. So it is not surprising that there arise in our minds at times concerns and anxieties as to the future. Part X meets these concerns and anxieties.

2. Structure and Sources

We distinguish two sections in Part X. The first deals in a general way with the means of preserving and developing the Society, laying down the basic principles (1-3, [812-814]). The second goes into detail by pointing out a number of particular or concrete means (4-13, [815-827]). In the source (which, as we shall say immediately, is the twelfth *Industria*), this division is clear. After having expounded the matter corresponding to the first three numbers of the Constitutions, Polanco begins his treatment of the material in the following numbers with the words: "getting down more to detail" (*veniendo más al particular*).

The first section begins by establishing the basic principle, namely, that the hope for the preservation and development of the Society must be placed in Christ alone ([812a]). The logical consequences are deduced: the necessity of prayer ([812b]), preference for spiritual means ([813]), and the motive for and the manner of employing human means as well ([814]).

The structure of the second section is more obscure. Nevertheless we do not think that some means have simply been placed before others without a preconceived order.[1] At least one may divide them into two blocks or sets. The first comprises numbers 4 to 9 ([815-821]); the second, the last four numbers, 10-13 ([822-827]). There is a notable difference in the importance attributed to the means of the first set and those of the second. It is said of the first set that they will be of great help, that they are of great and supreme importance, and that contrary defects are to be completely thrust aside or most diligently excluded. On the other hand, the author is content to say about the second set that they help or that they serve. Some might also see another difference, one we do not venture to assert: the first set of means could refer to the interior life of the Society, the second to its exterior activity.

The source, as we have mentioned, is the twelfth *Industria* of Polanco. With regard to the topic of ambition ([817]), a very early document of Ignatius exists in which some of the ideas expounded here are anticipated. On the other hand, the paragraph dealing with the fifth simple vow of the professed ([817b]) is original and later than the copy of text B. We will see further on why it was inserted here.

II. GENERAL MEANS

1. *The Omnipotent Hand of Christ ([812a])*

The first means for preserving and developing the body of the Society, first in every order of ideas and in a certain sense the sole means, is the supernatural action of "the omnipotent hand of Christ, God and our Lord"

---

1   The fact that the order of the numbers 4 to 8 [815-820] is exactly the inverse of that followed by Polanco in the 12th *Industria* shows that the author had an ordering principle in mind, although it is difficult for us to discern it.

([812]). The Society, in fact, "was not instituted by human means." It is not that a few men joined together on their own initiative the better to realize by their united efforts a common plan for the benefit of mankind. It was the omnipotent hand of Christ which "aroused Ignatius"[2] and was gently guiding him where he knew not so that, "being in his humility wisely unforeseeing" (*siendo sabiamente imprevisor en su humildad*), he would little by little open up the way for the founding of the Society.[3] It was the omnipotent hand of Christ which led the first companions, through the Exercises, to follow the "plan of life" (*propósito de vida*) of Ignatius.[4] For the rest, the providential and unforeseeable ways by which the group of "friends in the Lord" came to the feet of the pope and were led to change their Society into a religious order are well known.

An institution with such origins cannot be preserved or developed by "human means" ([812]). Only Christ, by his omnipotent hand, can ensure for it such preservation and development. It is to be hoped that he will do so. Certainly the Society does not possess the promise of indefectible continuity which Christ made to the Church. Our hope is founded on the provident goodness of Christ Himself, who will want to preserve and carry forward "what he deigned to begin for his service and praise and for the aid of souls" ([812]). By instituting the Society the Lord showed that he wanted to make use of it in his work of saving men. So it is to be hoped that he will continue making use of it for the same purpose.

Hope, then, and hope in him alone. It will be said that, such being the case, all the rest of Part X is superfluous. In a sense this is true, and we have already said that this action of the omnipotent hand of Christ is the sole means, inasmuch as it alone is totally efficacious by itself. Nevertheless, the other means are not to be ignored: they have an instrumental and dispositive value relative to the action of God's grace, which "requires cooperation from His creatures" ([134]).

2. Prayer for the Society ([812b])

In conformity with this hope, since on the one hand we cannot rely on human means but on the action of the omnipotent hand of Christ and on the other we do not have His promise of indefectible continuity, the first way to cooperate with this divine action, and "the best proportioned means" for obtaining what depends solely on it, must be "the prayers and Masses

---

2   The expression comes from Gregory XIII, *Quanto fructuosius* and *Ascendente Domino*. Pius XI, in *Paterna caritas*, spoke of St. Ignatius "divino afflatui parens."

3   See Nadal, *Dialogus II* (MHSI Nadal, V, 625-626).

4   See Nadal, *Exhortatio 6^a* (ibid., 842-843).

which ought to be offered for this holy intention."

The importance which Ignatius gave to prayer as a means appears also in other passages of the Constitutions. A rector, for instance, is "to sustain the whole college by his prayer and holy desires" ([424]); the general is to ensure the good of the whole Society "by his prayer which is assiduous and full of desires and by his sacrifices" which implore from God the grace of the preservation and development of this Society (see [723, 790]). And one of the means of helping the neighbor is prayer and the celebration of Holy Mass (see [638-640]). We find the same recourse to prayer recommended frequently in the letters of Ignatius.

Later on, the Society determined more precisely the number of Masses and other prayers which ought to be offered weekly, monthly, and annually for this intention.[5]

3. Uniting the Human Instrument with the Hand of God ([813])

In the next two numbers, 2 and 3 ([813-814]), two categories of means are distinguished which, relying on divine grace, we are to use for the preservation and development of the Society: means of a supernatural order and those of a natural order. The first are a virtuous life[6] (the virtue of charity, and pure intention of the divine service, and sincere zeal for souls being especially mentioned) and a life of prayer ("familiarity with God in spiritual exercises of devotion").[7] The second category is not defined, but is only exemplified as "learning and the other natural and human gifts" ([813]). Yet it is clear that the concept must be extended to many other fields of the natural order such as that of organization, publicity, influence, and so forth.

The first category is to be preferred: "Care should be taken in general that all the members of the Society may devote themselves to the solid and perfect virtues and to spiritual pursuits, and attach greater importance to them than to learning and other natural and human gifts" ([813]).[8]

In this context, in fact, it is not a question of preserving or developing

---

5   *Catalogus Missarum et orationum quae nostris praescribuntur.* It was published for the first time by Mercurian in the 1580 edition of the Rules.
6   Regarding the Spanish word "bondad" see what we wrote above in Part IX on treating of the qualities of the general (text corresponding to note 10).
7   The mention of zeal was added in the last text. This explains why it was placed at the end, while its logical place seems to be among the other virtues.
8   The *Diccionario de la Academia Española* gives two meanings for the adverbial expression "a una mano": (1) in a circular movement, always in the same direction, always from left to right, or always from right to left; (2) in conformity or conformably. We therefore understand it here with the meaning of equally, without distinction or difference.

only "the exterior" of the Society, what is here called its "body" (not, as at other times, in the social sense, but rather as contrasted to "spirit"), that is to say, the number of subjects, houses, and different works. If the exterior were the only concern, human means would be very efficacious, as we see they are in human enterprises. But at issue here is preserving and developing the Society "in its well-being" and thus preserving its "spirit," its spiritual vitality, which necessarily is specified by "the objective it seeks," namely, that of "aiding souls to reach their ultimate and supernatural end" ([813]). For this the natural means do not of themselves have any efficacy; all the efficacy comes from the spiritual or interior means.

We find ourselves always in this perspective: that it is the omnipotent hand of Christ alone that is to preserve and advance the Society in His divine service and the help of souls ([812]). The Society and its members are but weak instruments of this omnipotent hand. Very well, then, the spiritual means "join the instrument to God and ready it for being managed by His divine hand," while the other means ready it only for men, inasmuch as they make it humanly more perfect. The influence of the divine hand is passed on to the instrument which is closely joined to it, and being an omnipotent hand, it will achieve its work even though the instrument be humanly imperfect.[9]

4. Perfecting the Instrument ([814])

Nevertheless, the natural means are not to be despised or rejected; rather they should be sought "with diligence." This is another example of discretion in the Ignatian Constitutions.

Among these natural means, always bearing in mind the evangelizing purpose of the Society, are listed with special recommendation "well-grounded and solid learning" (that is, sound theological formation, firmly based on the sources of revelation) (see [358, 359]), "the manner" of presenting this doctrine to the people in sermons and sacred lectures ([402, 405, 645-647]), and "the manner of treating and conversing with persons" (see [414, 648]).

The reason why these natural means are to be acquired is found in the dispositions of the sovereign providence of God our Lord, who desires to be glorified both through the natural means which he gives as Creator and through the supernatural means which he gives as the Author of grace ([814])—with the gifts of nature and with the gifts of grace. Experience shows, in fact, that in his ordinary providence, between two people equally

---

9   See Ignatius to Miró, Dec. 17, 1552 (MI Epp, IV, 559-562).

virtuous and of equal interior life, God usually makes more use of the one who has better human qualities for helping souls spiritually.[10]

The constitution, however, lays down three conditions. First, that the attainment of these human means be based on what was said in the previous number ("based upon this foundation," [814]), that is, giving preference to supernatural means and understanding that those interior means are what is to give efficacy to the exterior ones ([813]). "Learning and all external appearance in dealing with others," said an early Ignatian document, are to be regarded as "chaff."[11] The same teaching was expounded earlier by the founder in a thoughtful page of the first text of the Examen, which unfortunately did not pass on to the following texts.[12] Indeed, in Sacred Scripture and in the history of the Church we find numerous cases in which God, precisely to show that the success of our undertakings does not depend on our own efforts but on His omnipotent hand, has made use of useless instruments. Enough to think of David and Goliath. Paul says: "He singled out the weak of this world to shame the strong."[13]

The second condition is that "these human means are acquired and exercised for the divine service alone," not selfishly for our own enrichment or advancement or in order that people may esteem us because of these personal values. We would then be at the first and second stages of the standard of Satan.[14]

The third condition is that we acquire and use these human means in order to follow God's sovereign providence, not because we trust in them as if the spiritual fruit of souls was in proportion to the measure in which we employed them. Hope is to be placed in Christ alone ([812]) and in the union of the instrument with the omnipotent hand of Christ ([813]).

In describing the methods of Ignatius, Ribadeneira thus expressed this doctrine in his own copious style: "In things of divine service of our Lord which he undertook, he used all human means to succeed in them with as much care and efficiency as if success depended on them, and he trusted in God and depended on His divine providence in such a way as if all the human means he used had no effect."[15] Later on, an effort was made to

---

10   The observation is by St. Ignatius, in the document we will cite later, note 11.
11   MI Const, I, 197, no. 1.
12   See Const, II, 125. The style is characteristically Ignatian. One who would want to learn the difference beween Polanco's style and that of St. Ignatius might compare that page with this no. 3 [814].
13   1 Cor. 1:27.
14   See *SpEx*, no. 142.
15   MI FontNarr, III, p. 631, no. 14 (with bibliographical indications in note 14).

synthesize the same thought in one of the most famous maxims attributed to Ignatius,[16] a maxim which spread beyond the Jesuit environment due to its inclusion among the aphorisms of Baltasar Gracián's *Oraculo manual y arte de prudencia*, where it is called "the rule of a great teacher."[17]

III. PARTICULAR MEANS

1. First Series of Particular Means ([815-821])

The body of the Society cannot be preserved or developed without the recruitment of new vocations which will fill vacancies and increase the number of laborers in the Lord's vineyard. It is then necessary to defend these laborers from the dangers which can threaten them, to select them carefully, to guide them rightly, and to keep them united. These are the five topics in the first group of particular means.

a. New Vocations.

This is envisioned in number 4 ([815]) where the colleges are treated, but considered insofar as they are "the seedbed for the professed Society and its coadjutors." It is the perspective of the Formula of the Institute[18] and of the first declaration of Part IV ([308]). For it is to be noted that neither here nor in the Formula of the Institute does the word *seminario* have the meaning of "seminary" that it acquired both in law and in Church practice after Trent, but rather the original meaning of "seedbed," a place where plants are sown and raised, plants which then have to be transplanted.

b. Dangers of Relaxation ([816-817]).

The mitigation of poverty, and ambition for posts of government have always provided two great dangers of relaxation in religious orders; as such nos. 5 and 6 present them ([816-817]). With regard to poverty, it is stated that "it is like a bulwark of religious institutes which preserves them in their existence and discipline and defends them from many enemies" and

---

16 See G. Hevenesi, *Scintillae ignatianae*, 1st ed. (Vienna 1705), maxim 2; I. Iparraguirre, S.J., *Orientaciones bibliográficas sobre san Ignacio de Loyola*, nos. 277 and 280; M. Ruiz Jurado, S.J., *Orientaciones*, II, no. 95.

17 *Oráculo manual*, aphorism 251: "Hanse de procurar los medios humanos como si no hubiese divinos, y los divinos como si no hubiese humanos." We may note that the first edition of *Oráculo manual* (1647) is almost sixty years prior to the first edition of the work by Hevenesi.

18 See Form. Inst. of 1550, no. 8.

that therefore "the devil uses corresponding effort to destroy this bulwark in one way or another" ([816], see [553]). Ambition is given the descriptive epithet "the mother of all evils in any community or congregation whatsoever" ([817]); a very early Ignatian document had called it "the pestilence which kills and devours souls."[19]

Not content with this, Ignatius points out in more detail the chief dangers which threaten the Society in these two fields. As far as poverty is concerned, the most frequent dangers would be those of admitting fixed revenue or stable goods (see [555, 561]), accepting alms for the ministries of "preaching or lecturing or for Masses or the administration of sacraments or similar things" (see [565]),[20] and converting the fixed revenues of the colleges, which are granted exclusively for the benefit of the scholastics, to the use of the Society (see [5, 326, 552]).[21] The most common objects of ambition will be dignities and positions of government both inside and outside the Society.

The solution which Ignatius devised against these dangers of relaxation was that of the vow, the formal commitment, that all professed members must make to Christ our Lord Himself (see [17]): (a) the vow "not to take part in altering what pertains to poverty in the Constitutions" ([553]): this is not treated here since it was already mentioned in Part VI; (b) the vow not to seek dignities or prelacies in the Society: in this case the penalty of ineligibility for office is added to the vow; (c) the vow of not seeking dignities or prelacies outside the Society, nor accepting them "unless one were obliged by obedience to one who can order it under pain of sin": this could only be the pope, for neither the general nor the Society can consent to it unless it is ordered by the pope ([756]);[22] (d) the vow of "manifesting" one who should seek a dignity.

General congregations later specified the matter of these vows in more detail,[23] and Urban VIII declared that not only ecclesiastical dignities and prelacies should be excluded, but also and much more so secular dignities

---

19   MI Const, I, 165.
20   This alms or stipend for ministries is here called a "salary," in the sense of a recompense for a service.
21   See Form. Inst., no. 8.
22   Later Paul V, *Ex incumbenti* (1618), and Urban VIII, *Vota quae Deo* (1632) and *Honorum dignitatumque* (1643), reserved to the Holy See the vow of not changing poverty and of not accepting offices outside the Society. If we consider [772], it seems to be the mind of Ignatius that for accepting a dignity outside the Society, any order of the pope is not enough; it is necessary that the pope wishes to oblige in conscience.
23   See *CollDecr*, d. 205.

and any office involving ecclesiastical or lay jurisdiction.[24] Leaving aside for the moment these decisions of a juridical character, let us note that the spirit of these vows goes much further: to refusal of honorific titles, highly honored positions according to the scale of human values, and so forth. The paragraph concludes as follows: "Our profession," that is, our vocation and charism, is one of "humility and lowliness": helping souls through the ministry of the word of God and the administration of the sacraments; not governing people, occupying posts of authority or prestige.[25]

The fifth vow, on listening to the advice of the general after someone has been elevated to a dignity or prelacy outside the Society, will appear quite singular and strange to us. It was something added later, after 1554. The declaration reveals its reason and origin, namely, the acceptance at that time by the Society of the patriarchate and two bishoprics in Ethiopia. A way was then sought to ensure that the patriarch and the two bishops would in some way remain linked to the Society. It seems that it was not as yet clear in canon law—as it now is—that a religious elevated to the cardinalate or episcopate continues to be a religious.[26] The first idea was that the pope would give a Jesuit papal authority over the patriarch and the bishops. Father Nunes Barreto, designated for the patriarchal office, thought that he would thus remain under the obedience of the Society. Clearly this was not compatible with the episcopal office. So recourse was then had to this vow of listening to the general. The one making the vow obliges himself "before God our Lord to do that which he finds to be better for His divine service, and to be happy to have someone who presents it to him with charity and Christian freedom, to the glory of God our Lord" ([817]).[27]

c. Selection ([819])

It was stated earlier that new vocations are necessary for the Society's preservation and increase. But numbers are not enough: quality must be taken into consideration. Above all, the only ones to be admitted to profession are "those who are selected for their spirit and learning, thoroughly and lengthily tested, and known with edification and satisfaction to all." This is one of the points which Ignatius saw with the greatest clarity

---

24   Urban VIII, *Vota quae Deo.*
25   See Ignatius to King Ferdinand of Austria, December 1546 (MI Epp, I, 451-452).
26   See *CIC*, can. 627.
27   On this whole subject see M. Costa, S.J., *Legge religiosa e discrezione spirituale* (Brescia 1973), pp. 184-218, where all the sources are mentioned.

and expressed with special emphasis in the Formula of the Institute.[28] It is in this part of the twelth *Industria* that Polanco mentions having heard Ignatius say on a number of occasions that "he would desire [longer] life, if it had to be desired, in order to be difficult and cautious in admitting." The very desire to preserve and increase the Society can induce a certain slackness (see [143]), especially when subjects are lacking to continue works already undertaken. Ignatius sets us right here. Far from helping the preservation and development of the Society, this slackness would bring about its destruction. With "this procedure," the constitution says—namely, if those incorporated into the Society are such as has been described— "even though the numbers are multiplied, the spirit will not be diminished or weakened." This is a clear indication that, in the opposite case, the number will perhaps be increased but with great harm to the spirit because the spiritual and religious level could not avoid sinking.

d. Good Government ([820])

Number 8 is an admirable synthesis of the entire Part IX and of its fundamental ideas. It begins with two observations which are the fruit of experience: that "the well-being or illness of the head has its consequences in the whole body" and that subjects will in a general way be what superiors are.[29] The influence of the head will contribute positively to the preservation and development of the Society if the four following conditions are fulfilled. First, that superiors be well chosen. Second, that they have much authority. Third, that this authority be well controlled.[30] Fourth, that superiors have good assistants and ministers. It is the system of government which we saw in Part IX. But here the motivation is added in a profound maxim applicable to other cases as well, even apart from government and even outside the Society: that they "may have full power for good and that, if they do poorly, they may be kept under complete control" ([820]).

---

28   Form. Inst., chap. V, no. 9 (since the first wording of 1539).
29   Regarding the Spanish expression "a una mano" see above, note 8.
30   The words "and, on the other hand, the Society in regard to the general, as is explained in Part IX," are due to a correction written by Ignatius himself. Already in Part IX, on speaking of "the providence of the Society in regard to the general" (note 19), we noted the change introduced by St. Ignatius in both places, writing "authority of the Society *in regard to* (*cerca*) the general" instead of *over* (*sobre*) the general.

e. Union ([821])

It was already strongly emphasized in the first number of Part VIII that "the Society cannot be preserved or governed or, consequently, attain the end it seeks for the greater glory of God unless its members are united among themselves and with their head" ([655]). Some of the means which were indicated there are here enumerated. However, the coordination of the clauses in the paragraph, and the two adverbial expressions "especially" and "in the first place," can create a difficulty, as if obedience is to be preferred to charity or as if it should be said that the bond of obedience serves to foster charity.[31] Nadal rightly rejects both interpretations and shows that two orders of ideas are being treated.[32] For interior and fundamental union the bond of wills, which is charity and love for each other (see [671a]), "especially" helps; uniformity (interior and exterior) (see [671b]) and mutual contact (see [673]) serve to foster union. The organic unity of the body of the Society is obtained "in the first place" by way of the bond of obedience, of an obedience hierarchical or subordinate, which unites the individuals with the local superiors, the local superiors with the provincials, and all of them with the general (see [659, 662, 666]).

2. Second Series of Particular Means ([822-827])

As already noted, to judge by the expressions used, the author seems to give less importance to this second group of means. He only says that "they will help" for preserving and developing the Society. This allows us to be more brief, delaying only on what might present some difficulty.

The means are: (a) "temperate restraint in spiritual and bodily labors," that is, in apostolic activity and in mortifications and penances ([822], see [298, 300]); (b) "moderation in the Constitutions" ([822]); (c) "striving to retain the good will and charity of all" ([823-824], see [446, 622]); (d) "discreet and moderate use of the favors granted by the Apostolic See" ([825]); (e) "seeking with sincerity nothing else than the aid of souls" ([825]); (f) "attention to the preservation of health" ([826, 827], see [492]).

(1) In the Spanish text the word *mediocridad*, "moderation," in number 10 ([822]) is a *hapax legomenon*, a one-time use in the Constitutions.[33] It does not of course have the pejorative meaning acquired in some Romance languages. As can clearly be deduced from the context, it means the just mean

---

31   "This is *especially* the case with the bond of wills which is charity. This bond is
      strengthened [Spanish *sirve*] *above all* by the link of obedience."
32   *Scholia*, on no. [821].
33   It does not appear in the <u>Exercises,</u> nor do we recall having read it in other
      Ignatian writings. It is probably due to the editor Polanco.

between the two extremes of excessive "rigor" and "laxity." If the Constitutions are excessively rigorous, in the long run they will not be observed; if they are lax or excessively indulgent, they will be of little efficacy in promoting religious perfection.

Two points are to be noted. Firstly, here, as in all Part X, what is envisaged is the future. Thus, the term "constitutions" has a generic sense, referring to laws or ordinances which will be made in the Society in the future, not properly to Ignatius' own Constitutions, which Polanco in a question to Ignatius had termed "the first constitutions"[34]—even though of course Ignatius implicitly shows that he himself tried to include this moderation (*mediocridad*) in his Constitutions. They are outstanding for their discretion, as we stated at the beginning of this work. Secondly, "moderation" (*mediocridad*) is recommended in the legislation, not in the observance. As far as the latter is concerned, the Society wants "all the Constitutions and Declarations and its regime of living observed in every regard according to our Institute, without deviation in anything" ([602]). Further, it wants "all of us to exert ourselves not to miss any point of perfection which we can with God's grace attain in the observance of all the Constitutions and in our manner of proceeding" ([547]).

(2) Number 11 ([823]), and even more its declaration ([824]), could cause surprise and even scandal if the legislator's intention is not taken into account. One could see here a worldly diplomacy, ambition to prevail, and even, projecting back into those times our present preoccupations, an alignment with the powerful instead of solidarity with the poor and oppressed. We need to note the clearly expressed motivation in these paragraphs in order to come to a genuine understanding of the author's thought. "First of all" an effort is to be made to retain the benevolence of the Apostolic See because "the Society should especially serve" it ([824]). We read in the Formula of the Institute that "this Society and all who make profession in it are campaigning for God in faithful obedience to Paul III and his successors in the Roman pontificate." Clearly, if the pope does not have confidence in the Society, it will be difficult for him to use it in his service. The motive for maintaining the benevolence of "temporal princes and great and prominent persons" is different. The reason, repeated twice, is that "the favor or disfavor of such persons" (their "good or bad will") "is of great importance for opening or closing the gate leading to the service of God and the good of souls." This must be understood partly in the historical circumstances in which it was written, partly as something valid for every age. In the sixteenth century, secular princes enjoyed almost

34   See MI Const, I, 320, no. 7.

absolute power and could put obstacles in the way of the evangelization of their peoples and even prevent it entirely; they could also remove the obstacles others had thrown up. But in every age it is an important human means for the divine service and the good of souls to have the support of "noble and powerful persons" (*personas grandes y de valor*), provided that it be obtained as explained in number 3 ([814]). As to enemies, the declaration is even more explicit: the reason for seeking their friendship, or at least preventing hostility, is "not because contradictions and ill-treatment are feared, but that God our Lord may be more served and glorified in all things" ([824]).

Likewise the warning that "there should neither be nor be seen partiality to one side or another among Christian princes or rulers, but in its stead a universal love which embraces in our Lord all parties (even though they are adversaries to one another)" ([823]) is valid for all times, despite the reference to "Christian princes or rulers." General Congregation XXVII (1923) gave an apt interpretation by applying this to divisions or parties existing "among Catholics." In fact, one is dealing here simply with questions of human politics which the Society ought to avoid, keeping in mind its spiritual aim of helping souls "to reach their ultimate and supernatural end" ([813]).

(3) Number 12 ([825]) has remained rather obscure in its final wording, either out of a desire for brevity or to avoid the repetition of ideas already touched on in number 2 ([813]), or perhaps through some error in a copy. The means of preserving and developing the Society proposed here are two, as appears clear in the source (the twelfth *Industria*) and in the first text. The first means is "a discreet and moderate use of the favors granted by the Apostolic See"; an immoderate or indiscreet use can, in fact, create hostility, as history attests. The second means is more general: it consists in the Society's persevering in its original vocation (the first text said "in the spirit in which it began"), "seeking with all sincerity nothing else than the aid of souls." The reason is that this manner of procedure will, as regards God, attract divine graces ("God our Lord will carry forward what he has begun") and, as regards man, "the fragrance" (or good repute, not vain) "arising from the genuineness of the good works" "will increase the benevolent desire of others to avail themselves of the Society's aid and to help the Society for the end which it seeks, the glory and service of His Divine Majesty." Avail themselves of the Society: in what manner? The first text said: "by entering it." Afterwards the less precise expression "to avail themselves of the Society's aid" was used, either in order to generalize the concept or perhaps so as not to express it in so concrete a form.

We consider as distinct from these series of means the one included in the second half of number 13 ([826]): the knowledge and observance of the Constitutions and the consequent necessity of reading them assiduously. It seems to us that it is a universal means which includes all the others. It is surprising to find it expressed in a clause depending on the only verb in the whole paragraph: "it will be helpful." But this very fact shows that the intention is simply to mention or record something evident and well known. The Constitutions were in fact composed in order to cooperate with the action of the supreme wisdom and goodness of Christ our Lord in preserving, guiding, and developing this least Society of Jesus, just as He deigned to start it (see [134]).

IV. Final Observation

The subject matter of Part X is, obviously, the institution, the body of the Society, and how to preserve and develop it.

The body of the Society has an exterior and visible aspect ([813]). It is composed of men ([819]), whose number is to be increased by means of colleges ([815]); it is a body organically constituted through the hierarchical subordination of the members ([820, 821]).

But it is not a merely human institution, conceived of and realized by men, with human or humanitarian objectives. To consider it in that sense would be the best way to bring about its destruction. The Society's author is Christ our Lord, and it is the omnipotent hand of Christ which we hope will preserve and continue what He deigned to begin for His service and praise ([812]).

This body is enlivened by a supernatural "spirit" ([813]), which must be protected from the laxity which some other religious orders suffered through mitigation of poverty or through ambition for rule ([816-817]); efforts must be made that the spirit may not be diminished or weakened by the admission of harmful or unsuitable persons ([819]) or by excessive rigor or laxity in the Constitutions ([822]).

It is a body or an institution wholly directed toward a supernatural objective: "to aid souls to reach their ultimate and supernatural end" ([813]). At this point appears the charism of the Society, the life of apostolic mission which is never absent from Ignatius' field of vision. This explains how the general means mentioned in [813] and [814] are conceived more as means of helping the Society to achieve "the objective it seeks" than as means for preserving and developing the body of the Society. They are means for helping a Jesuit to become a more suitable instrument in the salvific work accomplished by Christ. Therefore what is important is that the instrument be well joined to His divine hand and thus able to be used by it. However, efforts must be made to perfect the instrument itself, not because it adds efficacy to the supernatural action of Christ, but in order to accommodate ourselves to the ordinary dispositions of divine providence. In brief magisterial lines Ignatius gives us here an excellent pastoral plan for evangelization.

The special requirement of union ([821]) is also a consequence of the "missionary" life of the Society, as we saw in Part VIII. Likewise, such a life explains the effort to retain the good will and charity of all, especially of those whose good or bad will is so important for opening or closing the door to divine service ([823-825]). The same is true for the discreet and moderate use of the favors granted by the Holy See and for "the fragrance arising from the genuineness of the good works" ([825]).

This "fragrance of Christ," this aroma of the knowledge of God diffused throughout the world through our instrumentality,[35] is the final characteristic presented by the Constitutions of Ignatius in the outline of the charism of the Society.

---

35 See 2 Cor. 2:14-15.

INDEX OF NAMES